All of the electronic resources you need—in one pla

The Second Edition of *Bookmarks* contains marginal icons that refer you to
Companion Website, located at **http://www.ablongman.com/bookmark**

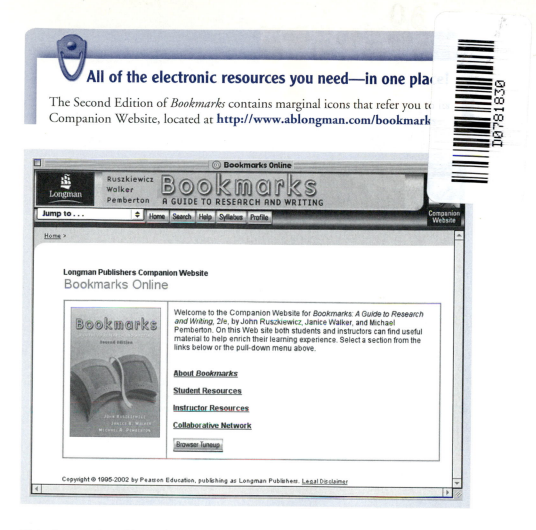

This site contains additional exercises, helpful research tools, and sample documents to
aid in the research and writing process. Find information in a variety of areas, including:

 Annotated links for each of the Web Sites Worth Knowing that appear at the
end of each chapter in Parts I–V. Find out which sites will help you get the information you need for your research project.

 Additional writing and research activities that will help you to hone in on
your weak areas and strengthen your skills through a mixture of interactive
questions, tasks, and collaborative efforts.

 Exercises that will assist you in planning and preparing your research project.
Learn how to fine-tune your topic, work with others, and conduct a successful
interview.

 Additional aids, including sample research documents at various stages of the
research process and a time line to keep you in check with your due dates.

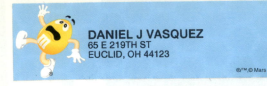

BOOKMARKS

A Guide to Research and Writing

SECOND EDITION

John Ruszkiewicz
University of Texas at Austin

Janice R. Walker
Georgia Southern University

Michael A. Pemberton
Georgia Southern University

Longman

New York   San Francisco   Boston
London   Toronto   Sydney   Tokyo   Singapore   Madrid
Mexico City   Munich   Paris   Cape Town   Hong Kong   Montreal

Vice President and Editor-in-Chief: Joseph Opiela
Acquisitions Editor: Lynn M. Huddon
Development Director: Janet Lanphier
Development Editors: Anne Brunell and Adam Beroud
Supplements Editor: Donna Campion
Media Supplements Editor: Nancy Garcia
Marketing Manager: Christopher Bennem
Senior Production Manager: Bob Ginsberg
Project Coordination, Text Design, and Electronic Page Makeup: Nesbitt Graphics, Inc.
Cover Design Manager: Wendy Ann Fredericks
Cover Designer: Kay Petronio
Cover Illustration: © Jeff Nishinaka/Artville
Photo Researcher: Photosearch, Inc.
Manufacturing Buyer: Roy Pickering
Printer and Binder: Quebecor World/Eusey
Cover Printer: Coral Graphics, Inc.

For permission to use copyrighted material, grateful acknowledgment is made to the copyright holders on pp. 431–432, which are hereby made part of this copyright page.

Library of Congress Cataloging-in-Publication Data

Ruszkiewicz, John J. 1950–
    Bookmarks: a guide to research and writing / John Ruszkiewicz, Janice R. Walker,
  Michael A. Pemberton.—2nd ed.
        p. cm.
    Includes bibliographical references and index.
    ISBN 0-321-10598-2
      1. Report writing—Handbooks, manuals, etc. 2. Report writing—Computer network
  resources—Handbooks, manuals, etc. 3. Research—Handbooks, manuals, etc.
  4. Research—Computer network resources—Handbooks, manuals, etc.
  I. Walker, Janice R. II. Pemberton, Michael A. III. Title.

  LB2369 .R88 2003
  808'.027—dc21   2002067900

Please visit our Web site at http://www.ablongman.com/bookmarks

ISBN 0-321-10598-2

2345678910—DOH—050403

Contents

PART **I**
Beginning Research   1

PART **III**
Working with Sources 112

9 Understanding Academic Responsibility and Intellectual Property 114

10 Evaluating Sources 124

PART IV
Developing the Project   178

15 Reflecting on What You Have   180

16 Refining Your Claim   186

PART **V**
Completing Your Project   232

PART **VI**
Documentation 300

Preface

What's a *bookmark?* A decade ago the answer would have been simple: a strip of metal, fabric, or paper inserted between the pages of a book to hold a reader's place. Today a bookmark can also be understood as a feature in a Web browser, a way to store Web addresses one expects to consult often, and even a digital tag in an e-book to help you find where you stopped reading in an electronic manuscript. Someone familiar with the World Wide Web might even use the term as a verb: *to bookmark.*

What has happened to this simple word provides a rationale for *Bookmarks: A Guide to Research and Writing.* Just as electronic technology has complicated the meaning of *bookmark,* it has similarly transformed every aspect of *research* for college writers and instructors. So we offer *Bookmarks* as a new generation research handbook, one built on the assumption that students need to know how electronic sources, materials, and methods are altering their relationship to knowledge.

One of the intriguing—and sometimes frustrating—features of digital technology in our era is that those technologies are constantly changing. Older software is upgraded to include new features, almost on a monthly basis; cutting-edge computing systems are fit for the scrap heap after only a couple of years; dynamic new Web tools appear, sweeping the Internet in a fraction of the time required by older ones; and useful, familiar Web pages disappear, with virtually no sign of why or how. This second edition of *Bookmarks,* then, endeavors to stay current with the dynamic information resource we know as the World Wide Web, to point you to the newest tools, sites, technologies, and programs that will enable your research.

Yet we insist that not everything has changed. Bookmarks still hold readers' places, and research still involves familiar activities such as finding topics, browsing indexes, summarizing and paraphrasing sources, and organizing ten-page papers. For this reason we have carefully designed *Bookmarks* as a bridge between old and new traditions—a guide for researchers who expect to work regularly in both print and electronic environments.

It will be obvious that *Bookmarks* has been written with the presence of technology assumed. Throughout the volume we refer to research "projects," not papers, and we treat Web pages, brochures, and multimedia presentations as plausible options for reporting research findings in many situations. We take technology seriously because it creates new opportunities for undergraduates to do serious research in both their local and their professional communities. At the University of Texas at Austin, the University of South Florida, the University of Illinois, and Georgia Southern University, we have watched students who use the Web and other technologies grow as writers and researchers, and we have been excited by their achievements.

We've also been chastened occasionally by Web projects that were more glitter than substance—offered by writers who failed to read, organize, document, or edit carefully. While much of *Bookmarks* is genuinely new, the framework for describing research processes and the detailed chapters on documentation draw on materials refined over more than a decade. The result, we are confident, is a research guide that offers writers state-of-the-art advice about college research: the best of an older tradition merged with a thoughtful assessment of the new. In keeping with this philosophy, the second edition of *Bookmarks* now attends to audience and rhetorical issues to an even greater extent than the first, considering the many ways in which digital technologies impact process, research, and presentation.

Our focus in this book is on offering **comprehensive, practical advice for student researchers,** including:

❏ An opening section **encouraging students to think of themselves as researchers** (Section 1a). More than twenty manageable chapters explain the process of research.

❏ Specific advice for **sizing up research projects and assignments** (Section 1b). In particular, writers learn how to read and interpret assignments.

❏ A chapter on **field research** (Chapter 7). Not all research occurs in the library or online, so *Bookmarks* includes suggestions for conducting interviews, using questionnaires, and making systematic observations.

❏ A complete chapter on **handling quotations** (Chapter 14), offering guidelines for selecting and using quotations.

Bookmarks pays unusual **attention to rhetorical matters**, offering:

❏ A full chapter on **finding a topic** (Chapter 2) as well as a chapter that helps writers to **focus and narrow** their theses (Chapter 4).

❏ A full chapter on establishing the **purpose of a research project** (Chapter 3). **Research hypotheses and claims** steer the development of thesis sentences and other aspects of the research process.

❏ A new chapter asking writers to **reflect on what they have** (Chapter 15) encourages them to review the results of their research at a critical point, before they begin committing themselves to a draft.

❏ A chapter on **drafting the project** (Chapter 18) that helps researchers develop cogent arguments for a particular audience.

❏ A new chapter that helps students **choose the format** that best suits the rhetorical situation for their project (Chapter 20).

❏ Two new chapters that **focus on design principles** for completing print-based (Chapter 21) and Web-based (Chapter 22) projects.

Bookmarks emphasizes the process of **evaluating and working with sources**, research skills critical for success today. We include:

❏ A full chapter on **evaluating sources** (Chapter 10), with a chart that explains the differences between research materials.

❏ A chapter on **annotating research materials** (Chapter 11). The chapter shows writers how to engage in an active dialogue with their reference sources.

❏ A thorough discussion of **intellectual property issues** (Chapter 9), with guidelines for using academic sources responsibly.

❏   A full chapter on **using search engines** (Chapter 6). The chapter helps writers manage electronic indexes and search engines efficiently.

❏   A chapter on **positioning sources** (Chapter 12). Writers learn how to detect and assess the biases in the materials they are using.

❏   A full chapter on **summarizing and paraphrasing** (Chapter 13).

To illustrate how the techniques and guidelines discussed in these chapters apply to a real writing situation, this edition of *Bookmarks* traces a single research topic—the effects of high-stakes standardized testing on the classroom—from the beginning stages of the process (finding a topic) to the production of a final draft (completing your project). Throughout the text this topic is used in examples and illustrations of the research process, and at the end of each part, writers can see how this project develops by following the advice in the preceding chapters.

A key feature of *Bookmarks* is its extraordinarily **comprehensive coverage of documentation** formats, including **Columbia Online Style (COS)**. This new system of documentation for electronic sources is presented authoritatively by its creator (Chapter 23). In addition, *Bookmarks* includes detailed treatment of **MLA, APA, CMS, and CSE** documentation styles (Chapters 24–27) with comprehensive indexes to documentation items and clear examples of citations as they should appear both in the body of a paper and in the list of Works Cited or References. *Bookmarks* includes complete **sample papers** in MLA, APA, and CMS styles, as well as excerpts from papers illustrating COS and CSE styles. Handy checklists help writers set up important items in research papers including title pages, Works Cited pages, and abstracts.

Bookmarks itself exemplifies the way technology is reshaping the writing process. The book features a **strong visual component**, with graphical elements highlighting important parts of the research process.

Each part begins with a **Technology Spotlight**, which hones readers in on an important aspect of technology as it applies to the research process.

A feature unique to this new edition is the **Focus On . . .** box that appears throughout the book. These boxes are designed to highlight noteworthy information on a range of research-related topics including ethics, collaboration, and writing.

Each chapter in Parts I through V concludes with **Web Sites Worth Knowing**, a useful feature that guides researchers to reliable and intriguing online sources.

In addition, **photographs and diagrams** throughout the book illustrate the research process.

Two complete sets of exercises follow each of Chapters 1–22. The first set introduces writers to specific research skills (**Getting Involved**) and the second leads them step-by-step through their own academic work (**Managing Your Project**).

A Glossary of terms inside the back cover provides easy reference for new or unfamiliar terminology.

Supplements

Accompanying *Bookmarks* is a large array of supplements for both instructors and students:

For instuctors and students

- The Companion Website, *Bookmarks Online* (at **http://www.ablongman.com/bookmarks**), includes numerous writing activities, links to helpful Web sites, sample projects, and other useful tools.
- *CourseCompass* is an interactive online course-management system powered by *BlackBoard*. This easy-to-use and easy-to-customize program enables instructors to tailor content and features to their own course needs. For more information, or to see a demo, visit **www.coursecompass.com**.

For instructors

- An updated *Instructor's Manual* is available to adopters of this Second Edition of *Bookmarks*.
- *An Introduction to Teaching Composition in an Electronic Environment,* by Eric Hoffman and Carol Scheidenhelm of Northern Illinois University, provides guidance for both experienced and inexperienced instructors who seek to use technology creatively.
- *Teaching in Progress,* Third Edition, by Josephine Tarvers of Winthrop University and Cindy Moore of St. Cloud State University, introduces both the basics and the latest trends in composition theory.
- *The Allyn & Bacon Sourcebook for College Writing Teachers,* Second Edition, edited by James McDonald of the University of Louisiana at Lafayette, offers varied essays by composition and rhetoric scholars on both theoretical and practical subjects.

For students

- *Researching Online,* Fifth Edition, by David Munger and Shireen Campbell of Davidson College, gives students detailed, step-by-step instructions for performing electronic searches; for researching with email, discussion lists, newsgroups, and synchronous communication; and for evaluating electronic sources.
- *The Longman Researcher's Journal,* by Mimi Markus of Broward Community College, provides helpful information, record-keeping strategies, checklists, graphic organizers, and pages for taking notes from sources, as well as space for students to write their own thoughts and reactions.
- The *iSearch Guide for Composition, 2003 Edition,* by H. Eric Branscomb and Linda R. Barr. This resource guide for the Internet covers the basics of using the Internet, conducting Web searches, and critically evaluating and documenting Internet sources. It also contains Internet activities and URLs specific to the discipline of English composition.
- The Literacy Library Series—*Public Literacy,* Second Edition, by Elizabeth Ervin; *Workplace Literacy,* Second Edition, by Rachel Spilka; and *Academic*

Literacy, by Stacia Neeley—offers instruction and models for writing in three different contexts.

- *Take Note!* is a cross-platform CD-ROM providing an information-management tool for students as they take notes from sources, outline, and prepare a bibliography.

- *ContentSelect* is an online research database that gives students instant access to thousands of academic journals and periodicals from across the disciplines. This site also offers detailed advice to students on the process of writing a research paper, tutorials on using search engines, and evaluating sources, and models for citing sources in various documentation styles. More information can be found at **http://contentselect.pearsoncmg.com/.**

- Additional Longman Resources for Students include *The Longman Writer's Journal,* by Mimi Markus; *Visual Communication,* Second Edition, by Susan Hilligoss and Tharon Howard; *Analyzing Literature: A Guide for Students,* Second Edition, by Sharon James McGee; and *A Guide for Peer Response,* Second Edition, by Tori Haring-Smith and Helon Raines.

Bookmarks may also be packaged with other books at a discount. Two dictionaries are available: *Merriam-Webster's Collegiate Dictionary,* Tenth Edition, a hardcover desk dictionary; and *The New American Webster Handy College Dictionary,* Third Edition, a briefer paperback. In conjunction with Penguin Putnam, Longman offers a variety of Penguin titles such as Arthur Miller's *Death of a Salesman,* Julia Alvarez's *How the Garcia Girls Lost Their Accents,* and Mike Rose's *Lives on the Boundary.*

Acknowledgments

Many people contributed to the development of *Bookmarks.* In particular we would like to thank the following reviewers, who have given us the benefit of their expertise: Thomas Ambrose, Seattle Pacific University; Allen Bradshaw, Mesa Community College; Craig Branham, St. Louis University; Cheryl M. Clark, Miami-Dade Community College; Alisa Cooper, South Mountain Community College; Gerard Donnelley-Smith, Clark College; Charlene A. Dykman, University of Houston; Jill D. Evans, Kettering College of Medical Arts; Thomas Fish, Cumberland College; Gloria Floren, MiraCosta College; Jim Frazer, University of Arkansas; Susanmarie Harrington, Indiana University-Purdue University Indianapolis; Bill Hart-Davidson, Purdue University; Ted E. Johnston, El Paso Community College; Traci Kelley, University of Minnesota, Crookston; Scott A. Leonard, Youngstown State University; Hilbert Levitz, Florida State University; Joe McCarren, Slippery Rock University; Lawrence McCauley, The College of New Jersey; John McLaughlin, East Stroudsburg University of Pennsylvania; Victoria E. McLure, South Plains College; M. C. Morgan, Bemidji State University; Ed Moritz, Indiana University-Purdue University Fort Wayne; Gerald Nelms, Southern Illinois University at Carbondale; Elizabeth Oakes, Western Kentucky University; Debora A. Person, University of Wyoming; Randall L. Popken, Tarleton State University; Dean Rehberger, Michigan State University; Donna Reiss,

Tidewater Community College; James Stokes, University of Wisconsin, Stevens Point; Molly Turner-Lammers, Dakota State University; Traci Hales Vass, University of Colorado, Denver; and Ken Zimmerman, Lane Community College.

We would also like to acknowledge the fine work of Dan Seward and the material borrowed from *SF Writer*, Second Edition, by John Ruszkiewicz, Maxine Hairston, and Dan Seward (Longman, 2002) on document design. We would like to thank our colleagues working in both libraries and online environments for their professional guidance on this project as well. Much of what we present in *Bookmarks* is based on information gathered over decades of teaching and research—both in dusty stacks and in front of terminals. The faculty and especially the graduate students at the University of Texas at Austin's Computer Writing and Research Labs deserve a special round of thanks. This facility of the Division of Rhetoric and Composition has pioneered many of the electronic research and pedagogical strategies described in *Bookmarks*. A special thanks as well to the Information Literacy Committees at the University of South Florida and Georgia Southern University libraries for helping to keep us informed of student and faculty concerns about research and writing from sources in the information age. Our appreciation also extends to the Technology and Writing Committee in Georgia Southern University's Writing and Linguistics Department for their continuing suggestions and advice about how to integrate computing technologies comfortably into a writing curriculum.

We are grateful, too, to the editorial team at Longman, especially to Lynn Huddon, who spearheaded the drive to take *Bookmarks* into a second edition. Anne Brunell was a superb editor to work with; her meticulous attention to detail, her carefully considered suggestions, and her gently annoying reminders about deadlines helped to keep us on track and productive. We also owe a debt of gratitude to Adam Beroud, whose detailed suggestions and commentaries were instrumental in giving shape to the revisions undertaken in the second edition. The contributions of Anne E. Smith, Sharon Balbos, Bob Ginsberg, Kelly Mountain, David Munger, Heidi Beirle, and Jennifer Bracco to the first edition of *Bookmarks* were substantial, and the strength of their work is continually evident throughout this text. No list acknowledging all the people and communities who have contributed to a work such as this can ever be complete, but we would certainly be remiss if we didn't express our indebtedness and gratitude to all those involved in the online conversations we have participated in throughout the years, whose questions, commentary, suggestions, and support have all contributed to this book.

Last, but certainly not least, we would like to thank our students in dozens of research-based writing courses for helping us to understand how college research projects typically begin, develop, advance, collapse, and recover. We hope that the practical knowledge we gained from them is evident throughout this project.

JOHN RUSZKIEWICZ
JANICE R. WALKER
MICHAEL A. PEMBERTON

To the Writer

Welcome to *Bookmarks: A Guide to Research and Writing*. This textbook provides a fresh perspective on undergraduate research because the work you'll do in college has changed. Papers are not just papers anymore. Today instructors expect you to delve deeply into new research materials and use a wide variety of innovative resources, both textual and graphic. They aren't surprised by illustrations, charts, and graphics in papers—in fact, they anticipate them. Some instructors may even encourage you to put your work online. Yet these same teachers will likely assume that you command all the traditional research skills, from reading an assignment sheet carefully to formatting a Works Cited page properly.

Bookmarks provides comprehensive information to guide you through contemporary college projects. It will help you choose a topic, find and evaluate sources, and prepare your research project efficiently, using up-to-date research and writing tools. Whether your path leads you to printed or electronic sources or to conduct your own field research, *Bookmarks* can do more than help you avoid the pitfalls of a research project. It can make the project an exciting introduction to genuine research.

Bookmarks provides ready access to the materials you will need. The chapters are arranged in a step-by-step sequence that helps you work systematically. The opening sections introduce preliminary skills such as reading an assignment sheet, discovering what is in your library, and choosing a topic. There's also an essential chapter on managing a research project (Chapter 1)—don't miss it. Then the research process advances, chapter by chapter, from finding a topic right through the completion and editing of a final project. The concluding section offers a comprehensive guide to the major systems of documentation, with a full chapter given to each type: COS, MLA, APA, CMS, and CSE.

You may treat *Bookmarks* as a reference tool as well. Use the comprehensive table of contents and the index to locate any information you need from *Bookmarks*. The part openers and chapter introductions give you a glimpse at the material contained in each section, and the convenient glossary of terms inside the back cover will explain unfamiliar terminology. Throughout the book you will find comprehensive treatment of electronic research forms, including illustrations of suggested Web sites, detailed instructions on using search engines, and important information on intellectual property for the modern researcher.

Be sure to visit the Companion Website for this text, at **http://www.ablongman .com/bookmarks**. This site offers a valuable annotated listing of links to essential Web resources to help you find information online, as well as sample papers and other useful tools.

As we hope you'll discover, undergraduate research is becoming more exciting because it is, more and more, real research with consequences for readers beyond individual classrooms. We sincerely hope that you enjoy using *Bookmarks* as much as we have enjoyed working with students like you to develop it.

JOHN RUSZKIEWICZ
JANICE R. WALKER
MICHAEL A. PEMBERTON

I

Beginning Research

Don't Miss . . .

- **The guide to project scheduling in Section 1f.** Time management is important to the success of any research project.
- **The list of specialized encyclopedias in Section 2c.** Encyclopedias offer useful background information and can point you to research topics.
- **The chart of useful research sources in Section 4d.** Make sure you consult the best sources in the most productive areas.

Technology Spotlight

PERSONAL COMPUTERS

It was not until 1977 that the first true personal computers (the Apple II and the TRS-80) were marketed to the general public—an amazing fact when you consider how commonplace PCs are today, little more than twenty-five years later. Though the Apple II and TRS-80 were not, strictly speaking, the first personal computers (that distinction goes to the Altair and a few hand-held calculators available in the early 1970s), they were the first to be embraced by the general public and the harbingers of a computer revolution that would soon sweep the world.

In 1978 the first floppy disk drives appeared; in 1981 the first modems were made available to retail consumers and the first IBM PCs appeared on store shelves with a whopping 16 kilobytes of memory (expandable to 256K!!). By the early 1980s nearly a hundred companies were offering personal computers for sale, most of them running their own software and operating systems, and many of them incompatible with one another.

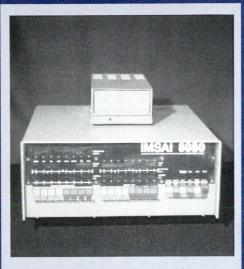

First introduced in the mid 1970s, Altair computers were sold to hobbyists as kits. Today, personal computers have revolutionized writing and research.

Today there are still hundreds of companies manufacturing and selling PCs, and thousands more are developing and producing software that will play games, design homes, create pictures, manipulate videos, generate sounds, and help people with their writing. From a morass of incompatible platforms, we are down to a modest few, with IBM-compatible PCs and Apple MacIntoshes accounting for nearly all the personal computer sales made to average consumers. Computer technology is now inescapable, integrated into our daily lives in ways that could only have been imagined twenty-five years ago. Microprocessors can be found not just in computers but in our cars, our household appliances, and in some cases even our bodies.

Just as inescapably, personal computers have become an important part of the way we do research, investigate the world, discover topics of interest, and produce much of our writing. Who can imagine what they will be capable of twenty-five years from today?

Starting Your Research Project

In college, your research will ordinarily have two dimensions: you will discover information and you will discuss what you have discovered—with friends and family, classmates and teachers, and perhaps with others through the medium of the Internet. Eventually you might address an entire professional group when you publish your findings in a journal or on a Web site. Yet scholarly research isn't only about reporting on what others have already said; it's about joining the conversation, discovering, clarifying, refuting, extending, or adding to the body of knowledge in a field. Research doesn't become real knowledge until your discoveries are shared, digested, tested, and reformulated by a community of people; the discussions which follow will then spur more ideas and more discoveries.

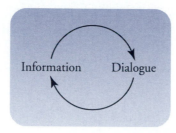

Consider what happened after Dolly, a sheep, was cloned in 1997. The discovery by Scottish scientists that it was possible to clone life forms as complex as mammals immediately settled some questions, but it raised just as many new ones. Should human beings be cloned? Would a cloned person have a soul? Would it be ethical to clone people just to harvest body parts? Could cloning help people who are unable to have children? The dialogue begun by Dolly will be churning long after she's stuffed and mounted in a museum.

Cloned by scientists in Scotland in 1997, Dolly created a firestorm in the media and raised questions about the ethics of this type of medical research. Will humans be cloned next?

Your research projects may not be quite so consequential as the one that produced Dolly, but they can have real significance if the process of discovery you initiate continues after a paper is turned in or a project submitted. College projects can open conversations that last a lifetime; many students find themselves redirecting their careers or changing majors as a result of the topics they selected for college projects. That's normal and proper.

Developments in electronic technology have made us more aware that intellectual conversations never cease. So if you think of research as an active process of creating knowledge rather than a passive one of reporting information, you'll be more comfortable with another notion: that almost every college paper and project should be supported by research. The information explosion of recent years makes this prospect exciting. Today, in the library or online, you can locate more useful (as well as not so useful) material than you can digest on almost every subject. Just as important, you'll have real opportunities to explore your subject with other writers locally and across the world. You may even be able to select the medium by which you'll share what you discover and create in a research assignment, exploring the rhetoric of document design, hypertext, or multimedia.

Of course, along with these new opportunities come new responsibilities: as a researcher, you'll find it important that you choose your sources wisely and that you accurately credit the sources you include in your project. Perhaps even more important, you will learn that, as a researcher, you have ethical responsibilities—to your subjects, to your readers, and to your ideas. From the time of Plato and Aristotle, philosophers and rhetoricians have held that a writer's goal must always be the pursuit of truth, and it will be your responsibility as a writer and researcher to remain faithful to that pursuit. Throughout this book we will consider ways in which ethics will impact your research and writing process, particularly in Chapter 9 where we discuss matters of intellectual property and plagiarism.

1a Think of yourself as a researcher and writer

Many of us imagine researchers and writers as being people different from ourselves. That may be because of the stereotypes of scientists, professors, and other professional people we see in films and on television. So consumed by their work that they barely find time to eat or fall in love, they come across as lab-coated eccentrics—comically inept, absentminded, disconnected from the problems of the "real world."

But all of us are capable of doing research, and we often do it without realizing that's what we're doing. The youngster who absorbs everything she can about the Chicago Bulls, the guy who can offer informed opinions about any car on the road, and the amateur botanists who have yet to find wildflowers they can't identify have all sought out, evaluated, and cataloged information on their favorite subjects. They have acquired surprising levels of expertise on topics that matter to them. Likely, they could—if asked—write about these subjects with authority and even passion. And that's what professional researchers do. Research develops from curiosity, the simple need to learn things and to share discoveries with others.

While research may take patience, skill, method, and some training, it's not beyond the talents of anyone intrigued enough by a subject or a problem to do something about it. People learn to do research just as they learn to write, and they get better at both skills the more they practice them. Just as important, people in the professional world usually do research as part of a team. They work toward common goals, argue about how to get there, collaborate on their reports, and (usually) share the credit.

WWW

1.1

So don't begin a research project—especially one that will involve writing—by underrating your talent and potential. Expect to be challenged and to work hard. Expect to involve others in your work. And expect to succeed.

1b　Size up your assignment carefully

Writing is a response to a particular set of requirements and demands, what is often referred to as the *rhetorical situation*. In many cases, a college research project assignment will be spelled out on an assignment sheet. In others, you may be expected to determine the shape of the assignment for yourself, usually within certain parameters. That is, your instructor may specify the number of words or pages and a due date but leave other considerations for you to decide. Make sure you understand what you may do. If you do not have an assignment sheet, ask questions. Pay attention to the key words in the assignment that will help you define the scope of your project; each of these terms has its own significance. Think of the assignment sheet as a contract, and annotate and highlight its key features. As in any contract, rules, regulations, and requirements will be spelled out—and there may even be some fine print. Read your assignment sheet carefully and consider the following.

Scope. An instructor may give you options for presenting a project—as a conventional paper, an oral report, an electronic presentation, a Web project. Understand those options in terms of what you must do and at what length. Find out whether the project has word or page limits or time limits at *both* ends (no less than, no more than). Most instructors don't want to read twenty-page papers when the assignment calls for four or five pages, and if you're asked to produce at least five pages, instructors will certainly be annoyed if your report has only three or four.

CHART

Key Research Terms

Analyze. Examine. Break your subject into its parts or components. Discuss their relationship or function.

Classify. Define. Place your subject into a more general category. Distinguish it from other objects in that category. What are its significant features? What makes it unique? recognizable?

Discuss. Talk about the problems or issues your subject raises. Which issues are the most significant? What actions might be taken? Look at the subject from several points of view.

Evaluate. Think about the subject critically. What criteria would you use to judge it? How well does it meet those standards? How does it compare to similar subjects?

Review of the literature. Examine a field or subject to see what the key issues are and what positions have been staked out by various researchers.

Explain. Show what your subject does or how it operates. Provide background information about it. Put your subject in its historical or political context so readers understand it better.

Compare. Show how your subject resembles other things or ideas.

Contrast. Show how your subject differs from other things or ideas.

Prove. Provide evidence in support of an idea or assertion.

Disprove. Provide evidence to contradict or undermine an idea or assertion.

Persuade. Come to a conclusion about your subject and explain why you believe what you do. Use evidence to convince others to agree, or provide good reasons for someone to think or act in a particular way.

Survey. Measure opinion on a question by using appropriate methods to guarantee an adequate, random, and representative sample of the population.

Due dates. There may be due dates for separate parts of the project: topic proposal, annotated bibliography, outline, first draft, final draft. Take each due date seriously, and assume that an assignment is due at the *beginning* of class on the date appointed, not by the end of class or later in the school day. Plan your time accordingly.

Rhetorical approach. Sometimes an instructor will specify the rhetorical approach you should take in your paper, indicated by the presence of certain *key research terms* in the assignment sheet. (See the chart, "Key Research Terms," above.) Evaluating a research subject is very different from analyzing it, and the shape of your research—as well as your final project—will be different too. Make sure you understand what you are expected to *show* through your research and how you are expected to present it.

Audience. Consider the needs and expectations of an audience. Why would someone be interested in the information you plan to present? What is your purpose in presenting this information? What can you assume that your audience already knows about your topic? What information will you need to provide in order for them to understand your position? Consider what kinds of evidence you will need in order to convince your audience; not everyone will be persuaded by the same facts or arguments. Remember, too, that while your instructor is an important audience, he or she should not usually be your *only* audience.

Presentation. Note exactly what your final paper or project must include. The instructor may require such items as a cover sheet, an abstract, appendices, bibliographies, illustrations, charts, and links. Highlight such requirements so you don't forget them. Check, too, whether your instructor expects you to turn in all your materials at the end of a project, including notes, drafts, photocopied sources, and peer editing sheets. If so, keep this material in a folder or an envelope or keep an electronic copy on disk from the start of the project. Don't wait until the last minute to get organized.

Format. Will your project be typed or printed, or will it be submitted or published electronically? Consider the requirements of the assignment as well as the needs of your audience in determining the proper format. Notice specific requirements the instructor may have for margins, placement of page numbers, line spacing, titles, headings, illustrations, graphics, and so on, or specific formats required for electronic projects. Are there requirements for Web page layout, compatibility with multiple Web browsers, file sizes, colors, or page links? If an instructor doesn't give specific directions for such items, you may want to follow the guidelines for your discipline of study. These guidelines often include more considerations than how to format a paper or cite sources; if in doubt, consult the style manual for your field. We provide samples of papers that follow various conventions, depending on purpose and discipline: Columbia Online Style (COS) for projects using electronic sources, for both the humanities (MLA and Chicago styles) and the sciences (APA and CSE styles); Modern Language Association (MLA) style for projects in English and the humanities; American Psychological Association (APA) style for projects in psychology and the social sciences; the *Chicago Manual of Style* (CMS) for projects in the humanities and other fields; and the Council of Science Editors (CSE) style for projects in the natural sciences.

Documentation. Be sure you understand your instructor's preferences for documenting a project. Some instructors may specify MLA, APA, or COS documentation; others may give you the option of choosing any system, providing that you handle it consistently. Make the decision about your documentation system early because you'll want to use it for your bibliography and notes or in your electronic files. You should get early feedback on your documentation, too, so commit yourself to getting the notes right at the beginning.

Collaboration. Instructors may encourage or require collaboration on research projects. If that's the case with your project, learn the ground rules to see how the work

1.2

can be divided and what reports and self-assessments may be required from project participants. Pay attention, too, to how the project itself will be evaluated.

❧ FOCUS ON . . . Collaboration

You may be expected or invited to work as part of a team for some college projects. If so, use the occasion to learn how to work productively to achieve a common goal. You'll quickly discover that careful management is an important part of any collaborative effort. Here is advice for organizing a group effort.

Decide how to make decisions. In most cases you will want a process that is flexible enough to encourage input from every member of the team but also responsive enough to allow timely decisions. A team might choose a project leader or decide to meet regularly during the project (even by email) and reach a consensus through discussions or voting. In any case, it is crucial that people on a team agree on how to make decisions and then respect that process.

Make sure someone has an overview of the process. Whether or not a project has a leader, someone must keep track of what each person is doing. Even groups as small as three or four people can lose sight of project goals, resources, or timelines and waste time by duplicating efforts. Choose one team member to allocate resources and adjust schedules to bring a project in on time.

Talk with each other. Members of a team need to talk with one another throughout a project so that they get a feel for each other's ideas, concepts, and goals. As much as possible, teams should practice "simultaneous engineering"—that is, a team should be aware of the impact their choices might have on each component of a project, especially in the early stages.

Assess the strengths of team members. When you work collaboratively, you can take advantage of what team members know individually and at the same time compensate for their weaknesses. While every member of the team should be exposed to almost every part of the project, people should work chiefly on those parts of a project for which they have skill, talent, and experience. Members can be assigned their major responsibilities either by a project leader or by group consensus, but a team has to be sure people don't undertake responsibilities they can't handle. A little diplomacy and honesty early in a project can save a lot of heartache later.

Be frank about sharing responsibilities. Quite often, students working collaboratively on a project may be asked to assess each other's work. So it is important that team members understand their assignments and those of their colleagues—and expect to be held responsible for them. If you can't pull your weight on a project, let your colleagues know immediately so they can make adjustments. Perhaps you can take on a job you can handle better. The worst tactic is to string your team members along, leading them to expect work you can't or won't produce.

1c Establish the hard points of your project

Hard points are those features of a project you can't change—they are usually described in the assignment. When an instructor asks for a ten-page paper on genetic engineering using CSE style and due in two weeks, you have four hard points.

1. Format: ten-page paper
2. Topic: genetic engineering
3. Documentation: CSE
4. Due date: two weeks from today

All four points will shape your planning, but perhaps none more so than the due date. You know that researching and writing ten pages in two weeks is a lot of work.

Many college assignments will have only one due date: the day the project must be submitted. When that's the case, you'll have to schedule the remainder of the project yourself. But do take that due date seriously. Instructors rarely show tolerance for late projects, particularly when there has been plenty of time to complete them.

Some instructors, however, may give you a series of due dates for a major project, asking that you submit items such as the following at specific times:

- Project proposal, prospectus, or thesis
- Annotated working bibliography
- Storyboards (for projects with graphics)
- First draft
- Web site design specifications
- Responses to peer editing

```
PROJECT              ANNOTATED              FIRST              FINAL
PROPOSAL    --->     BIBLIOGRAPHY   --->    DRAFT     --->     DRAFT
OCT. 2               OCT. 16                OCT. 23            NOV. 6
```

1.3

When you are given multiple due dates, they can be arranged to form a timeline into which you can fit the remaining hard points of your project.

1d Define the stages of your project

If you've never done a full research project, you might find yourself guessing about many of these steps. But your hard points provide a starting point. Each goal in the plan has to be met before your site will be ready for your target audience.

Different kinds of projects may follow vastly different paths. If you are gathering information in a library, you might have to allow time for creating a bibliography, locating documents, and then taking notes from them. If you are planning a field project that involves interviews, you have to determine *whom* to interview about *what,* prepare the questions, conduct the interviews, and then review and report your findings. If you are searching the World Wide Web for articles and resource documents, you will need time to search the Web, determine which resources are the most useful, print out hard copies of Web pages or save them to a disk, and keep track of their locations.

At the outset, however, there is no sure way of knowing all the elements a project might involve. The best you can do is estimate your work. In planning a project, it will certainly help to talk to more experienced researchers, to librarians, to instructors, and to colleagues. You might also review sample research projects, asking yourself, What did the authors have to do to create this work or get these results?

Finally, you might review the activities that research projects typically require. No project would include all the items listed in the checklist below, and many projects might include tasks and activities not mentioned here. Use the checklist to stimulate your own thinking and to help you arrange your activities in a rough sequence.

CHECKLIST
Research Activities

Stage 1: Beginning Research
- ○ Size up the assignment
- ○ Establish the hard points of your project
- ○ Choose a topic that fits the assignment and matches your interests
- ○ Determine your purpose and audience
- ○ Create a management plan
- ○ Prepare a proposal or prospectus for your research project
- ○ If people will be used as subjects in your study, check campus research policies

Stage 2: Gathering Ideas and Information
- ○ Determine what information you need
- ○ Decide where to look for information
- ○ Consult bibliographies
- ○ Locate sources of information (in libraries, online databases, on the World Wide Web, etc.)
- ○ Request materials through interlibrary loan, if necessary
- ○ Prepare questionnaires and/or surveys, if appropriate
- ○ Create a plan for systematic observation of subjects or objects of study
- ○ Keep track of information systematically
- ○ Establish a database or method of compiling results
- ○ Determine the best format to present your findings; if necessary, contact printers, Web consultants, research librarians, or other experts

(Continued)

Research Activities *(Continued)*

Stage 3: Working with Sources
- ○ Generate a working bibliography
- ○ Evaluate your sources
- ○ Annotate research materials
- ○ Prepare an annotated bibliography
- ○ Read and position sources
- ○ Summarize and paraphrase sources
- ○ Conduct interviews
- ○ Distribute questionnaires or surveys
- ○ Conduct studies or observations

Stage 4: Developing the Project
- ○ Refine your claim
- ○ Organize your materials
- ○ Decide on a design for your project
- ○ Begin drafting your project
- ○ Submit a draft or prototype
- ○ Get feedback on your project
- ○ Respond to feedback and make any necessary changes or revisions
- ○ Meticulously document all sources used in your project
- ○ Fine-tune your project, making any last-minute revisions or edits
- ○ Test and carefully proofread your final project
- ○ Submit your final project

1e   Assess your strengths and weaknesses

Once you have a comprehensive idea of what your research project will require from you (or your team), plot those responsibilities against your timeline and decide how much effort to devote to each stage. If you know you are a competent researcher but a slow writer, or if you are prone to procrastination, you might allot extra time to draft a research paper. Similarly, if you are a novice at interviewing, you may want to schedule more interviews than absolutely necessary, figuring that the earlier ones might not be entirely successful. (See also Chapter 8, "Keeping Track of Information.")

This is the point at which to acknowledge any personal limitations. For example, if you have no experience with document design or managing graphics, you should rethink the wisdom of creating a project heavy on illustrations. Or perhaps you'd like to prepare a paper comparing great American novels, but you realize that you aren't a particularly fast reader. A paper about great American short stories might be more successful.

You also have to measure your resources. What kinds of materials can you find in your local community? Do you have the tools and the money to produce exactly what you want? Do the members of your team have the experience to do the kind of project you envision? Adjust your plan accordingly and expect to make similar adjustments throughout the project.

Sometimes circumstances outside your project will change the timeline. Try to anticipate minor calamities: interlibrary loan operating more slowly than expected, fewer respondents replying to your survey than predicted, campus computer access growing more difficult at the end of the term. Factor in a little extra time for problems such as writer's block or a tendency to procrastinate.

A few tricks may help you overcome these problems. You might try freewriting, for instance. Write about your topic for ten minutes as quickly as you can without pausing to correct mistakes or revise wording. That way you'll have some words on paper to get you started or to keep you going. Try keeping a journal to record ideas you may have while watching a television show or eating lunch. To overcome a tendency to procrastinate, you might make a commitment to write *something* every day, no matter what. Or try breaking a large task down into smaller, more manageable components. For example, instead of attempting to produce an entire draft, why not write just a one- or two-paragraph introduction? You could even "talk" your draft into a tape recorder, then transcribe it. One way to overcome procrastination is by setting a schedule and sticking to it. For more tips, see "Web Sites Worth Knowing" at the end of this chapter.

WWW

1.4

1f Create a schedule for your project

When you have established your hard points, listed the steps and stages of your project, and assessed your capabilities, you are ready to sketch out your project in a calendar or timeline. You can create a calendar simply by listing the due dates of a project and leaving sufficient space between them to insert the activities necessary to meet those deadlines. Then estimate the time necessary and/or available for each step in the project. Your initial calendar should not be too detailed; you'll waste time if you try to account for every movement in what is largely an unpredictable process.

You can also mark off your research project on an actual calendar—the kind that provides a box for listing each day's activities. With such a calendar you can get a clear sense of the time available to do your work, perhaps coordinating it with your other commitments. Again, begin by marking down the due dates. Then look at the time available to complete the entire job, counting the actual days if it helps. If you are given only a completion date, estimate the halfway point of your project and decide what you must accomplish by that point—perhaps a complete first draft or a working Web site design. Whatever type of calendar you create, allow some slack toward the end to make up for time you will almost certainly lose earlier in the project.

A third type of project calendar is a timeline, also known as a Gantt chart. Here the trick is to imagine a line moving steadily forward while various activities proceed through stages that may be overlapping or even circular. You can design a timeline that

```
   PROJECT              ANNOTATED             FIRST               FINAL
   PROPOSAL    --->     BIBLIOGRAPHY  --->    DRAFT      --->     DRAFT
   OCT. 2               OCT. 16               OCT. 23             NOV. 6

 <--Choose a topic-->

    <--Prepare proposal-->

       <-----------Find sources----------->

       <----------Evaluate sources----------->

       <---Prepare annotated bibliography------>

             <-----Read and position sources----->

                         <--Refine claim-->

                  <----Prepare a draft---->

                                    <---Revise--->

                                       <---Edit--->
```

illustrates this process by mapping ongoing responsibilities below the more linear due dates, as in the example above.

Whatever form of calendar you create for your paper or project, allow flexibility. Sometimes a carefully considered plan will have to be reshaped when things don't go quite as you expect. Always remember that the point of having a schedule is to produce a product; all is not lost if you have to change a schedule to fit altered circumstances. Few projects meet all their initial goals.

More than anything else, we want to impress on you the value of forethought as you plan out your research project, even before you decide exactly what your topic is going to be. An understanding of your assignment, its requirements, and the time frame you're working in will definitely pay off in the long run. Armed with a clear sense of what you have to accomplish, you're ready to move onto the next step: choosing a topic.

WWW Web Sites Worth Knowing

1.5

- Procrastination and Writer's Block, **http://owl.english.purdue.edu/workshops/hypertext/ResearchW/procrast.html**
- Group Work and Collaborative Writing, **http://www-honors.ucdavis.edu/vohs/**
- Time and the Writer, **http://www.writing-world.com/basics/time.html**

GETTING INVOLVED

1. Describe a subject about which you might be said to have expert knowledge. The subject can be in any realm, from baseball cards to horticulture. Explain how you acquired knowledge of your subject. Could you write a book about the subject? How would you prepare to write such a book—what additional research might you have to do?

2. People often form opinions or urge action on the basis of faulty information. Describe a problem in your local community (school, town, workplace) that might be clarified if people had better information or shared it more effectively. For example, students on one campus might be complaining that their fees for courses and activities are too high. But just how high are those fees? Are they out of line with fees at comparable institutions? Have the fees been rising at a rate faster than inflation? In this case, researching the facts about fees might make claims about fees better informed. But consider also how such information might be effectively shared. Or explore why there is not meaningful dialogue on the subject. Look for similar cases or situations in your community.

MANAGING YOUR PROJECT

1. Photocopy your assignment sheet for a project, then annotate it thoroughly. Highlight the actual assignment and the due dates. Note the special features the project must have. What parts of the assignment emphasize information? What parts encourage dialogue, conversation, or collaboration?

2. Identify the two or three parts of the assignment that you expect will cause you the most difficulty, and then explain to yourself exactly why you are nervous about those requirements or expectations. For each such problem, consider what steps you might take to make the difficulty more manageable. Will more reading help? Could the instructor or a librarian help? Might the project be easier if you found someone to collaborate with?

3. Examine your entire project carefully and break it down into four or five major stages. You might imagine steps such as the following.

For a Paper	For a Web Project
Finding/focusing on a topic	Determining purpose
Locating information	Determining basic site design
Reading and assessing sources	Assigning and developing pages
Producing a first draft	Establishing links
Getting feedback	Getting feedback and testing
Revising and editing	Fine-tuning the design

Look at your stages in terms of the time available for completion, and establish a firm timeline for completing the paper. Be sure that the calendar leaves ample time for feedback from colleagues. The more time you allow for revision and fine tuning, the better your final project will be. That's because major projects often require a lot of work at the end: creating a Works Cited page, gathering notes, testing a design for "bugs," getting clean and handsome copies, and so on. Don't wait until the last minute.

C H A P T E R

2

Finding a Topic

Why is it that in a world of six billion people, virtually unlimited channels of information, thousands of years of history, hundreds of resource opportunities, and new controversies daily in most professions, a surprising proportion of students in the United States, given the power to research any topic, will choose capital punishment, abortion, the legalization of marijuana/hemp, euthanasia, or school prayer? A cynic might suggest that it's because an enterprising writer can lift a project on one of these topics from just about anywhere—a sorority file, a big brother, a term paper company, a Web site. Change the author's name, alter the date, add a recent source or two, and the work is done. Little effort is expended . . . and nothing is learned.

A more charitable view might be that writers seek topics that are both decently controversial and comfortably familiar because then they can be sure to find both an angle on the subject and plenty of respectable sources. Most people *do* have opinions about capital punishment or abortion and can rehash arguments they've been hearing all their lives. Such topics are the intellectual equivalent of the Dairy Queen—filling, familiar, and always just around the corner. Little is ventured to produce such a project and little gained. The effort is forgotten as soon as it is completed.

Expect more from a subject and from yourself. Have more confidence in your ability and that of your colleagues to make discoveries about fresh issues and problems closer to you and your community—whether that community is a college seminar on medieval history, a crowded lecture section on American literature since 1820, a film society considering the appeal of silent classics, or a neighborhood watch group looking for proven techniques to reduce vandalism. No matter who you are or where you're from, you have areas of interest, expertise, and knowledge that you can bring to bear on a research topic; trust in yourself and your ability to write about a subject in ways that will intrigue and captivate your audience.

A good subject in itself won't make a research project successful. But you'll find that the energy that comes from discovering a topic that means something to you and your colleagues will make all the difference. Finding a topic to write about begins with your own questions and ideas, usually prompted by class discussions and readings. By listening to what others have to say, you can start to get a good sense of your audience.

Choosing a topic for your project may sometimes seem like an insurmountable challenge. However, by focusing on those ideas that matter to you, perhaps in your local community, you can cut a seemingly daunting task down to size.

What are their concerns? What are their questions? What do they already understand about a topic, and what do they need or want to know? Why are they interested in a subject, and what sort of approach are they most likely to listen to? Knowing something about your audience is vitally important as you begin working on your research project. It will not only help you decide on a research plan, but it will also guide you in organizing and presenting your information as you write.

Discussions of this sort—with classmates, instructors, friends, and others you know well—can help you clarify your own thinking. What aspects of the subject do you already know a lot about, and which do you feel less certain of? Do other people raise points you hadn't thought of? Do they introduce related issues or make connections that you find intriguing? Do they agree with your views completely, or are there areas where they disagree with you dramatically? The cues you get from these discussions can be a valuable part of your initial discovery and research process.

But you must also extend these discussions beyond the classroom by participating in further conversations and discussions, face-to-face or online, through outside reading, watching television, browsing electronic newsgroups or the World Wide Web, and thinking about your topic.

2a Find a topic in your world

Many college research projects are open-ended—that is, your topic will be connected in some way to the general subject of the course, but its specific focus will be determined by you. You're expected to explore topics related to course themes—typically, subjects such as gender, multiculturalism, the environment, religion, education. In a history class you might write about an era or a movement or a conflict (the Gilded Age, the Civil War); in a philosophy course, a movement (Thomism, Existentialism); in government, a theme or concept (balance of power); in the natural sciences, an experiment; in the social sciences, a field project. Within these broad areas, however, you will have much room to choose specific topics.

When it's appropriate, you should try to connect an assignment to your own experiences and to issues of consequence in local, regional, or national communities. For ex-

🌀 FOCUS ON . . . Purpose

Finding a topic has a great deal to do with discovering a purpose for your research. As you consider topics, consider what you would like to accomplish by reading and writing about a topic. Perhaps you want to express your feelings about something, to learn more about it, to inform other people about it, or to persuade other people of something. Remember, however, that your purpose goes beyond the desire to narrate, inform, persuade, etc. Your purpose is the reason *why* you want to do these things, what you hope to accomplish.

For example, if you are writing to express your feelings about the required first-year writing courses at your university, perhaps you hope that by so doing you will be able to persuade your audience to effect some change in university policy related to those courses, or perhaps you want to persuade fellow students of the benefits of these courses so that they will expend more time and effort on them. You may find there are many topics in which you are interested, but the difficulty lies in finding those for which you can also discover a clear and certain purpose. Without that purpose, however, your research and writing will be drudge work, and your audience will likely come away from reading your work wondering why you have written about your topic at all.

ample, you may be uneasy after watching a *Crossfire* debate on standardized testing in schools. Do the participants' views reflect your experience in taking such tests? Are the facts and assumptions you have heard accurate, the claims justified? A serious project might grow from such a query. Similarly, a history assignment on the civil rights movement could lead you to inquire about local concerns: Was your school or community ever segregated? How did your city or town react to civil rights initiatives or legislation? Do contemporary concerns for women or gay rights have roots in this earlier political movement?

We suggest placing issues in local, even individual, contexts—not just to make them more challenging personally, but also because you're more likely to do original research when your project explores real turf, not abstract territories. A generic paper on capital punishment will likely rehash arguments a century old, but investigating a local death penalty case could produce significant insights.

Don't, however, expect a cogent topic to drop from the sky, and don't rely on sudden inspiration to strike you. Open yourself up to the world by reading critically everything you can get your hands on: local newspapers, university journals, trade magazines, minutes of influential committees, fliers distributed by offbeat groups, online discussion forums. Watch TV this way too, especially the news channels (CNN, MSNBC, Fox News) and that most valuable and unfiltered political source, C-SPAN. Surf the Net, checking out political, cultural, and social sites of interest to you—or even those that offend you. (You're more likely to be moved to action by encountering something you don't like.) And talk with people, face-to-face or via electronic forums. Remember that you will not be doing your research or writing about your project in isolation. You need to find out what others think, what's important to them, and how they will respond to what you want to say.

2b Connect your topic to a wider community

From the start, you should invite others to join in the exploration of your topic. Look for campus events, clubs, or forums that might be related to the subject. Consult the local papers for information about lectures, film groups, or community meetings where you might meet people interested in your work. When you find such people, network with them to find more people and organizations invested in your subject. To begin research on a paper about standardized testing and its impact on the classroom, for example, you could contact the local chapter of the PTA or attend a meeting of the local Board of Education. The people you encounter at these meetings might be able to point you to resources and reference materials far more quickly and efficiently than you could manage on your own.

2.2

    If you are in a course with access to a local electronic network or chat room, invite classmates to join you in a session to discuss research ideas. As you explain your topic to others, you'll grasp it better yourself: its features will stand in sharper relief when viewed side by side with the projects your colleagues are planning. You can also explore subjects via a class listserv (if your instructor sets one up) or through conventional email exchanges with instructors and colleagues. Or you may be able to set up your own electronic discussion list through such sites as *Yahoo! Groups* or *Tile.net* (see "Web Sites Worth Knowing").

    Consider, too, how the project you are planning might be framed for a real audience, preferably one that includes many more people than yourself and an instructor. Take your assignment public. For example: the best medium for exploring the costs of local environmental cleanups might be a Web site; your paper describing local reading projects might have more impact redesigned as a feature story in a campus publication or as a multimedia presentation for recruiting literacy volunteers; a critique of "high stakes" standardized testing might best be directed to an influential state politician. Not all research efforts can be shaped this way, but even the most conventional paper can be written for more than just a grade.

2.3

2c Browse the library in your topic area

Look for a subject about which you can honestly say, "I want to learn much more about it." The enthusiasm you bring to a project will be evident in the work you produce. Of course, not all subjects hold the same potential. Avoid stale controversies that have been on the national or local news without resolution for a long time—don't be one of a half dozen students submitting projects on an unresolvable campus concern with parking or football tickets. You'll find plenty of material on such subjects, but it is unlikely you'll add much to the debate. Think too about how your instructor will react to a paper that rehashes the same facts about the same boring topic that he or she has read about dozens of times over the years. You want your paper to be different, to spark interest, to stand out from the others in the stack. The best way to do that is to go beyond "obvious" content, and the best way to do that is to learn as much as you can about your subject.

Get closer to your subject by spending a few hours browsing in the library or on the World Wide Web. (See Section 2d and Chapter 6 for a full discussion of online resources.) A little preliminary research, reading, and talking about ideas can help you discover what to say about a topic that hasn't already been said over and over. Exploring

---

CHECKLIST

Specialized Encyclopedias

Doing a paper on . . . ?	Begin by checking . . .
American history	○ *Encyclopedia of American History*
Anthropology	○ *International Encyclopedia of the Social Sciences*
Art	○ *Encyclopedia of World Art*
Astronomy	○ *Encyclopedia of Astronomy*
Communication	○ *International Encyclopedia of Communication*
Computers	○ *Encyclopedia of Computer Science*
Crime	○ *Encyclopedia of Crime and Justice*
Economics	○ *Encyclopedia of American Economic History*
Environment	○ *Encyclopedia of the Environment*
Ethics in life sciences	○ *Encyclopedia of Bioethics*
Film	○ *International Encyclopedia of Film*
Health, medicine	○ *Health and Medical Horizons*
History	○ *Dictionary of American History*
Law	○ *The Guide to American Law*
Literature	○ *Cassell's Encyclopedia of World Literature*
Multiculturalism	○ *Encyclopedia of Multiculturalism*
Music	○ *The New Grove Dictionary of American Music*
Philosophy	○ *Encyclopedia of Philosophy*
Political science	○ *Encyclopedia of American Political History*
Politics	○ *Oxford Companion to Politics of the World*
Psychology, psychiatry	○ *International Encyclopedia of Psychiatry, Psychology, Psychoanalysis and Neurology; Encyclopedia of Psychology*
Religion	○ *The Encyclopedia of Religion; Encyclopedia Judaica; New Catholic Encyclopedia*
Science	○ *McGraw-Hill Encyclopedia of Science and Technology*
Social sciences	○ *Encyclopedia of the Social Sciences*

your topic in this way can also help you determine what the actual controversies are by helping you to focus your ideas.

Efficient sources for the preliminary exploration of academic topics are encyclopedias, beginning with those that deal specifically with your subject. Encyclopedias provide broad overviews of many subjects, outlining the important issues within a particular field and focusing more on general concepts than on details. In this way, they help you get a sense of the big picture within which your own research project will fit. The more specialized the encyclopedia, the better its coverage of a subject area will be. Library reference rooms have dozens of specialized encyclopedias covering many fields, and many libraries also offer electronic access to them. Ask reference librarians for their help. The checklist on page 19 points you to some of the most commonly available specialized encyclopedias.

When no specialized encyclopedia is available, or if the volume you select proves too technical, use one of the general encyclopedias available in print or electronic format.

Print	Electronic
The Encyclopaedia Britannica	*Britannica Online*
Encyclopedia Americana	*Encarta*
Collier's Encyclopedia	*Grolier Multimedia Encyclopedia*
Columbia Encyclopedia	*Academic American Encyclopedia*

To get a feel for your topic area, examine books and journals in the field as well. What are the major issues? Who is affected by them? Who is writing on the topic? You can learn more than you might expect from quick but purposeful browsing. One thing you will learn fairly easily is whether or not sufficient reliable resources exist to support your project in the time available. If you have a difficult time finding information about your research topic, you might consider changing it. On the other hand, if a wealth of information is available, you should survey your subject so you can identify key issues and narrow the scope of your project as appropriate. Even more important, you should use the time you spend browsing to confirm whether you are in fact interested in your topic and want to read about it more deeply.

2d Browse the Internet

Check out your subject by examining online resources such as Web sites and discussion groups. To see what others have posted on your subject, you can explore Web sites using search engines (see Chapter 6) to find the best locations. The quality of materials in this vast environment varies enormously (see Chapter 10). Still, a well-constructed Web site should provide a helpful overview of a subject as well as links to other sources. Many libraries also offer access to databases and other reference sources through the World Wide Web (see Section 5b).

Like Web sites, Internet discussion groups can help you understand the dimensions of a subject—what it involves and what the issues are. Internet discussion groups include both *asynchronous* communications, such as email, listservs, newsgroups, and bulletin boards like those available in WebCT or Blackboard courseware, and real-time *synchronous* communications, such as IRC (Internet Relay Chat), MUDs (Multi-User Domains) and MOOs (MUDs Object Oriented), and chat rooms. In an asynchronous discussion, participants read messages that have been posted earlier and leave messages of their own for others to read at their convenience. In a real-time discussion, the participants are online at the same time, reading and responding immediately to each other, as they might in an actual conversation.

Email, listservs, and newsgroups. Many people use the Internet to communicate about a wide variety of topics. Internet discussion lists enable people with common interests to share information via email exchanges. Electronic mail, listservs, and Internet newsgroups can all be sources of material for a research project, and you might begin a discussion to help you discover what to explore. They can also be good places to ask questions and to learn about other potential sources. However, before using information obtained from email or listserv messages, make sure you get permission, and always give proper credit (see Chapter 14).

Some email lists and newsgroups are informal or classroom discussion lists. Others, such as *ClariNet,* are fee-for-subscription services that offer up-to-the-hour news reporting. Newsgroups come in all shapes and sizes, from raunchy or eccentric *alt.whatever* groups to moderated groups offering expert information on a wide variety of topics. Almost all Internet providers, on campus and off, allow access to newsgroups, and most browser programs (including *Netscape* and Microsoft *Internet Explorer*) contain newsreader functions that will let you read and participate in them easily. Some people prefer to use specialized newsreader programs such as *Forté FreeAgent* (**http://www.forteinc.com/agent/download.php**) for this purpose.

Whichever route you follow or program you use to gain access, however, understand that there are far more newsgroups than you will ever be able to read—more than 55,000 at the time of writing. A very small sampling will illustrate something of the range these groups cover:

alt.algebra.help

alt.dorks

humanities.classics

info.academic-freedom

rec.animals.wildlife

rec.folk-dancing

soc.history.ancient

talk.environment

The sheer number of available newsgroups need not be daunting. You can usually do a quick text search in the list of available groups to find those that might be related to your subject area. For example, if your subject is related to religion in the United States, a search for the word "religion" would reveal dozens of postings under *alt.religion, soc.religion,* and *talk.religion.* You might locate ongoing conversations about standardized tests and classroom teaching in *alt.education.higher*, *k12.ed.comp.literacy*, and *misc.education.language.english* by searching under "education," "literacy," and "language," respectively. You can find discussions of current news events on the newsgroup *alt.current-events.usa*. Not all such sources will be equally helpful, but remember that you aren't seeking research material at this stage; you're deciding whether an issue merits more scrutiny.

In contrast to newsgroups, which are publicly accessible in the broadest sense—virtually anyone anywhere can post anything and read everything—listservs tend to be more private and more focused. A listserv is an email discussion group, sometimes called a "list," that interested parties can subscribe to and unsubscribe from at will. Participants with common interests join the list (which is usually a matter of sending a "subscribe" message to the computer that handles such things), and messages sent to the list are automatically distributed to every subscribed member. You can find listservs with search engines such as *Tile.Net* or you can search through newsgroups using a specialized search engine such as *Google Groups* (**http://groups.google.com/**). Some listservs and newsgroups such as *HyperNews* can be read on the World Wide Web using a browser, or you may be able to read them in your Internet email editor (see Chapter 5).

Make sure you follow proper *netiquette* (the etiquette of the Net); although many listserv and newsgroup discussions are open forums, discussion lists often focus on specific topics, and list members do not want students or others posting queries. It is usually best to "lurk" for a while, read the FAQs (frequently asked questions) and other information about the list, and get a sense of the conversation before asking questions.

Telnet sites.   Telnet is an application that allows you to log on to a remote computer and access its files and programs. Most telnet sites will require that you have an account on their server, with a log-in name and password. You may use telnet protocols to log on to your school computer from home. Once connected, you can work on that computer just as if you had accessed it directly. Many libraries allow telnet access to their catalogs, and most MOOs and MUDs (real-time synchronous communication sites on the Internet) use telnet protocols. Telnet sites, like most Internet sites, can also be accessed using a World Wide Web browser and the address form *telnet://address* (for example, *telnet://damoo.csun.edu:8888*). Various client programs are available for telnet applications as well. Some may already be installed on your host computer, and others are available on the Internet for free downloading.

MOOs and MUDs are similar to the chat rooms with which you may already be familiar. In addition to holding scholarly conferences and meetings in MOOs, many teachers meet with students online. The format can range from informal classroom discussions to very formal scholarly conference presentations.

Internet Relay Chat (IRC) and chat rooms.   Internet Relay Chat (IRC) is one of the most popular and best known forms of synchronous communication, or real-time conferencing. Recent technological developments and the proliferation of multimedia computers have brought developments in IRC client programs as well, and many chat rooms and messenger programs, such as *Yahoo!*, now allow for real-time audio and video conferencing and easy file sharing.

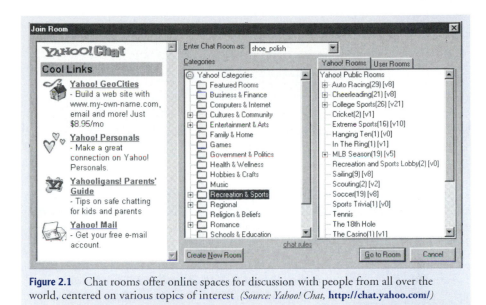

Figure 2.1 Chat rooms offer online spaces for discussion with people from all over the world, centered on various topics of interest *(Source: Yahoo! Chat,* **http://chat.yahoo.com/***)*

Like MOOs and MUDs, IRC channels and Internet chat rooms are sites to meet with people from around the world and discuss various topics in real time. You can conduct online interviews in these spaces with a wide variety of people, conduct surveys or ethnographic studies, and meet with group members to discuss your findings. Different "channels" or "rooms" represent distinct communities or topics. Figure 2.1, for example, shows the list of public rooms available in *Yahoo! Chat's* "Recreation and Sports" category. Before logging a conversation or using information in your research, however, make sure you ask permission, and make sure that you cite your sources accurately.

Web boards. Some professional Web sites have discussion areas or "electronic bulletin boards" where others can share opinions, ask questions, pool resources, and help newcomers. You might look in on these areas as you browse the Web for relevant sites and sources of information. Cable Network News (CNN), *Time* magazine, and *U.S. News and World Report* have Web sites that invite people to share their views of current events on a Web board. Professional organizations like the National Council of Teachers of English (NCTE) offer similar services—and members at the NCTE site, for example, might be very responsive to an inquiry on a topic such as standardized testing. Before posting a question as a new user, however, be sure to look through the archived discussions (which are usually available online) to make sure that the topic has not already been raised—and discussed thoroughly—within recent weeks.

Finding a topic for your research project is not always an easy task. Although it's possible you will find a topic relatively quickly, one rich in resource material that interests both you and others, it is equally possible that you will have to give some time to rethinking and refining your subject (see Chapter 4). Take the time to find a topic with a high potential for success; then you will be ready to consider how to give that topic—and your research project—a well-defined purpose.

WWW Web Sites Worth Knowing

- Writing Center at Colorado State University's Guide to Writing Processes: Audience, **http://writing.colostate.edu/references/processes/audmod/**
- Purdue's Online Writing Lab: Writing a Research Paper: Introduction to Topic, **http://owl.english.purdue.edu/workshops/hypertext/ResearchW/topic.html**
- Tile.Net Discussion List and Newsgroup Search Engine, **http://tile.net/**

GETTING INVOLVED

1. Browse the World Wide Web to locate term paper sites such as *School Sucks* at **http://www.schoolsucks.com**. Examine the sites critically to get a sense of the types of subjects covered. Do the papers they offer look like serious research projects? Why or why not?

2. Working in a group, spend a day comparing the news coverage from several news sources. You might assign one person to each news outlet. Before beginning your research, agree on what you will compare. For example, you might decide to compare the stories covered and the time devoted to each by the various network news shows and news stations: ABC, CBS, NBC, CNN, Fox, and so on. Or you might compare the front-page stories in half a dozen newspapers (or on their Web sites). Or you might analyze the coverage of one story given by various media.

3. In the reference room of the library, locate and browse the specialized encyclopedias. Compare these specialized volumes to more general encyclopedias such as *Collier's* and *The Encyclopaedia Britannica*. When would you be better off using a specialized encyclopedia (where available) to find a topic? When might you benefit most from a general encyclopedia?

MANAGING YOUR PROJECT

1. What issues or problems most concern your campus at the present time? Can any of these issues be connected to a research project you might do for a course? Do any of these issues have a history you might explore in a class project or research paper? Could you do library work or fieldwork that might illuminate the issue or add an important voice to an ongoing conversation?

2. What connections might you make between the project you are considering for a course and your local community? Could you do a project that draws on the resources of people around you or that involves local people or institutions? With which groups or institutions do you most identify? How might a group or institution benefit from your research into archives, local or regional history, or current issues or controversies?

3. Investigate any special resources, collections, museums, institutions, or groups in your community that might help you in shaping a project.

4. Use the World Wide Web to look at newsgroups, listservs, or telnet sites that focus on your topic. For information on searching and evaluating such resources, see Chapters 6 and 10.

CHAPTER

3

Establishing a Purpose

Have you ever gone into a major chain bookstore like Borders or Barnes & Noble and scanned the magazine rack for a title or subject area that interested you? If so, you've probably been taken aback by the sheer number of magazines available in virtually every area of recreational or professional interest. If you're into contemporary music, you can choose from *Beat, Rolling Stone, Crawdaddy, Vibe,* and *Billboard;* a fan of computer games can look into *Computer Gaming World, GamePro,* and *PC Gamer;* a news junkie can browse *Time, Newsweek, U.S. News and World Report, Atlantic, Foreign Affairs,* and even the *Onion* (for a humorous twist on current events). So many magazines, and so many of them writing on similar topics—how do they all manage to create and sustain a demand for their publications, and how do they manage to avoid repeating themselves (and each other) month after month after month?

The answer is that these magazines all have different purposes, different audiences, and different takes on the subjects they cover. They appeal to their audiences in a variety of ways, depending on their goals, their style, and their assessment of what the target audience wants. Sometimes their purpose is to provide factual information; sometimes it's to persuade people to accept a particular point of view; sometimes it's purely to provide entertainment. As you might suspect, there's an analogy here to your own research. Just as these publications have had to make important decisions about how to focus their articles and how to appeal to a specific group of readers, you too must make decisions about the purposes your paper or project might serve.

There are probably as many ways of defining the purpose of a research project—regardless of your topic—as there are types of magazines. To make your choice manageable, we'll focus on just five. Given a research topic that engages you, but which you don't yet know how to handle, consider examining it as

- a question of fact,
- a question of definition,
- a question of value,

- a question of causality, or
- a question of consequence.

These five approaches have their roots in classical rhetoric as the means of deciding the issues a lawyer might argue in a courtroom. We'll illustrate these strategies, examining the approaches one at a time, through an imaginary research project on standardized testing. You should understand, however, that these questions will almost always overlap in your work, one question leading naturally to another.

Imagine that you and a group of friends want to use a writing course assignment to investigate the value and effectiveness of mandatory standardized testing in public schools. There have been increasing demands at national and state levels to "hold teachers accountable" for their students' performance, and you remember having to spend a lot of class time in high school preparing to take—and then taking—those tests. Many students and teachers seem to think this is a waste of class time that could be better spent on other things. What can you do? Advocates of standardized testing point to the value of identifying "troubled" schools with low test scores, saying students will benefit in the long run if poor teachers can be weeded out and good teachers rewarded. At a time when educational excellence is a national priority, this point of view seems to be getting a lot of support. You're concerned, however, about what this means for the classroom. Teachers worried about losing their jobs might "teach to the test" even more than they have been doing, thereby squeezing out activities that might be more beneficial to student learning. You and your colleagues agree to collaborate on a campus information project to explore the details of this push for national testing and, depending on your research, to present alternatives.

Given this scenario, exactly what issues might you address, and how might you best approach them? You'll certainly need to consider your potential audience, and one important aspect of that audience will be the *discipline* to which they belong. The issues that interest politicians and political scientists on the subject of testing are likely to be quite different from those that interest historians or mathematicians or psychologists or even college students thinking about becoming teachers. In the same way, the arguments and evidence that are persuasive to members of one discipline might be far less effective with another. Hard numbers, numerical data, and detailed budget figures could appeal to an economist, but a group of high school language arts teachers might

3.1

Stake out a claim to your territory by carefully establishing the purpose for your project. Determine your audience, your purpose, and the approach you will take to achieve your purpose.

❧ FOCUS ON . . . Audience

Whenever you write something down, you're writing for an audience. Sometimes that audience can be you alone—as with shopping lists, diary entries, and research notes—but more often you will intend what you write to be read by someone else. The size of your audience can range from one person to thousands, even millions in some cases, but regardless of its size, you will always be making judgments about how to communicate to that audience most effectively. Some people, when they're writing, imagine that they're writing to one person in particular; others try to imagine a specific, well-defined audience—readers of *Seventeen* magazine or a group of *Star Trek* fans, for example. Whichever approach works best for you, ask these questions about your audience and use your answers to guide you as you research and write:

- What will my readers already know about my topic?
- What will they likely want to know about my topic?
- What beliefs will they already have about my topic, and how can I address those beliefs?
- What parts of my topic will concern them most?
- How can I persuade them to value the results of my research?

---

find these numbers far removed from their own concerns. Always keep your audience in mind as you reflect on how to approach and present your subject to your readers.

But even though differences between disciplines exist, there are important commonalities. The five questions mentioned above, for example, reflect rhetorical approaches found in all disciplines, and as such they can give you direction as you think about how to develop and research your project.

3a Consider the topic as a question of fact

You can approach almost any subject by exploring factual questions, reporting what is known about a subject or what remains to be discovered. You might find this information in books, articles, surveys, and reports, or you may have to generate it on your own. Queries of fact include the familiar journalist's questions: *who, what, where, when,* and *how.* By answering these questions you could develop the topic and purpose for a project.

For example, in researching the case for additional standardized testing, you might explore the need for such testing in the first place: How much testing is being done now, in what subjects, and at what grade levels? Have test scores been rising, falling, or staying the same over the last ten or twenty years? Are there places where an increase in the number of tests being given has resulted in better teaching, higher scores, or higher graduation rates? To answer these questions you may have to visit offices and archives. At the Board of Education, you might dig up test results from local schools as well as the results from counties across the state (or even across the nation). Then you'd have to determine whether those results indicated a significant trend that additional testing could address. The office of a local or state official might have records of legislative debates or copies of bills to fund such testing. Gathering and correlating these facts would be genuine research.

In crunching these numbers, you'd likely recognize a need to present them to potential readers (or voters) clearly. So part of your research team may have to work with media and document design issues. If you decide to reach students through handouts or brochures, you may need graphics and tables to state your case clearly. If facts suggest that test scores in math and language arts have indeed been falling, you might want to generate tables or charts to establish this.

Factual questions such as the following provide a great way to begin your exploration of a topic.

- What is known about this subject?
- What remains to be discovered?
- What might readers find new or surprising about this subject?
- Are important factual matters relating to this subject in dispute?

As a result of considering these queries you may decide to frame your project as a report, a brochure, or an informational Web site. Or, should your research show that the facts are in dispute, you may write an argument favoring one set of facts over another.

S U M M A R Y

Questions of Fact

You are dealing with factual matters when your research leads you to verify what is already known about a subject. In other words, there's information that you can find, evaluate, and report. You'll likely begin your research with specific questions—and other questions will arise as you learn more about your topic.

Projects based on questions of fact . . .

- Tell readers something they don't know.
- Prove that something known *is* so.
- Discredit false information.
- Explain how something came to be.
- Enumerate the parts or elements of a situation.
- Explain how something occurred.

3b Consider the topic as a question of definition

You can examine almost any subject by studying the meaning of its key concepts. You might find the standard meanings of these crucial terms in dictionaries and encyclopedias, or you might have to come up with definitions on your own—for example, by creating questionnaires to discover how the public understands the terms, concepts, or ideas.

Many civic debates turn on questions of definition, often expressed through the difference between paired terms—citizen/alien, welfare/handout, white lie/perjury, expenditure/investment, contribution/bribe, censorship/obscenity, and so on. Within such controversies you may find compelling material for extensive research into the historical meaning of terms, their legal status, or their changing implications. Although this binary approach is often simplistic, it can be a useful starting point.

An issue such as standardized testing may not raise obvious questions of definition. But certain terms might quickly become controversial if your research places them in the public sphere. Should administrators or government officials use the terms *accountability* and *good teaching,* you might examine the question by looking more closely at the meaning of those terms. Teachers, on the other hand, might refer to *high-stakes testing* and *academic freedom,* and these terms too may lead to matters of definition. If you do not believe that the qualities of good teaching—or good teachers—can be adequately measured by students' performance on a set of formal, timed, standardized tests, then you might explore whether good teachers could be fired for the wrong reasons, thereby undermining the purpose of administering the tests in the first place.

Questions of definition may lead either to reports or to arguments. Your research effort might, for example, provide an extended definition of a concept in which you both define an idea and furnish examples and illustrations to help readers understand it. Or a research project based on issues of definition may become an argument when the terms of the definition are in dispute.

SUMMARY

Questions of Definition

You are dealing with matters of definition when you examine questions about the nature of things. You'll be trying to understand definitions, create them, or refute them. Or you may be trying to decide whether something fits the criteria of an established definition. Your exploration may begin with general sources (dictionaries) but will likely branch out to include more specialized information.

Projects based on questions of definition . . .

- Explore the classes to which things belong.
- Enumerate distinguishing features.
- Examine basic similarities.
- Point out fundamental differences.
- Move to include someone or something in a group.
- Move to exclude someone or something from a group.

3c Consider the topic as a question of value

You can examine almost any subject by framing it as a question of value. In fact, almost every day you make snap judgments about dozens of things—movies, food, music, athletes, politicians, automobiles. These informal evaluations are not all that different from the more studied judgments you might make in a full research project, where you evaluate the work of a contemporary poet or judge the merit of a new social program. In these more formal situations, you will need to support your evaluations with convincing evidence because you become more accountable when you go public with an opinion, whether in print or online.

Many situations call for judgments and evaluations. You may be asked to assess a person's work or achievements; to judge the quality of a performance, a product, or an idea; or to compare persons, objects, or ideas in order to rank them.

How might issues of quality shape your research into the wisdom of standardized testing? You'll have to explore many aspects of quality: the impact additional testing would have on classroom instruction, the quality of students' educational experience, the value of learning how to do well on a particular type of standardized test, or even the benefits of tests now being given. The purpose of research here is to go well beyond mere opinion. You would have to find strong evidence to support any claims of value you might offer, getting testimony from the opinions of experts, from public surveys and questionnaires, from systematic observation, and from articles and reports on the subject.

S U M M A R Y

Questions of Value

You are exploring a question of value when you judge the merit of an idea, concept, policy, institution, public figure, or activity. You'll have to decide what are the valid criteria for judgment and then determine whether what you are evaluating meets those standards. In a few cases, particularly in the sciences, standards of performance or quality may be defined precisely. In other arenas, criteria of evaluation may be controversial. You'll need to understand the controversies in order to make convincing judgments of your own.

Projects based on questions of evaluation . . .

- Assess strengths and weaknesses.
- Explain why something has or has not worked well.
- Advise others in a course of action.
- Improve a product, activity, or performance by understanding its strengths and weaknesses.
- Assess the competition.
- Praise or blame someone or something.

You'd have to think carefully about how to present your findings. To show all sides of the issue, you might write a feature article for the campus newspaper or create a Web site that offers a variety of opinions—using tables, charts, or graphics to display information. However, most evaluations will end up as persuasive pieces, with researchers taking definite stands supported by completely developed arguments, using evidence they have gathered to support their judgment.

3d Consider the topic as a question of cause and effect

Examining why things happen the way they do is one of the most important jobs of researchers. Done appropriately, cause-and-effect analyses are among our culture's most powerful (and habitual) operations. If that sounds overstated, consider how regularly our leaders and the news media trace effects back to causes in order to dole out praise and blame: in describing the success or failure of policy decisions, in tracing the reasons for disasters, in tracking the environmental consequences of various actions, in attributing behavior to societal influences.

You can find specific topics easily by thinking about cause-and-effect relationships. For example, you might design a project to explain how curricula or the school calendar would have to be changed to accommodate additional testing dates. What effects would testing have on student promotion rates, and how might that impact class sizes? What financial effects would poor test results have on an already poor school district? How would teachers' job security or tenure be affected? Would fewer people be interested in becoming teachers? Would some of the best teachers be so discouraged that they would consider leaving the profession? What other changes might occur in schools or classrooms as a result?

Questions of cause and effect can lead to reports when the causal analysis is more factual than speculative. The more speculative your analysis, the more likely it will move in the direction of argument. But even such arguments can be informative when, for example, research suggests many possible causes for a particular phenomenon.

S U M M A R Y
Questions of Cause and Effect

You are exploring a cause-and-effect question when you seek to know why something happened. You can explore such questions from two directions: by looking at an existing event or phenomenon and researching its causes or by examining a potential force and speculating what its consequences might be. For example, you might explore the factors causing a national increase in single-parent families, or you might examine the future consequences of this change in family structure.

Projects based on cause-and-effect questions . . .
- Explain why something happened.
- Consider what might happen as a result of certain trends or movements.

- Challenge accepted explanations for certain phenomena.
- Challenge stereotypical thinking.
- Affirm the validity of certain explanations in the face of new challenges.
- Explore the relationships between causes and effects.
- Probe the complexity of political and social relationships.
- Overturn superstitions or simplistic explanations for complex phenomena.
- Undermine or question complex explanations for simple phenomena.
- Raise questions about cultural assumptions by examining their implications.

3e Consider the topic as a question of consequence

You might approach any subject by making it the subject of a proposal for action. Proposals often begin with a problem, a gap, or an uncertainty. You might begin with evidence that a given situation—in school, at home, in the country—must change. First you have to define the problem, appreciating its complexities; then you have to think creatively about its implications. For example, were you to oppose either an increase in the frequency of standardized testing or the threat it posed to teachers' job security, you might have to offer alternatives that would achieve the desired effects: improvements in teaching quality and improvements in student learning. So you'd have to research options for identifying schools or teachers that are having trouble and suggest a more effective means for helping them succeed. One approach to the problem might be to learn what other counties or states have done to improve teaching or to demonstrate student learning without relying on standardized tests. Another approach might be to look at the recommendations made by professional organizations such as the National Science Teachers Association and the National Council of Teachers of Mathematics and then survey teachers, school administrators, and PTA members for their opinions. Finally you'd have to consider the best way to convey your information: a detailed report both in print and online might be an impressive strategy.

In thinking through the consequences of a proposal, remember that it's important to analyze public or professional attitudes toward your subject. You'll often need to explain what's wrong with current thinking on a subject before you can persuade readers to consider new proposals. And of course you'll have to defend your own proposal thoroughly—its consequences, its feasibility, its advantages. But the examination of a subject in terms of the action it might produce is usually a fertile way of deciding what to write about.

Questions of consequence often lead to papers or projects that are exploratory. Such work asks people to consider alternatives to existing situations along with offering a particular solution. If your research leads you to recommend strongly a specific course of action, then you might write a formal proposal.

> ### SUMMARY
> ## Questions of Consequence
>
> You are addressing a question of consequence when you study a problem (local or national) to determine why current solutions aren't working and to suggest alternatives. First, you will have to establish the facts of the present situation and examine different perspectives on the problem. Then you'll offer a solution of your own, backed by information on its costs, feasibility, and likelihood of acceptance.
>
> Projects based on questions of consequence . . .
>
> - Present solutions to problems.
> - Offer alternatives to the status quo.
> - Consider the advantages of change.
> - Consider the consequences of change.
> - Consider the costs of change.
> - Ponder the likelihood of change.

3.2

Selecting a rhetorical purpose for your project allows you to make important decisions about how to proceed as you do your research and prepare to present your information. The goals you decide upon, as we have shown here, will determine the sorts of questions you ask, what you look for, what counts as useful information, and how you might present your results to an audience. Decisions about purpose may also have a direct impact on your research topic; you will probably need to consider narrowing or focusing it to better fit the purpose you have chosen.

WWW Web Sites Worth Knowing

3.3

- The Forest of Rhetoric,
  http://humanities.byu.edu/rhetoric/
- Writing Center at Colorado State University's Guide to Writing Processes: Purpose,
  http://writing.colostate.edu/references/processes/purpose/

GETTING INVOLVED

1. Examine a daily newspaper or newsmagazine to find stories or features that respond to each of the five types of questions discussed in this chapter.

   Questions of fact
   Questions of definition
   Questions of value

Questions of causality
Questions of consequence

Also look for articles in which different purposes are combined. Do you find that particular types of writing dominate in particular sections of the paper or magazine? Why?

2. None of the questions discussed in this chapter would lead toward a project designed to entertain or amuse. Would an academic research project likely have entertainment as a primary goal? Might it have entertainment as a subsidiary goal?

MANAGING YOUR PROJECT

1. Identify two general subjects that might be appropriate topics for a research paper, and explore each one using the five approaches described in this chapter—as we did with the topic of standardized testing. You'll likely find that some perspectives work better with your subject than others.

2. List the most interesting questions or perspectives your topic generates (see Exercise 1). Then look for connections between the questions to see whether different questions might be pursued in the same paper.

3. When you have connected your potential topic to a specific purpose, locate an example of research that resembles the project you have in mind. If you decide to create a factual Web site, look for a Web site that presents documentary evidence. If you expect to prepare a proposal document, look for a proposal argument. When you locate an appealing model, note its features and decide which ones you might emulate and which ones may not fit your project.

Focusing Your Project

Once you have a general topic for a research project and a sense of purpose, you can be-gin to focus the project, either by putting it into words or by sketching it out. Some writers narrow and focus their topics by posing a *research question* or *query* for which they do not yet have a satisfactory answer.

Research Question
Why is criminal violence increasing among juveniles at a time when the overall crime rate is decreasing?

Other writers prefer to guide even their early research by constructing a *hypothesis*, a statement that makes a *claim* that will be tested in the project.

Hypothesis
Despite a drop in the overall crime rate, violence among juveniles is increasing because of the pernicious influence of television.

Just as a scientist may need to focus in on microscopic details, researchers need to focus their topics on specific parts of a larger controversy in order to deal with them adequately.

Either a research question or a preliminary hypothesis will help to focus your research. As a general rule, a research question might be better when you want to consider a variety of explanations to an interesting or puzzling phenomenon. A hypothesis might be more useful if you have a pretty clear understanding (or a strong opinion) about your subject and you want to focus on proving or disproving it. You don't have to commit to a position at this stage, however. Until the evidence comes in, be open-minded and always ready to revise your claim.

The question or hypothesis you decide upon will also be important if your instructor asks you to prepare a proposal or prospectus as part of your research plan (see Section 4g). How you frame your research subject—as an open-ended query or a narrowly focused claim—will guide the decisions you make about what sources to consult, what kinds of evidence to gather, and what information will be pertinent to your project. If your hypothesis asserts a connection between juvenile crime and television, you will probably want to center your research on sources that consider that issue in particular. A research question that asks why the juvenile crime rate is increasing will probably consider the influence of television as only one of several possible explanations.

www

4.1

4a Pose questions

To gain more perspective on a topic, ask specific questions. Use your preliminary reading and discussions to learn what the issues are in a field or topic area. In your reading or field research, be curious about the following matters.

- The focal points of chapter titles and section headings
- The names of important people or experts
- The names of events or institutions related to the subject
- Issues or questions that come up repeatedly
- Issues about which there is controversy
- Issues about which there is doubt and uncertainty

↻ FOCUS ON . . . Ethics

When you begin your research, you may have strong feelings about your subject and you may want to focus on a hypothesis right away. It's fine to do so, but be careful! More than a few students (and professionals) have discovered that the positions with which they began were contradicted by the scientific evidence and expert opinions they uncovered in their research. Don't forget that you have an ethical responsibility to present evidence fairly, not to ignore or conceal information when it doesn't agree with what you want to believe, and to choose sources that do the same (see Chapter 9). Feel free, especially in the early stages of your research, to modify, refine, or completely change your hypothesis on the basis of what you learn.

Consider, too, what the implications of an issue might be. Ask questions and write down your observations. Above all, while reading and discussing your topic, maintain an attitude of healthy skepticism. Be curious and adventurous in the questions you pose as you consider a subject.

TOPIC: MARINE PARKS

Does the confinement of whales and dolphins at marine parks constitute cruelty to animals?

Do marine mammals live longer in the wild than in protected environments? If so, why?

Who profits from keeping marine mammals in captivity—scientists or business-people?

TOPIC: STANDARDIZED TESTING

Do teachers object to all standardized tests or just some of them? Why?

Which companies write the tests used in schools and who approves them? What procedures do they follow?

Do standardized tests discriminate against minorities or ethnic groups?

TOPIC: VOTING

Has voter turnout for national elections been much higher than it is now?

Who would benefit from increased voter turnout in national elections?

What reasons do people give for not voting?

You can turn some questions into tentative hypotheses by making them claims.

The confinement of whales and dolphins at marine parks constitutes cruelty to animals.

But you couldn't turn some other questions into hypotheses without additional information. (For example, you might not know for sure whether voter turnout has been higher in previous decades or who exactly would benefit from increased voter turnout.) Spend time just thinking about your subject, comparing what you've learned from your sources, and then decide what you can offer readers.

In most cases, narrowing subjects early in the writing process can make subsequent searches of print and electronic resources more efficient. If you've narrowed a subject too much, you'll know it soon enough.

4b Consider the acceptable level of generality

When you think about the research question or claim you want to address in your project, consider the *level of generality* at which you will be expected to write.

CLAIM   Cars are better than trucks.

CLAIM   The Mercedes S500 is superior to the Lexus LS430.

The second of these two claims is clearly more specific than the first. While the first claim compares two types of four-wheel transportation vehicles, the second compares two specific brands and models of luxury-class cars. Because the first claim is made at a more general level, the comparisons you make in supporting it will likely be more general too (gas mileage, size, comfort, price). If your claim is too general, comparisons you offer may be more difficult to make. Because the second claim is more specific, the comparisons you offer can be more specific as well (relative sizes of the wheel base, ergonomic design, airbag deployment, emission controls).

Topics that are too general and topics that are too specific can both lead to research problems down the road. When your topic is too general, you may have a hard time distinguishing between relevant and irrelevant information. When it's too specific, you may not find much information published about it. Ideally, you should aim for a topic general enough to provide lots of information but narrow enough that you can sift through the information easily and determine what's important.

If you are working on a class project, read the assignment sheet carefully. Sometimes there are clues or even suggested topics that will indicate the level of generality that the instructor will accept. If you are uncertain about your topic choice, your preliminary research and reading will help you decide whether to make it more specific or more general. And you can always run the topic by your instructor for advice and suggestions.

4c Identify the information your project requires

As we demonstrate in Chapter 3, different projects serve different purposes and require different kinds of research. Your research techniques and sources will often depend on whether your preliminary question or hypothesis involves a question of fact, of definition, of value, of cause, or of policy.

Questions or claims of fact have as their primary goal the demonstration of what is true, with "true" being defined as something that can be proved or disproved by clear, unambiguous evidence and data.

Examples of fact-based queries and claims

QUERY   How do children raised in day-care environments compare emotionally or intellectually with children raised at home by parents?

CLAIM   Violence among teenagers is higher now than in any decade in modern American history.

In the case of the first research question or query, you would probably want to look at published studies comparing children from each environment and then write about the most striking results. In the case of the hypothesis or claim, you would search for crime statistics that made comparisons—decade by decade—of young people aged 13–19 and then determine whether or not there has been an increase. The information you discovered, as long as it came from reputable, reliable sources (see Chapter 10), would probably be sufficient to establish your position as either true or false.

Questions or claims of definition, on the other hand, have as their focus the clarification of an ambiguous term or concept. Our world is filled with abstract ideas that we use and talk about frequently—freedom, justice, obscenity, good manners, discrimination—but which many people understand or define quite differently. Even relatively concrete concepts such as bilingual education, standardized testing, and affirmative action can be subject to disagreements about how they should be defined.

Examples of definition-based queries and claims

QUERY   How do individual states interpret affirmative action and apply it to hiring policies?

CLAIM   Solitary confinement in prisons constitutes a form of cruel and unusual punishment forbidden by the Constitution. (What is "cruel and unusual punishment"?)

The first query suggests that the definition of "affirmative action" may not be the same in all states and that variations in definition may lead to variations in how affirmative action programs are designed and regulated. To answer this question, you might want to locate government documents that define affirmative action for each state. Perhaps you could contact a local affirmative action office and ask for assistance in finding this information.

To support a claim about "cruel and unusual punishment," you would need to explore what authoritative sources have had to say about the subject. Court documents, legal records, and editorials in magazines and newspapers should provide rich resources for discussions of "cruel and unusual punishment" and the experience of solitary confinement. As you research and write about a definition-based project, you will be trying to help readers understand a concept more fully.

A query or claim about value makes a judgment about something on the basis of reasonable criteria. We make judgments every day—I like that teacher; I want to buy the Sony receiver, not the Aiwa; the Beatles were much better musicians than Elvis—and we always have reasons for making those judgments, reasons that are based on personal criteria, or standards, for evaluation. Sometimes you make your standards explicit when you talk about them, sometimes you don't. In an evaluative project your goal is to spell out your criteria, justify them, and show how the focus of your project measures up.

Examples of value-based queries and claims

QUERY   Is the quality of American filmmaking in decline?

CLAIM   Diomedes, not Achilles, is the real hero of *The Iliad*.

The query about the quality of American filmmaking leads naturally to a question about how one determines "quality" in films. Some people might consider screenwriting or cinematography or special effects the most important element; other people might talk about production values, the effects of merchandising, or box-office revenues. Ultimately the choice of criteria is up to you, but you'll have to make sure yours are reasonable criteria that your readers will value as well. Not everyone would agree, for example, that an increased amount of violence in the movies necessarily means a decline in quality. You might have to convince your audience to accept the validity of your criteria.

The claim about Diomedes being the "true" hero of *The Iliad* begs the question, "What are the qualities of a hero?" A project attempting to justify this claim will need to determine what a hero is—how a hero acts, how a hero differs from a "brave warrior," what features distinguish a hero from other people. To substantiate this claim, you could read what scholars have to say about heroes and heroism in literature, compare Diomedes to other heroes in literature or in real life, and research the criteria that others have used to describe heroes.

A query or claim about cause, as we said earlier, explores cause-and-effect relationships that are linked in time. We want to know *why* something happened in the past, and we want to be able to predict what *will* happen in the future if we follow a particular course of action. For this reason, projects which focus on cause will often begin either with an effect (something of special interest in the present) and consider what causes brought it about, or with a cause (again, something of special interest in the present) and speculate what its eventual effects might be.

Examples of queries and claims based on cause

QUERY   Why is the quality of American filmmaking in decline?

CLAIM   Enforcing new EPA pollution standards will endanger the economy of regions that rely on mining.

We could easily rephrase the above query to ask, "What reasons or events in the past caused the quality of American filmmaking to decline?" To answer this question, you would have to research the claims or reasons that have been advanced by film scholars or industry professionals to explain the decline (assuming of course, that such a "decline" exists). You may want to investigate the history of a single studio, or you may want to look at significant events in history (the JFK assassination, the Vietnam war, the proliferation of VCRs) that could have had a significant impact on the movie industry.

In contrast to the backward-looking question about the film industry, the forward-looking claim about pollution standards predicts what will happen as a result of strictly enforced pollution standards. Even so, it is possible to use evidence from the past to make predictions about the future. You might want to research the effects of pollution standard enforcements on small mining towns. Perhaps there are towns that have been seriously affected by existing standards; their history would make your argument about future effects all the more powerful. Web sites maintained by the mining industry and the EPA could provide useful information about predicted effects as well.

A query or claim about policy is also forward-looking in that it argues in favor of (or against) a course of action. To some extent, projects based on this type of research question or hypothesis will incorporate elements of cause and effect. If you want to argue why we should do something in a certain way, you need to argue that the outcomes or effects will be beneficial. But the purpose of a policy-based project goes one step further: it doesn't just predict what the effects will be, it demands that we pursue them.

Examples of policy-based queries and claims

QUERY   What can be done to improve math education in American secondary schools?

Claim   Science literacy in local high schools might be improved by creating adjunct teaching positions for practicing scientists.

The query about improving math education implies that we need to consider a variety of alternatives and gauge which among them are best. You could interview math teachers and read math journals for possibilities, or you could survey teachers for their opinions about weaknesses in math education. Professional Web sites by groups such as the National Council of Teachers of Mathematics, or even by universities that train future math teachers, might provide a wealth of material.

The claim about creating adjunct teaching positions as a way of improving scientific literacy would require research into whether this has been tried and studied in the past and whether concrete benefits have been documented. Is there evidence to support the belief that "practicing scientists" would want to do this in sufficient numbers for it to be a reasonable solution to the problem? If you can provide evidence like this and present it carefully, you will go a long way toward convincing your audience to support your recommendation.

4d Determine where to locate the information your project requires

Given the glut of information available in books, articles, newspapers, databases, and the Internet on every subject imaginable, you're likely to find something about your topic no matter which resource you turn to first or which rhetorical approach you decide to use. If you had all the time in the world to research your subject, one starting place would be as good as any other and it wouldn't matter where you began. Unfortunately, deadlines and due dates make it important that you be selective in doing your research and focus on resources that are likely to have the best and most pertinent information for your project's goals.

The chart below can help point you to the most profitable research sources, depending on the type of research question or hypothesis you form. This is not to say that other sources in the chart should be overlooked or ignored, just that you are likely to find more immediately useful information for your project in the sources identified here.

CHART
Useful Sources for Research Material

Research Source Materials	Fact	Definition	Value	Cause
Encyclopedias	✓	✓		
Dictionaries		✓		
Other reference works, almanacs	✓			
Books, both scholarly and popular	✓	✓	✓	✓
Journal articles and magazines	✓	✓	✓	✓

Research Source Materials	Fact	Definition	Value	Cause
Popular and special-interest magazines			✓	✓
Newspapers and online news services	✓			
Newspaper editorials and columns			✓	✓
Book reviews, film reviews, product reviews			✓	
Scientific experiments and observations				✓
Interviews with experts	✓		✓	
Fieldwork	✓			
Surveys of opinion		✓	✓	✓
Institutional and government Web sites	✓			
Issue-oriented Web sites	✓	✓	✓	
Listservs and Usenet groups		✓	✓	
Individual Web sites			✓	

4e Review the library catalog and Web directories

Library catalogs are designed to make information manageable and accessible to researchers. Catalogs can also be powerful tools for generating topic ideas because they break complex subjects into manageable parts. To find topic suggestions, learn to browse a catalog strategically. For example, under a very broad category such as "English literature" you may find the divisions "postcolonial authors," "Oriental influences," and "Renaissance." These subheads in turn may lead to still narrower divisions ("Renaissance playwrights," "Renaissance theaters") and perhaps to categories that pique your interest. Remember that each card or screen in the catalog provides information on a particular source, so the catalog could also lead you to your preliminary research materials. (For more information on using the library catalog, see Section 5b.)

You can do a similar survey of World Wide Web directories that outline major subject areas. *Yahoo!* offers indexes of such areas as "Arts and Humanities," "Business and Economy," "Computers and Internet," "Education," "Entertainment," "Government," "Health," and "News and Media." Under each of these categories are subcategories with links to online sites related to the topic, as well as further subcategories. "Arts and Humanities," for example, offers the subcategories "Countries and Cultures," "Electronic Literature," "History of Books and Printing," and "Storytelling." By noting which headings and subheadings in a directory have the most entries, you can get a rough sense of what areas or topics are most productive and controversial.

4f Talk to other people

Explain what you intend to explore in your project, and let the questions and comments of colleagues guide you to key issues. You'll be surprised how often a classmate will raise an issue you hadn't considered. Others may even be able to broaden your appreciation for a subject. If you were considering a research project about the long-term effects of childhood abuse, you might consider joining a newsgroup or chat room discussion to find firsthand accounts of the experience. Many such opportunities are available online, though you should approach them carefully and sensitively, using the information you find mainly to stimulate your own thinking. After all, people may not want their lives to become part of your research project. A conference with your teacher during the early stages of your project can help you be sure you're on the right track and provide the opportunity to get advice when you're unsure what to do next. Your instructor will often be able to point you to resources and help you over stumbling blocks. Writing a proposal or prospectus can also play an important role in this process.

4g Prepare a research proposal or prospectus

For many research assignments you may be asked to prepare a document outlining your topic, plans, resources, and qualifications for the project. Sometimes this is called a *research proposal*, other times a *prospectus*. By outlining your ideas early, you enable an instructor or supervisor to give you the advice or suggestions you need to keep a project on track.

We can't offer a single form to cover all types of projects you might explore. The prospectus for a minor project might fit on a single page; that for a senior thesis or a dissertation might run to many pages. However, any prospectus will likely include many of the following elements.

- **A topic or topic area.** Identify your topic area and, if required, provide a rationale for selecting this subject.

- **A hypothesis or research question.** State your hypothesis or question. The claim you make in this section will form the basis for the rest of the prospectus, particularly the kind of research you will do and the ultimate goal(s) of the project itself. If required, discuss the hypothesis in detail and establish its significance, relevance, or appropriateness.

- **Background information or a review of literature.** Identify the background reading and research that provides preliminary grounds for your research. For major projects, provide a full review of the professional work already done in your area of research, summarizing the articles and other scholarly materials that provide the context for your research.

- **A review of necessary sources and archival materials.** Identify the kinds of materials you expect to review for this project: books, articles, newspapers, documents, manuscripts, recordings, videos, artworks, databases, Web sites, email lists, and so on. You might also be asked to assess the availability of these materials and identify where and how you expect to gain access to them.

- **A description of your research methodology.** Outline the procedures you will follow in your research and justify your choice of methodology. For many types of research, this section will be the most demanding part of the prospectus. You have to convince an instructor or supervisor that your approach will treat your subject adequately and provide valid and repeatable results. For example, if you intend to do a survey, you need to explain how you will generate and test your survey questions, how you will tally and validate responses to them, and how you will select your respondents to assure a valid and adequate sample.

- **A description of your qualifications to undertake the project.** Show that you or members of your research team either possess or can acquire the knowledge and skills needed to carry out a project. You might point to courses you have taken (say, in statistics), expertise you have (perhaps in languages), or skills you can purchase (for example, the expertise of a printer or a Web designer).

- **An assessment of the ethics of your project if it might involve experiments on other people.** Most universities have strict guidelines for research that deals with human subjects. Your instructor will likely make you aware of these rules, especially in fields in which human research is common, such as psychology and the social sciences.

- **An assessment of resources and/or costs.** Identify any special equipment, library resources, and other materials you expect to need for the project. Outline any travel that the work may entail. Provide a detailed estimate of costs for equipment, salaries, and printing. In major research projects the budget may be a separate part of the prospectus.

- **A schedule or timeline.** Estimate the stages of your project and provide firm dates for each item that must be submitted.

A prospectus, then, builds the research query or hypothesis into a complete research plan. It incorporates nearly all parts of the research process you have completed up to this point: choosing a topic, reviewing resources, thinking about audience, finding a focus, and managing your time. The sample proposal on pages 47–49 might be produced for a research project on the topic of standardized testing.

With a research query/hypothesis or prospectus in hand, you will be well prepared to leap into the most exciting and rewarding part of your project: doing the research itself. This is where you will take on the role of detective and investigator, searching for clues, teasing out facts, learning everything you can about the topic you have chosen. But be warned! Investigators are only as good as the tools they use and their skill in using them. You will have to learn about the full range of research tools available to you, and you must pick your tools well and wisely. In Part II of this book we will look at all the strategies, techniques, and options you have in your research toolbox.

WWW Web Sites Worth Knowing

- Online Newspapers, **http://www.onlinenewspapers.com/**
- Links to Public Opinion Surveys (Cornell Institute for Social and Economic Research), **http://www.ciser.cornell.edu/info/polls.html**
- Proposal Writing: Selected Web Sites list (University of Pittsburgh), **http://www.pitt.edu/~offres/proposal/propwriting/websites.html**
- Preparing a Prospectus for a Project (Brigham Young University), **http://www.byu.edu/ipt/program/ms_prospectus_guide.html**

4.3

GETTING INVOLVED

1. Here's a list of generic topics likely to be shrugged off as dull by most readers. For two of them, come up with specific research questions that might spark interest. If necessary, do some library or online research.

domestic cats	common cold
France	calculus
cheating	attention deficit disorder
Vikings	First Amendment

2. Examine textbooks from several of your college courses to see whether you can discern from the tables of contents, chapter headings, and graphics what the crucial issues, controversies, or subjects of research might be within each field or discipline. Do some types of textbooks or subjects reveal the research interests of their fields more readily than others? Why might that be so?

MANAGING YOUR PROJECT

1. Put your preliminary topic in the form of a research question. This is the question your paper might answer ("Is it likely that explorers will find water under the surface of Mars?"), or it will be the question that guides a brochure or Web site you are designing ("What volunteer opportunities do students have for improving literacy in our community?").

2. Put your preliminary topic in the form of a hypothesis. This is the statement your paper may support ("Explorers are likely to find water under the surface of Mars"), or it will be the statement that provides a rationale for your brochure, Web site, or other project ("The community provides many opportunities for students to volunteer for literacy projects").

3. Draft a proposal for your project. Include a clear statement of your research question or hypothesis, a description of why this is an interesting and/or critical area to study, and your plan for finding resources. Share this proposal with classmates and the instructor—in class, during office hours, or by email—and get feedback to use as you continue your research.

Annotated Research Proposal

Henry Pym

English 1102

Dr. Jellico

PROSPECTUS FOR RESEARCH PROJECT

Overview

1 For my research project, I plan to study some of the effects of standardized testing on classroom teaching. I believe that the current emphasis placed on these tests as a way to measure teaching effectiveness is misguided and can lead to a decline in the quality of teaching and

2 student learning. A number of teachers I know have complained about how these tests interfere with what they want to do in their classrooms, but there is also a big push in several states, including Texas, to require even more standardized testing than there is already.

The arguments made by politicians and some school administrators that testing benefits schools (by identifying school districts that are doing poorly and are therefore in need of additional assistance) are contradicted by scholars such as Jack Kaufhold, H. Dickson Corbett, and Bruce L. Wilson, who claim that the tests do little more than threaten teachers' job security and turn

3 classrooms into learn-how-to-pass-the-test centers. Clearly, there are serious disagreements between the two sides of this controversy, and my goal in this project will be to investigate the facts used to support both sides and argue--if the evidence supports it--that the effects of "high-stakes" standardized testing cause more problems than

4 they solve.

Research Plan

I intend to research a wide variety of resources for this project, beginning with books and articles that discuss the effects of standardized testing in classrooms. Two books I have found already seem especially helpful in addressing

5 this issue: <u>Testing, Reform, and Rebellion</u> (Corbett and Wilson 1991) and <u>The Competency Movement: Problems and Solutions</u> (Neill 1978). I will also look into recent publications by the Texas Education Agency that focus on testing standards as well as professional journals for teachers, such as <u>English Journal</u> and the <u>Journal of Teaching Writing</u>, that would likely include articles expressing a teacher's point of view.

There are several online sources I plan to research as well. The National Center for Fair & Honest Testing at **http://www.fairtest.org/** maintains an issue-oriented Web site against standardized tests, and the Eisenhower National Clearinghouse keeps a list of many links to sites that deal with the issue of testing at **http://www.enc.org/**

6 **topics/assessment/testing/.** Closer to home, the Teachers.Net Web site has a chat board specifically for Texas teachers, and I will use this board to see what teachers in my own state have to say about the issue. If I find some of the comments on the chat board to be useful for my paper, I will make sure to get the authors'

7 permissions before quoting them directly.

I believe that this approach will allow me to see both

8 what scholars are saying about standardized testing as a national issue and what teachers are saying about it as a local issue that affects their own classrooms and jobs. I anticipate no special difficulties in being able to conduct this research, as the materials are either available in the library or easily accessible online.

Project Timeline

I anticipate that the preliminary research and notetaking for my project will take two weeks to complete and that I will have my annotated bibliography done by 11/2. The first draft of the project will be finished by class time on the due date, 11/16, when I will share it with class members

for their review and comments. I would like to schedule a
conference with you by 11/21 to discuss my project's
progress and set an agenda for my work on the next draft. I
plan to have the second draft finished by 12/1 and will
make an appointment in the Writing Center to go over the
paper once more. The final draft will be turned in on the
9   due date, 12/7.

Annotations

1. This prospectus begins with an Overview that incorporates several of the elements detailed in the earlier list: the statement of the topic and hypothesis and a brief description of the positions held by opposing sides in the controversy.

2. The writer clearly states the position that he intends to defend in his research project.

3. The writer points out two opposing points of views on this issue, and he also identifies some of the sources he's consulted in his preliminary research.

4. The writer reaffirms his goal for the paper, introduces the term "high-stakes standardized testing," and indicates a willingness to modify his hypothesis if the evidence proves him wrong.

5. The writer mentions specific book and journal titles he intends to review, including those that will give him a variety of perspectives on the issue.

6. The type of Web site and the nature of the information that can be found there are included.

7. The writer shows an awareness of the ethical issues involved in quoting people on an open forum like a chat board.

8. This paragraph justifies the scope of the research plan and its likelihood of success.

9. All deadlines and due dates are specified, including those set by the author himself.

II

Gathering Ideas and Information

Don't miss . . .

- **The library tour in Section 5a.** Explore your library and learn how to use its diverse collections and facilities.
- **The explanation of keyword and Boolean searches in Chapter 6.** Learn how to focus your Web searches with a few simple strategies and commands. Get the results you really want, not just thousands of useless "hits."
- **The discussion of field research in Chapter 7.** Not all research involves finding out what other people have said. Sometimes you will have to conduct your own surveys or interviews.
- **The guidelines for annotated bibliographies in Section 8c.** Summarizing your resources' main points is an excellent way to keep track of critical information.

Technology
Spotlight

EMAIL

What was the first email message? Any guesses?

According to one account, the first email message was "QWER-TYIOP," sent from one lab computer to another in a small office in 1971. Bolt Beranek and Newman (BBN) engineer Ray Tomlinson is generally credited with being the person who "invented" email by developing a simple program that engineers in his company could use to leave messages for one another. Since BBN was the company charged with the development of ARPANET— later to be known as the Internet— Tomlinson was quick to see how this simple program could be modified to send instant messages to other sites on the network, no matter how far away they might be. By 1973, a mere two years later, a study revealed that nearly 75% of all network traffic on ARPANET consisted of email messages.

It is estimated that there are over 148 million people sending 7 trillion email per year in the U.S. alone. Learning to manage the information glut is an essential survival skill.

While some critics claim that email has brought the death of the personal letter, others argue that email has made personal communication more popular than ever. Today email is a standard means for exchanging friendly greetings, formal business documents, pictures, programs, and proposals. Whether you're using a sophisticated program with a graphic interface (such as *Eudora*) or a text-based Unix program (such as *PINE* or *ELM*), you now have a tool that allows you to contact virtually anyone else in the world with access to a personal computer. As you conduct your own research, remember that an email inquiry can be the fastest and most direct way to get the answers to your questions!

CHAPTER
5

Finding
Information

Once you have a research question or hypothesis, your next goal for many projects will be to locate potential sources and to prepare a *working bibliography*, that is, a preliminary list of materials relevant to your topic. (See Chapter 8 for more on preparing a working bibliography.) The type of information you will need depends on the specific rhetorical situation for your project, that is, on your audience, purpose, and topic. Different audiences will require different types of evidence. For example, you would most likely search scholarly books and journals to find information acceptable to an academic audience. Your purpose will guide you to different types of information as well. If you are explaining a technical concept to engineers, you may need to locate "white papers" or technical specifications, whereas if you plan to try to persuade legislators to vote for a bill, you may need to search the Congressional Record or survey voters in your district. Your topic will also dictate what kinds of sources may be appropriate. You will need to search newspapers, news magazines, or Web sites to locate information on current events, while a paper on educational assessment might require you to scour scholarly journals in the field of education.

Although it might be possible to go to your university library and browse the shelves until you find sources useful to a research project, that technique would be inefficient and would provide you with only the barest beginnings. The books you find on the shelf would likely represent only a small portion of the information available in the library, and many of those books would be out-of-date. Obviously, you don't want to rely on chance or serendipity to support serious research in a library. You need to work systematically with bibliographies, indexes, library catalogs, and librarians to find the information you need.

Systematic research is even more important today when you have to deal with an explosion of electronic sources, many of which were not designed with researchers and scholars in mind. The very strength of the World Wide Web—its robust connection of millions of computers, files, and databases—is also its weakness: it presents a jumble of

You may sometimes feel a bit like the researchers pictured here examining materials in a Kenyan mine pit as you search for information to support your ideas. Luckily, many of the sources you eventually find will lead you to others by way of the bibliographies they include.

information, leaving users to screen nuggets of gold from mountains of slag. So it's essential that your searches be more efficient and knowledgeable than ever.

In this chapter we explain the basic tools and resources you will use when sorting through these stacks of information. We urge you to be systematic and dogged in your work. It's too easy—and usually wrong—to decide there's nothing available on your topic. Instead, you want to push deeper into the archives, libraries, and networks. Try different search terms or databases, and ask the reference librarians for help. You will learn more about organizing your materials in Chapter 17; for now, you want to learn how to find relevant and reliable sources that fulfill the requirements of your specific rhetorical situation as quickly and efficiently as possible—without sacrificing thoroughness.

5a Learn about your library

A first priority for any college student is to become familiar with the arrangement of campus libraries and research facilities. Most libraries nowadays offer powerful electronic catalogs to search for books or periodicals and to provide access to electronic databases, government documents, special collections, audio and video materials, and to bibliographies and indexes that help you locate additional material. Most university libraries offer tours or workshops to help you learn how to use their resources. Many libraries even offer these services online, accessible from your dormitory room or from home through the Internet or a dial-in connection. Don't be intimidated. Take a tour of these buildings and learn how to take advantage of all available help.

The following library resources are discussed later in this chapter, but to give you an overview of the resources available and the questions you may need to ask, we've compiled this list.

- **Library catalog.** Most libraries now provide access to their collections via computer terminals that allow powerful electronic searches. Learn how to use these terminals. Find out whether you can access the catalog from home or from computer labs on campus. Some older materials may not be indexed in the electronic catalog; for those materials a card catalog may provide your only access.

Find out whether that is the case, and know where the card catalog is located and how to use it.

- **Reference room.** Large libraries often have a reference desk or area staffed by librarians especially knowledgeable about finding information in many fields. Study this collection carefully, noting how materials are arranged and where heavily used items—encyclopedias, almanacs, phone books, databases—are located. Note where the reference librarian is stationed.

- **Bibliographies and databases.** Most libraries house their most important bibliographies and indexes in their reference collections. The bibliographies in various fields will often be large multivolume collections. Many of these bibliographies and indexes, especially the more current ones, may be available online through your library Web site, electronic catalog, or on CD-ROM. Electronic databases offer fast and powerful searches, and some even offer full-text or full-image access to articles and abstracts. Find out if your library offers workshops or handouts to help you use these databases.

- **Statistics.** For many topics you will want to include statistical information (facts and figures). Make sure, however, that the statistics you use are accurate and up-to-date. Your reference librarians can help point you to reliable sources of information in the library reference room and online.

- **Microforms collections.** Many important materials, including government documents, newspapers, and periodicals, are collected on rolls of film called *microfilm* or rectangular sheets of film called *microfiche*. Know where these collections are, how they are arranged, and how you can get to them. Learn to use microfilm readers, both the type that handles film and the type that reads cards.

- **Periodical collections.** You'll need to know both where current journals, magazines, and other periodical publications are located and where bound or microfilmed materials are kept.

- **Newspapers.** Current newspapers are usually available in a reading room. Older newspapers will usually be available on microfilm, and then you will likely have access to only a limited number of major papers, depending on the size of your library's collection. Online archives of newspapers are a recent innovation; you won't be able to search back more than a few years.

- **Book and film reviews.** You can locate book and film reviews using printed or electronic indexes to newspapers and periodicals, and you can locate reviews of current books and films on the World Wide Web. There are many specialized indexes that specifically index and sometimes abstract reviews and criticism. Find out where these indexes are located.

- **Special collections.** Libraries often have rooms or sections for their rare or special items such as pictures, photographs, maps, government documents, and so on. You may be able to view rare books and manuscripts, special artifacts such as presidential campaign or Civil War memorabilia, stamp collections, even collections of comic books and dime novels. Learn the location of important collections in your library and how to access them.

- **Government documents.** Find out if your library is a Federal Government Document Depository. Over 1,400 of them are located throughout the country, offering free access to government information in various forms, including books, periodicals, microfiche, CD-ROM, and Internet-based sources. Even if your library is not an official depository, it will almost certainly subscribe to important government publications such as the Congressional Record.

In addition to the resources listed above, your library will offer some or all of the following services.

- **Circulation desk; library services.** Be sure you know where the circulation desk is and what other services the library offers you as a researcher. For instance, you may be able to recall materials that are on loan if you need them for your project. In addition, most libraries are involved in interlibrary loan programs that enable you to borrow materials your library does not own from other participating libraries throughout the country. (Those orders take time, so don't wait until the last minute to make such a request.) Some libraries will also answer questions online; find out if your library offers this assistance, or try the "Ask a Librarian" service on the Library of Congress Web site at **http:// www.loc.gov/rr/askalib/**

- **Directories.** Large libraries can be complicated facilities. Take advantage of any directories or pamphlets that your library offers to help you locate collections. Also note how the collections are arranged, where library call numbers are displayed, how the shelves themselves are arranged, and other aspects of the physical arrangement. Find out if handouts are available to help you learn your way around the library or if a library Web page offers this information.

- **Photocopiers, computers, study areas.** Learn where in the library you can reliably copy information. (It's smart to track down two or three copying locations because copiers get heavy use.) Also check to see whether computer terminals or modem ports are available in the library and whether areas are set off for study and research.

- **Study carrels.** Many colleges and university libraries provide special partitioned desks or enclosures, called carrels, in the library for people pursuing serious research. Find out whether you are eligible for a carrel.

5b Use library catalogs efficiently

Library catalogs can usually be searched by author, by title, by subject, by Library of Congress classification (see Section 5g), and by keywords. If you know the title or author of a work, a catalog can tell you whether the library owns the item and, if so, where to locate it in the stacks. A subject search will help you locate sources in which a given topic is the main focus; a keyword search can help you locate sources in which your topic is mentioned, even though it may not be the focus of the piece. Thus a keyword search provides a potentially richer range of source material. Keyword searches can be very powerful; to learn how to use them effectively, see Chapter 6. When the catalog is electronic (as most now are), you can also determine immediately whether a document is checked out, lost, or otherwise unavailable, thereby saving you much time. If your library has an electronic catalog, learn its basic search techniques and commands.

Figure 5.1 shows the search menu screen for the online library catalog at the University of Texas at Austin at **http://dpweb1.dp.utexas.edu/lib/utnetcat/keyword.html**

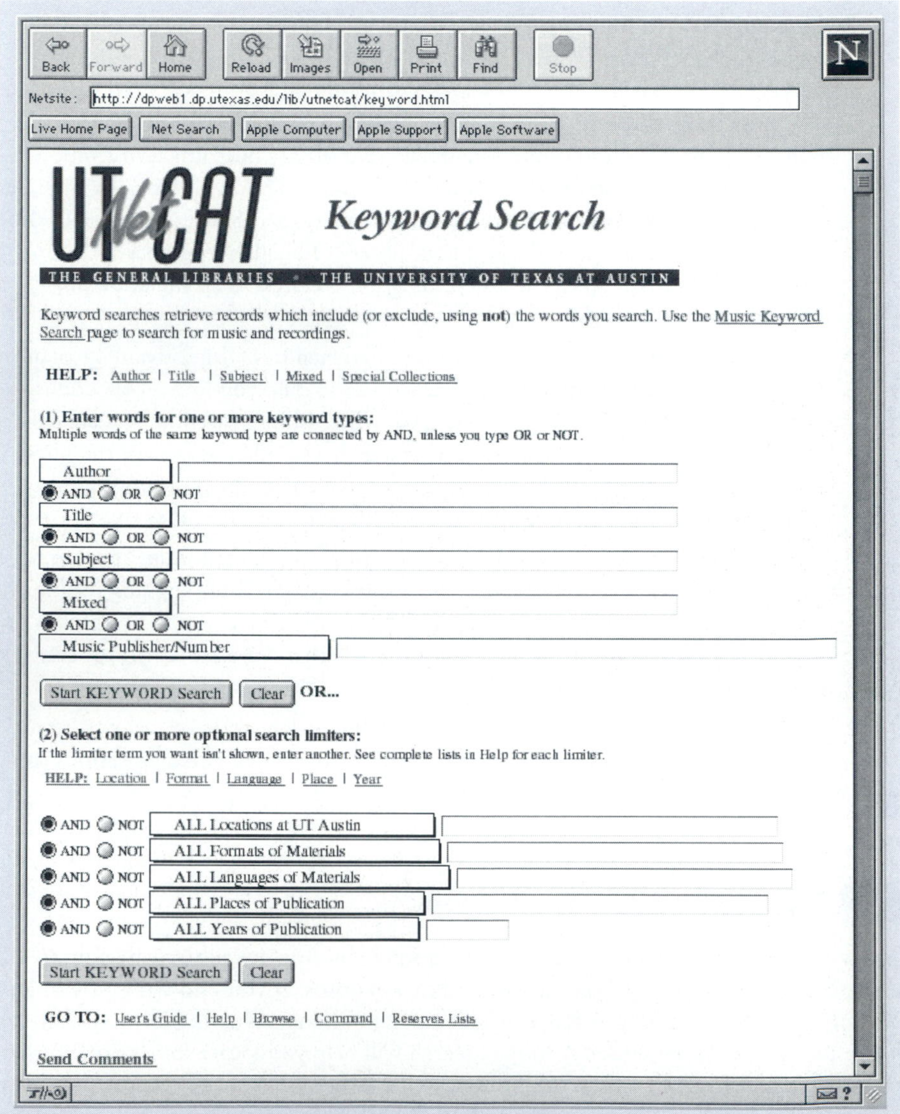

Figure 5.1   Search menu screen for an online library catalog.

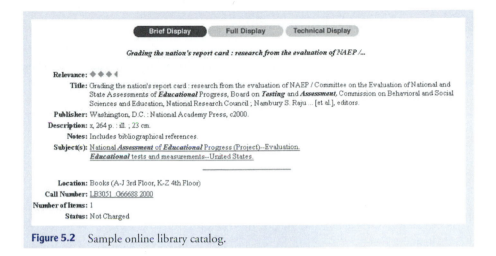

Figure 5.2 Sample online library catalog.

Notice that the screen supports a variety of keyword combinations and permits a user to specify the location, format, and language of the research material.

Thanks to the Internet, you can easily search the catalogs of other libraries. For a list of online library catalogs, examine LIBCAT at **http://www.metronet.lib.mn.us/lc/lc1.cfm**. This can be especially useful if your library is small or your topic unusual. You may be able to borrow items your library doesn't own through the Interlibrary Loan (ILL) program; find out if your library participates and how to request items.

Online library catalogs will usually give a short entry first—typically the author, title, publishing information, date, and call number—with an option to select a fuller listing. The fuller listing will describe additional features of the book—whether the book is illustrated and whether it has an index or a bibliography, for example. Be sure to follow up any new subject headings provided: they can be keywords for additional searches. In Figure 5.2, additional subject headings are links to more sources of information that you might not have found with your original keyword search. The book also includes a bibliography that can point you to further sources. The screen tells you the location of the book, the call number, and whether or not it is checked out.

5c Locate the reference room

Most libraries have a special section or room that houses reference materials, including dictionaries, encyclopedias, indexes, bibliographies, and many other types of sources. Usually these materials cannot be checked out. You will want to learn what materials are available to you here and how to access them. Reference librarians are there to help you; don't hesitate to ask. In addition to printed sources, most libraries offer access to electronic reference sources, either online or on CD-ROM. You may need to sign up for time on computer terminals to search CD-ROM resources; find out your library's policy. Find out, too, if you need to purchase a card to use the photocopy machines or printers and whether or not your library allows you to use your own diskettes in the computer terminals.

5d Locate suitable bibliographies

Bibliographies are lists of books, articles, and other documentary materials that deal with particular subjects or subject areas. You can save considerable time if you can locate an existing bibliography—preferably an annotated one—on your subject, rather than attempting to search through all the literature on your own.

There are four major types of bibliographies. Depending on your topic, you may need to consult one or more of the following.

- *Complete bibliographies* attempt to list all the major works in a given field or subject.

- *Selective bibliographies* usually list the best known or most respected books in a subject area.

- *Annotated bibliographies* briefly describe the works they list and may evaluate them.

- *Annual bibliographies* catalog the works produced within a field or discipline in a given year.

To determine whether a bibliography has been compiled on your subject, check the reference room of your library. Or you may be able to locate bibliographies using the library catalog. Chances are, however, that you won't find a bibliography on your

---

CHECKLIST

Bibliographies of Selected Disciplines

Doing a project on . . . ?	**Check this bibliography . . .**
American history	○ *Bibliographies in American History*
Anthropology	○ *Anthropological Bibliographies: A Selected Guide*
Art	○ *Guide to the Literature of Art History*
Astronomy	○ *A Guide to the Literature of Astronomy; Astronomy and Astrophysics: A Bibliographic Guide*
Classics	○ *Greek and Roman Authors: A Checklist of Criticism*
Communications	○ *Communication: A Guide to Information Sources*
Engineering	○ *Science and Engineering Literature*
Literature	○ *MLA International Bibliography*
Mathematics	○ *Using the Mathematical Literature*
Music	○ *Music Reference and Research Materials*
Philosophy	○ *A Bibliography of Philosophical Bibliographies*
Physics	○ *Use of Physics Literature*
Psychology	○ *Harvard List of Books in Psychology*
Social work	○ *Social Work Education: A Bibliography*

precise subject area; instead, you may have to use one of the general bibliographies available for almost every field. Only a few of the hundreds of bibliographic resources in specific disciplines are listed here to help you get started.

Your instructor or a reference librarian should be able to suggest an appropriate bibliography or computerized index for your subject area.

Although printed bibliographies are quickly losing ground to up-to-date electronic indexes and databases, they are still available on many subjects. In addition, the bibliographies you'll find at the back of scholarly books, articles, and dissertations may prove invaluable. They represent a selective look at a field and are usually compiled by an expert, not by a search engine. Pay special attention as well to works that are cited repeatedly; they may be important references that you should not overlook

5e Locate suitable periodical indexes or databases

Library catalogs will list the titles of journals and periodicals that are included in the library collection, but in order to search for specific articles in these journals and periodicals, you will need to use an index. Indexes list many useful items that cannot be recorded in a library catalog: journal articles, magazine articles, stories from newspapers. This material is called the *periodical literature* on a subject. You shouldn't undertake a college-level research paper without surveying this rich body of information. For example, to explore the subject of school vouchers, you'd likely want information from magazines such as *Newsweek* and *U.S. News and World Report* and newspapers such as *The New York Times* and *The Washington Post*. To find such information, you would go to indexes, not traditional library catalogs.

In the past, all periodical indexes were printed works, and you may still need to rely on those volumes to find older sources. For more current materials, however, you'll likely use electronic indexes. Many of them provide not only the bibliographical facts on an article—who published it, where, and when—but even abstracts of the pieces. Some electronic indexes furnish the full texts of news stories, magazine articles, literary works, and historical documents to print out or download to your computer (depending on copyright rules). Many databases also include listings for books in specific topic areas as well as cataloging the contents of journals, magazines, and newspapers. You can search through the abstracts of theses and dissertations using an index like *Dissertation Abstracts International*.

Ordinarily you can access indexes in your library reference room, the online library catalog, or the library Web site, and a few are available on the World Wide Web for free. Most indexes, printed or electronic, are relatively easy to manage—provided that you read the explanatory information that typically accompanies them. Electronic indexes usually support title, author, and keyword searches (see Chapter 6), and they may permit searching by other "fields"—that is, the categories by which data is entered. For example, a database may be searchable not only by author and title but also by publisher, place of publication, subject heading, accession number (a unique number assigned to items in databases that can be used to locate the specific item), government document number, and so on. Powerful indexes and databases such as *LEXIS-NEXIS* may require special commands and search techniques.

You may want to begin periodical searches with general and multidisciplinary indexes such as the following.

Academic Search Premier. Abstracts and indexing for over 3,800 scholarly journals and general magazines.

ArticleFirst. Bibliographic citations for articles in journals of science, technology, medicine, social science, business, the humanities, and popular culture.

CARL Uncover. Citations for over 25,000 multidisciplinary journals.

EBSCO Host (electronic). A collection of online databases in business, education, the sciences, and more.

JSTOR. Full text, full image collection of core journals in the humanities, sciences, and social sciences.

Lexis-Nexis' Academic Universe. Indexes approximately 5,000 publications, mostly full text, including newspapers, legal news, general interest magazines, medical journals, company financial information, wire service reports, government publications, and more.

Periodical Abstracts. Multidisciplinary index of over 1,600 publications in the humanities, social sciences, and general sciences, including scholarly journals, popular magazines, and business publications.

Project MUSE. Index of journals from Johns Hopkins University Press.

Readers' Guide to Periodical Literature (print). Index to popular magazines and periodicals.

Readers' Guide Abstracts (electronic). Like the *Readers' Guide to Periodical Literature, Readers' Guide Abstracts* indexes popular magazines and periodicals, but unlike its print counterpart, it includes an abstract of each article.

All major academic fields have specialized indexes for their periodical literature, most of them now computerized. Because new indexes may be added to a library's collection at any time, check with your reference librarian about the best sources for a given subject and how to access them. The checklist on page 61 gives just a sampling of the many specialized indexes to specific academic areas that are available.

Learning to use these powerful research tools is essential. Figure 5.3 shows the results of a simple keyword search in the *WorldCat* online database. The list provides important information about each entry, including the title, the year of publication, and the name of the author, where applicable. Reviewing this information is a necessary first step in narrowing the focus of your search. For example, the title can give you some idea of whether the content of an article will be useful before you look for the article itself. Similarly, if you want only more recent information, the dates of publication will help you eliminate sources.

Some databases, such as *ERIC*, may provide abstracts of articles along with full bibliographic records for each entry (see Figure 5.4). The screen may also enable you to access other information, such as a listing of libraries that own a particular source, options for obtaining the source via fax or email, and links to view the document on the World Wide Web. You can also email the bibliographic record to yourself (or to someone else) to review later.

CHECKLIST
Specialized Academic Indexes and Databases

Doing a project on . . . ?	Check this index . . .
Anthropology	○ *Anthropological Literature*
Architecture	○ *Avery Index*
Art	○ *Art Abstracts*
Biography	○ *Biography Index*
Biology	○ *Biological and Agricultural Abstracts; BIOSIS Previews*
Business	○ *Business Periodicals Index; ABI/Inform*
Chemistry	○ *CAS*
Computer science	○ *Computer Literature Index*
Current affairs	○ *LEXIS-NEXIS*
Economics	○ *PAIS (Public Affairs Information Service); EconLit*
Education	○ *Education Index; ERIC (Educational Resources Information Center)*
Engineering	○ *INSPEC*
Film	○ *Film Index International; Art Index*
History	○ *Historical Abstracts; America: History and Life*
Humanities	○ *Francis; Humanities Abstracts; Humanities Index*
Law	○ *LegalTrac*
Literature	○ *Essay and General Literature Index; MLA Bibliography; Contemporary Authors*
Mathematics	○ *MathSciNet*
Medicine	○ *MEDLINE*
Music	○ *Music Index; RILM Abstracts of Music*
Philosophy	○ *Philosopher's Index*
Psychology	○ *Psychological Abstracts; PsycLit; PsycINFO*
Public affairs	○ *PAIS*
Physics	○ *INSPEC*
Religion	○ *ATLA Religion Database*
Science	○ *General Science Index; General Science Abstracts*
Social sciences	○ *Social Science and Humanities Index; Social Sciences Index; Social Sciences Abstracts*
Technology	○ *Applied Science and Technology Abstracts*
Women	○ *Contemporary Women's Issues*

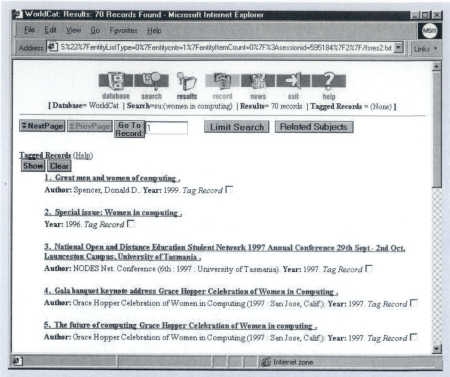

Figure 5.3 Results of a keyword search using the *WorldCat* online database.

```
Telnet - luis.nerdc.ufl.edu                                    _ □ ×
Connect  Edit  Terminal  Help
Search Request: t=encouraging enrollment and retention      Long View
CITATION - Record  1 of 1                      ERIC (RIE) (1988 to date)
---------------------------- + Screen 1 of 5 ----------------------------
Authors:          Sturm, Deborah
                  Moroh, Marsha
Title:            Encouraging Enrollment and Retention of Women in Computer
                  Science Classes. / by Sturm, Deborah; Moroh, Marsha
Pub.Date:         1994
Pages; Fiche:     6; 1
Document no.:     ED396688

FOUND IN ERIC microfiche unless noted otherwise:
                  EDRS Price - MF01/PC01 Plus Postage.

Abstract:         Women computer science students at the College of Staten
                  Island (CSI) in New York have a substantially higher pass
                  rate than their male classmates; however, their enrollment
                  and retention rates are low. During the last year and a
---------------------------------------------- CONTINUED ON NEXT SCREEN ---
START   Restart    BR   Brief view   TAG   Tagged view  F    Forward
I       Index      R    Review Searc HIST  See Searches H    Help
MENU    Databases  LIB  Owning libs  SUS   SUS location SET  Set values

NEXT COMMAND: ▮
```

Figure 5.4 Sample abstract of an article from a database.

You may be able to search some electronic databases remotely, from home or from terminals in open-use labs; other databases may be available only on certain library terminals or on CD-ROM. Some electronic indexes and databases may require that you enter your library or student ID number for access. Check with your reference librarian for details.

A library terminal may provide access to several databases or indexes, so be sure you are logged on to the appropriate index for your subject. Since not all databases and indexes work the same way, you will need to read carefully the descriptions of the index and the help screens to learn how to access its information.

When searching by keyword, see whether a list of subject headings is available. To save time, match your search terms to those on the list before you begin. If your search doesn't return the number of items you had hoped for, or if you need to ensure that your search has been thorough, try your search again using synonyms of your initial keyword(s). For more on keyword searching, see Chapter 6.

5f Consult biographical resources

Often in preparing a research project you'll need information about famous people, living and dead. Powerful sources are available in the reference room to help you. Good places to start are the *Biography Index: A Cumulative Index to Biographic Material in Books and Magazines; Bio-Base; LEXIS-NEXIS; Current Biography;* and *The McGraw-Hill Encyclopedia of World Biography.*

CHECKLIST
Specialized Biographical Resources

Your subject is in . . . ?   **Check this source . . .**

Art   ○ *Index to Artistic Biography*

Education   ○ *Biographical Dictionary of American Educators*

Music   ○ *The New Grove Dictionary of Music and Musicians*

Politics   ○ *Politics in America; Almanac of American Politics*

Psychology   ○ *Biographical Dictionary of Psychology*

Religion   ○ *Dictionary of American Religious Biography*

Science   ○ *Dictionary of Scientific Biography*

Your subject is . . . ?   **Check this source . . .**

African   ○ *Dictionary of African Biography*

African American   ○ *Dictionary of American Negro Biography*

Asian   ○ *Encyclopedia of Asian History*

Australian   ○ *Australian Dictionary of Biography*

Canadian   ○ *Dictionary of Canadian Biography*

Female   ○ *Index to Women; Notable American Women*

Mexican American   ○ *Mexican American Biographies; Chicano Scholars and Writers: A Bibliographic Directory*

Various *Who's Who* volumes cover living British, American, and world notables, including African Americans and women. Deceased figures may appear in *Who Was Who*. Probably the two most famous dictionaries of biography are the *Dictionary of National Biography* (British) and the *Dictionary of American Biography*.

On the World Wide Web you might check out the database maintained by the A&E program *Biography* at **http://www.biography.com**. For the wisdom of famous people, see the Web version of the 1910 edition of *Bartlett's Familiar Quotations* at **http://www.bartleby.com/100/** or, for more recent remarks, *The Quotation Page* at **http://www.starlingtech.com/quotes**. To search for private individuals, you can use features such as *Yahoo!*'s "People Search" on the World Wide Web; it provides addresses and phone numbers with almost frightening ease. And for information about writers and authors, consult the Internet Public Library's "Authors Resources" at **http://www.ipl.org/ref/RR/static/hum60.10.00.html** where you can find links to sites that provide bibliographies, abstracts, and even full-text biographies of famous authors.

5.1

Examples of the specialized biographical resources available to you are included in the checklist on page 63. Check with your instructor or reference librarian for additional resources.

5g Consult guides to reference works

The reference room in most libraries is filled with helpful materials. How do you know what the best books are for your needs? Ask a reference librarian whether guides to the literature for your topic are available, or check the reference section using the call number that you used to locate circulating books. Most libraries arrange books according to the Library of Congress Classification System (see below). Reference books are usually shelved in a non-circulating section or room but are usually arranged following the same classification system. You can use these classifications to help guide you to the location of additional works in your library or reference room that you may have missed in your electronic catalog or database searches.

Library of Congress Classification System

A	General Works
B	Philosophy, Psychology, Religion
C–F	History
G	Geography, Anthropology
H	Social Sciences, Business
J	Political Science
K	U.S. Law
L	Education
M	Music
N	Fine Arts
P	Language and Literature

Q   Mathematics, Science

R   Medicine

S   Agriculture

T   Technology, Engineering

U   Military Science

V   Naval Science

Z   Bibliography, Library Science

Also useful in some situations are printed or electronic indexes that list all books currently available (that is, books that are in print), their publishers, and their prices. Updated frequently, such indexes include *Books in Print* (print or electronic) and *Paperbound Books in Print.*

Dictionaries, encyclopedias, atlases, and other reference works can be good starting points for many research projects. Some Web versions may require access through your library server or a paid subscription, but others are available to anyone on the Internet. Commercial information providers such as *America Online* offer their subscribers access to online reference works. These resources can give you valuable background information on your subject, and some may provide a bibliography of further sources to pursue. Of course, you should not rely on dictionaries and encyclopedias alone for your research, but you should not ignore them either.

The following chart lists popular online reference works that will help you locate suitable information for your project.

CHART

Online Reference Works

American School Directory	**http://www.asd.com**
Bartlett's Familiar Quotations	**http://www.bartleby.com/100/**
CIA World Fact Book	**http://www.odci.gov/cia/publications/ factbook/index.html**
Electronic Statistics Textbook	**http://www.statsoft.com/textbook/ stathome.html**
Encyclopaedia Britannica Online	**http://www.eb.com**
IEEE Standards Library	**http://standards.ieee.org/reading/index.html**
Occupational Outlook Handbook	**http://www.bls.gov/oco/**
Perry Castaneda Map Collection	**http://www.lib.utexas.edu/maps/index.html**
U.S. Census Bureau American Fact Finder	**http://factfinder.census.gov/servlet/ BasicFactsServlet**
U.S. Code	**http://uscode.house.gov/usc.htm**
WWWebster's Dictionary	**http://www.m-w.com/dictionary**

WWW

5.2

5h Locate statistics

Statistics on every imaginable topic are available in library reference rooms and online. Be sure to find up-to-date and reliable figures, however. Consult resources such as *New York Times on the Web* "Navigator" at **http://www.nytimes.com/library/tech/reference/ cynavi.html** or the General Reference Collection at *The Internet Public Library* at **http://ipl.sils.umich.edu/ref/RR/**. Even *The Old Farmer's Almanac* is on the Web at **http://www.almanac.com**. Commercial online services such as *America Online* and *Prodigy* may offer access to additional reference sources. Other electronic sources may be available on CD-ROM, online through your library's home page or university network, or for free on the World Wide Web. For statistical information on specific topics, try the resources named in the checklist below or ask your reference librarian for additional sources.

CHECKLIST

Resources for Statistical Information

To find . . .	Check this source . . .
General statistics	○ *World Almanac; Current Index to Statistics* (electronic; check with your library for access)
Statistics about the United States	○ *Historical Statistics of the United States; Statistical Abstract of the United States* (online at **http:// www.census.gov/prod/www/statistical-abstract- us.html**); *Stat USA* (electronic; check with your library for access); *GPO Access* (online at **http:// www.access.gpo.gov/su_docs/index.html**)
World information	○ *The Statesman's Yearbook; National Intelligence Factbook; UN Demographic Yearbook; UNESCO Statistical Yearbook*
Business facts	○ *Handbook of Basic Economic Statistics; Survey of Current Business; Dow Jones–Irwin Business Almanac*
Public opinion polls	○ *Gallup Poll*
Census data	○ *Population Index* (electronic; check with your library for access)

5i Check news sources

Sometimes you'll need information from newspapers, particularly when your subject is current and your aim argumentative or persuasive. For information before about 1995, you'll have to rely on printed papers or microfilm copies since electronic newspapers and news services are a more recent phenomenon. When you know the date of an event, you can usually locate the information you want, or you can use a periodical index or search newspaper indexes to locate information. Only a few printed papers are fully indexed. One newspaper you are likely to encounter in most American libraries is *The New York Times,* usually available on microfilm. *The New York Times Index* provides chronological summaries of articles on a given subject. A second U.S. newspaper with an index is *The Wall Street Journal.*

A useful reference tool for more recent events is *NewsBank,* an index available since 1982 in electronic format. It covers more than 400 newspapers from across the country, keyed to a microfiche collection. *Facts on File* summarizes national and international news weekly. For background information on major problems and controversies, check *CQ Researcher*; to report on what editors are thinking, examine *Editorials on File,* a sampling of world and national opinion.

For very current events, you can search hundreds of newspapers and news services online. Figure 5.5 shows a search screen from *The New York Times on the Web.*

A directory such as *Yahoo!* at **http://www.yahoo.com/News_and_Media/ Newspapers** can point you to hundreds more online newspapers of every sort. Be care-

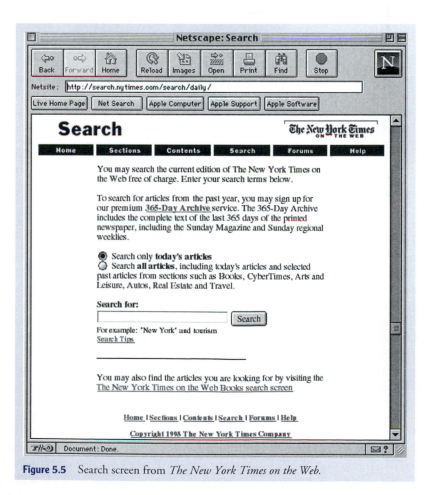

Figure 5.5   Search screen from *The New York Times on the Web.*

ful, however; not all news sources are unbiased or even credible. For more on evaluating sources, see Chapter 10.

The following chart lists online news resources worth consulting.

5.3

CHART

Online News Sources

CNN Interactive	**http://www.cnn.com**
C-SPAN Online	**http://www.c-span.org**
Fox News	**http://www.foxnews.com**
London Times	**http://www.timesonline.co.uk**
MSNBC	**http://www.msnbc.com/news**
National Public Radio	**http://www.npr.org**
The New York Times	**http://www.nytimes.com**
Reuters	**http://www.reuters.com/**
USA Today News	**http://www.usatoday.com**
The Wall Street Journal	**http://www.wsj.com**
The Washington Times	**http://www.washtimes.com/**

5.4

Another important online resource is the *ClariNet* news service at **http://www.clari.net/** which offers up-to-the-minute news reporting. And many schools offer a useful Web version of *LEXIS-NEXIS* that you may find helpful, especially with topics currently in the news.

5j Check special collections

In addition to circulating materials and reference collections, your library may offer access to rare books, original manuscripts, special exhibits, or interesting artifacts. For example, the Zach S. Henderson Library at Georgia Southern University has on exhibit such items as a 1940 campaign banner for Franklin Delano Roosevelt's bid for reelection as president, an original fifteenth-century manuscript of a Dutch prayerbook, and a handwritten slave deed dated February 17, 1845. These holdings are usually kept in a special room or area where they can be protected. Some items may be subject to copyright or other access restrictions, but most items in special collections are available for you to review. Your library catalog may allow you to search for items in special collections, or the library may index these items in a special catalog. Check with your reference librarian for information. Be sure to note any rules for using materials housed in special collections (such as limitations on photocopying) and be prepared to abide by them.

5k Consult government documents

5.5

Nowadays you can find many government documents online through the Web site for the Government Printing Office at **http://www.gpo.gov** or the World Wide Web sites for various government agencies. Many libraries are designated as official depositories for government documents, including documents or publications not available online. Your library may also house public records and official documents for local, state, or regional governments. Check with your reference librarian for more information.

5l Check book and film reviews

To locate reviews of books, see *Book Review Digest* (since 1905), *Book Review Index* (since 1965), and *Current Book Review Citations* (since 1976). *Book Review Digest* does not list as many reviews as the other two collections, but it summarizes those it does include—a useful feature. Many electronic periodical indexes also catalog book reviews, including *Academic Periodical Index* (since 1988) and *Readers' Guide to Periodical Literature* (since 1983). You can also find numerous book reviews online. Try searching with the *Yahoo!* directory at **http://dir.yahoo.com/Arts/Humanities/Literature/Reviews/** or try searching for online book reviews on bookseller sites such as *Amazon.com*.

5.6

For film reviews and criticism, see the printed volumes *Film Review Index* (since 1986) or *Film Criticism: An Index to Critics' Anthologies* (since 1975) as well as the electronic *Film Index International*, or find reviews online at **http://dir.yahoo.com/Entertainment/Movies_and_Film/Reviews/**.

5m Join in electronic conversations

Some online resources have no print equivalent; they represent ongoing discussions about ideas or work in progress. You will find such resources on the Internet's Usenet newsgroups and listserv discussion groups. You may have interactions in other electronic forums as well: in MOOs you can interact within imaginary environments, many online course packages such as *WebCT* and *Blackboard* offer discussion boards or chat rooms, and many online chat rooms such as *Yahoo! Chat*, or online service providers such as *America Online*, offer real-time chats with public figures, including authors, actors, and musicians.

Usenet groups, listservs, and similar tools can furnish you with interactive and up-to-the-second information on a topic from many points of view. These electronic conversations may introduce you to experts on your subject from all over the world or to knowledgeable amateurs—or to people simply blowing steam. They offer you the chance to question people who are doing the research or living the experiences you are writing about. But you must be careful when you take factual information from these environments: make it a habit to confirm any statistic, fact, or claim with information from a second and different type of authority—a book, an article, a reference work, or another credible source.

Some Web search engines now cover Usenet groups so that you can find and even join online conversations on your topic when such a discussion group exists (try searching *Google Groups* at **http://groups.google.com/**).

5.7

Usenet groups and other electronic conversations can help you give a dialogic dimension to a project, allowing you to place your own work within an existing community of thought. They can provide a close-up view of your subject. But keep the bigger picture in mind too; rely on traditional resources—journals, books, encyclopedias—to keep the full subject in perspective and to balance individual and idiosyncratic points of view you may find online.

The following checklist describes major characteristics of and uses for listservs and Usenet newsgroups and offers tips for searching these resources for information.

CHECKLIST

Listservs and Usenet Newsgroups

A **listserv** is a type of mail program that maintains lists of subscribers interested in discussing a specific topic. Users must subscribe in order to read or post messages.

Major characteristics: Lists are run on large computers; subscribers may be experts working in fields related to the list topic or simply interested participants. Some lists may be moderated to screen out irrelevant material or "noise." Old messages may sometimes be archived and available to anyone who is interested.

Use for: Excellent window on current issues. Good for listening in on the practitioners' conversations, discovering opinions, noting solutions to common problems, and learning about other available print or online resources.

Searching: When you subscribe, check the welcome message for instructions for searching the archives and for rules governing participation.

A **Usenet group** works like a listserv except that you need not subscribe to the list either to read its messages or to participate in the discussion.

Major characteristics: Thousands of groups focus on topics from *A* to *Z*. There is wide variation in the expertise of contributors. Anyone may read or post messages. Just browsing the list of Usenet groups can suggest topic ideas.

Use for: Conversations about popular topics and about little-known, obscure subjects. Almost every political group, social interest, religion, activity, hobby, and fantasy has a Usenet group.

Searching: Check the welcome messages and the FAQs (frequently asked questions) for information on how to search. Many lists have archives of older discussions.

5n Write or email professional organizations

Almost every subject, cause, concept, and idea is represented by a professional organization, society, bureau, office, or lobby. It makes good sense to write or email an appropriate organization for information on your topic; ask for pamphlets, leaflets, and reports. Many organizations offer detailed information on their Web sites as well. For mailing addresses of organizations, consult *The Encyclopedia of Associations,* published by Gale Research, or use a search engine to find Web sites.

Remember that the U.S. government publishes huge amounts of information on just about every subject of public interest. Check the *U.S. Government Periodicals Index*

FOCUS ON . . . Email etiquette

Most listservs welcome new members, but before subscribing to a list, check out its Frequently Asked Questions (FAQ) posting if there is one—or "lurk" for a while, reading the messages and getting a sense of the conversation. Although some groups may discourage students or researchers from asking questions, many listserv members are happy to share information with students whose questions show thought, knowledge, and advance preparation. Make sure that you acquire permission from the author(s) to use any information you obtain through listserv or Usenet discussions.

The following guidelines—called "Netiquette," or Internet etiquette—help make electronic discussions courteous and productive.

- Read the FAQ posting for the list or newsgroup, if there is one, to get a sense of the conversation and any limitations.
- Avoid using all-capital letters, usually considered the electronic equivalent of shouting.
- Do not send advertisements, chain letters, or personal messages to the entire list.
- Keep postings relevant to the topic of the list; for most lists, keep postings as brief as possible.
- When replying to previous messages, quote only those portions of the message to which you are referring.
- Ask permission before quoting from or re-posting messages from the list. Do not post copyrighted material from other sources to the list without permission from the copyright owner.
- Include a brief subject line that describes the topic of your message. If your message is part of an ongoing thread (that is, a discussion of a particular topic), use the reply key in your email editor to retain the same subject line as the message(s) to which you are replying.
- Keep signature files, if used, brief—usually no more than four lines. (Signature files allow writers to attach information about themselves to the end of each email message.)
- Avoid flaming (messages that attack other members of the list or their beliefs and ideas). Keep discussions and arguments on topic and courteous.
- Avoid "me too" messages. Do not reply to the list simply to express agreement; your posting should have something to contribute to the conversation.
- Use acronyms or emoticons (smiley faces and other symbols) sparingly. Make sure the members of the list are familiar with those you choose to use, and remember that humor and sarcasm may be hard to express in text-only formats like email.

or the *Monthly Catalog of U.S. Government Publications* for listings. Or use a Web site such as *Fedworld Information Network* at **http://www.fedworld.gov** to look for the material you need.

50 Use search engines to check the World Wide Web

The World Wide Web is a hypertext pathway into the vast resources of the Internet. In Chapter 6 you will learn how to use search engines to locate these resources efficiently. Web browser software such as *Netscape Communicator* and *Internet Explorer* presents the information via "pages" that can contain text, graphics, video, and sound as well as hypertext links; the browsers also support email, Usenet newsgroups, and other forms of electronic communication. The Web can distribute just about any information that can be digitized, including photo archives, artwork, maps, film clips, charts, music, and magazines. Web users move through different sites by selecting words or graphics linked to related resources.

Understand, however, that the Web is not a library. It has not been systematically designed to support research, so you cannot apply library research techniques or assume that what you find there is reliable. What goes online is not routinely cataloged, edited, or reviewed, so the quality of information on the Web varies greatly and its organization can be chaotic. As a result, you must approach the Web with caution when you use it as a tool for research. You may quickly find superb and up-to-date information on your subject, or you may struggle through a great deal of material that proves unreliable, malicious, biased, and wrong. In short, you need to apply critical skills to survey Web sites for information. (See Chapter 10 for further advice about evaluating sources.)

Once you have been introduced to the resources of the World Wide Web, you'll appreciate the need for search engines and directories—tools that help you cull wanted information from the hundreds of millions of Web pages now online. For example, the *Yahoo! Search Directory* categorizes information to help you locate information that can be difficult to find with keyword searches (see Chapter 6). Such guides, constantly being refined and upgraded, are readily available—just click the "Search" button on your Web browser. But you have to use them properly. Some of the best known Internet search engines are listed in the following chart.

CHART
Selected Internet Search Engines

About.com	http://home.about.com/index.htm
AltaVista	http://www.altavista.com/
AOL Anywhere	http://search.aol.com/
AskJeeves	http://www.askjeeves.com/
Excite	http://www.excite.com/
Google	http://www.google.com/
HotBot	http://www.hotbot.com/
LookSmart	http://www.looksmart.com/
Lycos	http://www.lycos.com/
WebCrawler	http://webcrawler.com/
Yahoo!	http://www.yahoo.com/

WWW

5.8

Most search engine sites include online guides to both basic and advanced search techniques. Take a few minutes to read the "Help" files to discover the remarkable and changing features of these highly competitive tools. Remember, too, that different search engines search differently; while some, such as AltaVista, will search the full texts of Web sites, others will search only information in titles or headers. Some search engines, usually called *directories*, will search only information which has been reviewed or categorized. For more on using search engines effectively, see Chapter 6.

Two points you should remember: (1) Web engines and directories all work a little differently and have different strengths and weaknesses, so you should explore your subject on more than one search engine. (2) Web search engines and directories may have huge databases with access to tens of millions of documents and Web pages, but there is no guarantee that any search engine will cover everything available on the Internet. Every engine is selective in how and what it covers. Again, explore your subject using more than one engine. Even searching on a different day can often return different results; sites may be down temporarily, and new sites are constantly being added and old ones deleted.

Commercial Web search engines aren't the only resource for finding information and links on the Web. Libraries, universities, and government institutions with more scholarly intentions have created hundreds of reference sites and search engines on the Internet as well. The following chart lists a few places to look to get you started.

5.9

C H A R T

Academic Directories and Search Engines Online

Argus Clearinghouse	**http://www.clearinghouse.net/**
Books on the Internet	**http://www.lib.utexas.edu/books/etext.html**
eserver.org	**http://eserver.org**
Infomine	**http://infomine.ucr.edu/**
InfoSurf	**http://www.library.ucsb.edu/subj/resource.html**
Internet Public Library	**http://www.ipl.org/**
Knowledge Source (SIRS)	**http://www.sirs.com/tree/tree.htm**
Librarian's Index to the Internet	**http://lii.org**
Library of Congress Subject Guide to Internet Resources	**http://lcweb.loc.gov/global/subject.html**
The Universal Library	**http://www.ul.cs.cmu.edu/**
Voice of the Shuttle	**http://vos.ucsb.edu/**

5.10

For more search engines and directories, check out *Yahoo!'s Searching the Web* at **http://www.yahoo.com/Computers_and_Internet/Internet/World_Wide_Web/Searching_the_Web**

Many commercial software packages can search the Net even while you sleep. Although no search engine or software can guarantee it will find sources that are authoritative and relevant to your topic, you can make searches more productive and less daunting by learning how to use the resources available.

5.11

Finding information is a time-consuming and sometimes frustrating process. Even with the aid of computers, which speed up certain kinds of searches beyond the wildest dreams of earlier scholars, researchers today still must explore a wide range of materials. However, with a little practice you can soon learn to locate the information you need more effectively. In the next chapter you will learn some techniques to make your electronic searches more efficient—whether you're searching the library catalog, a CD-ROM or online database, or the World Wide Web.

WWW Web Sites Worth Knowing

5.12

- ITools!, **http://iTools.com/**
- Library of Congress, **http://www.loc.gov/**
- Ask a Librarian, **http://www.loc.gov/rr/askalib/**
- Yale University Library "Research Guides by Subject," **http://www.library.yale.edu/guides/**
- Sink or Swim: Internet Search Tools & Techniques, **http://www.ouc.bc.ca/libr/connect96/search.htm**
- Internet Country Codes, **http://www.bcpl.net/~jspath/isocodes.html**

GETTING INVOLVED

1. Take a tour of your college library or research facility, especially if it is significantly larger than any library you have used before. Many larger libraries have brochures describing their resources and services. Some may offer tours, either self-guided or led by library staff.

2. Use the resources of your library to prepare a brief report about the week of your birth. Consult newspapers, magazines, books, and other resources to find information to help convey what the week was like. Don't limit your account to news events; find out what you can about the popular culture of the time—check the ads, the movie reviews, the sports pages, even the comics.

3. Working in a group, use the resources of the reference room to prepare a fact sheet or pamphlet on your city, town, or college or on a prominent local institution. Imagine that the brochure might be distributed in a packet given to newcomers. Decide what information might be useful (for example, population data, the average cost of a three-bedroom home, average temperatures) and then find it.

4. Check out the Web directory *Yahoo!* and examine how it categorizes information. Choose several subjects and see how long it takes you to find information using only the listings of subjects. (In other words, don't use the keyword search function.)

5. In class, come up with a list of five or ten barely famous people, persons of some accomplishment who are not household names. Then assign teams to find out basic biographical facts about the lives of these people—everything from their places of birth and birth dates to the names of their children.

MANAGING YOUR PROJECT

1. Explore your subject in your library's catalog. Begin by looking specifically for books on your subject. If you're having trouble locating books using a simple keyword or subject search, try some of the tips in Chapter 6.

2. Locate a bibliography particularly suited to your subject. The more specific the bibliography, the better. But don't ignore the general bibliographies available in many fields.

3. Make a list of the indexes that you must consult for your project, then learn how to use these tools. A little time spent reading about how these indexes work may save you a great deal of time later.

4. Explore your topic on the Web using a directory such as *Yahoo!* Do the categories in the directory point you to topic areas you hadn't considered?

5. Explore your topic on the Web using a search engine such as *Google*. But first come up with keywords that will help to both identify and narrow your subject. (For help, see Chapter 6.)

CHAPTER

6

Conducting
Electronic Searches

You need to know how to conduct electronic searches effectively in order to explore basic research resources such as online library catalogs, electronic indexes, and the Internet. When you use the "find" feature of a word processor, you are performing a simple keyword search. Increase the power of this technique and apply it to much larger databases and you have a search engine, an instrument that can seek not only the word(s) you specify but related terms and phrases as well.

Perhaps the best advice we can give for conducting electronic searches is to read the instructions for the database or search engine you are using, whether it is an electronic catalog, a Web "spider," or a directory. A Web spider searches out Web pages on its own; a directory is a database of Web pages compiled by people. As you might expect, spiders and directories will return different results depending on how they are structured and how they maintain their lists of searchable sites. Search engines that use directories will often include only those Web pages that have been submitted by site owners, so the total number of Web sites included in a particular directory may be relatively small. Search engines that use spiders will be much more comprehensive, but their ranking system—how the engine determines which sites to list first when returning results—may not provide you with the most useful sites at the top of the list. (Some engines will use the number of hits a site gets as a measure of importance; others may use the number of times your search term appears in a page.) The key to a successful search is to use a combination of "big" search engines and smaller specialized engines to look for information (see Section 6e). Among the biggest and most popular search engines and directories are *Yahoo!, Google, AltaVista, and HotBot.* More specialized search engines can be located at the *Big Search Engine Index* (**http://www.search-engine-index.co.uk/**), which currently indexes 910 search engines available on the Web. A few search portals, often called meta-search engines, such as *Dogpile* (**http://www.dogpile .com**), will run your keyword search through many search engines simultaneously.

Keyword searches are all similar in some respects, but the rules and "filters" that control any given system will differ. Your ability to focus a search and get the best re-

When doing keyword searches on electronic databases, be ingenious and persistent. Some preliminary reading on your topic may suggest helpful synonyms for your search term. Learn to use Boolean searches too. An effective Boolean search may reduce the number of worthless hits you receive in your search.

sults depends on knowing how to direct that search. You'll be surprised by the sophistication of some databases, particularly those on the World Wide Web (see Section 6e), which seem at times to anticipate your needs. But you can waste time if you ignore the information waiting beneath "Help," "Simple Search," or "Advanced Search" buttons on the screen.

One other tip: Be sure to type keywords carefully, especially proper nouns. A misspelled search term can prevent you from finding available information.

6a Understand how a simple keyword search works

A keyword search identifies files that contain the word(s) you have typed into a box or line on the screen. A librarian or instructor may be helpful in guiding you to appropriate keywords for your searches.

Or you can use research tools creatively to find powerful keywords. For example, when searching a library catalog, always look for cross listings for your subject—that is, other terms under which your subject is entered—and follow up on those terms. If your project on Civil War ironclad ships leads you to search with the term "Monitor" (the name of a famous Union ship), a particular catalog entry might include cross listings such as "Civil War"; "Merrimac"; "U.S. Navy, history"; and "Ericsson, John." You could then probe the catalog using each of these terms. Think about it like a detective following a trail of clues—each location you visit will contain new terms, new connections, and potential new directions for your investigation.

At times you will have to be ingenious and dogged in choosing keywords. For example, if you need to know whether alcohol is legally considered a drug, you could begin with the general keywords "alcohol" and "drugs." But you'd be swamped by the number of responses, and you might never find the particular information you need. Here is where a little preliminary reading might pay off (see Section 2c). If you learn that drugs are regulated by the Food and Drug Administration, you could try searching with that term or, even better, its familiar acronym: FDA. Once you locate the FDA's official site on the Web, you could search it for "alcohol" to find the information you were seeking.

WWW

6.1

"FDA" might not have been the first term to come to mind when you started your exploration, but it is a logical keyword given the information you were seeking.

So the keywords you choose—whether names, places, titles, concepts, or people—will shape your search. A comparatively small database, such as an online library catalog, may ask you to indicate whether a word you are searching is a title (t), author (a), subject (s), or some other type of term the system recognizes. Imagine that you are preparing to write a report on *Master and Commander* by Patrick O'Brian, a novel that takes place in the time of the Napoleonic wars. Typing the title of the book (*Master and Commander*), the name of its author (Patrick O'Brian), or a narrow subject keyword (Napoleonic wars) will often produce manageable numbers of items to examine and read.

t (title)	*Master and Commander*	8 items
a (author)	Patrick O'Brian	26 items
s (subject)	Napoleonic wars	25 items

You could easily look at all the items that appeared either on the computer screen or on the printout resulting from this search. Thus a simple keyword search may be adequate when the database you are exploring is small or the term you are searching is distinctive.

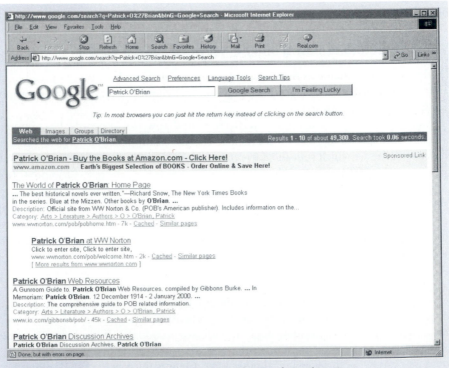

Figure 6.1   Search results for Patrick O'Brian on the *Google* search engine.

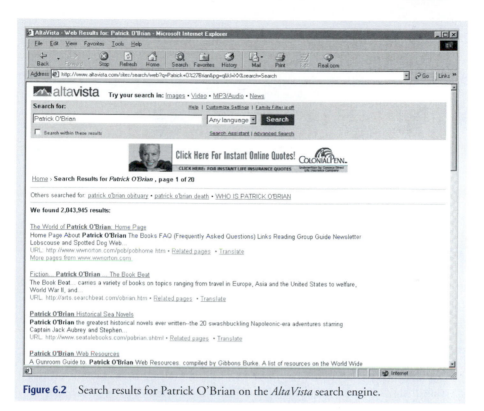

Figure 6.2   Search results for Patrick O'Brian on the *AltaVista* search engine.

However, a simple search of the same items on the World Wide Web, a huge database, might overwhelm you. Consider, for example, these results returned by three popular Web search engines as shown in Figures 6.1, 6.2, and 6.3:

	Google	AltaVista	HotBot
Master and Commander	297,000 items	8,693,249 items	181,700 items
Patrick O'Brian	49,300 items	2,043,945 items	14,900 items
Napoleonic wars	60,000 items	1,170,568 items	133,900 items

Similarly, typing even a narrowed subject listing into an online library catalog may provide too many items for you to read and research.

Naval history	1,800 items

In these situations you need more sophisticated search techniques. One such technique, called Boolean searching, uses "Boolean operators" to control and limit what a search does. These operators include simple logical commands such as AND, NOT, and OR that are useful for telling search engines what to include in a search and, even more important, what to leave out. A full discussion of Boolean searching can be found in Section 6c.

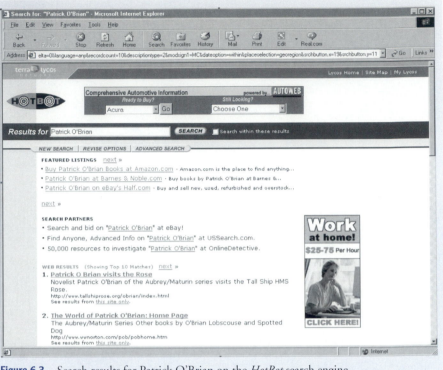

Figure 6.3 Search results for Patrick O'Brian on the *HotBot* search engine.

6b Truncate terms to extend your search

Computers can search only for the exact string of letters you type in. They cannot always recognize different forms of a word. In the above example, a search for the keywords "Napoleonic wars" would miss any articles or Web pages that contain variations of these words, such as "Napoleon" or "war." Truncating your terms (literally, shortening them) allows you to search for words with a common root. For example, the word *vote* has the variants *votes, voting, voter, voters*. List these words in a column and draw a line down the column following the last letter that is the same in all the words:

vote

votes

voting

voter

voters

The root common to all of the forms of the word is **vot.** Replacing the omitted (or variable) letters with an asterisk, the truncated term you would use in your search becomes **vot*.**

Most databases use an asterisk (*) to indicate truncation, although some use other characters, such as a question mark (?) or an exclamation point (!). Be sure to read the instructions for the search engine or database you are using.

Of course, you need to consider carefully the effect of truncation on your search. When you are combining search terms, truncation can be quite effective in helping you to narrow your search; truncation can also help broaden your search when specific forms of a word are returning too few hits. But use the technique with caution; searching for "vot*" will help to broaden your search for forms of the word "vote," but it may also return irrelevant hits for words such as "votive" and the French "*votre.*" To eliminate these terms, use Boolean operators such as NOT (e.g., vot* NOT votive) and select English-only if your database allows you to limit your search. Section 6c shows you how to use other Boolean operators to refine your search.

6c Refine your search with Boolean operators

There are close to two billion Web pages on the Internet, and chances are a great many of them will contain at least one of the words you're looking for. Because *AltaVista* indexes more Web pages than either *Yahoo!* or *HotBot*, it's likely to return a greater number of matches for any search. When *AltaVista* is told to search for the words *Master and Commander*, for example, it looks for every single Web page in its database that contains the words "master" and "commander" (it ignores the lowercase "and" altogether). These words could be separated by many paragraphs of text, but as long as they both appear somewhere in a page, the engine will call it a match. The result? Thousands of links to pages or articles that will be of no use to you whatsoever.

One way to avoid this and increase your chances of success in the search process is to use Boolean operators. When you do a Boolean search, you are actually doing two or more searches simultaneously and studying the point where those searches overlap. Most search engines in online catalogs, databases, and Web browsers use some form of Boolean searching.

You control a Boolean search through a set of specific terms or symbols. For example, by linking keywords with the term AND, you can search for more than one term at a time, identifying only those items in which the separate terms intersect. (It may help to visualize these items in terms of sets.) One way to initiate a Boolean search is to insert AND (in capital letters) between terms you wish to search.

Patrick AND O'Brian

miniature AND schnauzer AND training

Washington AND Jefferson AND Constitution

Another way is to select an appropriate command from the search engine, such as *AltaVista*'s "All of these Words" option. Asking the engine to search for only those items in which all the words you've specified occur usually reduces the information glut, but sometimes not enough to make the results manageable.

Master and Commander	from 8,693,249 to 121,823 items
Patrick O'Brian	from 2,043,945 to 9,799 items
Napoleonic wars	from 1,170,568 to 24,315 items

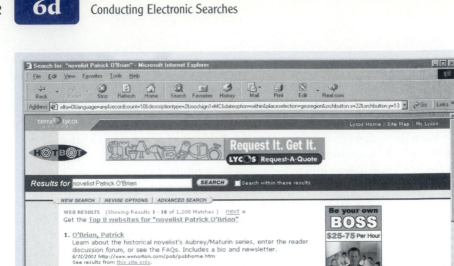

Figure 6.4 Search results for "novelist Patrick O'Brian" on the *HotBot* search engine.

You can further refine a Boolean search by increasing the number of search terms—the more specific the better. Consider what happens when you add "Great Britain" to our earlier online library catalog search for "naval history."

> Great Britain naval history   from 1,800 to 450 items

Or look at what happens when we specify O'Brian's profession, using *HotBot*'s "All the Words" filter on the Web (see Figure 6.4).

> Novelist Patrick O'Brian   1,200 items

At this point the logic of the *HotBot* search engine is trying to figure out which of the more than 1,200 items might be most helpful to us. As it turns out, the resulting search still produces no first-rate material, but that's not unusual in Web searches. You have to keep plugging away.

6d Refine your search with exact phrases

To narrow a search even more, you can look for a specific and distinctive phrase either by placing it between quotation marks or selecting the "exact phrase" option on a search screen. This technique is essential for Web research. Type "novels of Patrick O'Brian"

C H A R T

Commonly Used Boolean Commands

OR   Using OR between keywords directs the search engine to find examples of either keyword. Using OR would widen a search, but it would also allow you to locate all documents that cover related concepts.

> dog OR puppy
> Congress OR Senate

NOT   Using NOT between terms permits you to specify sites with one term but not another. This may be useful when you want to exclude certain meanings of a term irrelevant to your search.

> Indians **(NOT)** Cleveland
> apple **(NOT)** computer
> republican **(NOT)** party

( )   Putting items in parentheses allows for additional fine tuning of a search. In the first example below, you could locate documents that mentioned either Senator Gramm or Senator Hutchison but not Senator Kennedy or Senator Hatch. The second set of search terms will locate documents that contain the word "church" but that do not include either the word "Mormon" or the word "Catholic." Similarly, the last example will find information about pickup trucks as long as they are not made by either Ford or Dodge.

> Senator AND (Gramm OR Hutchison)
> church NOT (Mormon OR Catholic)
> pickup NOT (Ford OR Dodge)

Some search engines use + and – signs to select the same functions.

+   Putting + (a plus sign) immediately before an item, without a space after it, indicates that the word following it *must* be in the document being sought. Let's say, for example, you are looking on the World Wide Web for definitions of terms. You might format the requests this way.

> +wetlands +definition
> +"standardized test" +"definition of"

(Note that there is a space *before* the second plus sign, but there are no spaces *after* the plus signs)

–   Putting – (a minus sign) immediately before an item, without a space after it, indicates that the word following it *must not* be in the document being sought. Let's say you wanted to search for documents about Richard Nixon that didn't discuss Watergate or China. You could format the request this way.

> +Nixon –Watergate –China

(Note that here, too, there is a space before the second minus sign but not after it.)

into the search engine *AltaVista*, and it hunts its vast database for only those sites where that phrase occurs in its entirety (see Figure 6.5). The narrowing is dramatic:

> novels of Patrick O'Brian   287 items

And these items include a Patrick O'Brian Web page, a newsletter, and, best of all, a list of other O'Brian links that leads to a newsletter index and a mailing list for online conversation about O'Brian's maritime novels.

You can use exact phrase searches creatively in many ways. When you can't recall who is responsible for a particular expression or quotation—for example, "defining deviancy down"—you can make it the subject of an exact phrase search on the World Wide Web. Do so in the Web directory *Yahoo!* and you'll quickly find the expression attributed to Senator Daniel Patrick Moynihan, in the very first item located by a search of that directory. Many databases allow you to specify exact phrases in your searches.

You can also combine exact word searches with various Boolean commands to find precisely what you need when you can identify appropriate keywords. When you wanted to find Web pages about the movie *The Ten Commandments* that specifically mentioned either Charlton Heston or Yul Brynner, for example, your Boolean search would look like this:

> "Ten Commandments" AND ("Charlton Heston" OR "Yul Brynner")

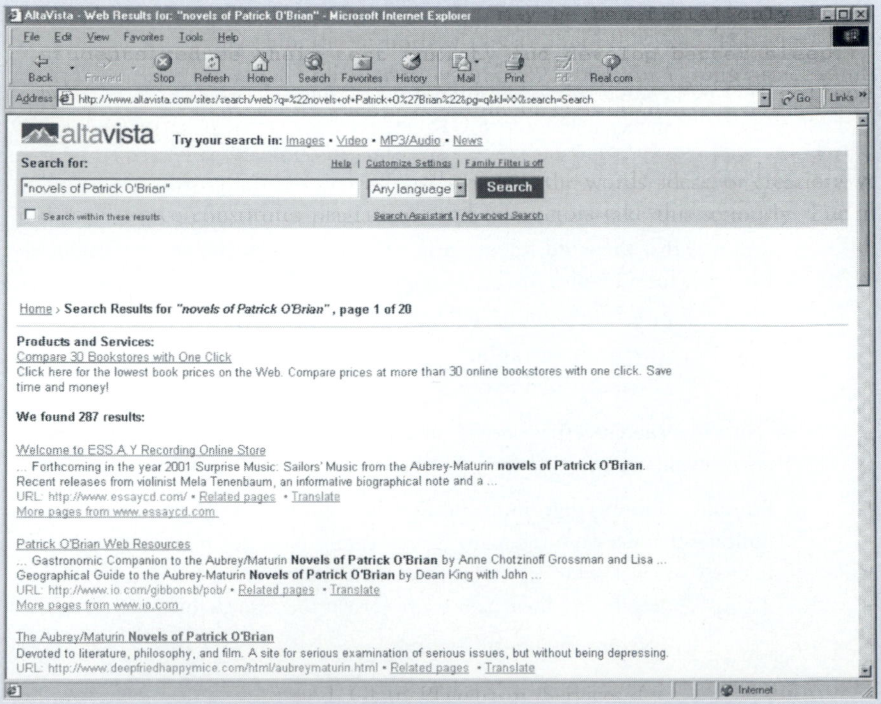

Figure 6.5 Search results for "novels of Patrick O'Brian" on the *AltaVista* search engine.

By the same token, a search for information on pickup trucks not manufactured by Ford or Dodge would take this form:

"pickup truck" NOT (Ford OR Dodge)

Some databases allow you to refine searches further by language or by publication type. The potential of such searches is limited only by your imagination and the speed of your modem or online connection.

As with mathematical equations, there is a distinct order of operations in Boolean searching: Boolean operations are evaluated from left to right, with operations in parentheses evaluated first. Make sure you read the directions for the particular software or search engine you are using, and experiment with it until you feel confident.

6e Use more than one search engine or database

No two search engines are alike—they perform their functions in different ways using different sets of criteria for finding and listing. Some engines (like *Yahoo!*) are very selective about the pages they index and search; others (like *AltaVista*) are almost completely nonselective, including virtually every Web page they can find on the Internet. As a researcher, then, you need to take advantage of the strengths and weaknesses of several search engines to get the best and most useful results.

A good way to illustrate this is to take a close look at two of the more popular search engines on the Web, *AltaVista* (see Figure 6.6) and *Google* (see Figure 6.7).

AltaVista, perhaps more than any other search engine, aims to index the Web as thoroughly and comprehensively as possible. It employs a Web "spider" or "crawler" to seek out, locate, and index new pages every day, constantly adding new information to its database. Although this may give you the power to access nearly everything published on the Web about your topic, the sheer scope of "everything" means you have to focus your searches very carefully with Boolean operators. Here are the results of searches on *AltaVista* on the topic of *standardized testing* before and after using Boolean terms:

standardized testing	4,171,690 items
standardized AND testing (*same for* +standardized +testing)	109,855 items
"standardized testing"	20,371 items
"standardized testing" AND effects	2,113 items
"standardized testing" AND effects AND teaching	1,308 items

Though the prospect of wading through more than a thousand results may seem daunting, you will often find that the first several pages of results will provide the most useful resources. In this case, the first ten results in the last search include links to a document on standardized testing from the *ERIC Digest* (a well-known source of educational research) as well as an article by Richard Phelps, "Why Testing Experts Hate Testing," that outlines many of the major arguments for and against standardized tests.

Like *AltaVista*, *Google* automatically seeks out Web pages with a crawler (called *Googlebot*), but it indexes a smaller proportion of the pages available on the Web ("smaller" being defined as 1,610,476,000). What makes *Google* distinctive is that it uses a sophisticated ranking system to list the pages most likely to be useful first.

Figure 6.6   Home page for *AltaVista* search engine. *(Source:* **http://www.altavista.com***)*

Here are the results of a search on *Google* using several Boolean operators:

standardized testing	463,000 items
"standardized testing"	53,900 items
"standardized testing" AND effects	6,580 items
"standardized testing" AND effects AND teaching	4,310 items

The results for the last search on *Google*, somewhat larger than the same search on *AltaVista*, list the *ERIC* paper first and the article by Richard Phelps ninetieth. Between the two listings, however, are a wealth of articles—some not included or easily found on *AltaVista*—that offer useful perspectives on the effects of standardized testing on teaching. Without conducting this second search, you might miss those articles.

For those who prefer a somewhat different approach to Web searching, *Google* offers a smaller directory of Web pages, submitted by Web site owners and reviewed for content, that can be browsed independently. Information on standardized testing, for example, can be found by looking under the category Society>Issues>Education>Standardized Testing.

Figure 6.7 Home page for Google Search Crawler. *(Source:* **http://www.google.com***)*

Again, use more than one search engine when researching a topic; what is overlooked by one may be highlighted by another. And if you're having trouble focusing the search and finding what you need, click on the "Help," "Advanced Search," and "Search Assistant" buttons available on most sites. They will guide you through the search process and give you extremely valuable tips on how to use the engine effectively.

6f Evaluate your electronic search

With search engines and directories you can get results quickly and determine whether (or how) new material illuminates your chosen subject: did you receive the results you expected or something quite different? Don't be satisfied with your initial searches, even when they supply ample information. Another combination of keywords or a different search path might provide still better material.

Each time you search and get an unexpected response, ask yourself why. Ideas may be hidden under synonyms of the word you searched. When the first try doesn't work, look for clues in the results you receive (or don't receive). Check spellings and try synonyms. Use different combinations of Boolean operators. Don't give up.

6g Keep a record of your search

Whether you are conducting research on the Web, using an online information service or database, or searching an online library catalog, probably the most important research strategy of all is to keep track of your work. In addition to keeping a record of potential sources, you will want to remember the search terms you have used and keep a record of the indexes, databases, or catalogs you have searched. This way, you will be able to locate information again if necessary later in the research process by using the same search strings, and you can save yourself time by ensuring that you do not duplicate effort. You may also want to consider compiling an annotated bibliography, that is, a listing of all the potential sources you found, along with a brief summary or description of each one. This can be valuable if your project later develops in ways you had not anticipated. Chapter 8 provides useful information and helpful tips on keeping track of and organizing your work.

Not all of your research will or should rely solely on published materials. Some projects will require that you conduct your own experiments or field research. Chapter 7 provides important information about conducting interviews, administering surveys and questionnaires, and using careful observation as additional sources of support for your project.

WWW Web Sites Worth Knowing

WWW
6.4

- *AltaVista* Search Assistant Help Page, **http://help.altavista.com/search/power_help**
- Purdue's OWL, "Searching the World Wide Web," **http://owl.english.purdue.edu/handouts/research/r_websearch2.html**
- Boolean Logic and Boolean Operators, **http://www.josts.net/tec3012/5a5.htm**
- Search Engine Watch: Tips About Internet Search Engines, **http://searchenginewatch.com/**
- Search Engine Showdown: The Users' Guide to Web Searching, **http://notess.com/search/**
- Search Engines

    Google, **http://www.google.com**

    Yahoo!, **http://www.yahoo.com**

    AltaVista, **http://www.altavista.com**

GETTING INVOLVED

1. Try out your local library's electronic catalog. What kinds of searches does it permit? What kinds of library materials will it search? What limits can you place on searches?

2. Pick a topic that interests you and conduct a series of searches using various combinations of Boolean operators and search terms. Try quotation marks, parentheses,

+ and –, AND, and OR. Explore the "Advanced Search" capabilities of the search engine you choose. Which searches or combinations of searches produce the most interesting or useful results?

3. Compare two Web search engines in detail. First read all you can about the search engines. The home page of a site will usually offer links to various options, including documentation on how to use the site, the search options available, and suggestions for how to use the engine. Compare the features of the site.

   Then choose keywords related to a subject that interests you and type them into the two search engines. Compare the kinds of results you get: the number of hits, how the hits are reported, how the hits are classified, the quality of the hits. Report your findings to classmates and compare your conclusions with theirs.

MANAGING YOUR PROJECT

1. Describe your project to your reference librarian, asking him or her to suggest appropriate *descriptors* (terms by which your subject might be described in catalogs and databases) for your subject.

2. Begin the exploration of your subject in the library catalog. In every preliminary item you find, check for other subject listings under which your topic is cataloged. Use these new terms as keywords for additional searches.

3. Consider various combinations of keywords that might help you narrow your search. Or vary the forms of words by which you are searching.

   alcohol → alcoholism → alcoholic
   democracy → democratic
   "moon shot" → "moon landing" → "Apollo 11"
   "House of Representatives"→ "U.S. House" → Congress
   "Lyndon B. Johnson" → LBJ → "President Johnson"

4. Explore your subject with at least two Web search engines or directories. Keep track of the tools you use and the search terms you try. Use the tools to narrow your search as necessary. Be sure to note what it is you are searching: complete Web sites, just the headings of Web pages, newsgroups, recent postings, and so on.

5. Begin to assemble your preliminary bibliography. Create note cards for printed sources you consider valuable. Also create note cards for important online material. Immediately print out or download any useful material from newsgroups or listservs; this material might not be available the next time you look for it. Keep track of all bibliographical data, including the date of access for electronic items. (The date of access is the day on which you examined an electronic source.)

6. Create a special "Bookmarks" or "Favorites" file for pages and sites from the World Wide Web you expect to visit again. You can organize this file in various ways, grouping related items and even annotating them.

CHAPTER

7

Conducting Field Research

Although much college research occurs in the library or online, some projects may lead you to seek information through your own interviews, surveys, and close observation. This *fieldwork* is common in disciplines such as psychology, anthropology, and education; if you are pursuing a degree in these areas, you'll learn formal techniques for field research. But informal fieldwork can be useful in other, less rigid research situations provided that you describe your procedures accurately and qualify your conclusions properly.

Why do fieldwork at all? You may find questions in your research project that can't be answered any other way. If you wanted to include information about the effects standardized testing has had on local classrooms or local teachers, for example, it is unlikely you would find much relevant information on the Web or in the library. Your best bet would be to pay a visit to local schools and interview teachers about the effects as they perceive them. Not only will that give you insights about standardized testing you probably couldn't find anywhere else, but current, poignant observations from local schoolteachers might be very persuasive to an audience made up of residents of the same community.

The sort(s) of fieldwork that will work best for you will depend on your project, your research question and/or hypothesis, and the time and resources you have available. Field research requires careful planning and perseverance to be successful, and the process of gathering and interpreting fieldwork data can be complex and time consuming. Budget your time wisely as you think about the kind of fieldwork that will contribute the most to your project's rhetorical goals. In this chapter we'll look only briefly at basic information for conducting interviews, using questionnaires, and making observations.

There are as many guides to fieldwork as there are fields of study. To give you an idea of the breadth and specificity of these guides, here are a few of them.

- *Handbook for Industrial Archaeologists: A Guide to Fieldwork and Research,* by Kenneth Hudson
- *Doing Fieldwork: Warnings and Advice,* by Rosalie H. Wax

- *Folklife and Fieldwork: A Layman's Introduction to Field Techniques,* by Peter Bartis
- *Fieldwork, Participation, and Practice: Ethics and Dilemmas in Qualitative Research,* by Marlene de Laine
- *Gender Issues in Ethnography,* by Carol A. B. Warren and Jennifer Kay Hackney
- *Getting the Facts: A Fieldwork Guide for Evaluators and Policy Analysts,* by Jerome T. Murphy
- *Hermeneutic Phenomenological Research: A Practical Guide for Nurse Researchers,* by Markene Zichi Cohen, David L. Kahn, and Richard H. Steeves

For more information, you'll want to consult a good research guide for your own field of study.

7a Conduct interviews

Sometimes people are the best sources of information. When you can discuss your subject with an expert, you'll add credibility, authenticity, and immediacy to a research report. If you are writing a paper about an aspect of medical care, talk to a medical professional. When exploring the financial dilemmas of community theaters, try to interview a local producer or theater manager. If writing about problems with standardized testing, find a teacher or school administrator with thirty minutes to spare.

If possible, you will want to meet in person to conduct your interview. However, you may need to interview people by telephone or by mail, and of course it is now possible to consult with knowledgeable people via email, newsgroups, and listservs (see Section 5m). Although online chats tend to be less formal than face-to-face conversations, your queries will still require appropriate preparation and courtesy. For a directory of experts willing to consult via email, check out *Pitsco's Ask an Expert* at **http://www.askanexpert.com/** or *Find/SVP* at **http://www.findsvp.com**.

Conducting a formal interview is not the same thing as chatting with a friend over the phone. You're there with a specific purpose, and you're often talking with someone you've never met before. You should make every effort to conduct the interview as professionally as possible, and the following checklist will assist you in achieving that goal.

Successful field research relies on communication with the appropriate subjects and authorities. The best interviews are face-to-face dialogues, but email, newsgroups, and listservs also provide valuable opportunities for conversation with research subjects and experts.

CHECKLIST

Conducting a One-on-One Interview

○ Write, telephone, or email your subject for an appointment, making clear why you want the interview.

○ Confirm your appointment the day before, and be on time for your appointment.

○ Be prepared for the meeting. Learn all you can about your subject's professional background, education, work history, and publications.

○ Dress appropriately; show that you take the interview seriously.

○ Have a list of questions and possible follow-ups ready in your notebook. Establish the basic facts: *who? what? where? when? how? why?* When appropriate, pose questions that require more than one-word answers.

○ Focus your queries on your research question: don't wander from the subject.

○ Be alert and interested: make frequent eye contact.

○ Ask follow-up questions as necessary; be prepared if your interviewer brings up important points you had not previously considered.

○ Take careful notes, especially if you intend to quote your source.

○ Double-check direct quotations, and be sure your source is willing to be cited "on the record."

○ If you plan to tape or log an interview, get your subject's approval first.

○ Thank your subjects for their time.

○ Send a copy of your completed project, along with a written thank-you note, to everyone you interviewed.

Asking questions in just the right way to get the responses you want can be tricky, especially when you may have strong views about a subject. Posing questions in an ethical way is a hallmark of good research design.

7b Conduct surveys

Research projects that focus on your local community may require surveys of public opinion and attitudes not available from other sources. So you may have to supply the information yourself by creating questionnaires and conducting studies. Yet polling is demanding, and even creating a useful questionnaire requires ingenuity; you'll have to work hard to produce research results that readers will respect.

The principles behind effective polls and surveys are not inscrutable. To begin with, you should have a clear idea about the information you are seeking. In other words, you distribute questionnaires not to see what turns up but as a way of answering research questions you have already formulated: Do people on my dormitory floor feel personally secure in their rooms? Would people in my neighborhood support the pres-

🌀 FOCUS ON . . . Ethics in Field Research

When conducting field research, resist the urge to inject your own opinions or biases into the research process. As an investigator, your role should be to gather information from as many sources as possible and to do so in honest and ethical ways. That means asking questions fairly and interpreting the responses without prejudice. In his well-known book *How to Lie with Statistics*, Darrell Huff shows how survey results can be skewed by deceptive or careless wording in questions. Try to make the wording of all your questions as bias-free as possible.

Remember that you are obligated to present your results fully and without an intent to deceive your readers. Your goal as a researcher should be the pursuit of the truth, not the promotion of your own beliefs or self-interest. Recall that the Challenger disaster in January 1986 was caused in part by a decision among project managers to hide the results of tests on the space shuttle's O-Rings. Though your own research project will probably not be as high profile as the space program (and the consequences of deception probably not as tragic), the basic lesson holds true: if you obscure relevant information or falsify your results, you violate the whole purpose of doing research. On the other hand, if you present the results of your research in a fair, balanced, logical, and ethical fashion, your audience will be more strongly inclined to accept your conclusions.

You also have an obligation to your research subjects. In addition to your ethical responsibility to present their opinions and statements fairly and accurately, you have an obligation to protect your respondents from repercussions by protecting personal information, assuring anonymity (when appropriate), and obtaining informed consent from your subjects to participate in your research project. You may also need parental consent if your subjects are under eighteen. Most colleges and universities have an Institutional Review Board (IRB) that you may need to check with before conducting research that involves human subjects; ask your instructor to see if that is the case.

ence of a halfway house for juvenile offenders? Are people willing to pay additional taxes for improved public transportation?

You have to formulate good questions, whether you are gathering factual information or sampling public opinion. Asking the right question isn't easy. You don't want to skew the answers by posing vague, leading, or biased questions.

7.1

VAGUE	What do you think about standardized testing?
REVISED	What are the effects (if any) of standardized testing on the way you teach?
LEADING	Are you in favor of the city's building a halfway house for juvenile criminals right in the middle of our peaceful Enfield neighborhood?
REVISED	Do you favor the city's plan to build a halfway house for former juvenile offenders in the Enfield neighborhood?

BIASED   Would you support yet another tax increase to fund a scheme for light rail in the city?

REVISED   Would you support a one-cent increase in the current sales tax to fund a light rail system for the city?

To make responses easy to tabulate, you will often want to provide readers with a range of options for answering your questions. This is called a Likert Scale.

```
How do you feel about the following statements?

Respond using the appropriate number.

    1 I disagree totally.

    2 I disagree somewhat.

    3 I agree somewhat.

    4 I agree totally.

Our bus system serves the whole community.   _____

Our bus system operates efficiently.         _____

Our bus system runs on time.                 _____

Bus fares are too high.                       _____

A sales tax increase for buses makes sense. _____

I am unfamiliar with our bus system.          _____
```

Experts recommend that you provide an even number of choices for responses; otherwise, answers often tend to hover in the middle.

In addition to exploring specific issues, you may want to gather demographic data on the people you are surveying; this information may be useful later in interpreting your findings. You must be able to protect the privacy of the people you survey and offer reasonable assurances that any information they volunteer will not be used against them in any way. But personal data can reveal surprising patterns, particularly when you ask questions about political and social topics.

```
About you. Knowing a little about respondents to this survey

will make interpretation of the data more significant. Please

answer the following questions as best you can. Leave off any

information you would rather not offer.

    1. What is your gender?

        _____ M          _____ F

    2. What is your marital status?

        _____ Married

        _____ Single, divorced/separated/widowed

        _____ Single, never married
```

3. What is your age?

   _____

4. What is your race or ethnicity?

   _____ Asian

   _____ Black/African American

   _____ Hispanic

   _____ White

   _____ Other

5. What is the highest level of your education?

   _____ elementary school or less

   _____ some high school

   _____ high school graduate

   _____ some college

   _____ college graduate

   _____ postgraduate or professional school

   _____ other

Try to anticipate the questions your queries might raise in a respondent's mind. For example, the list of educational achievement might be puzzling to someone who went to a technical or trade school out of high school. The category "other" often helps in doubtful cases.

Work for a reasonable mix of "quick response" and "open-ended" questions. People are not often willing to spend a lot of time completing surveys, and if you ask too many questions that require written responses, you may find that few of your surveys will get back to you. Whenever possible, ask questions in ways that your respondents can answer quickly and with minimal effort. Save the open-ended, free response questions for those issues that can't be satisfactorily answered any other way.

Be sure you survey enough people from your target group so that readers will find your sample adequate. Ordinarily you need to choose people at random for your survey, and yet those polled should represent a cross section of the whole population. In other words, "random" doesn't really mean random! Getting the right mix can be tricky. Surveying only your friends, only people who agree with you, or only people like yourself will almost certainly produce inadequate research.

You may have to provide an incentive to get people to cooperate with your survey. In most cases this means suggesting that their responses may help to solve a problem or serve others in some way. J. D. Powers, the company famous for surveying new-car owners, sends a crisp dollar bill with its survey to thank potential respondents. You may not be able to go that far, but you do need to consider whether you can offer some incentive for a response, particularly when your survey is lengthy (as the J. D. Powers survey is).

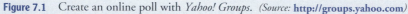

Figure 7.1   Create an online poll with *Yahoo! Groups*. *(Source:* **http://groups.yahoo.com***)*

Finally, you'll have to tabulate your findings accurately, present the results in a fashion that makes sense to readers, let readers know the techniques you used to gather your information, and, most important, report the limits of your study. Those limits provide the qualifications for any conclusions you draw. Don't overstate the results.

Like interviews, surveys and polls can be conducted face to face, by telephone, by mail, or online. Figure 7.1 shows a simple online poll created using the free *Yahoo! Groups,* which automatically tabulates results for you.

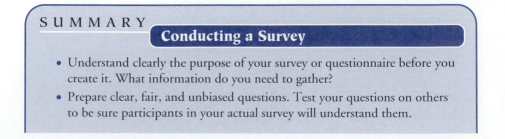

S U M M A R Y

Conducting a Survey

- Understand clearly the purpose of your survey or questionnaire before you create it. What information do you need to gather?
- Prepare clear, fair, and unbiased questions. Test your questions on others to be sure participants in your actual survey will understand them.

- Consider the types of responses you need from respondents. Should they respond to a scale? to a list of options you provide? Should they fill in blanks?
- Consider how much space might be adequate for responses and how much space might be too much.
- Create questionnaires that are easy to read, easy to fill out, and easy to tabulate.
- Create questionnaires that are convenient to return. If necessary, provide properly addressed envelopes and return postage.
- Give respondents appropriate assurances about the confidentiality of their responses and then abide by your commitment.
- Keep track of all your sampling procedures so you can report them accurately in your research.

7c Make systematic observations

Some of the best field research you can do may come simply from the careful study of a phenomenon. The techniques of observation you use for a college research project may not be so rigorous as those of professional ethnographers who make a science of such studies, but you do need to take the process seriously. On their own, people are notoriously unreliable in recounting what they have seen; their observations are often colored by their expectations, experiences, and assumptions. (Not surprisingly, the sworn testimonies of eyewitnesses to events are often conflicting.) So in making research observations—whether about the behavior of sports fans at a football game or the interactions between infants and staff at a day-care center—you want to employ techniques that counteract your biases as much as possible and ensure the reliability of your claims.

In recording your observations, you might begin with a double-column spiral notebook to separate your actual observations of a phenomenon from your immediate reactions to it. Your written notes should be quite detailed about time, place, duration of the study, conditions of the observation, and so on. You may have to summarize this information later.

You need not rely on notebooks alone for your records. To assure an accurate account of what you are studying, use any appropriate technology: photography, tape recording, video recording, transcription of online conversations, and so on. Remember to get permission to gather this type of information. If you make multiple observations over a period of time, follow the same procedures each time and note any changes that might affect your results. For example, students conducting a traffic count of persons entering a major campus facility would want to perform the counts on typical campus days—not during spring break or on days when the weather is unusually bad.

> **S U M M A R Y**
> ## Making Observations
>
> - Understand the purpose of your observation. What information do you hope to gather? In what forms can that data be gathered and reported?
> - Look at the literature on your subject and become familiar with the issues or subjects you are studying. What background information do you need to have on your subject(s) to make informed and perceptive observations?
> - Plan the method of your observation. How can you gather the information you need? How can you minimize your own impact on the situation you are observing? Will it be necessary for you to obtain permission from an institutional review board or another regulatory authority?
> - Practice techniques of observation. Determine what methods work best.
> - Work with others to confirm the reliability of your observations. Cross-check your field notes with those of fellow researchers.

Between going to the library, conducting searches on the Web, and collecting data from field research, you may soon begin to feel yourself awash in information. We've all had the experience at one time or another of sitting at a desk with papers, magazines, photocopies, books, and printouts everywhere, unable to remember where everything came from or which piece of paper had that absolutely perfect quote needed to make that really important point. With so many new sources of information available to us these days, it's all the more important to find ways to keep track of it all. In the next chapter we'll look at handy ways to make "keeping track" a bit easier.

WWW Web Sites Worth Knowing

7.3

- American Statistical Society: What Is a Survey?, **http://www.amstat.org/sections/srms/whatsurvey.html**
- Field Research: Planning an Efficient Out-and-About—Suite 101.com, **http://www.suite101.com/article.cfm/academic_writing/26071**
- Tips for Interviewers, **http://www.rscc.cc.tn.us/OWL/Interview2.html**
- U.S. Department of Health and Human Services, Office for Human Research Protections, **http://ohrp.osophs.dhhs.gov/**

GETTING INVOLVED

1. Carefully watch a news or entertainment interview on television, videotaping it if possible. Then study the session closely and try to work backward to determine what the interviewer would have had to find out in order to ask the questions he or she did. What research did the interviewer (or support staff) do? How much did

the interviewer rely on common knowledge? What questions did the interviewer pose that you couldn't have asked without more background information?

2. Write a one-page news release about a classmate and her or his accomplishments, background, and career objectives, using information you accumulate from a brief interview. For this interview, prepare a list of questions to help you find out as much as possible about an aspect of your classmate's life. (Your subject may decline to answer any question without explanation, so frame your questions with a sense of your audience.) After you have drafted your press release, show it to your class-mate for a critique. Revise the press release on the basis of your classmate's comments.

3. Recall a time recently when you were either surveyed orally (perhaps over the tele-phone) or asked to respond to a questionnaire prepared to discover public opinion. Why and how do you think you were selected for the survey? How much might the questioners have known about you demographically, and what demographic questions were posed? For example, were you asked about your age, income, gen-der, or employment? How many questions were posed? Were the questions bal-anced or open-ended—or did you feel you were being directed toward a particular conclusion? Could you tell from the survey or questionnaire what the people spon-soring the project were trying to establish?

4. Choose a local activity, behavior, or phenomenon to observe closely enough to record data and draw conclusions. Pick a relatively simple subject: How many stu-dents use a library database in a two-hour period? What techniques do students use to secure their bicycles near the university library? What types of vehicles do fac-ulty members tend to drive? Study the phenomenon or question for a very limited time, taking careful note of the questions or problems that arise as you do your sys-tematic observation. Then, in a report to classmates, explain the complications that you encountered in your study and what modifications you might have to make if you were to design a larger, more detailed, more systematic study.

MANAGING YOUR PROJECT

1. Decide how or whether your subject would benefit from interviews with experts or others involved in your topic. What might you learn from these interviews that you might not discover in printed or electronic sources?

2. Does your topic need information from a survey or questionnaire? Even if it seems that a formal survey is unnecessary, might your project benefit from the results of an informal survey of opinion that provides an opening for your work? For exam-ple, a survey might reveal apprehension or general ignorance about your subject, and you could introduce your subject by reporting the results of that survey.

3. Does your subject require systematic observation of any kind? If so, sketch out your methodology for the observation and share the report with your instructor or colleagues. Get feedback on the techniques you will use to be sure they are valid and reliable.

CHAPTER

8

Keeping Track of Information

Organizing your research materials may be as important as collecting them. Not only might you quickly acquire stacks of photocopies and printouts of Web sites, but you may also amass notes from interviews, data from surveys or experiments, lists of electronic addresses, disks of images in various formats, MOO transcripts, audio and video files, and software copies of your own work, perhaps in several versions. Somehow you'll have to bring all this information together and make sense of it.

Even before you begin your research, you need a strategy to record, classify, and protect information as you gather it. The basic principle is simple: Keep track of everything. With printed sources, be especially careful to record page numbers and dates of publication accurately. For electronic sources, be sure to record both electronic addresses and dates of access for online materials. Remember, the purpose of this information is twofold: to help you compile your list of Works Cited and to allow you to reaccess the sources if need be.

8a Classify the materials you will gather

By classifying your research resources, you can decide how and where to record them. If you'll be relying chiefly on print items, you can use a system of note cards, photocopies, and bibliography cards to manage much of the project. However, you are more likely to use a word processor or database to keep track of your list of sources. You may want to include charts, graphs, and illustrations in the paper, some of them created on software, some downloaded from electronic sources, and you will want to save them to disks. Or you may choose to use an electronic software package such as *EndNote* or *ProCite* to keep track of your research and help format your bibliography. Regardless, make sure you back up your work—it can be frustrating to save all your hard work to a disk and then leave it behind in a public lab! Invest in two diskettes and make a back-up copy of your work to keep in a safe place. And invest in a hard case for your working disk to protect it from dust and dirt that can damage it and cause you to lose data.

Information you gather is only useful if you can locate it when you are ready to use it. Make sure you organize the material you collect: photocopy print sources, bookmark or save electronic ones, or take careful notes, either by hand or by using one of the many software packages that help you keep track of information.

If you're working with large files, as when you are using multiple images in a project, you may need a Zip disk or CD-R (Compact Disc-Recordable) to store your files. Other types of work may require other resources and strategies. If your project involves interviews, you'll need notebooks for recording the responses of your subjects. If you tape-record these conversations, you may need to prepare transcripts to share the conversations with your readers. For projects that generate factual information, you may have to learn how to construct a database to study your findings, using existing database software such as Microsoft *Access* (see Figure 8.1) or Symantec's *Q&A*. Such software will help you see your results from many angles and then present it efficiently in charts and graphs.

Consider, too, where to keep all the stuff you accumulate while working on a project. A rugged, closable folder with ample pockets and safe storage for papers and disks is a good investment. Be sure it bears your name and a local phone number in case you

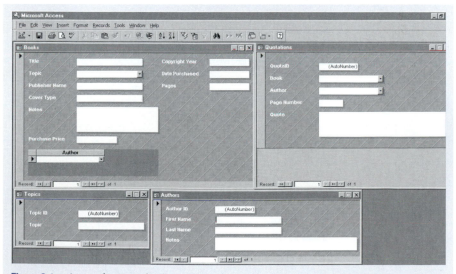

Figure 8.1   A sample *Access* database to keep track of sources, topics, and quotations. *(Source: Microsoft Access 2000, © 1992–1999, all rights reserved.)*

lose it. Also put your name, email address, and phone number on all computer disks before you use them; sooner or later, you'll leave an important disk in a machine at a computer facility.

It also helps to organize your computer information intelligently: keep your data in
one location on your hard disk, name your files in a logical way (such as "Testing Proj-
ect-Kohn Article Notes.doc"), and update files consistently so that you are always working with the latest version of a document. That's especially important if several people
will be involved in revising and editing the final product. (One way to do this is to keep
a "version number" at the top of the document [ver. 1.1] that you modify every time
you make even a minor change. Another approach would be to include a revision date
at the top [rev. 11/15/01] that you change in the same way.) You can also create directories (or folders) on your hard drive and disks to help you organize information (and
locate it again quickly!), and you can use your *Netscape* "Bookmarks" or Microsoft
Internet Explorer "Favorites" file to help you keep track of Web sites. *Netscape's* "Bookmarks" file even allows you to create folders to organize your bookmarks (see Figure
8.2), and you can save the file to a disk and carry it with you.

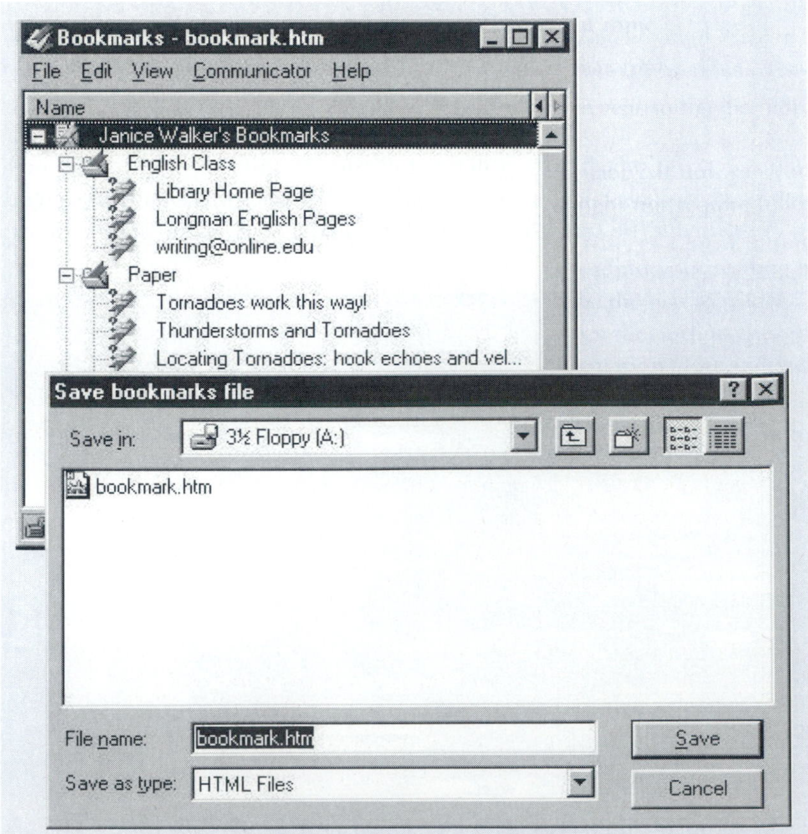

Figure 8.2   "Bookmarks" files help you to keep track of Web sites.

8b Prepare a working bibliography

It doesn't matter whether you are using print or electronic sources or whether your project will culminate in a paper, a Web site, or a brochure. You need to know where your information came from, and the best way to keep track is to record bibliographical data as you move through your sources, developing a working bibliography.

Regardless of what format you need to follow (MLA, APA, Chicago, etc.), you will have to record the same information about each source you use.

CHECKLIST

Bibliography Checklist

○ Name(s) of author(s), editor(s), translator(s), Webmaster(s), or others responsible for the publication, along with a notation of their contribution (e.g., "ed.")

○ Date of publication

○ Title information

○ City of publication and name of publisher (for books)

○ Journal, magazine, or newspaper title, along with volume and issue numbers (for journals) or section or edition name(s) for newspapers

○ URL (Uniform Resource Locator, or the Internet address) for World Wide Web sites

○ Database name and identifying file or accession numbers (for full-text or full-image articles accessed through an online database)

○ Date of access for electronic materials

○ Call number(s) for books

○ Page number(s) for articles or book chapters

Recording this information will ensure that you can re-locate the source if need be and that you will have the information you need to compile your list of References or Works Cited. You may also want to record notes about the source: whether or not it contains a bibliography or illustrations, for instance, and a brief summary or description of the information it contains. If you are using a database or bibliography software, you might want to include keywords to help you search your entries quickly. And you might want to record particularly succinct or well-stated sentences or phrases if you think you will want to use a quotation from this source. Make certain that you copy direct quotations accurately and that you carefully denote them as quotations! Include page numbers for any information you quote or summarize as well.

There still may be no simpler way to create the bibliography and track your sources than to keep an accurate set of 3-by-5-inch bibliography cards, one source per card. Each bibliography card should contain all the information you need to find a source again or to record when you accessed an electronic source such as a newsgroup or Web site. For printed sources, be sure to include a library call number or a location (current periodicals, for example, may not have call numbers). Typical bibliography cards might look like this:

WWW

8.1

```
TL
410
V36
1999
PCL Stacks

van der Plas, Rob. The Mountain Bike Book: Choosing, Riding,
    and Maintaining the Off-Road Bicycle. 3rd ed. San
    Francisco: Bicycle, 1993.
```

```
CNN Interactive. "Shuttle Atlantis makes repair call to Mir."
    17 May 1997. http://www.cnn.com/TECH/9705/16/shuttle/
    index.html (19 May 1997).
```

Nowadays most writers skip bibliography cards and instead print out a list of potential sources from online library catalogs, electronic databases, and Web search engines such as *AltaVista* or *Excite* (see Chapter 5). But this strategy can be risky because the information on a Web search page printout is usually insufficient for preparing a Works Cited page or References list. Printouts can also be misplaced among the many

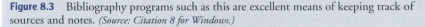

Figure 8.3   Bibliography programs such as this are excellent means of keeping track of sources and notes. *(Source: Citation 8 for Windows.)*

papers a research project typically generates. So if you rely on printouts for bibliographical information, keep the lists in one place and know what's on them. Use a highlighter to indicate important sources and annotate them when possible. If you download or print out Web pages, make sure you record carefully the URL information you need and the date of access in a separate file or handwrite the information on your printed copies (see Section 8d).

An even better alternative to note cards might be an electronic program that keeps track of your notes and sources. Database software of this kind is often easy to use and quite powerful, though you may need a laptop computer to take it into the library. If you access the library online from your own personal computer, however, such software can help simplify your note taking. Figure 8.3, for example, shows screens in *Citation 8 for Windows* that can automatically generate bibliographical lists or format in-text entries following whatever style you use. Built-in templates for various types of sources help you list the necessary information. Some software packages can be configured to work from inside your word processor to help you ensure that your citations are accurate.

8c Prepare an annotated bibliography

Your instructor may require you to prepare and submit an annotated bibliography of sources, that is, a listing of sources that includes a summary or description of each source. Even if your instructor doesn't require it, you may want to compile one. An annotated bibliography can be useful for keeping track of the information contained in the many sources you review. Of course, not all the sources you review will find their way into your completed project, but if at a later stage you realize that you need information

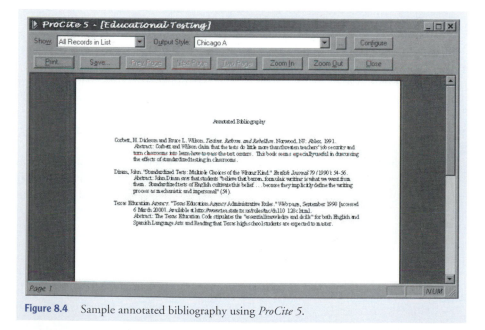

Figure 8.4 Sample annotated bibliography using *ProCite 5*.

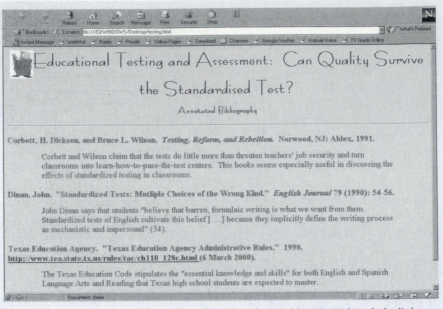

Figure 8.5   An annotated bibliography published on the World Wide Web includes links to online sources.

from a source you reviewed early on and discarded, you can scan the annotated bibliography to help you recognize the source and retrieve it. The nutshells, or summaries, of each source that you compile can also be useful when you need to include a summary of ideas from these sources in your paper or project. An example of an annotated bibliography appears on page 111.

Commercial software packages such as *EndNote* and *ProCite* (see Figure 8.4) have been designed to help you compile an annotated bibliography quickly, but you don't have to invest in this kind of specialized software if you don't want to. Your word processor or Web page editor has all the tools you need to create an annotated bibliography for your project (see Figure 8.5).

8.2

The primary advantages of commercial bibliography software lie in their features and flexibility—automatically inserting references into your document, automatically creating a bibliography page in any format you desire, etc.—but the truly important part of annotated bibliographies, recording the publication data and summarizing what you find there, can be accomplished with a pen and a sheet of paper.

8d Make copies of important sources

Photocopy or print out passages from sources you know you will quote from directly and extensively. While a case can be made for taking all notes on cards, the fact is that most researchers—faculty and students—now routinely either photocopy or download their major sources when they can. In such cases, see that your copies are complete and legible and make sure you can read the page numbers; write in any information that didn't photocopy well. When you are copying from a book or a magazine, record the title page and publication/editorial staff material. You'll be glad you did later.

In all cases, attach basic bibliographical information directly to photocopies and printouts so you know their source, making sure each document is keyed to a full bibliographic record. You can create subdirectories on your hard drive or disk to file information, or you can staple or paper clip printed information together (be careful, though; paper clips have a way of disappearing). In this way, you'll later be able to connect information to its source. (If you are extraordinarily well organized, you might even color-code information from key sources by topic.) Use highlighter pens to mark those passages in photocopies and printouts you expect to refer to later, and keep all materials in a folder. Some word-processing programs allow you to highlight passages in different colors, or you may be able to insert comments that are keyed to specific words or passages. Never highlight original material or write in library books.

It is possible to copy many electronic sources directly to disk, and copyright regulations usually allow you to make copies for personal use. Do back up all such copies, keeping them, for example, on both a floppy disk and your hard drive. Be especially careful that you know where all downloaded images come from and who owns their copyrights. As with printed sources, you must document and credit all copyrighted pictures, photographs, and images borrowed from the Web, whether you use them in a paper or in an electronic project. In addition, if your project is to be published on the Web or distributed outside the classroom, you may need to acquire permission from the copyright owner to use the material (see Chapter 9).

A particularly efficient way to organize information gathered mainly from the Web is to use your browser's "Bookmarks" or "Favorites" feature. Bookmarking a site simply adds it to a menu list so that you can return to it again easily. Web browsers also enable you to organize such bookmarked items and even (in some cases) to annotate them. When you begin a project, you may want to create a folder for it on the bookmark menu and move all Web sites relevant to your search into the designated slot, annotating each entry to remind you of its relevance to your research. Note, too, that you can save your list of bookmarks to a disk and thus transport them from machine to machine.

8e Take careful notes

To avoid unintentional plagiarism, make sure you carefully designate the sources of all ideas, statistics, and other information in your notes. At a minimum, you'll want to record the author's name and the page number or Web site address in your notes, and make sure you put quotation marks around all words, phrases, or passages which you copy word for word.

When your project will be completely electronic—a Web site, for example—you'll be working with some sources differently. Rather than recording information from

FOCUS ON . . . Note Taking

While it may seem like the easiest thing in the world to cite the URL of a Web site—copying and pasting it from the address bar of your Web browser—you have to be careful about just what sort of URL you're citing, especially when the information comes from an online database or newsbank. The primary reason for citing a source, remember, is to allow someone else to find it easily; unfortunately, the information that appears in the address bar after an online database search will not always permit others to locate that material. Sometimes this is because the database you used is *password-protected* or *site-limited*. You have access because your school has subscribed to the database; off-campus users will not be allowed to link to it. At other times the URL information may be created "on the fly" and will change depending on the particular user and date of access.

A search through the State of Georgia's GALILEO portal (a site that provides access to online databases) for full-text articles on "standardized testing," for instance, turns up the article "Guiding Your Child Through Testing Mania," by Sally Squires and Kathleen Jacobs. The URL for this article, **http://ehostvgw18.epnet.com/fulltext.asp ?resultSetId=R00000000&hitNum=3&booleanTerm=%22standardized%20testing %22&fuzzyTerm=** shows that it comes from a licensed database, *EBSCO Host*, and includes details on all the Boolean and other search terms used to find it. If nonregistered users try to find the same article with this URL, they will get only an error message. In such cases it is important to cite the article using all the information from the original publication (in this case, the November 2001 issue of *Family Life*) and indicate that it was located via the *EBSCO Host* database.

other Web sites, you'll likely link directly to them or make electronic copies of images you intend to use in your project. But remember that when you borrow information or images from other sources that can't be reached online via a link, you must provide traditional documentation.

8f **Back up your work frequently**

It's happened to all of us: a notebook or disk left behind in the library or a public lab. And if there's one thing that computers can always be relied on to do, it's to crash at inopportune times. Sometimes you're lucky and you can recover the lost notebook, disk, or file intact. But better than relying on luck is taking the time to back up your work frequently. If you've made substantial changes to a paper, click "save." When you finish a work session, copy all your files—word-processed documents, bibliographic files, bookmarks files, graphics files, etc.—to another disk or to your hard drive. Make two sets of photocopies and keep one in your desk drawer. And remember to update your backup files and copies regularly; otherwise, while you might save some duplication of effort, you may have to retrace all the work you did for however long it has been since your last backup.

An old adage summarizes much of what we've covered in this chapter: An ounce of prevention is worth a pound of cure. Paying attention to detail at the beginning can save you a lot of frustration at the end. If you are a thorough researcher and organize your information carefully, you'll find yourself well prepared to *use* that information in your own research project. As you think about ways to do so, you will have to be certain you incorporate outside sources fairly and ethically.

8.3

 Web Sites Worth Knowing

8.4

- How to Write Annotated Bibliographies,
  http://www.mun.ca/library/research_help/qeii/annotated_bibl.html

- ASU-WAC-Writing Annotated Bibliographies (Power Point presentation),
  http://www.asu.edu/duas/wac/annbib.html

- Note Taking,
  http://student.bvsd.k12.co.us/~blackl/school/nvhsresearch/notetaking/notetaking.html

- Bibliographical Management and Note Taking,
  http://www.kcl.ac.uk/humanities/cch/pg/course/bib_management/bib_management.html

- Introduction to Communicator: Organizing Your Bookmarks,
  http://help.netscape.com/products/client/communicator/IntroComm/chap02.html#1008140

GETTING INVOLVED

1. Do a campus survey of electronic and computer resources. Find out these basic facts:
   - From where, when, and how can you gain access to your college library catalog? Can you search the catalog via the Web?
   - Does your library allow access to online databases through the World Wide Web or from other on-campus labs? Find out how to access the databases and whether or not you need a password.
   - Does the library catalog indicate whether books or other materials are checked out? What is your library's policy on recalling books?
   - What hours are campus computer facilities open? Will these facilities be readily available at crunch times—for example, when papers and projects are due at midterm or near the end of the term?
   - What access do you have to printers and copiers? Will these facilities be available during crunch periods?
   - What restrictions might you face in using lab facilities or software? For example, before committing yourself to a complex multimedia project, be sure you will have access to equipment you need.

2. Investigate your library's interlibrary loan policies. Find out how you can acquire materials your own library might not have, how long it might take to acquire materials, and what costs you might have to pay.

MANAGING YOUR PROJECT

1. Plan your research strategy. Begin by considering how you will keep track of your bibliography information (the data you will list for each source on a Works Cited or References page). Typically this information will include author, title, publication information, volume numbers, dates, page numbers, and date of access (for electronic items). Set up a routine for listing all sources you examine, even those you might not use at all. As a project grows, you'll appreciate having a record of all sources you've looked at so you don't waste time inspecting some materials twice.

2. Set up a procedure for taking notes from your sources. If you are using handwritten or word-processed notes, make sure the link between your notes or photocopies and your bibliography is always clear. If you are keeping track of information via a computer program such as *TakeNote*, the software will make the linkage between notes and bibliographic information for you.

3. Always consider the possibility that some part of your project might be lost or erased. Would you be able to recover the information? Plan a strategy to avoid such problems (such as a regular schedule of backups).

4. Compile an annotated bibliography of potential sources. If you have access to database or bibliographic software, you may be able to use the software to facilitate the process. Or you may want to use a word processor or Web page editor to compile your annotated bibliography. If you are working on a group project, share your resources with other members of the group. You will want to photocopy important sources, especially any material you anticipate quoting. You can also take notes directly on the photocopied text. Be sure to photocopy the title page of a source because it will have bibliographic information you'll need later.

Annotated Bibliography

Kohn, Alfie. "Standardized Testing and Its Victims." *Education Week* 20.4, 60, 46–47.

> A very strong anti-testing tract by someone who is often cited in other such articles. Kohn begins by listing eight "facts" that condemn the practice of standardized testing, including "Standardized-test scores often measure superficial thinking" and "Virtually all specialists condemn the practice of giving standardized tests to children younger than 8 or 9 years old." He goes on to attack the tests for their inherent bias and consequences such as, "Those allegedly being helped will be driven out."

Patten, Peggy. "Standardized Testing in Schools." *NPIN Parent News* for January-February 2000. National Parent Information Network. 21 Dec. 2001. **<http://npin.org/pnews/2000/pnew100/feat100.html>.**

> In this article the author lists four reasons for the popularity of standardized tests, but then she offers three more detailed explanations for the ways in which standardized testing falls short and/or leads to unwanted results. She maintains a balanced treatment of the issue but seems to come down firmly on the side of testing critics.

National Association for the Education of Young Children (NAEYC). "Standardized Testing of Young Children 3 Through 8 Years of Age." 16 Mar. 1998. 21 Dec. 2001. **<http://www.naeyc.org/resources/position_statements/ pstestin.htm>.**

> This position statement argues for valuing standardized testing according to what they call the utility criterion: "The purpose of testing must be to improve services for children and ensure that children benefit from their educational experiences." They provide a list of seven bulleted guidelines for using tests effectively in collaboration with other measures of student performance.

III

Working with Sources

Don't miss . . .

- **The discussion of copyright and intellectual property in Chapter 9.** When documents and pictures are put on the Web, that doesn't necessarily mean they're free for the taking. Learn why you must cite borrowings from all your sources.
- **The exploration of biases in sources raised in Section 10e.** As a researcher, you must weigh the special interests served by even the most "objective" sources.
- **The advice about positioning sources in Section 12b.** Recognize which sides of an issue your sources support, and work toward a fair, balanced presentation of your topic.
- **The guidelines for paraphrasing in Section 13c.** When you paraphrase information from your sources, be certain you do so accurately.

Technology Spotlight

WORLD WIDE WEB

How old is the World Wide Web? It depends on whether you define the Web as a concept or a technology, and even then there is room for debate. Some scholars trace the Web's origins to a 1945 article by Vannevar Bush in *Atlantic Monthly* that described an imaginary device called a Memex that could follow hyperlinks. Others point to Tim Berners-Lee's development of a simple hypertext program, "ENQUIRE," in 1980 or his later work designing the first browser (named, prophetically, *World Wide Web*) in 1990. For many of us, however, the World Wide Web as we know it today began with the release of *Mosaic*, a Web browser written by University of Illinois graduate student Marc Andreessen in 1993.

Since that time the popularity of the Web has expanded tremendously, and so have its capabilities. New protocols and new plug-ins allow Web sites to include animation, sound, video, and other special effects. Sophisticated browsers such as *Netscape* and *Internet Explorer* are distributed freely, opening the door to the Web for nearly everyone, and commercial portal sites like *America Online* and *CompuServe* have made Web navigation simple even for novice users.

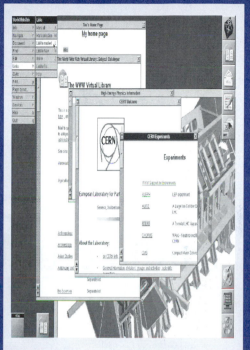

The development of the World Wide Web, from a text-only to the now-ubiquitous graphical and interactive interface most users are familiar with, may only be a harbinger of things to come.

Researchers, too, have begun to see the Web as an indispensable tool—not just for finding the information they need but also for publishing the results of their investigations. Where once it took months, sometimes years, for scientific work to be published in obscure journals, today experimental results and compilations of data can be made available to millions almost as soon as they can be produced. The World Wide Web has, quite literally, become the marketplace of ideas, and with tens of millions of Web pages currently accessible around the globe, the number of ideas we have to sift through has become staggering! As a researcher, you'll have to make careful judgments about the value of Web resources to your project.

CHAPTER

9

Understanding Academic Responsibility and Intellectual Property

College writers often bridle when they hear terms like *plagiarism* (stealing another writer's words) and *collusion* (conspiring with another to cheat or defraud), knowing that being accused of either offense can undermine one's integrity and ruin a career. Worse, many students worry so much about inadvertently violating the seemingly arcane rules that surround academic sources that they avoid research entirely when they can. Research ought to be regarded as an exciting journey, not as an obstacle course full of traps. You'll enjoy research a lot more if you can learn to regard the principle of academic responsibility as an ally, protecting your work and that of others.

9.1

Simply crediting the sources you use in a research project is often not enough, especially if you borrow materials from electronic environments such as the World Wide Web. You can be meticulous and thorough in your citations and still be in violation of copyright law. Legislators and other interested parties are now debating how copyright legislation should change to reflect the changing nature of the publication and communication of ideas, but some proposals threaten our ability to use sources at all. It is therefore important that we follow guidelines for the use of electronic sources based on common sense, ethics, and the unique nature of electronic publications.

9a Understand the ethics of research

You should summarize, paraphrase, quote, and document research materials carefully, not to avoid charges of plagiarism but because you have an ethical responsibility to rep-

Just as hearsay evidence is not allowed in a courtroom, academic researchers need to reference original work whenever possible. Remember that you have an ethical responsibility to your readers as well as to the authors of the sources you use, to present your results both honestly and thoroughly.

resent the ideas of other writers accurately, to back up your own claims, and to assist readers in verifying your research or gathering additional information.

Readers and writers alike depend on the integrity of their sources. The elaborate networks of information we have built can be trusted only if researchers themselves are trustworthy. Thus you need to ensure not only that you are using sources ethically, but that the sources on which you rely are honest as well (see Chapter 10). As collaborative and electronic projects make authorship more complex, we need to depend more than ever on the good faith of researchers and writers. Most students do understand that it is wrong to buy a paper, to let someone heavily edit a paper, or to submit someone else's work as their own, but many students do not realize that taking notes carelessly or documenting sources inadequately may also raise doubts about the integrity of a paper. The example below shows how easily you can be guilty of unintentional plagiarism when you are not careful in copying and pasting information from an online source into your notes.

ORIGINAL SOURCE

Quality of sleep habits was found to be a factor in self-perceived academic competence. If college students experience REM sleep deprivation more than the average population, then the findings of this study need to be passed on to college students. The findings in this study suggest that college students with poor sleep habits may perceive themselves as having lower academic competency. The study also showed that self-perceived academic competency was positively correlated to academic performance. Thus, according to Hobson (1989), Webb & Bonnet (1979), and this study, those college students who do have poor sleep habits will negatively affect their academic performance.

It was also found that test anxiety and grade point average are negatively correlated, and that quality of sleep and grade point average are positively correlated. This, and the fact that quality of sleep and test anxiety are negatively related, suggest interrelationships among the variables test anxiety, sleep habits, self-perceived academic competency and academic performance. This highlights the fact that professors need to instruct their students on how to manage test anxiety. Students also need to be aware of the effects that poor sleep and low self-perceived academic competency have on academic performance. Thus, the phrase, "I think I can, I think I can . . ." may be beneficial only if students reduce their test anxiety and develop better sleep habits. More research needs to be done to find other variables that affect self-perceived academic competence.

The following are two paragraphs based much too closely on material from the original essay, now archived on the Web. This reformulation of the material amounts to plagiarism, even though the author of the plagiarized paragraphs credits the source. The bold-faced material looks like it was copied and pasted directly from the online original.

PLAGIARIZED PARAGRAPHS

Getting a good night's sleep before an examination makes sense psychologically. According to Briggs (1999), **quality of sleep habits was found to be a factor in self-perceived academic competence.** That is to say that college students with poor sleep habits may perceive themselves as having lower academic competency. **Those college students who do have poor sleep habits will negatively affect their academic performance.**

There also seems to be a connection between self-perceived academic competency and academic performance. **This highlights the fact that professors need to instruct their students on how to manage test anxiety. Students also need to be aware of the effects that poor sleep and low self-perceived academic competency have on academic performance. Thus, the phrase, "I think I can, I think I can . . ." may be beneficial only if students reduce their test anxiety and develop better sleep habits.** So a student really can improve performance in college courses by making more time for sleep.

Representing as your own, intentionally or not, the words, ideas, or creations you found in a source constitutes plagiarism, and instructors take this seriously. Luckily, plagiarism is easily avoided when you take good notes and follow the guidelines discussed in the following section.

9b Avoid plagiarism

Sometimes when people have trouble with a writing assignment, not knowing how to begin or feeling overwhelmed with other schoolwork, they think about taking short-cuts—some of them unethical. The ease with which entire papers can be found on Web sites or in databases can be a powerful temptation to cheat: a quick search, a quick cut, a quick paste, a quick printout, and *presto*, the paper is done! Who's to know, right?

Wrong. The Web has also made it much easier for instructors to catch plagiarism. Often all they have to do is take a short phrase from a paper, type it into a search engine, and every Web document that includes that phrase appears in the results page. The process can take less than a minute. Some companies, such as Turnitin.com (**http://www.turnitin.com**) and Glatt Plagiarism Services (**http://www.plagiarism.com**) specialize in plagiarism checking, comparing student papers to the thousands upon thousands they have in their databases; other companies, like Canexus (**http://www.canexus.com**), perform detailed Web searches for instructors on request.

More than a few students have discovered to their surprise that the time they "saved" on research and writing resulted in an F on their transcripts and, in some cases, expulsion from school. Students who plagiarize ultimately cheat only themselves. College writing courses offer the opportunity to learn how to communicate your own ideas in writing, a skill that you will need throughout your life. You may get through your first year composition courses by turning in someone else's work, but getting through the rest of your life that way will be much more difficult!

Most students recognize that intentional plagiarism is cheating, whether one buys a paper from a term paper mill or copies it from a friend or a fraternity cache. However, you need to understand that copying *any* portion of a source word for word or presenting ideas, facts, and figures from other sources—even in your own words—constitutes plagiarism. Luckily, it's simple to avoid this kind of plagiarism: you make sure to take careful notes and scrupulously cite your sources. In Chapter 13 you will learn how to summarize and paraphrase sources and how to correctly acknowledge your borrowings. Chapter 14 explains how to handle quotations in your paper accurately and honestly. For more help, try the tutorial on recognizing and avoiding plagiarism at **http://www.indiana.edu/~wts/wts/plagiarism.html.**

9.2

9c Understand the special nature of collaborative projects

Whether working with writers in your classroom or with students in other locations across a network, you'll find that in truly collaborative projects it can be tough to remember who wrote what. As long as everyone understands the ground rules, joint authorship is not a problem, but legitimate questions do arise.

- Must we write the whole project together?
- Can we break the project into separately authored sections?
- Can one person research a section, another write it, and a third edit and proofread it?
- What do we do when someone is not pulling his or her weight?
- Do we all get the same grade?

The time to ask these questions is at the beginning of a collaborative project. First, determine what your instructor's guidelines are. Then sit down with the members of your group and hammer out the rules.

Collaborative work is an important part of many writing projects in the classroom as well as in the workplace. Sometimes the group takes credit for the entire project; at other times, individual authors are credited for discrete sections or components of a project. Collaboration is not the same thing as collusion, however. Check with your instructor before you decide to work with someone else on a project.

Be careful, too, when consulting with others on a project. Many colleges and universities offer professional consultations for students free of charge in Writing Centers or Academic Tutoring Centers (see Chapter 18). These consultants are trained to offer guidance and feedback to students without taking over a project. Sometimes, however, a well-intentioned friend or family member (or even an over-zealous tutor) will offer too much "help," essentially writing the paper for you. Remember, *you* are the author; while you do want to take advantage of proffered feedback and assistance, you want to ensure that your project reflects your own voice and ideas, not those of someone else.

The authorship and source problems of collaborative projects done on paper pale when compared with the intellectual property issues raised by electronic projects. Hypertext authors may link words and images from dozens of authors and artists and various sources and media. Every part of the resulting collage might be borrowed, but the arrangement of the parts will be unique. Who then should be credited as *author* of the hypertext? Conventional documentation formats may not be adequate to handle the unique problems of electronic environments.

9d Understand intellectual property rights

Patents, trademarks, and copyrights are all ways of protecting original creations and ideas. When we create an original machine or process, we patent it, which means we own the rights to produce the invention: we can sell (or rent) those rights to others, and we can receive compensation for such use. When we create an original work of words or art, online or in print, the same premises apply, only the concept is called *copyright* instead of patent. We still own the rights to reproduce our work; we can sell (or rent) those rights to others, and we have the right to receive compensation or recognition for such use.

Copyrighted material may be included in other works, such as research projects, without prior permission or payment of royalties, under the doctrine known as *fair use.*

> The fair use of a copyrighted work, including such use by reproduction in copies or phonorecords or by any other means specified [. . .], for purposes such as criticism, comment, news reporting, teaching (including multiple copies for classroom use), scholarship, or research, is not an infringement of copyright. (17 U.S.C. Sec. 107)

Whether or not a given use is protected by this definition is based on four considerations:

1. The purpose and character of the use, including whether such use is of a commercial nature or is for nonprofit educational purposes;

2. The nature of the copyrighted work;

3. The amount and substantiality of the portion used in relation to the copyrighted work as a whole; and

4. The effect of the use upon the potential market for or value of the copyrighted work. (17 U.S.C. Sec. 107)

Usually, fair use involves taking no more than ten percent of a work (a poem, paper, or other document) and giving proper credit to the author or creator (see Chapter 19). Violations of fair use can bring legal penalties and charges of plagiarism.

9e Understand the special nature of online resources

Even though governments around the world (including our own) have yet to decide what the laws will be regarding copyrights, fair use, and electronic sources, some guidelines for handling electronic materials have been developed, based on current laws. For example, the recent controversy surrounding the Napster Web site (which allowed users to share copyrighted music files without paying royalties) hinges on legal definitions of "fair use." Even so, what is legal is not always ethical. You will need to understand the guidelines and principles of fair use and consider carefully how you use information, ideas, graphics, and other elements created by others in your own projects. Use the checklist below as a guide.

The World Wide Web is an international publishing space. As such, many images, texts, and other files may fall under the copyright laws of other nations, whose attitude toward ownership of intellectual property may be different from our own. Thus a key word in our consideration of intellectual property should be *respect*—respect for the moral and ethical as well as the economic and legal rights of authors, creators, and publishers.

CHECKLIST
Guidelines for Fair Use

○ **Follow guidelines already established for published (that is, print) sources where possible.** For print, the rule of thumb has been that quoting ten percent or less of a work constitutes fair use. For online sources, you should abide by this same guideline. For print papers that will be used only in the classroom, you may not actually need to obtain permission; however, you should be aware of the steps necessary to do so. For work to be distributed outside the classroom (for instance, to be published on the World Wide Web), it is imperative that you at least make an attempt to acquire permission. The Academic Computer Center at Dartmouth University offers a Web site at **http://www.dartmouth.edu/~webteach/articles/legal.html** with a good explanation of how to stay legal that includes links to downloadable samples of request-for-permission letters that you can modify to suit your own needs.

○ **Point to (or link to) text files, images, audio, and video files in online projects rather than downloading them where possible.** Some sites offer graphic images to users at no charge and may specifically request that users download them. Requests such as these should be honored. However, graphics and other files should not be downloaded without permission. Users may instead point to images and other types of files rather than downloading them. Yet courtesy suggests that users request permission even to link to an image or file, since this link may add to traffic on the file server where the image is stored. See Chapter 20 for more on including graphics or other images in your project.

(Continued)

Guidelines for Fair Use *(Continued)*

○ **Always cite sources carefully, giving as much information as possible to allow the reader to locate the source.** In addition to citing the source of any text you use in your project, you should properly cite all graphics, audio, and video files included in your work (see Chapter 19). The citations for electronic sources should include the name of the person responsible (the author, creator, or maintainer of the site); the title of the work and/or the title of the Web site, as applicable; the date of publication or creation (if known); the protocol and address along with any directions or commands necesssary to access the work; and the date on which you accessed it. Most of the major documentation styles have attempted to present guidelines for the citation of electronic sources. A particularly clear and effective style is the Columbia Online Style, which can be used along with all the major styles developed for print citation (see Chapter 23).

○ **When in doubt, ask.** If it is unclear whether or not a given use of electronic material is permitted, ask the owner or author of the site, if possible, explaining the nature of the intended use and noting the portion or portions of the work to be included in your work. If asked by a copyright owner to remove material or links from your project, do so promptly.

9f Follow guidelines for the classroom

With more and more student research projects being published on the World Wide Web or using sources from the Web, it is important that we develop guidelines for using sources. The following suggestions should help until authors, publishers, legislators, and international policy makers come up with more concrete regulations.

Always give credit where credit is due. We deserve credit for our ideas and inventions. Even without laws and teachers' red pens, it would not be ethical to take credit for someone else's ideas. Citing sources serves several purposes beyond avoiding academic penalties and/or lawsuits:

1. It gives credit to the originator of the idea.
2. It shows that you have done your research (you know what you're talking about).
3. It tells readers where to find your sources if they want further information.

Whenever possible, use primary sources. *Primary sources* are those sources where the idea or text you are citing (or quoting) originated. *Secondary sources* are those which use the words or ideas of others. For example, an eyewitness to an event testifying in a trial is a primary source. The newspaper account of what the eyewitness said is a secondary source. When you write about literature, the book or story you are writing about is your primary source (for example, Shirley Jackson's "The Lottery"); works *about* the story (Jonathan Burns's "The Hidden Truth: An Analysis of Shirley Jackson's 'The Lottery'") are secondary sources.

In a courtroom, eyewitness accounts are preferred to hearsay. The same should hold true when you are conducting research and compiling research projects. How can you be sure a secondary source has accurately quoted or interpreted the original? The answer is simple: check the original for yourself.

Of course, that is not always possible; an original source may not be available or may be too difficult or time-consuming to access. This is especially true with electronic sources; electronic discussion forums, forwarded files, and disappearing Web sites can make it necessary to reference secondary sources. Your citations should always make that clear. (For more on citing sources, see Chapter 19.)

If it's on the Web, it's published. When you make documents and graphics available on the World Wide Web, you are publishing them. In the traditional classroom, students produce papers for an audience of one: the teacher. They are usually free to include graphics, pictures, quotations, and paraphrases from other sources without permission or payment of royalties, provided the sources are properly cited.

When you publish your work on the Web, however, it is immediately available to anyone in the world who has access. Because intellectual property is considered to have economic value, the publication of someone else's work, even with proper credit, can affect the economic value of that work. Why would people buy a book if they can read it online for free?

Copyrights don't last forever; when they expire, works go into the *public domain*. Many works of literature are now freely available on the World Wide Web, and some newspapers and journals have chosen to make online versions of their publications available for free. Others require a subscription or payment for access. It is important that you know the difference. Works in the public domain may be used without permission or payment of royalties (although it is still necessary—and ethical—to accurately cite the source); copyrighted materials, on the other hand, may not be republished without permission even if they are freely available. For instance, forwarding a copyrighted news article to an email discussion list or newsgroup may constitute violation of intellectual property laws and could carry legal ramifications, even when the article may be read for free on the news source's Web site.

If you are feeling intimidated at this point, don't worry. Most instructors know that learning how to use and cite sources correctly takes time, and no one's going to throw you out of school if you inadvertently forget a quotation mark or two as you work on your research project. In the next few chapters we'll show you how writers commonly bring research material into their texts and how you can do so without falling into "the plagiarism trap."

WWW Web Sites Worth Knowing

WWW
9.3

- "10 Big Myths About Copyright Explained,"
  http://www.templetons.com/brad/copymyths.html
- University of Texas at Austin, "Academic Integrity,"
  http://www.utexas.edu/depts/dos/sjs/academicintegrity.html
- KU Writing Guide, "Academic Integrity,"
  http://www.writing.ku.edu/students/docs/integrity.html
- Center for Academic Integrity, http://www.academicintegrity.org/

GETTING INVOLVED

1. Most schools have formal written policies on scholastic responsibility and plagiarism. Locate a copy of your institution's official documents or, perhaps, brochures on the subject published by a school office. Do the guidelines mention copyright law? If they do, in regard to what sorts of materials? Do the statements mention electronic texts and materials such as audio and video files?

2. How would you feel about students at other schools linking to a Web site you created—let's say a set of pages describing your hobby, your favorite sports team, or volunteer projects in the community? What reservations might you have about such links? Would you routinely grant permission for links to your site if you received such requests? What if someone asked to "mirror" your site (copy the entire contents to a different Web address)?

3. Imagine that you are running a site for a major political party or interest group. How much control would you want over outside groups linking to your site? What concerns might you have about outside groups tying themselves to your presence on the World Wide Web?

4. The overwhelming majority of newspaper and magazine pieces you read are not written using any of the formal academic systems of documentation described in this book (MLA, APA, CMS, CSE, COS). In fact, you'd probably be startled to see in-text notes in *Newsweek* or a Works Cited page on the sports page. But look carefully at a serious article in a major publication. How does the piece earn the right to be taken seriously? What signals within and around the article assure readers that it was properly researched and is based on credible materials? Examine several pieces from different kinds of periodicals: a feature from *The New York Times*, a story from *Popular Science*, a column from *National Review*, a road test from *Car and Driver*. Do you see differences in the way the periodicals treat information, talk about their sources, or give credit for borrowed information?

5. Newspapers and other news media often report information from sources described as "unnamed" or "reliable" or "inside"; the anonymity of such sources is thereby protected. How much faith are you, as a reader, willing to place in an

unidentified source? Why do you think news media routinely report off-the-record information? Discuss the use of unnamed sources with your colleagues. When—if ever—might such sources appear in a research paper or project?

6. Charges of plagiarism have been attached to the names of numerous public figures over the years, including writers and elected officials. Can you recall such accusations? Why do you think that these charges are reported even decades after the alleged act of dishonesty?

MANAGING YOUR PROJECT

1. If you expect to rely heavily on materials borrowed from online sources, be sure to acquire permission early in your project. If you wait until the last minute, you may be in trouble if you are denied permission to use material central to your thesis or project. In making such a request in a letter or, more likely, in email, be sure to mention

   - Who you are
   - Your academic institution
   - The character of your work
   - The nature and scope of the material you are borrowing
   - The context in which you intend to use the material

2. What fears and apprehensions about plagiarism and scholastic responsibility do you have when facing a research project or using outside sources in a paper? Discuss these feelings with your colleagues or instructor *before* you turn in a draft of your project. Clear up any doubts you have about how to use sources appropriately.

3. If you are involved in a collaborative project, sit down with your colleagues and discuss how the work will be distributed and then credited. Have this discussion before you get too deeply into the project. Decide not only who will do what but how performance within the group will be monitored during the project and then reported when the project is done.

CHAPTER

10

Evaluating Sources

Experience teaches us to trust some people more than we do others. The same is true for research resources. No matter what your project is, you want supporting materials that will seem authoritative to people reviewing your work.

For many subjects, traditional research resources—books, articles, and newspapers—now form just the tip of an iceberg. You may also have to consider pamphlets, microfilm, maps, field data, transcripts of interviews, CD-ROMs, databases, Web sites, videos, listservs, email, and more. Many judgments about the credibility of research materials that used to fall on publishers and librarians now fall squarely on your shoulders. That's because some electronic sources come to you almost directly from their authors, unreviewed and unrefereed. Yet the complications caused by online sources only highlight responsibilities that writers have always shouldered. Before you use any source, you have to determine its strengths, its limits, and its appropriateness.

Before you can expect your readers to rely on the information you give them, you must be certain that the sources from which you gathered your information are reliable and relevant. In this chapter we present information that will help you answer these questions and ensure that your use of information gleaned from outside sources is successful.

10a Consider the relevance of your sources

Search tools such as electronic catalogs and indexes may point you to thousands of potential resources. When you find yourself with an embarrassment of riches, first try narrowing the scope of your project even more than you did initially (see Chapter 4), or scan the titles in your working bibliography (see Section 8b); you'll usually be able to cut irrelevant items. For example, if you did a keyword search in your library catalog on "Washington" for a project on the first U.S. president, you'd immediately cut entries on George Washington University or Washington, D.C. Remember, too, that you can tell most search engines to exclude unwanted items with a NOT command: "NOT University NOT D.C." (See Chapter 6 on conducting electronic searches.)

Some library catalogs, indexes, and search engines provide summaries or abstracts of the works they contain. Such summaries may also suggest whether a full article or site

CHECKLIST

Evaluating Sources: Questions to Consider

Authority
- ○ Does the author have firsthand knowledge or experience?
- ○ Are arguments and supports presented logically and in an easy-to-follow format?
- ○ Are facts and figures from reliable sources used to support the author's position when necessary?

Timeliness
- ○ How current is the information?
- ○ Has more recent work substantiated claims or provided more information that is pertinent?
- ○ Are the statistics or other information still relevant?

Relevance
- ○ Does the information answer important questions that you have raised?
- ○ Does it support your propositions or present counterarguments that you need to address?
- ○ Does it present examples or illustrate important points in your project?

Author's Purpose and Audience
- ○ Is the author's purpose apparent or explicit?
- ○ Can you detect any biases that may affect the author's choice to present or omit facts or ideas?
- ○ Does the author's choice of audience affect the presentation?

deserves your attention. Recognize the limits of these brief descriptions—you may still have to examine the source itself to appreciate its value.

Many scholarly sources, especially in the social and natural sciences, routinely include abstracts of lengthier research studies. These abstracts usually convey a clearer sense of the content than the brief descriptions of a piece you might find in a database or a search index listing. Some instructors may even allow you to cite an abstract itself in your paper if you cannot locate the article summarized in it. In this way, abstracts can be valuable tools for narrowing a list of potential sources. However, most research projects will require that you carefully review the entire work because an abstract will not contain all the supporting information on which the claims it may make are based.

There is no magic formula for determining how relevant a source is to your topic—other than exercising critical judgment. You are conducting research to find answers to questions or to support your arguments. Each source you include should provide such answers or add something that will help you build your case. You must decide what the material in question adds to your project: crucial information? supportive

Early in a project, take some time to assess the variety of resources available to you. Establish their reliability, strengths, limitations, and appropriateness to your project. In some cases you may want to draw on a special library collection such as maps or government documents.

commentary? an alternative perspective? Indeed, if a source makes points you had not previously considered, or if it convincingly challenges your own views, ethics dictate that you acknowledge it in your work.

Never include sources in your project simply to pad your bibliography. Above all, do not let your sources or existing work dictate your research agenda. There is no point in assembling a project that merely summarizes the research others have done or that supports only one side of a proposition while ignoring the truth or merit on other sides. Choose sources carefully; push yourself to learn more and be prepared when necessary to reconsider your approach. Often you will need to reconsider your entire hypothesis.

After you've cut obviously irrelevant materials from your preliminary bibliography, you will have more important decisions to make. One of them is deciding what types of sources are most appropriate to your project.

10b Consider the purpose of a source

The value of a source will depend both on its trustworthiness and on the uses you intend to make of it. If you were writing a report on the official positions taken by the two major political parties in a distant presidential election, you'd probably depend on scholarly books and articles published by reputable writers and on newspaper accounts archived in the library. But if you were developing a project about a current political campaign, you might examine less scholarly materials and read the views expressed in current campaign literature, recent magazines, and even Web sites and Usenet groups. You could also conduct interviews or cite polls. These sources might lack the authority and perspective of scholarly books or even official party materials, but they could still provide an excellent survey of political attitudes.

Ultimately you have to decide what research materials suit your topic best and then be prepared to defend their relevance should readers resist them—as they might when you quote from personal home pages or Usenet discussions.

Even when sources can't be described simply as good or bad without considering their purposes, they will have characteristics you must weigh. We've summarized some of those features in the chart on pages 128–29, but our guidelines should be taken with the understanding that any single source can differ from our characterizations. One suggestion: in researching a subject, the best sources for you are likely to be those just a step or two above your current level of knowledge—you want to push yourself to learn more without exceeding your depth.

10c Consider the authority and reputation of a source

Reputable books and other reference tools will be cited in the literature you accumulate on a project; you'll soon recognize the names of important scholars and key works because you will find them cited repeatedly in other works. If you haven't included these sources in your own collection of data, go back to the library and pick them up. Do the same with electronic sources; Web sites on a topic usually provide links to other, similar materials. Inevitably the most useful sites will appear often. Don't rely only on someone else's summary of the ideas or arguments they contain—track them down and determine their usefulness for yourself.

There are also growing numbers of review tools for online materials. *The Argus Clearinghouse* at **http://www.clearinghouse.net/** offers a collection of guides to Web sites on a wide variety of topics, along with ratings of the information contained there. You can use similar criteria to evaluate sites you find on your own. The *Librarian's Index to the Internet* at **http://lii.org** and *ICYouSee* at **http://www.ithaca.edu/library/Training/hott.html** are additional sites that could be useful in locating and evaluating online sources. And, as you should realize by now, many of the same criteria should be considered when evaluating print sources.

10d Consider the credentials of experts, authors, and sponsoring agencies

As you read about any subject you'll pick up the names of people mentioned frequently as experts or authorities. You may even hear your instructors speak of writers who deal with your topic. When scanning a printout of potential sources, look for those familiar authors. But don't be drawn in by celebrity alone, particularly when the names of famous people are linked to subjects about which they may have no special expertise.

With Web sites, listservs, and other online materials, you may find yourself in a quandary about the credentials of your "authors." At times you may have no more to go on than the word and email addresses of people involved in Usenet group discussions. When you report factual information from such sources, you will usually want to confirm the information through second, more familiar sources. (Reporting opinion is a different matter.) On personal Web sites, check the credentials that writers claim for themselves, then try to verify them. When Web authors offer email addresses, you can follow up their claims with a one-on-one exchange, asking for the sources they used to support claims on their pages. Be open-minded but skeptical.

You can be more confident about electronic information when the sponsoring agency of the source is one you would trust in a printed environment. Acquiring information online from Reuters News Service or *USA Today* is almost equivalent to seeing the same information in print. That means you should remain sensitive to issues that apply to any source: questions of bias, timeliness, and completeness.

C H A R T

Assessing Sources

Source	Purpose	Authors	Audience/ Language
Scholarly books	Advance or report new knowledge	Experts	Academic/Technical
Scholarly articles	Advance or report new knowledge	Experts	Academic/Technical
Serious books and articles	Report or summarize information	Experts or professional writers	Educated public/ Formal
Popular magazines	Report or summarize information	Professional writers or journalists	General public/ Informal
Newspapers	Report current information	Journalists	Popular/Informal
Sponsored Web sites	Varies from report information to advertise	Varies	Varies/Usually informal
Individual Web sites	Varies	Anyone	Varies/Depends
Interviews	Consult with experts	Experts	Varies/Technical to colloquial
Listservs	Discuss specific subjects	Experts to interested amateurs	Varies/Technical to colloquial
Usenet newsgroups	Discuss specific subjects	Open to everyone	Varies/Technical to colloquial

10e Consider the biases of a source

You'll need to consider political, social, and religious leanings when you deal with controversial subjects. In deciding which items on a long list to read or what people to interview or survey, it may help to select opinions from across the spectrum. Otherwise you may write your entire paper unaware that important perspectives are being ignored.

It is important to understand that almost all sources have points of view that shape the information they contain (and determine what they exclude). Sometimes those biases are apparent. You do not have to read much to realize, for example, that the editorial page of *The New York Times* tends to be liberal in its politics and that of *The Wall Street Journal* conservative. It may be harder to detect similar biases in scholarly journals, popular magazines, and news services on the Web, but be assured that they are there. If you are in doubt about the broad-mindedness of the sources you have selected, consult with instructors or librarians—being aware that they, too, have points of view and may try to influence your selection.

Publisher or Medium	Reviewed/ Documented?	Current/ Stable?	Dialogic/ Interactive?
University or scholarly press	Yes/Yes	No/Yes	No/No
Scholarly or professional journal	Yes/Yes	Usually no/Yes	No/No (unless online)
Commercial publishers	Yes/Not usually	Depends on subject/ Yes	No/No (unless online)
Commercial publishers	Yes/No	Yes/Yes	No/No (unless online)
Commercial press or online	Yes/No	Yes/Yes	No/No (unless online)
Online WWW/ Commercial sponsor	Sometimes/ Links to other sites	Yes, if regularly updated/Sometimes	Sometimes/Often
Online WWW	Usually no/ Links to other sites	Varies/Varies	Sometimes/ Sometimes
Notes, recordings, email	No/No	Yes/No	Yes/Yes
Online email	Not usually/No	Yes/Sometimes	Yes/Yes
Online email	Not usually/No	Yes/Sometimes	Yes/Yes

During your research you will likely read many sources on your topic, some of which will arrive at distinctly different conclusions. You will discover that even cold facts and hard figures can be interpreted in various ways. That is because authors do not write in a vacuum; we all come to our work with biases, preconceptions, and agendas. Sometimes an author's bias or purpose is explicit: the thesis statement clearly defines what the author wants to prove and from what point of view. At other times, only careful reading will uncover the author's intentions.

Two opposing points on the political spectrum offer thought-provoking online assessments of media bias. See "FAIR: Fairness and Accuracy in Reporting" at **http://www.fair.org** for a left-wing take on issues of balance and fairness in the news. See Media Research Center at **http://www.mediaresearch.org** for a conservative right-wing perspective. You can easily see that not only do credible sources often reflect the bias of their authors, but that you will need to consider your own biases when you evaluate sources.

10f Consider the timeliness and stability of a source

Timeliness is relative. You will want your projects to be supported by the most current and reputable information in a field, but your instructors and librarians may point you to classic pieces, too, that have shaped thinking in your topic area. For many college papers you should have a mix of sources—some from the past, some quite recent. While specific books and articles may at times be difficult to acquire, a complex infrastructure of library collections and catalogs assures the relative stability of the material.

Timeliness is a different matter for electronic environments, complicated by the unstable nature of many online sources. No conventions currently govern the millions of Web pages, so not every site you visit will provide dates for the original posting or the most recent update. You'll want to check for both since the Web is full of outdated sites, posted and largely forgotten by their authors. Currency is less a factor in listservs, Usenet groups, and other email postings because the turnover of material is rapid, changing from day to day. That also means that something you read today may be gone tomorrow—or sooner. Obviously you need to print out or download relevant postings from such sources or check to see whether the source you are using archives its materials. Many researchers prefer to use material from sites that archive their postings, since that ensures that the information will continue to be available.

Web sites pose similar problems. Some sponsored sites enable you to search their archives for past stories or postings, but those archives may not be complete or may not go back many years. We are a long way from having electronic sources that are as stable, comprehensive, and dependable over the long run as printed books and articles. The stability of electronic sources is a matter to ponder deeply, especially when you are considering a long-term research project. At the same time, you cannot ignore important information online merely because it may not be permanently available.

One more note about timeliness: If you are researching a topic that is currently in the news or that has been the focus of a lot of attention over the past several years—genetic engineering, computer animation, or terrorism, for example—make certain that you draw as much of your information as possible from equally current and up-to-date sources. If you want to sound well-informed, you'll need to be aware of—and ready to discuss—the most recent developments and innovations in the field.

10g Consider how well a source presents key information

The design of a source is probably of greater concern with Web sites than with printed books and articles, for which the conventions were established years ago. Still evolving as an information tool, the Web brings together the complex resources of print, visual, and audio media, sometimes brilliantly, sometimes garishly. A well-designed Web site identifies its purpose clearly, arranges information logically, uses graphics to enhance its mission, gives access to its materials without exhausting the capacity of its users' technology, furnishes relevant and selective links to other responsible resources, and provides basic bibliographical information: the identity and email address of the author or sponsor, the date of the posting, the date of the most recent update, and so on. Yet standards for Web documentation are still developing. You cannot automatically discount a site that does not include this information, for an author's authority is not dependent on his or her knowledge of technology and the constraints of electronic publishing, but you will need to consider what a lack of documentation may mean to your research.

10h Consider commercial intrusions into a source

Books today rarely contain advertising, and we are accustomed to dealing with ads in print magazines. But commercial intrusion into Web sites is growing enough to warrant our concern when assessing resources. Sponsored Web sites—especially search engines—are often so thick with commercial appeals that they can be difficult to use. Moreover, your search itself may bring up specific advertising messages in an effort to direct you to a sponsor's material. No library catalog ever exerted this kind of pressure.

Sponsored sites may also reflect the commercial connections of their owners, especially when news organizations are owned by larger companies with commercial interests. What appears—or doesn't appear—on a site may be determined by who is paying for the message. You shouldn't automatically discount commercially sponsored sites, but you should consider how advertising may affect the information you find and what effect using information from these sources will have on your reader's evaluation of your own credibility.

10i Consult librarians and instructors

Librarians and instructors can help you assess the quality or appropriateness of a source. They have the expertise to cut right through a long list of references to suggest the three or four you should not miss. Those leads will often enable you to make subsequent judgments on your own.

Librarians and instructors may even correct biases in your own research strategies, directing you to sources you might have avoided or considered suspect. And they may suggest solutions to problems you are having with experiments, interviews, or statistical sampling.

10j Consider interviews and email

Interviews with authorities are important sources of information, but the information created in these circumstances, both the answers you received and the questions you asked, must be accurately recorded. Remember that an expert speaking or writing to you may be less precise and less accountable than the same person offering information in print. You may want to make arrangements to show your final paper or project to the people you interviewed, allowing them the opportunity to correct any misinformation.

Interviews can be especially useful in obtaining personal opinions and insights, depending on the person you choose to interview. The opinion of an educator about the usefulness of standardized testing in schools, for instance, would carry more weight than the opinion of a student; however, the student's opinion might provide an important point of view that needs to be considered as well. The information you gather from interviews will be useful to the extent that you have carefully selected interviewees to suit your purpose, carefully chosen your questions, and carefully recorded the responses. See Chapter 7 for more on conducting effective interviews.

10k Consider listservs and Usenet groups

A *listserv* is a program working online that allows a group of people who subscribe to the list to have extended email conversations. Listservs enable people with specific interests to share their ideas and their research. If you join a group germane to your subject, you can quickly learn a great deal about the nature of current interests and debate. However, listservs have all the advantages and disadvantages of any extended conversation: participants may vary widely in what they know; facts and figures may be reported unreliably; the credentials of participants may not be well known.

FOCUS ON . . . **Evaluating Web Sites**

One advantage of conducting research online is that you may find sources not available in library collections, and thereby you give your work a fresh perspective. Often these sources reflect points of view—political, social, economic, philosophical—that need to be considered, whether or not they are recognized as "authoritative." Unfortunately, along with the advantages of conducting research online, there are distinct disadvantages. Much of the information you may find has not been reviewed for you. You will need to apply careful critical reading skills to determine the logic and validity of the information you find before you consider relying on that information in your own work. That's one reason why articles in professional journals can be so valuable to researchers: these articles ordinarily meet clear professional standards, right down to their punctuation. Electronic sources should be held to similarly high standards: links in World Wide Web documents should be easy to follow; navigational aids and transitional statements should guide readers through arguments; and sources should be documented so that users can verify the claims presented or find additional information. Authors or author affiliations (for example, a sponsoring organization such as a news service, an educational institution, or a government agency) should be clearly designated, along with the date of publication or last revision.

When considering information from online sources, ask yourself these questions:

- Is the site sponsored by a reputable group you can identify?
- Do the authors of the site give evidence of their credentials?
- Is the site conveniently searchable?
- Is information in the site logically arranged?
- Is the site easy to navigate?
- Does the site provide an email address where you might send questions?
- Is the site updated regularly or properly maintained?
- Does the site archive older information?
- Is the content of the site affected by commercial sponsorship?

A Usenet group works like a listserv except that you need not subscribe to the list either to read its messages or to participate in the discussion. Anyone with access to the Internet can participate in any of the thousands of Usenet groups. As you might guess, these groups are often more valuable for what they reveal about the range and depth of feeling on a subject than for any information you may find there. You'll have reasons to cite Usenet discussions in some projects, but you'll use these materials with caution because you cannot confirm their credibility.

10.1

As you locate information, you will want to take careful notes and record summaries of the information contained in them, along with your responses or questions that the material raises that you will want to find answers to. Chapter 11 presents useful strategies for annotating research materials to help make your research efforts more productive.

WWW Web Sites Worth Knowing

- "Critically Analyzing Information Sources," **http://www.library.cornell.edu/okuref/research/skill26.htm**

  10.2
- "Evaluating Web Sites," **http://www.library.cornell.edu/okuref/research/webeval.html**
- "Using Cybersources," **http://www.devry-phx.edu/lrnresrc/dowsc/integrty.htm**
- *The Good, the Bad, and the Ugly: or Why It's a Good Idea to Evaluate Web Sources,* **http://lib.nmsu.edu/instruction/eval.html**
- "Thinking Critically about World Wide Web Resources," **http://www.library.ucla.edu/libraries/college/help/critical/index.htm**

GETTING INVOLVED

1. On what types of sources might you rely if you were looking for information on the following subjects?

   - the most recent World Series
   - the Persian Gulf War
   - the human genome project
   - literary movements in American literature

   - current trends in popular music
   - solvency of the Social Security system
   - the history of the European Monetary Union
   - the National Electrical Code

2. Browse several Web sites sponsored by the federal government. Locate them using *Yahoo!* at **http://www.yahoo.com/Government/U_S__Government/.** How authoritative do these sites seem? What types of information are available? Do you detect political biases in any sites? For presentation in class, write a brief assessment of the site you regard as most useful to a researcher.

3. Browse several corporate sites. You can locate them using *Yahoo!* at **http://www.yahoo.com/Business/Companies/.** How authoritative and thorough do

these sites seem? What types of information are available? What limitations and biases do you detect on any of the sites? For presentation in class, write a brief assessment of the site you regard as most useful to a researcher.

4. In the periodical room of your local library, look for journals or magazines targeted to specific groups of people—either ethnic, religious, social, economic, or political. Where or how are the biases of the periodical made evident? Be sure to consider such factors as the advertisements, layout, images, and language of the magazines.

5. Most search engines display advertisements. Open a search engine on your Web browser and explore the advertisements you see. What types of products are highlighted? What effects might this advertising have on a visitor to the Web site? In what ways might a reader on the Web be influenced by these and similar ads?

MANAGING YOUR PROJECT

1. As you recall your preliminary reading and scan your preliminary bibliography, do certain names stand out—people of authority on your subject whose names are cited often? Find out all you can about these authors. Be sure they are cited for the right reasons, and check what they have to say about your topic.

2. For each source, answer any of the following questions that apply.
   - Is the source appropriately timely? Would a more recent source be more up-to-date or less reflective?
   - Is this a source a reader will be able to follow up reliably? If not, can you still afford to use it? Does it serve some purpose that might not require following up?
   - What are the biases of this source? How should you adjust your reading of the source to account for the bias? How will you describe the bias to readers?
   - How does the source present its information? Does the author cite sources and provide evidence for all assertions? Is the presentation clear and well organized? Can you reliably find what you need?

11

Annotating Research Materials

Once you have collected print and online sources and evaluated them for timeliness, reliability, authority, and usefulness, you can begin mining them for information. One way to do that is to *annotate* the material you've gathered—that is, to attach comments, questions, and reactions to it. The point of such annotation is to identify ideas and information worth returning to and, more important, to engage in a dialogue with the authors and sources you are reading. Some instructors refer to this process as *critical reading*—not just accepting information at face value but always questioning it, looking for biases, and thinking about how credible the evidence is. Most important, annotation focuses you on the question, How does this information relate to my research question or affect my hypothesis?

Annotation is not an option when you are reading library books and materials; it is irresponsible to mark up books and magazines that do not belong to you, and it is a form of vandalism for which you can be prosecuted. When responding to library texts, you will want to record your reactions in notes, summaries, and paraphrases (see Chapter 13). Much research material today is also photocopied, downloaded, or read online—and these media support different forms of annotation.

The annotations you make while reading critically have a distinctly different rhetorical purpose from those you made in your annotated bibliography (see Section 8c). In an annotated bibliography your notes *capture* the substance of an entire text briefly yet as accurately as possible. Critical reading annotations, on the other hand, *expand* the text you are reading by adding your own responses and making connections to other texts.

11a Highlight key information

Many researchers working with photocopied material use highlighting pens to tag important passages, but often their highlighting is both too frequent and too random to be useful. If you underscore every passage that strikes you as interesting, you will end up

Use highlighter pens or marginal notes to mark up your research materials, inserting your own comments and helping you locate important information when you need to refer back to it. Make sure, however, that you do not mark up library materials; make photocopies if necessary.

with pages glowing pointlessly with color. Use color chiefly to help you locate material you intend to use later. Consider these strategies for marking a printed text:

- Highlight sentences you expect to quote directly. Potential quotations should be *very* limited in number. Don't highlight material that is generally interesting or even, in some respects, important—give attention to such information in your notes or with marginal comments.

- Highlight important dates, facts, and figures that you might have difficulty locating later. Such highlighting can be smart when you're dealing with especially dense passages of prose.

- Highlight sentences that might contain a thesis or an important summary of the piece. Such sentences should be relatively rare. Don't merely highlight the topic sentences of paragraphs; you'll brighten too much material if you do.

- Highlight key names or sources you might wish to consult later.

11.1
- Never mark a text that is not your own property.

11b Use marginal comments to start a dialogue with your sources

A marginal comment is a more powerful tool for critical reading than a highlight. To make a comment, you have to respond actively to a text, not just point out what someone has said. That's why you should make it a habit to read with pencil in hand, either annotating the text itself or immediately taking notes on cards or notebook paper. If you feel comfortable doing so, read with a word processor at hand and type responses to the text as you read; these comments can later be printed out for review and even worked into the body of your report where appropriate. Some bibliography and database software also allow you to record notes, summaries, paraphrases, and pithy quotations keyed to your source information (see Section 8b).

Ask pointed questions as you read. Record your reactions to the materials you are reading, note connections you see to other material, and jot down ideas that pop into your head. Each section you highlight should be accompanied by a marginal comment that explains the importance of the passage or gives your reaction to it.

You can use the annotation features of word-processing programs to record your reactions to files you download from your computer, but again your comments are the essential element. These annotations can be incorporated into the paper or project itself if they are thoughtful and entirely in your own words.

Even pages from the World Wide Web can be marked with comments and, in some cases, annotated as part of an ongoing online discussion. You can use *Netscape Navigator*'s "Bookmarks" or *Internet Explorer's* "Favorites" feature to gather together all Web sites or pages relevant to your project, arranging the items in folders that reflect its overall structure, one folder per major section or theme. It is even possible to annotate each bookmark to remind yourself why the site or page is important.

The following sample shows how a source (an editorial from the *Oakland Tribune*, May 5, 2001) might be annotated in its margins.

Tests Undermine Teachers

Anthony Cody

As we enter the testing season, teachers and students are once more submitting to inspection. Those pushing for high standards have apparently concluded that the only way to achieve them is through uniform adherence to specific curricular objectives.

Language suggests testing is a threat or demeaning?

The only way to promote adherence, in turn, is tests to measure how many of these facts and skills have been absorbed, and rewards and punishments based on these test results. As a teacher in a "low-performing school," which has further been designated for the honor of "immediate intervention," I have very mixed feelings.

Cody is a teacher himself; sarcastic use of "honor"

On the one hand, I am confident we can raise our scores. On the other hand, I don't think our designation as low-performing has done anything at all to motivate us to improve. Instead it has created a feeling of resentment toward the tests and those who would presume to judge our efforts based on so narrow a measurement.

Criticizes tests and those who support them.

Is this carrot-and-stick approach to school reform the only way? Are we even rewarding the best teaching? One way to look at our situation is as a choice between two models. The standardized testing model says you motivate people, teachers and students alike, by telling them exactly what to do, then rewarding them for doing it and punishing them for failing to do it.

He doesn't make it sound attractive—follow orders or be punished?

Figure 11.1 Annotated Source   *(continued)*

Everything in the system is rewired to focus on the standards, which translates into standardized test scores. This is where energy for reform has been directed much of the past decade.

What has been ignored and sacrificed? First of all, the best teachers are thoughtful, creative people. They naturally resist coercion, especially if it goes against their beliefs about how children ought to be taught. But they are forced to fight to defend their methods, rather than being encouraged and supported. Alfie Kohn said in his speech in Oakland several weeks ago, "People don't resist change. They resist being changed." There is an important distinction, and it applies to students as well as teachers. Second, the whole emphasis is on something external to the central action in the learning process. Rather than focus on the quality of the teacher/student relationship, the quality of instruction and the conditions and support needed for optimum learning, the standards advocates have, along with the testing technicians, erected a huge supervisorial superstructure that looms outside and over the classroom, attempting to dominate and control instruction.

Contrasts "creative" teachers with "dominating superstructure"

An alternative model is one that emphasizes teacher professionalism. This model says teachers will do their best not when threatened or coerced, but when given support and the opportunity to grow. Teachers are and must be accountable. The National Board of Professional Teaching Standards suggests that accomplished teachers are responsible for the learning in their classroom. They need to be able to organize and present curriculum, to give feedback to students, to assess growth, communicate with parents and participate in a professional community of educators. This is how they are accountable. They are not bound and determined to raise test scores. They are bound and determined to increase student learning, which is measured many different ways.

Is the issue really as black and white as he makes it sound?

Sees the goal of education as "student learning," not higher test scores.

Figure 11.1   Annotated Source *(continued)*

As you read and make your annotations, you are assessing the author's position on your subject as well as her or his credibility and authority. Does the author agree with your views, disagree with them, or fall somewhere in the middle? Is the author an expert in the field or someone expressing a personal opinion? The answers to these questions will be central when you decide how to *use* sources in your research project, and that is the topic of our next chapter.

WWW Web Sites Worth Knowing

- Critical Reading Strategies, **http://mind.phil.vt.edu/www/1204crs.html**
- Critical Thinking—Critical Reading (Power Point Slideshow), **http://www.kcmetro.cc.mo.us/longview/ctac/powerpoint/ct.ppt**
- Underlining, Marking & Annotating: Definitions & Purpose, **http://virtual.parkland.cc.il.us/studyskills/Reading&StudySystem/ Underlining,Marking,Annotating.purpose.htm**

GETTING INVOLVED

1. Take a close look at newspaper or magazine articles (or Web sites) that use "pull quotes"—sentences or phrases drawn from the article that are highlighted in a box or in another way to attract a reader's attention. In some ways, pull quotes work just as highlighting does to identify the words or phrases that best represent what an author has said. But look at pull quotes carefully: do they always represent the significant content of a piece accurately, or do they tend to focus on its sensational aspects?

2. Look for a book or another printed source that uses running annotations as part of its basic structure. (If necessary, ask a librarian for help.) Some textbooks and computer manuals are designed this way, as are many editions of the Bible. Marginal commentary (or glosses) was common in older books and manuscripts. When you find an example of a "glossed" text, examine how the running comments function. Do they highlight what is in the text? What other functions does the commentary have?

3. One of the "extra" features on DVD versions of some movies is a "commentary" soundtrack in which the director offers voice annotations as the movie is playing. Do these added highlights and remarks add to (or detract from) your experience of the movie? How so?

MANAGING YOUR PROJECT

1. If you prefer highlighter pens for marking sources, pay attention to the suggestions in this chapter for limiting your comments. Highlight only those passages or bits

of information you need to find quickly or cannot afford to lose when you come to assemble your project or write your paper.

2. Annotate in the margins of photocopied material carefully. Making the comments should help you practice reading texts actively. Record your responses, whether you agree with your sources or find yourself doubting what you read. You may well want to read both ways, what the scholar Peter Elbow describes as "believing and doubting."

3. Review your note-taking process carefully at this stage. Are the methods you are employing working? Are you keeping track of your sources and your comments on them? Modify any procedures that are not working now, before you get deeper into your project.

CHAPTER

12

Reviewing and Positioning Sources

As you gather or create materials for a project, review them critically in terms of your research question or hypothesis (see Chapter 4). To incorporate any material into your research effort, you must understand its impact on your work: Does source material or the data you generate advance your argument or undermine it? fill a hole in your background information or raise new questions? suggest novel perspectives or reinforce existing ones? change your opinion or validate it? Approach all research materials actively and intensely, reading and responding to them carefully, thinking deeply about their implications and ideas. This critical activity might—perhaps *should*—lead you to refine your initial thinking and to do even more reading and research.

When you review and position sources, you're thinking about three things in particular: *what* your sources have to say, how *credible* the information is, and how well it *fits* with your research query or hypothesis. Reviewing and positioning are activities that are chiefly concerned with the specific content of what is being said and with how that information extends, clarifies, or otherwise affects *your* arguments and ideas.

12a Review data and resources critically

Skimming materials may make sense when you are browsing a subject early in the research process, but your subsequent research (as you learned when annotating) requires careful, *critical* reading. Critical work involves interrogating your sources and methods, asking the questions that will help you understand the context, claims, and authority of each item of information you find or generate. Begin by critically reviewing your own methodologies as well as those of the sources you are considering. You can learn a lot about a source by asking the questions in the checklist on page 142.

Sometimes you can find clues to the authority of a source outside the work itself. For printed sources, the title page or book jacket gives important information: a university press such as Columbia University Press or Oxford University Press will probably

CHECKLIST

Critical Review of Data and Resources

Ask yourself about your own methodologies.

○ Are my findings valid and repeatable?

○ Was I careful not to skew my methods to generate data favorable to my thesis or hypothesis?

○ Was I careful to incorporate a variety of perspectives into my research or reading?

Question all facts and figures you encounter in your sources.

○ Do the authors have firsthand knowledge or experience of their subject matter?

○ Are all critical claims adequately documented?

○ Are my sources in conflict about important basic claims? If so, what might explain those conflicts?

○ Do my sources appeal to logic, or do they make unwarranted appeals to emotions?

○ If facts and figures are presented, where did they come from?

○ Are figures the result of government or university studies?

○ Are the figures presented in a biased way? Could the figures be used to support different arguments?

○ Are the samples used in surveys complete and representative?

○ Can controversial facts and figures be verified by other sources?

Consider carefully the sources included in bibliographies.

○ Are the references used authoritative?

○ Does the author include references to works that might disagree with his or her point of view?

○ Are the facts and figures presented in the work from reliable and diverse sources?

WWW

12.1

wield more authority than a trade press that targets a popular market (see Section 10b). Yet no single press or place of publication is ideal for all subjects. Authorities on extreme sports or haute couture are more likely to write for monthly magazines than for Harvard University Press. Even a comic book or a video game might be an authoritative source for a project on popular culture.

Establishing the authority of online sources can be more of a challenge. Virtually anyone with the technological skills can become a "published" author on the World Wide Web without the benefit of comments from editors, corrections from fact checkers, advice from reviewers, or support from publishers. For better or worse, much online material goes unscreened from authors to readers.

Just as political candidates represent different sides in a debate, the sources that you use may represent different positions on your topic. Make sure you understand how authors' possible biases or purposes may affect what they have to say.

However, the World Wide Web does offer a kind of book jacket in the *domain name*. The domain name, which is usually the first part of the Internet address (called the *uniform resource locator,* or URL), can provide important clues to the location of the author (and hence perhaps to her or his authority). The URL itself breaks down into specific parts: the type of protocol used to access the resource, the domain name where the file resides, any directories and/or subdirectories, and the file name and type. URLs may lack some or all of these parts; however, when citing sources, it is important that you include the entire URL shown in your browser's location or address bar.

The following table illustrates how three URLs break down into their component parts.

http://www.cas.usf.edu/english/walker/mla.html
http://www.m-w.com
http://www.columbia.edu/acis/documentation/ghttp/search-info.html

Protocol	Domain	Directory	Subdirectories	File	File Type
http://	www.cas.usf.edu	english	walker	mla	.html
http://	www.m-w.com				
http://	www.columbia.edu	acis	documentation/ghttp	search-info	.html

Generally, the domain name identifies where the information resides. A document at **http://www.cas.usf.edu** resides on the World Wide Web server (*www*) for the College of Arts and Sciences (*cas*) at the University of South Florida (*usf*), an educational institution (*edu*). The last part of the domain name gives important information about the type of site. The most common designations are:

.com	Commercial site
.edu	Educational site
.gov	Government site
.mil	Military site
.org	Organization (usually a nonprofit) site

No source is automatically credible, or even useful, merely because the domain at which it is published is an educational site, nor is a commercial site necessarily biased or useless. For more on determining the authority of print and online sources, see Chapter 10.

12b Position your research materials

After you've decided that source materials or data are appropriate and reliable, you'll want to "position" them within your project to identify their perspectives and biases. Where do they fit in your project? Do the sources support your arguments, provide examples or definitions, represent opposing viewpoints you need to consider? Positioning a source helps you use sources with your eyes wide open, conscious of contexts that can shape and influence information.

Sources do reflect generational, political, social, and economic biases and attitudes. Differences of gender, religion, or worldview may shape the materials you gather in ways that bear on your research. Even the methods used in creating the source material will influence how you present them: Was a survey scientific? Was a study sponsored by a group with a stake in its outcome? Does a document you cite represent a person's carefully considered judgment, or is it a paid endorsement, a political creed, even a parody? You need to know before you go public with it.

The answers to such questions will help you define how to use sources responsibly. You owe it to readers to be honest with information and to share what you learn about your sources when that information affects your conclusions. At times you might have to investigate your sources to be sure they are reliable. When an expert who provides statistics in support of nationalized health care is a scholar at a liberal think tank, you and your readers should know; if a columnist you quote as supporting a flat tax proposal is wealthy enough to benefit significantly from the policy change, that's relevant information. The Web sites in Figure 12.1 are positioned in ways that reflect their origins as well as their political biases.

Keep an eye on the positional balance of the articles and Web sites you collect. If you realize that many of them lean overwhelmingly in one direction, you might want to refocus your research strategy to find information that presents alternative points of view. Not everyone in your audience will readily agree with your perspective; you have to show that you have at least considered other ways of looking at an issue, other solutions to problems, or other opinions that may not fit well with your own. One of the most effective strategies for persuading an audience to see things your way is to show you have made an effort to be fair, to be open to a range of possibilities. If your readers sense that you're overlooking important points or not giving other perspectives a fair shake, your arguments will lose much of their persuasive force.

Following are examples of how two short articles might be positioned. Your own efforts to position a source might be much less formal than these. Positioning is not so much a written assignment as it is a mental exercise to be performed with all your research materials and methods. The examples are offered to help you formulate the questions you need to ask in order to appreciate what a source is and does. The first article is an editorial from *USA Today,* July 7, 1997; the second article, another editorial, ran in the *Oakland Tribune* on May 5, 2001.

Utne Reader at **http://www.utne.com/** appeals to a predominantly left-of-center readership concerned with issues of culture, earth, body, spirit, and politics. You might discover its point of view most readily by studying its links to other sources.

The titles of articles in *The Weekly Standard* at **http://www.weeklystandard.com/** might suggest its right-of-center politics. Or you might recognize the names of some of its authors. Better yet, check the revealing "About Us" link.

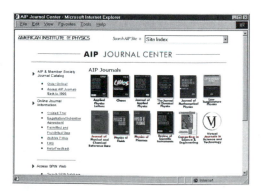

The American Institute of Physics publishes a dozen specialized journals, described at **http://www.aip.org/ojs/service.html**. The titles of journals such as *Chaos* or *Physics of Fluids* will quickly reveal the journals' academic orientation. (Reprinted with permission. Copyright 2002, American Institute of Physics. (AIP).)

Figure 12.1   Positioning Web sites.

Example

> ### "Leave the People Home"
> #### by Alex Roland
>
> The debacle currently unfolding aboard the *Mir* space station argues against sending people to Mars any time soon. To think about a manned Mars mission now is like planning your next cruise during an abandon-ship exercise.
>
> The problem is putting people in space.
>
> All the really useful things done in space have been achieved with automated spacecraft controlled by people on Earth. The record is long and impressive—scientific probes to the planets and beyond, communications satellites, weather satellites, reconnaissance satellites, the global positioning system.
>
> Two bad things happen when humans come aboard. First, cost increases by an order of magnitude, mostly to pay for life-support equipment and safety precautions. Second, the spacecraft becomes a lifeboat. Whatever mission it was intended to conduct—research, exploration, commerce—takes second place to saving the crew and returning them to Earth. The people, supposedly a means to some end, become the end themselves.
>
> The *Pathfinder* spacecraft, due to touch down on Mars July 4th, is a case in point. At a tiny fraction of what a manned mission would cost (indeed, at a small fraction of the cost of a single shuttle mission), this resourceful spacecraft, and the roving *Sojourner* vehicle it carries, will do more and better research than astronauts could do. Machines can reach more places, stay longer, and take more risks.
>
> But machines, you say, are not as dramatic, not as interesting as people. It is not the practicality of a manned Mars mission that appeals, but the romance. Sending people to Mars is a feel-good mission that speaks to the basic human longing to explore.
>
> Well, our next feel-good mission is already booked.
>
> Later this year, components of the international space station are scheduled to rocket into orbit. In 1999, three years before construction is complete, people will begin to inhabit it permanently. If it proves useful, more durable and safer than *Mir,* there will be plenty of time and a better argument for sending people to Mars.
>
> For now, however, we have all we can do to find a reason, a budget, and a technology to keep people in orbit.

POSITIONING　"Leave the People Home" is an editorial that appeared in *USA Today* on July 7, 1997, following the successful landing on Mars of a research robot. The piece, written by Alex Roland, appears as a rebuttal to the paper's official editorial position endorsing exploration of Mars by human explorers. Owned by Gannett, *USA Today* is a daily newspaper available throughout the country, with a predominantly liberal editorial page. It routinely publishes counterpoints to its editorials. *USA Today* notes that Alex Roland, "chair of the history department at Duke University, teaches technology history and is a former NASA historian." Roland's academic credentials and work with the American space agency appear to give him authority to write on this subject. The editorial was accessed online on July 7, 1997, for a Web project exploring the pros and cons of a human mission to Mars.

Example

Tests Undermine Teachers
Anthony Cody

As we enter the testing season, teachers and students are once more submitting to inspection. Those pushing for high standards have apparently concluded that the only way to achieve them is through uniform adherence to specific curricular objectives.

The only way to promote adherence, in turn, is tests to measure how many of these facts and skills have been absorbed, and rewards and punishments based on these test results. As a teacher in a "low-performing school," which has further been designated for the honor of "immediate intervention," I have very mixed feelings.

On the one hand, I am confident we can raise our scores. On the other hand, I don't think our designation as low-performing has done anything at all to motivate us to improve. Instead it has created a feeling of resentment toward the tests and those who would presume to judge our efforts based on so narrow a measurement.

Is this carrot-and-stick approach to school reform the only way? Are we even rewarding the best teaching? One way to look at our situation is as a choice between two models. The standardized testing model says you motivate people, teachers and students alike, by telling them exactly what to do then rewarding them for doing it and punishing them for failing to do it.

Everything in the system is rewired to focus on the standards, which translates into standardized test scores. This is where energy for reform has been directed much of the past decade.

What has been ignored and sacrificed? First of all, the best teachers are thoughtful, creative people. They naturally resist coercion, especially if it goes against their beliefs about how children ought to be taught. But they are forced to fight to defend their methods, rather than being encouraged and supported. Alfie Kohn said in his speech in Oakland several weeks ago, "People don't resist change. They resist being changed." There is an important distinction, and it applies to students as well as teachers. Second, the whole emphasis is on something external to the central action in the learning process. Rather than focus on the quality of the teacher/student relationship, the quality of instruction and the conditions and support needed for optimum learning, the standards advocates have, along with the testing technicians, erected a huge, supervisorial superstructure that looms outside and over the classroom attempting to dominate and control instruction. *(continued)*

An alternative model is one that emphasizes teacher professionalism. This model says teachers will do their best not when threatened or coerced but when given support and the opportunity to grow. Teachers are and must be accountable. The National Board of Professional Teaching Standards suggests that accomplished teachers are responsible for the learning in their classroom. They need to be able to organize and present curriculum, to give feedback to students, to assess growth, communicate with parents and participate in a professional community of educators. This is how they are accountable. They are not bound and determined to raise test scores. They are bound and determined to increase student learning, which is measured many different ways.

POSITIONING   This short editorial, which appeared in the *Oakland Tribune* on May 5, 2001, was written by Anthony Cody, who has been teaching at Bret Harte Middle School in Oakland for 14 years. The fact that he teaches at a school that has been identified as "low-performing" may affect his perspective on the standardized testing issue, as might the demographics of the student body he works with. One of the criticisms often leveled against standardized tests is that they discriminate against minority cultures and languages, and Mr. Cody may see that effect in his own students' experience. The length of time he has been teaching in this school district gives him the authority to speak about this issue. The editorial was accessed online on November 29, 2001, for a group project on the effects of standardized testing on classrooms.

CHECKLIST
Positioning Your Sources

○ What are the background and interests of the author(s)?
○ What are the interests and biases of the publisher?
○ How much authority does the source claim?
○ Are the assertions of authority justified?
○ Does the source or method purport to be objective and/or scientific?
○ Does the source present itself as subjective and/or personal?
○ Whose interests does the source or method represent?
○ Whose interests does the source or method seem to ignore?
○ What do readers need to know about the source or method?

As you can see, positioning is more than deciding which side of an argument a piece of writing falls on. You have to assess an author's background and expertise as well as a publication's potential editorial bias. Good research requires a healthy dose of skepticism, and that means not always believing everything you read or taking information at face value.

As you annotate, review, and position your sources, you will always be on the lookout for ways to bring information *from* those sources into your own project. One easy way of doing this is by summarizing important points or paraphrasing what other writers have had to say. Using summary and paraphrase wisely can be a little more complicated, however, and the next chapter will review guidelines to keep in mind as you proceed.

12.2

WWW Web Sites Worth Knowing

- The Gale Group: Bibliographic Instruction Support Program—Content Positioning, **http://www.galegroup.com/customer_service/alise/content_position.htm**
- Purdue University's OWL: Evaluating Content in the Source, **http://owl.english.purdue.edu/handouts/research/r_evalsource3.html**
- The Writing Center at Colorado State University—Using Outside Sources in your Writing, **http://writing.colostate.edu/references/sources/working/index.cfm**

12.3

GETTING INVOLVED

1. Locate a recent newspaper article or column that cites facts or statistics. Then play fact checker: underline or highlight the specific facts and use your skills as a researcher to verify the facts or numbers as best you can. Use the resources of a library reference room and the World Wide Web (if necessary). How accurate are the claims that the article or columnist makes? Were the facts presented clearly and in their full context? Or did the piece you studied use information selectively or present it unfairly? Especially good pieces for this exercise are newspaper and magazine columns that address contentious political issues.

2. Following are Web addresses that focus on the issue of standardized testing. Study them thoroughly and then describe what you can learn about the site from the address alone. What type of site might it be? Is it likely to be authoritative? What might its biases be? How regularly will it be updated and maintained? How long is it likely to be around?

   http://www.ets.org/
   http://www.parentsoup.com/edcentral/testing/
   http://www.fairtest.org/
   http://www.texasnaacp.org/taas.htm

   When you've completed your speculation, look at the actual sites and compare your expectations with the reality of the sites.

MANAGING YOUR PROJECT

1. After you have assembled a working bibliography (see Section 8b), use the check-list in this chapter to position your major sources, describing them as best you can. Observe that positioning a source is different from evaluating it. When you position a source, you are describing the research context of the materials: Who is offering the material? What are their points of view and biases? What baggage do the sources carry?

2. After positioning your sources, check that they are sufficiently diverse. You want your source material to suggest the breadth and depth of your reading. If all your sources reflect the same perspectives, come from the same publishers, and show similar biases, you may need to expand your preliminary bibliography.

3. If your project relies on materials you generated yourself, position your methods of inquiry. For example, if you are relying on a survey, what are the strengths and weaknesses of that approach? If you are designing a scientific experiment, what are its underlying assumptions? If you decide to interview subjects rather than gather factual data on an issue, what is the rationale for that approach, and how might it affect the information you are gathering? (That is, what kind of information might an interview reveal that a survey will not—and vice versa?)

4. Position yourself within your project. What assumptions and biases do you bring to the material? Do you favor a scientific methodology in your work, or do you prefer a more humanistic approach to your subject? Is your work influenced by a particular social, ethnic, religious, sexual, or political orientation? What experiences or training directed you toward this inquiry? To help you position yourself, think about how someone outside the project might view you.

5. Assess what you have learned from positioning your sources and methods. If you've done a thorough job locating your sources, you may discover that the main-stream research in a field reflects selected interests or points of view. Or certain ideas or voices may be ignored while others receive unexpected emphasis. Consider why this may be so. Are the possible reasons institutional, political, cultural, economic? Ponder this information and use it as you see fit in your own treatment of the research materials.

C H A P T E R
13

Summarizing and Paraphrasing Sources

To some researchers, summaries and paraphrases of source materials may seem like holdovers from a time when photocopiers and computers weren't widely available. In that ancient era you had to take detailed notes because you couldn't count on having the necessary books and articles on your desk when you did a project. Why bother taking detailed notes today when you can mark up copies of actual sources or download the texts and images you want?

The answer is that in summarizing or paraphrasing research materials, you get to know them. You're far more likely to understand sources when you have read them carefully enough to put their claims into your own words; you're more likely to appreciate or question evidence when your own fingers trace out an assertion, a fact, a statistic. In moving from reading to writing you also demonstrate how well you understand key concepts in research materials. Even more important, you help your readers better understand how sources connect with your own ideas when you include summaries or paraphrases of your sources.

When you are presenting information from field research, you need to summarize or paraphrase the information you gathered in interviews, surveys, and questionnaires, and you may need to summarize information contained in tables, figures, and other visual sources both to ensure that your readers understand this information and to relate the information to your own ideas.

Summarizing and paraphrasing are far more active processes than scribbling comments in margins or sweeping photocopied texts with highlighter pens—although both techniques may help you in summarizing and paraphrasing. (For how to highlight and comment on texts effectively, see Chapter 11.)

Make it a habit to either summarize or paraphrase all your major sources.

Movie posters often include quotes from reviewers such as those pictured here. For academic projects, however, you will need to ensure your reader that your borrowings are not only accurate, but that they reflect the original source's intentions as well.

13a　Summarize or paraphrase a source

Your choice of summary or paraphrase will be determined by both the source and the use you intend to make of it.

A *summary* captures the gist of a source or some portion of it, boiling it down to a few words or sentences. Summaries tend to be short, extracting only what is immediately relevant from a source and highlighting key concepts. You'll summarize those materials that support your thesis but do not provide an extended argument or idea you need to share in detail with readers. You might also want to summarize the main idea of articles from which you plan to use important facts and figures, information, or direct quotations in order to position these materials (see Chapter 12) and connect them to your own ideas.

When an article is quite long, you might look for topic ideas in each major section. If you have a photocopy of the source, highlight sentences that state or emphasize key themes. Then assemble these ideas into a short, coherent statement about the whole piece. You may also need to summarize the key idea or concept depicted in visuals (tables, charts, graphics) to ensure that your reader understands the information depicted in the way that you intend. (For more on including visual components in your project, see Section 20c.)

An effective summary will meet these conditions:

- The summary accurately reflects the source's key facts or ideas.
- The summary is shorter than the original but detailed enough to stand on its own and make sense weeks after you examined the material.
- The summary is necessary to help your reader understand the context of the information or statements you include from the source.
- The summary does not confuse your reader by including your own ideas or response without clearly designating which ideas are yours and which are your source's.

- The summary is written entirely in your own words, except for key words or phrases that are enclosed in quotation marks and accurately cited.

- The summary appropriately acknowledges the original source (see Section 13e).

A *paraphrase* reviews a complete source in much greater detail than a summary, recording both important ideas and supporting details. When paraphrasing a work, you report its key information or restate its core arguments point by point *in your own words.* You will typically want to paraphrase any materials that provide specific facts or ideas your readers will need. Predictably, paraphrases run much longer than summaries.

Paraphrases generally follow the same structure as the original source, and often they include details or supporting evidence in addition to arguments. As in summaries, material that is paraphrased must be cited and connected to your own ideas. Prepare a paraphrase by working through the original source more systematically than you would with a summary.

An effective paraphrase will meet these conditions:

- The paraphrase reflects the structure of the original piece.

- The paraphrase reflects the ideas of the original author, not your ruminations on them.

- Each important fact or direct quotation is accompanied by a specific page number from the source when that is possible.

13.1

- The material you record is relevant to your theme. (Don't waste time paraphrasing those parts that are of no use to your project.)

- The material is entirely in your own words—except for clearly marked quotations.

Practically speaking, making the distinction between summaries and paraphrases is often less important than simply taking the notes you need for a project. In gathering this information, you'll often find yourself switching between summary and paraphrase, depending on what you are reading. Now let's look at a source first summarized and then paraphrased.

13b Summarize sources to highlight key concepts

In Chapter 12 we read Alex Roland's editorial "Leave the People Home" with an eye to positioning it rhetorically. In this section we will refer to the same article (page 146) to frame our discussion of summary and paraphrase.

To prepare the editorial for either a summary or a paraphrase, you might first highlight and annotate the information most relevant to your project (in this case, focused on the research question, "Should humans explore Mars?").

To prepare a summary you would assemble the key claim and supporting elements into a concise restatement of the overall argument. The summary should make sense on its own—as a complete statement you might use later in your project itself. Don't be surprised if you try out several versions of that sentence before you come up with one that satisfies you.

EFFECTIVE **SUMMARY**	Alex Roland, chair of history at Duke University and a former historian at NASA, argues in USA Today (7 July 1997) that using automated unmanned spacecraft to explore planets such as Mars makes better sense than sending people on such missions because humans in space increase costs and risks and reduce the potential for long-term productive science.

How can something as simple as a summary go wrong? In a number of ways. You might make the summary too succinct and leave out crucial details; a summary scribbled on a note card might be useless when you try to make sense of it days later.

INEFFECTIVE **SUMMARY**	He argues that using people increases costs and reduces the science. International space station, 1997. Better reason to send after? Budget and technology.

Or your summary might fail because it misses the central point of a piece by focusing on details not relevant to the argument. Useful in a different context, these facts are misleading when they don't capture the substance of what the author wrote.

INACCURATE **SUMMARY**	Alex Roland, chair of history at Duke University and a former historian at NASA, argues in USA Today (7 July 1997) that the Pathfinder mission to Mars was very inexpensive and that, very soon, we will be launching an international space station.

Yet another danger is that you might use the actual words of the original author in your summary. If unacknowledged borrowings make their way into your project without both quotation marks and documentation, you would be guilty of plagiarism (see Chapter 9). In the example following, language taken directly and inappropriately from Roland's editorial is boldfaced.

PLAGIARIZED **SUMMARY**	Alex Roland, chair of history at Duke University and a former historian at NASA, argues in USA Today (7 July 1997) that **all the really useful things done in space have been achieved with automated spacecraft controlled by people on Earth. Machines can reach more places, stay longer, and take more risks than people**.

You can appreciate how tempting it might be to slip these plagiarized words from this summary into the body of a paper, forgetting that you didn't write them yourself. To avoid plagiarism, the safest practice is *always* to use your own words in summaries.

13c Paraphrase sources to record important ideas

A paraphrase of "Leave the People Home" (page 146) would be appreciably longer than a summary because a researcher would expect to use the information differently, probably wanting to refer to the source in greater detail. Here's one possible paraphrase of the editorial.

EFFECTIVE
PARAPHRASE

Recent problems on the Russian space station <u>Mir</u>, Alex Roland argues in a <u>USA Today</u> editorial (7 July 1997), make it clear why a human mission to Mars may not be a good idea: people in space cause problems that robots don't. Automated spacecraft perform almost all the really important work in space (communications, weather satellites, global positioning). Spacecraft that carry astronauts must also take along everything that keeps them alive, adding tremendously to the weight and complexity of missions. When something goes wrong, the whole project is jeopardized by the need to preserve the lives of astronauts. The Mars <u>Pathfinder</u> expedition, in contrast, was accomplished far more cheaply than even a routine space shuttle launch and yet can do more science over the long term than a human expedition because it isn't as vulnerable. We may like the adventure and romance that come along with human space exploration, and we'll have that experience with the international space station to be launched in 1999. But humans in space are an expensive and possibly unnecessary luxury.

You'll notice that this paraphrase covers all the major points in the editorial in the same order as the ideas originally occurred. It also borrows none of the author's language. With proper documentation, any part of the paraphrase could become part of a final research project without the need for quotation marks (see Sections 19a and 19b).

13.2

How can paraphrases go wrong? One way is by confusing the claims in a source with your own opinions. A paraphrase should accurately reflect the thinking of the original author, so reserve your comments and asides for annotations or other, separate notes. Consider how the following paraphrase might misreport the views of Alex Roland if the researcher later forgets that the boldfaced comments in the example are in fact personal notes and annotations.

INACCURATE
PARAPHRASE

Recent problems on the Russian space station Mir, Alex Roland argues in a USA Today editorial (7 July 1997), make it clear why a human mission to Mars may not be a good idea: people in space cause problems that robots don't. **You could argue, though, that people can fix problems robots can't: one reason Mir has been in space so long is that cosmonauts can repair the station.** True, automated spacecraft perform almost all the really important work in space (communications, weather satellites, global positioning)--**if you ignore the more complicated experiments performed by astronauts. No robot could have fixed the Hubble Space Telescope, for example.** Spacecraft that carry astronauts must also take along everything that keeps them alive, adding tremendously to the weight and complexity of missions. . . .

The reactions to the editorial are valid, but they don't represent an accurate paraphrase of the original article.

A paraphrase also should not reorganize or improve on the structure or argument of the original piece. The following paraphrase doesn't add material to Roland's editorial, but it rearranges information radically.

INACCURATE
PARAPHRASE

Americans may like the adventure and romance that comes along with human space exploration, and we'll have that experience again soon with the international space station to be launched in 1999. But humans in space are an expensive and possibly unnecessary luxury, argues Alex Roland in a USA Today editorial (7 July 1997). Spacecraft that carry astronauts must also take along everything that keeps them alive, adding tremendously to the weight and complexity of missions. When something goes wrong, the whole project is jeopardized by the need to preserve the lives of astronauts. That's the lesson we should have learned from recent problems on the Russian space station Mir. The Mars Pathfinder expedition, in contrast, was accomplished far more cheaply than even a routine space shuttle launch and yet

```
can do more science over the long term than a human

expedition because it isn't as vulnerable. So a human

mission to Mars may not be a good idea: people in space

cause problems that robots don't. Automated spacecraft

perform almost all the really important work in space

(communications, weather satellites, global

positioning).
```

The most dangerous and academically dishonest sort of paraphrase is one in which a researcher borrows the ideas, structure, and details of a source wholesale, changing a few words here and there in order to claim originality later. This sort of paraphrase would be plagiarism even if the material were documented in the research project. Writers can't just change a few words in their sources and claim the resulting material as their own work.

PLAGIARIZED
PARAPHRASE

```
The catastrophe now unfolding aboard the Mir space

station argues against launching people to Mars any time

soon. To consider a manned Mars mission now is like

planning your next flight during a midair crisis.

        The difficulty is sending people into outer space.

        Most of the really useful things achieved in space

have been done with automated spaceships controlled by

technicians on Earth. The record is quite impressive--

scientific probes to the planets and beyond,

communications satellites, weather satellites,

reconnaissance satellites, the global positioning

system. . . .
```

You'll see the fault readily if you compare these plagiarized paragraphs with the opening paragraphs of Roland's editorial.

13d Summarize and paraphrase carefully

A proper summary or paraphrase of a source should be entirely in your own words (see Section 13a). Suppose that in preparing a research paper on mountain biking you come across this passage in *The Mountain Bike Book* by Rob van der Plas:

> In fact, access and right-of-way are the two intangibles in trail cycling these days. The sport is getting too popular fast, and in defense, or out of fear, authorities have banned cyclists from many potentially suitable areas.
>   You will probably use forest service or fire roads intended for hikers most of the time. Don't stray off these trails, since this may cause damage, both to

the environment and to our reputation. As long as you stay on the trails and do it with a modicum of consideration for others, you have nothing to fear and should not risk being banned from them by public agencies.

In many areas a distinction is made between single-track trails and wider ones. Single tracks are often considered off-limits to mountain bikers, although in most cases they are perfectly suitable and there are not enough hikers and other trail users to worry about potential conflicts. In fact, single trails naturally limit the biker's speed to an acceptable level.

Some writers mistakenly believe that they can avoid a charge of plagiarism by rearranging or changing a few words in a selection. The following passage would be considered plagiarism—with or without a parenthetical note—because it simply takes the source's basic words and ideas and varies them slightly.

PLAGIARIZED
VERSION

```
In trail cycling today, access and right-of-way are the
two intangibles. The sport of mountain biking is getting
too popular too quickly, so defensive authorities have
banned cyclists from many potentially suitable areas out
of fear.

    Mountain bikers typically use forest service or
fire roads and trails intended for hikers most of the
time. They shouldn't stray off these trails, since this
may cause damage, both to the environment and to the
reputation of cyclists. As long as mountain bikers
remain on the trails and do it with a modicum of
consideration for others, they need not fear and should
not risk being restricted from them by public agencies.
```

These few minor changes are not enough to avoid a charge of plagiarism. Make sure that the words you use are truly your own.

13e Acknowledge all borrowings

When you quote all or part of a selection in your essay, you must use quotation marks (or indention) to indicate that you are borrowing a writer's exact words. You must also identify author, work, publisher, date, and location of the passage. In MLA documentation style (see Chapter 24), the parenthetical note and corresponding Works Cited entry would look like this:

```
    As Rob van der Plas reminds bikers, they need only use
common sense in riding public trails: "As long as you stay
the trails and do it with a modicum of consideration for
```

others, you have nothing to fear and should not risk being
banned from them by public agencies" (106).

Works Cited

van der Plas, Rob. <u>The Mountain Bike Book: Choosing, Riding,</u>
    <u>and Maintaining the Off-Road Bicycle</u>. 3rd ed. San
    Francisco: Bicycle, 1993.

You must use *both* quotation marks and the parenthetical note when you quote directly (see Chapter 14). Quotation marks alone would not tell your readers where your source was to be found. A note alone would acknowledge that you are using a source, but it would not explain that a given portion of the words in your paper are not your own.

Alternatively, you may need to use the selection above indirectly, borrowing the information in van der Plas's paragraphs but not his words or arrangement of ideas. Here are two acceptable summaries of the passage on mountain biking (see pages 157–58) that report its facts appropriately and originally. Notice that both versions include a parenthetical note acknowledging van der Plas as the source of information.

Rob van der Plas asserts that mountain bikers need not fear
limitations on their right-of-way if they ride trails
responsibly (106).

Though using so-called single-track trails might put mountain
bikers in conflict with the hikers, such tracks are often empty
and underutilized (van der Plas 106).

🌀 FOCUS ON . . . Rhetorical Strategies for Using Sources

Your work with sources doesn't end when you've finished paraphrasing or summarizing them. You must now consider them thoughtfully in relationship to one another. Think of your project as a lively conversation and see that no single voice dominates that conversation or goes unchallenged. This means that you shouldn't compose a major part of your work without drawing on a variety of sources. And every part of the project should reflect the depth of your research and reading.

In some projects you'll want to cite sources that reinforce each other, especially when you're trying to build a persuasive case. In other situations you may find authoritative sources that differ significantly; then you have to decide which to endorse, or perhaps you'll leave that choice to readers. When sources have pronounced biases (political or otherwise), be sure to read them "against" pieces with alternative views to keep your own perspectives broad. And when you borrow material from online discussion groups, always find more conventional sources to confirm the facts, figures, and claims you find there.

Without documentation, both versions above might be considered plagiarized even though only van der Plas's ideas—and not his actual words—are borrowed. You *must* acknowledge ideas and information you take from your sources (unless you are dealing with common knowledge; see Section 19b) even though the exact words you use to express the ideas may be your own.

You are the author of your paper, and your paper should reflect *your* ideas and opinions. Don't make the mistake of patching together a paper that consists of nothing but the ideas and opinions of others, even if you summarize and paraphrase them entirely in your own words. Don't overlook the importance of including direct quotations when they are especially well phrased or when the reputation of the speaker will lend authority to your own arguments. In the next chapter you will learn more about handling quotations in your research project.

WWW Web Sites Worth Knowing

WWW

13.3

- University of Wisconsin–Madison Writing Center *Writer's Handbook*, "Creating a Successful Summary or Paraphrase,"
  http://www.wisc.edu/writing/Handbook/QuoSuccessfulSummary.html

- Purdue University OWL, "Quoting, Paraphrasing, and Summarizing,"
  http://owl.english.purdue.edu/handouts/research/r_quotprsum.html

- University of Northern British Columbia Learning Skills Centre, "Why Summarize, Paraphrase, or Quote?" **http://quarles.unbc.ca/lsc/rpsummar.html**

- Ohio University ESL, "Quotation, Paraphrase, Summary,"
  http://www.ohiou.edu/esl/help/quotation.html

GETTING INVOLVED

1. In the library, browse the collection of recent magazines and journals to find one or two that provide formal abstracts: you may have to choose a scholarly journal to find this feature. Read over the abstracts in these journals and decide whether you'd classify such an abstract as a summary or a paraphrase. How useful are these abstracts? In what ways might you use them in preparing your own research project?

2. While in the magazine section of your library, look for two or three magazines that annotate their tables of contents, briefly explaining the substance of their main articles and features. Compare several of these summaries to the articles in the magazines. Would you describe these table-of-contents blurbs as accurate summaries, or do they serve other functions such as enticing readers into the magazine? Where else do you find similar kinds of brief—and enticing—summaries?

3. Working in class in groups of five or six, choose a substantive article from the campus newspaper. Have each member of the group prepare a summary of the piece

no more than 150 words long. Then compare and contrast the summaries. What—if anything—did every member of the group include in the summary? Over what matters was there considerable variance?

MANAGING YOUR PROJECT

1. Survey your working bibliography and decide which sources you expect will require full paraphrases, which ones will be handled adequately through summaries, and which ones may require a combination of approaches.

2. Using a word processor or note cards, write a summary for the sources in your working bibliography that you plan to use extensively in your project. For particularly important or complicated points, write a paraphrase of the original, including the main ideas and supporting information and following the structure of the original. Make sure you include page numbers and source information so you can accurately document the summaries and paraphrases if you use them in your project.

3. Explore the features of note-taking programs such as *TakeNote* if you have access to one. These programs handle the logistics well, linking notes and bibliographical information effortlessly. Such programs may encourage you to take more thorough notes than you do usually and may help you see more connections between your materials. Include a brief summary of the sources you include in your database or note-taking software.

CHAPTER

14

Quoting Sources

In many research projects, especially those in the arts and humanities, you'll have frequent occasion to quote directly from sources. You will want to do so effectively because quotations can add texture and authority to your project. Think of sources as voices that confirm your positions, challenge them, or extend them. No stylistic touch makes a research project work quite so well as quotations deftly handled.

However, including too many quotations can be distracting and ineffective—your voice should be the one that readers hear—yet there are good reasons why you *should* include quotations. This chapter will help you select and use quotations to fulfill your own rhetorical purposes.

14a Select direct quotations strategically

Every quotation in an article should contribute something your own words cannot. Use quotations for various reasons:

- To focus on a particularly well stated key idea in a source
- To show what others think about a subject—either experts, people involved with the issue, or the general public
- To give credence to important facts or concepts
- To add color, power, or character to your argument or report
- To show a range of opinion
- To clarify a difficult or contested point
- To demonstrate the complexity of an issue
- To emphasize a point

Never use quotations to avoid putting ideas in your own words or to pad your work. You already know that you need to scrupulously acknowledge *all* borrowings from other sources: ideas, opinions, facts, information (unless it is common knowledge). When you use tables, figures, or artwork, you must also acknowledge the source

Don't let quotations squeeze out your own writing. Readers want and need to hear what *you* have to say, including how you interpret and connect ideas gleaned from other sources.

from which you obtained them (see Section 14c). Just as important, you need to make sure that your readers understand how you are using the quotations you select—what they mean in the context of your own project.

14b Introduce all direct and indirect borrowings

Although quotation marks (see Section 14d) and indentions (see Section 14i) will identify direct quotations, these typographical devices don't tell a reader who wrote a passage, why it is important, or how it stands in relationship to the rest of an essay. And indirect borrowings (summaries, paraphrases, statistical information, graphics) have no quotation marks at all. So short introductions, attributions, and commentaries are needed to orient readers to materials you've gathered from sources. To be sure readers pay attention, give all borrowed words and ideas a context or *frame*.

Frames can be relatively simple; they can precede, follow, or interrupt the borrowed words or ideas. The frame need not even be in the same sentence as the quotation; it may be part of the surrounding paragraph. Here are some ways that material can be introduced, the frames appearing in boldface.

Frame precedes borrowed material

A few years ago, my wife and I were startled by a teaser for a story on a network news program, which asked what was meant to be a provocative question: "When is a church more than just a place of worship?"

—Stephen Carter

Frame follows borrowed material

"One reason you may have more colds if you hold back tears is that, when you're under stress, your body puts out steroids which affect your immune system and reduce your resistance to disease," **Dr. Broomfield comments.**

—Barbara Lang Stern

Frame interrupts borrowed material

"Your best action," **an Atomic Energy Commission booklet read,** "is not to be worried about fallout." —Terry Tempest Williams

"They are taking away the night," **I thought.** "They are taking away the last moments of mystery. Is nothing sacred?" —J. Michael Bishop

Surrounding sentences frame borrowed material

Even taste is affected by zero gravity. "Body fluids migrate to your upper body, and you end up with engorged tissue around the nasal passages and ear," **explains Gerald Carr, who was commander of the third and longest (84 days) Skylab mission.** "You carry with you a constant state of nasal and head congestion in weightless environment. It feels pretty much like you have a cold all the time." —Douglas Colligan

If so, says Solow, we should be seeing much warmer temperatures than we have seen so far. "For example, for the planet to warm by 2°C in the next hundred years, the average rate of warming would have to be four times greater than that in the historical record." Greenhouse warming is expected to be greatest at high latitudes and more rapid in the north than in the south, but this pattern hasn't appeared either, **he says.**
—Jane S. Shaw and Richard L. Stroup

Borrowed material integrated with passage

The study concludes that a faulty work ethic is not responsible for the decline in our productivity; quite the contrary, the study identifies "a widespread commitment among U.S. workers to improve productivity" **and suggests that** "there are large reservoirs of potential upon which management can draw to improve performance and increase productivity."
—Daniel Yankelovich

Borrowings in your research paper should be attributed in similar fashion. Either name (directly or indirectly) the author, the speaker, or the work the passage is from, or explain why the words you quote are significant. Many phrases of introduction or attribution are available, and they can shape significantly the way readers perceive a quotation. Verbs of attribution such as those in the following examples are more powerful than the repetition of the bland phrases "he said" and "she explained."

President Bush **claimed** that ". . .

One expert **reported,** ". . .

The members of the board **declared** that ". . .

Representatives of the airline industry **contend** that ". . .

Marva Collins **asserts**, ". . .

Senator Kennedy **was quoted** as saying, ". . .

"The figures," **according to** the GAO, "are . . .

The following chart lists verbs of attribution that you might consider using when the context makes them appropriate. (For more on using quotation marks correctly, see Sections 14d and 14e.)

CHART
Verbs of Attribution

accept	argue	emphasize	reveal
add	believe	insist	say
admit	confirm	mention	state
affirm	deny	posit	think
allege	disagree	propose	verify

Vary these terms sensibly; you needn't change the verb of attribution with every direct quotation.

You may need to identify the speaker's authority as well. In the sample paper "Can Quality Survive the Standardized Test?" on page 260, the author includes a quotation from Linda Rief, who says, "I expect good reading and writing, in which process and product are woven tightly into literate tapestries of wonder and awe." Without identifying Rief's authority to speak about her expectations, how effective would this quotation be? How many of your readers would know that Rief is an author and teacher? While you can avoid charges of plagiarism by simply naming the source of your quotation, you may need to note the author's credentials for his or her words to have the effect you desire. The sample bibliography with both positioning information and sample quotes at the end of this chapter will aid you in documenting information effectively.

In academic papers you will usually be expected to include in-text documentation (called *parenthetical citations*) when using direct and indirect quotes. The format for such documentation is discussed in Section 14j.

14c Integrate graphical elements correctly

You will need to frame your use of graphics, figures, tables, and other artwork. Usually that means referring to them in the text, summarizing the information they contain, to ensure that your reader understands them in the way that you intend. Most style guides have explicit rules for labeling tables, figures, and other graphical elements as well. And you must cite the source from which you borrowed a graphical element or the source of the information you include in tables. The following table is labeled above the item; the source of the information is identified under the table.

Table 1

Percentage of Students Passing All Texas Assessment of
   Academic Skills Exams (TAAS)

	1994	1995	1996	1997	1998	4 Yr. Gain
Grade 3	58	66	70	74	76	18
Grade 4	54	64	67	72	78	24
Grade 5	58	66	73	79	83	25
Grade 6	56	60	69	77	79	23
Grade 7	55	58	67	75	78	23
Grade 8	49	50	59	67	72	23
Grade 10	52	54	60	68	72	20

Source: Texas Business and Education Coalition. School
   Gains. 1999. 27 Feb. 2000. <http://www.tbec.org/gains.HTML>.

In some circumstances, particularly when you want to give readers a lot of numerical data that encompass many variables or an extended time period, it may be preferable to use a chart or graph rather than try to present all the information in a narrative or text form. Graphical elements can often demonstrate the relationships among many factors more easily and vividly than words can, but it is always important not to let graphical elements "speak for themselves." All pictures need to be introduced, and all graphics need to be explained, reviewed, or interpreted to make your point. Include a credit line citing the source of a graphic or include a separate listing of all graphical borrowings at the end of your paper or project.

14d Handle quotation marks correctly

Quotation marks—which always occur in pairs—draw attention to the words, sentences, or passages they enclose. Use double quotation marks (" ") around most quoted material; use single quotation marks (' ') to mark quotations within quotations. Quotation marks are used around any material you borrow word for word from sources, even if you borrow only one particularly cogent term or a two-word or three-word phrase.

Take care with the punctuation before and after quotations. A quotation introduced or followed by *said, remarked, observed,* or similar expressions takes a comma.

```
Benjamin Disraeli observed, "It is much easier to be critical
than to be correct."
```

```
"Next to the originator of a good sentence is the first quoter
of it," said Ralph Waldo Emerson.
```

Commas are used, too, when a one-sentence quotation is interrupted by a phrase.

```
"If the world were a logical place," Rita Mae Brown notes, "men
would ride side-saddle."
```

When a tag line comes between two successive sentences from a single source, a comma and period are required.

```
"There is no such thing as a moral or an immoral book," says
Oscar Wilde. "Books are well written, or badly written. That is
all."
```

No punctuation is required when a quotation runs smoothly into a sentence you have written.

```
Abraham Lincoln observed that "in giving freedom to the slave
we assure freedom to the free."
```

Take care, too, to place quotation marks correctly with other marks of punctuation. Commas and periods go *inside* closing quotation marks except when a parenthetical note is given.

```
"This must be what the sixties were like," I thought.
```

```
Down a corridor lined with antiwar posters, I heard someone
humming "Blowin' in the Wind."
```

When a sentence ends with in-text documentation, the period follows the parenthetical note.

```
Mike Rose argues that we hurt education if we think of it "in
limited or limiting ways" (3).
```

Colons and semicolons go *outside* closing quotation marks.

```
Riley claimed to be "a human calculator": he did quadratic
equations in his head.
```

```
The young Cassius Clay bragged about being "the greatest"; his
opponents in the ring soon learned he wasn't just boasting.
```

Question marks and exclamation points fall *inside* the closing quotation marks when they are the correct punctuation for the phrase in quotation but not for the sentence as a whole.

> When Mrs. Rattle saw her hotel room, she muttered, "Good
>
> grief!"
>
> She turned to her husband and said, "Do you really expect me to
>
> stay here?"

They fall *outside* the closing quotation marks when they are appropriate for the entire sentence.

> Who was it that said, "Truth is always the strongest argument"?

Quotation marks are also used to indicate dialogue. When writing a passage with several speakers, follow convention and begin a new paragraph each time the speaker changes.

> Mrs. Bennet deigned not to make any reply; but unable to contain herself, began scolding one of her daughters.
>
> "Don't keep coughing so, Kitty, for heaven's sake! Have a little compassion on my nerves. You tear them to pieces."
>
> "Kitty has no discretion in her coughs," said her father; "she times them ill."
>
> "I do not cough for my own amusement," replied Kitty fretfully.
>
> —Jane Austen, PRIDE AND PREJUDICE

14e Tailor your quotations to fit your sentences

To make quotations fit smoothly into your text, you may have to tinker with the introduction to the quotation or modify the quotation itself by careful selections, ellipses (see Section 14f), or bracketed additions (see Section 14g).

AWKWARD   The chemical capsaicin that makes chili hot: "it is so
        hot it is used to make antidog and antimugger sprays"
        (Bork 184).

REVISED   Capsaicin, the chemical that makes chili hot, is so
        strong "it is used to make antidog and antimugger
        sprays" (Bork 184).

AWKWARD   Computers have not succeeded as translators of languages
        because, says Douglas Hofstadter, "nor is the difficulty

caused by a lack of knowledge of idiomatic phrases. The
fact is that translation involves having a mental model
of the world being discussed, and manipulating symbols
in the model" (603).

REVISED   "[A] lack of knowledge of idiomatic phrases" is not the
reason computers have failed as translators of
languages. "The fact is," says Douglas Hofstadter, "that
translation involves having a mental model of the world
being discussed, and manipulating symbols in the model"
(603).

Take care that you do not change the context of the original or skew its meaning. There
is obviously a significant difference in the meaning of these two statements:

MISLEADING   Thomas Paine argued that soldiers and patriots will
"shrink from the service of their country."

REVISED   Thomas Paine argued that the "summer soldier and the
sunshine patriot will, in this crisis, shrink from the
service of their country."

You have an obligation both to your sources and to your readers to ensure that the use
you make of material from sources is ethical and accurate (see Chapter 9).

14f Use ellipses to indicate omissions

Three spaced periods (one space after each period) mark an ellipsis (. . .), a gap in a
sentence or passage. The missing material may be a word, a phrase, a complete sentence, or more. In MLA style (demonstrated below), ellipses you add to a passage are
enclosed in brackets.

COMPLETE   Abraham Lincoln closed his First Inaugural Address
PASSAGE   (March 4, 1861) with these words: "We are not enemies,
but friends. We must not be enemies. Though passion may
have strained, it must not break, our bonds of
affection. The mystic chords of memory, stretching from
every battlefield and patriot grave to every living
heart and hearthstone all over this broad land, will yet
swell the chorus of the Union when again touched, as
surely they will be, by the better angels of our
nature."

Passage
with
omissions

```
Abraham Lincoln closed his First Inaugural Address
(March 4, 1861) with these words: "We are not enemies,
but friends. [. . .] The mystic chords of memory [. . .]
will yet swell the chorus of the Union when again
touched, as surely they will be, by the better angels of
our nature."
```

Be sure to use the correct spacing and punctuation before and after ellipsis marks. When an ellipsis mark appears in the middle of a sentence, leave a space before the first and after the last period and remember that the periods themselves are spaced. For MLA style, note where brackets are placed in the second example.

```
chords of memory . . . will yet swell

chords of memory [. . .] will yet swell
```

If a punctuation mark occurs immediately before the ellipsis, include the mark when it makes your sentence easier to read. The punctuation mark is followed by a space, then the ellipsis mark (or the bracket in MLA style).

```
We are not enemies, . . . must not be enemies

We are not enemies, [. . .] must not be enemies
```

When an ellipsis occurs at the end of a complete sentence or when you delete a full sentence or more from a passage, place a period at the end of the sentence, followed by a space and then the ellipsis.

```
We must not be enemies. . . . The mystic chords

We must not be enemies. [. . .] The mystic chords
```

When an ellipsis appears at the end of a sentence or passage, the final period follows the ellipsis unless there is a parenthetic note.

```
"These are the times that try men's souls. The summer soldier
and the sunshine patriot will, in this crisis, shrink from the
service of their country [. . .]."
                                                    —Thomas Paine
```

When a parenthetical reference follows a sentence that ends with an ellipsis, leave a space between the last word in the sentence and the ellipsis. Then provide the parenthetical reference, followed by the closing punctuation mark.

```
passion may have strained it [. . .]" (102).
```

In most cases you should avoid ellipses at the ends of sentences when they indicate only that more material follows. Most readers understand that is likely to be the case whenever you quote. Keep your use of ellipses to a minimum.

An ellipsis may appear at the beginning of quoted sentences to indicate that an opening clause or phrase has been omitted. Three spaced periods precede the sentence, with a space left between the third period and the first letter of the sentence. Any punctuation at the end of the clause or sentence preceding the quotation is retained.

> "The text of the Old Testament is in places the stuff of
> scholarly nightmares. [. . .] the books of the Old Testament
> were composed and edited over a period of about a thousand
> [years]."
>
> —Barry Hoberman, "Translating the Bible"

You needn't use an ellipsis, however, every time you break into a sentence. The quotation in the following passage, for example, reads more smoothly without the ellipsis.

> In fact, according to Lee Iacocca, "[. . .] Chrysler didn't
> really function like a company at all" when he arrived in 1978.
>
> In fact, according to Lee Iacocca, "Chrysler didn't really
> function like a company at all" when he arrived in 1978.

Other styles (APA, CMS, and CSE) use ellipses to indicate omitted material, but they do not enclose them in square brackets.

> In his First Inaugural Address, Abraham Lincoln said, "The
> mystic chords of memory . . . will yet swell the chorus of the
> Union when again touched, as surely they will be, by the better
> angels of our nature."

Whenever you use ellipses, be sure your shortened quotation accurately reflects the meaning of the uncut passage. It is irresponsible and dishonest to alter the meaning of a source by excising critical words or phrases.

14g Use square brackets to add necessary information to a quotation

Sometimes you may want to explain who or what a pronoun refers to, or you may have to provide a short explanation, furnish a date, or explain or translate a puzzling word. Enclose such material in square brackets: [ ].

```
Some critics clearly prefer Wagner's Tannhäuser to Lohengrin:
"the well-written choruses [of Tannhäuser] are combined with
solo singing and orchestral background into long, unified
musical scenes" (Grout 629).

And so Iacocca accepted Chrysler's offer: "We agreed that I
would come in as president but would become chairman and CEO
[Chief Executive Officer] on January 1, 1980" (Iacocca 145).
```

Any change you make to material in a quotation—even changing an uppercase letter to a lowercase one or changing a mark of punctuation—must be designated by enclosing it in square brackets. But don't overdo it. Readers will resent the explanation of obvious details, and too many changes may lead the reader to question your use of the material.

14h Use [sic] to acknowledge errors in sources

Quotations must be copied accurately, word by word from your source—errors and all. To show that you have copied a passage faithfully, place the expression *sic* (the Latin word for *thus* or *so*) in brackets one space after any mistake in the original.

```
Mr. Vincent's letter went on: "I would have preferred a
younger bride, but I decided to marry the old window [sic]
anyway."
```

If *sic* can be placed outside the quotation itself, it appears between parentheses, not brackets.

```
Molly's paper was titled "Understanding King Leer" (sic).
```

14i Present quotations correctly

Short quotations are arranged differently on a page than longer ones, but the exact format will depend on which documentation style you are using. MLA, APA, and Chicago styles vary slightly; be sure you follow the appropriate guidelines for the style you are using.

Place prose quotations of four typed lines or fewer (MLA) or forty words or less (APA) between quotation marks.

```
In On Liberty (1859), John Stuart Mill declares, "If all
mankind minus one were of one opinion, mankind would be no more
justified in silencing that one person than he, if he had the
power, would be justified in silencing mankind."
```

Indent prose quotations longer than four typed lines (MLA) or forty words (APA). MLA form recommends an indention of ten spaces or one inch from the left-hand margin; APA form requires five spaces. (The right-hand margin is not indented.) Quotation marks are *not* used around indented material. If the long quotation extends beyond a single paragraph, the first lines of subsequent paragraphs are indented an additional three typed spaces (MLA) or five spaces (APA). In MLA papers, the indented material—like the rest of the essay—is always double spaced. Both APA and Chicago style permit quotations to be single spaced in student projects.

When you are quoting poetry, indent the lines when the passage runs more than three lines (MLA). Up to three lines of poetry may be handled just like a prose passage, with slashes marking the separate lines with a single space before and after each slash. Quotation marks are used when the lines are not indented.

```
As death approaches, Cleopatra grows in grandeur and dignity:

"Husband, I come! / Now to that name my courage prove my

title! / I am fire and air" (V.ii.287-89).
```

More than three lines of poetry are indented ten spaces and quotation marks are not used. (If the lines of poetry are unusually long, you may indent fewer than ten spaces.) Double-space the indented passage (MLA), and be sure to copy the passage accurately, right down to the punctuation.

www

14.2

```
Among the most famous lines in English literature are those

that open William Blake's "The Tyger":

        Tyger tyger, burning bright,

        In the forests of the night;

        What immortal hand or eye,

        Could frame thy fearful symmetry? (1-4)
```

14j Document the source of all quotations

You must use quotation marks (or indention) to indicate that you are borrowing a writer's exact words. You must also identify author, work, publisher, date, and location of the passage. In MLA documentation style (see Chapter 24), the parenthetical note and corresponding Works Cited entry would appear in this form:

```
As Rob van der Plas reminds bikers, they need only use common

sense in riding public trails: "As long as you stay on the

trails and do it with a modicum of consideration for others,

you have nothing to fear and should not risk being banned from

them by public agencies" (106).
```

```
                          Works Cited

    van der Plas, Rob. The Mountain Bike Book: Choosing, Riding,

        and Maintaining the Off-Road Bicycle. 3rd ed. San

        Francisco: Bicycle, 1993.
```

You must use *both* quotation marks and the parenthetical note when you quote directly. Quotation marks alone would not tell your readers where your source was. A note alone would acknowledge that you are using a source, but it would not explain that a given portion of the words in your paper are not your own. For the same reason, providing complete references in hypertexts is still necessary, even though you can (and often should) link a quotation to the original if it is available online. Online sources may move or disappear, and readers often print out or save hypertexts to disks, making links inoperable.

By now you may have completed a substantial draft of your project, but don't make the mistake of printing it out, correcting typographical and grammatical errors, and thinking you are done. Now is the time to carefully read through your project. You may find that you have not provided sufficient support for your arguments to be persuasive: perhaps you need to do more research. Or you may even find that, as a result of what you have learned in the course of your research, you need to change your argument. Part IV will guide you through developing your project, reflecting on what you already have, refining, organizing, drafting, documenting, and—finally—completing it.

WWW Web Sites Worth Knowing

14.3

- "Bartlett's Familiar Quotations," **http://www.bartleby.com/100/**
- "Big Dog's MLA Quick Guide," (Netscape browsers only).
  http://aliscot/bigdog/mla.htm
- "Incorporating Quotations,"
  http://www.wisc.edu/writing/Handbook/QuoLitIncorporating.html

GETTING INVOLVED

1. Comb several full pages of a daily newspaper—including the front, editorial, and lead sports pages—looking for verbs of attribution that introduce direct or even indirect quotations (see Section 14b). Which words or expressions appear most often? What is the most unusual lead-in you find for a quotation?

2. Only recently has the Modern Language Association (MLA) decided that ellipses added to passages should be enclosed in brackets. Given the function of brackets, explained in Section 14g, argue for or against this practice.

MANAGING YOUR PROJECT

1. Review your notes and photocopied or downloaded material for passages, tables, charts, or images that you regard as essential to your project. These may be the materials you will either have to quote directly or reproduce entirely in your work. Be sure you have a rationale for each direct borrowing (see Section 14a).

2. After you have drafted a version of your project, check to see that you have framed every direct quotation in some way (see Section 14b) or provided an appropriate label or title for any table, chart, or figure. Remember that no borrowed element should simply be dropped into the paper without an explanation or context.

3. Review every point of entry into a quotation for readability. Be sure that reading is not disrupted by a shift in verb tense, person, or sentence structure (see Section 14e). Revise your frame or modify the quotation appropriately to make any difficult passage more readable.

Sample Bibliography with Positioning Information and Sample Quotes

By the time you have reached this point in the research process, you should have found a substantial number of resources, kept track of their bibliographic information, positioned them carefully, and mined them for appropriate quotes and information. On individual sheets of paper or word processed documents, you will have detailed summaries, annotations, and direct quotes such as these that you will later be able to incorporate into a draft of your final project:

```
Rief, Linda. Seeking Diversity. Portsmouth: Heinemann,
     1992.

     Linda Rief, a middle school language arts teacher,
     takes an idealistic point of view about writing and
     language instruction, grounded in her longtime
     experience in the classroom. She strongly objects to
     standardized testing and does whatever she can to
     subvert its demands. She seems frustrated by the
     meaningless tasks asked of students by test
     questions. Her many years of experience as a teacher
     give her the authority to speak on this issue, and
     Heinemann is a respected press for educational issues
     whose books are all subjected to rigorous scholarly
     review.

     "I expect good reading and writing, in which process
     and product are woven tightly into literate
     tapestries of wonder and awe" (10).

     "I cannot immerse my students in literature I don't
     like, anymore than any of us can write effectively on
     topics in which we have little interest" (19).

     Her replacement for a meaningless writing topic:
     "Write about anything you care deeply about. Try to
     convince the reader how much you care" (121).
```

Shaughnessy, Anne. "Teaching to the Test: Sometimes a Good
Practice." English Journal 83 (Apr. 1994): 54-56.

Anne Shaughnessy, a longtime teacher, discusses how
she prepared her eighth-grade students to take the
Florida Writing Assessment Test. She definitely does
not think that a single score on a single
standardized test is an adequate measure of students'
writing ability, but she tries to find a way to make
the test meaningful to students. She demonstrates how
their own criteria for good writing are reflected in
the test's scoring rubric and has them apply it to
their own writing. English Journal is a peer-reviewed
publication of the National Council of Teachers of
English and likely reflects the perspective of many
middle- and secondary-school teachers across the
country. Articles published in this journal are
rarely, if ever, complimentary to standardized
testing.

"Clearly I was teaching to the test, but I was also
introducing activities that extended rather than
displaced the writing curriculum" (56).

IV

Developing the Project

Don't miss . . .

- **The questions for reflecting on what you have in Chapter 15.** Don't rush into the final stages of your project before you're ready. Take a few moments to gauge what you've done and what you still need to do.

- **The strategies for organizing your material in Section 17b.** Tailor the organization of your project to fit your rhetorical goals.

- **The discussion of audience in Section 18b.** Thinking about your audience will help you decide what information to include in your project and how to present it.

- **The advice about visiting the writing center in Chapter 18.** Your campus writing center is a valuable resource. Take advantage of the feedback and suggestions that writing consultants can provide.

Technology Spotlight

WORD PROCESSORS

The term *word processing* was coined by IBM in 1964, the same year that ASCII (American Standard Code for Information Interchange) was adopted as a standard for electronic character data, but *word processing* meant something very different in the 1960s. In that decade, word processors were little more than electric typewriters with specialized tape recorders mounted on the side. Controlled by a series of coded pulses recorded on tape, the typewriters could produce form letters automatically, but they were difficult to program and extremely limited in what they could do.

By the late 1970s, however, the personal computer had forever changed our notions of word processing and led us into a new era of document design. The first true word-processing program, *Electric Pencil*, was written by Michael Shrayer in 1976, but the first commercially successful word processor was *WordStar*, written for the CP/M operating system by Rob Barnaby three years later. *WordStar* allowed on-screen typing, editing, and revising, and documents could be stored in electronic form on floppy disks or printed out on 9-pin impact printers.

Modern word processing software allows users to create documents that rival those created by professionals.

Today, with programs like *Microsoft Word* and *Word Perfect* at our disposal, we can easily manipulate fonts, change margins, create templates, incorporate graphics, type form letters, and even link parts of our documents to databases. Yet the options and flexibility this new technology provides do not affect the basic work that writers must do: a project must still be well researched, well organized, and well written. Pretty pictures and fancy fonts won't make up for inadequate work; you need to craft your project carefully.

CHAPTER
15

Reflecting on What You Have

Now that you have taken your first good pass through the research process and gathered a comprehensive assortment of materials on your topic, you will probably have a good feeling for what kinds of resources are available, what the major issues are, and how well the information you've found is likely to fit into your research project. Before you move into the next phase of the project, though, step back, take a critical look at what you've got, and consider what—if anything—you may still need. This is when you should assess the scope and balance of your materials. Are they sufficient to support your research hypothesis? Do they come from sources that your readers will respect? Do they present opposing views fairly? Do you need to revise your original position or purpose based on what you have learned? You should consider these questions carefully now so you don't find yourself in the awkward position of having to backtrack when your project is reaching its final stages.

15a Consider whether you need to do more research

Look at the material you've collected on your topic, particularly the material and resources that relate directly to your research hypothesis. How comprehensive are they? Do your resources provide you with both a broad overview of the subject area and a detailed look at the specific topic you're researching? In the case of standardized testing, for example, you would probably want to have information about the history of standardized testing, general commentaries on its educational benefits and drawbacks, as well as articles and research studies that focus on the specific effects that testing has on classroom curricula and teaching. In order to write convincingly about the little picture, you need to know what the big picture looks like (and vice versa). Examine your materials and ask yourself these questions:

- Do my materials give me a sense of the larger subject area in which my project is based?

- Do I have a sufficient number of studies and articles that focus specifically on my research topic?
- Do I have a sufficient number of studies and articles on my topic to support my hypothesis?
- Does the information I've gathered come primarily from reputable authorities my readers will accept?
- Have I gathered my information from an appropriate range of print, online, and other resources?
- Are there other avenues of research or published resources my readers would expect me to include?

If your answers to these questions leave you with lingering doubts about the completeness of your research, you will probably want to continue your investigations until you can answer the questions more confidently.

15.1

15b Consider whether you have a fair balance of sources and opinions

Look again at the reviewing and positioning you did in Chapter 12 and think about the results in terms of rhetorical balance. Do virtually all the articles, Web sites, and book chapters you've uncovered take basically the same position or talk about the subject in the same way? If so, then you should probably return to your research to look specifically for views, perspectives, and opinions that express alternative points of view. It doesn't matter if you're researching brake pedal design, the Napoleonic wars, Ebonics, standardized testing, or the number of African swallows it takes to carry a coconut; there are always points of disagreement, and there are always resources to be found where those disagreements are expressed. Sometimes a little creativity with the key terms you use in search engines (see Chapter 6) can turn up different perspectives; sometimes Web sites will provide links to pages that express positions you might not expect. You might even ask friends or instructors to look over your hypothesis, evidence, and arguments and come up with every possible objection they can to your posi-

Take the time to think about what you have learned about your topic. Consider how your ideas have changed or developed.

tion. If nothing else, they may be able to help you see gaps in your research or points you'll need to address in your project that you hadn't thought of.

Remember, to be fair and ethical in your research and to be persuasive to your audience, you will need to show respect for other voices and other opinions. If you find that you've been favoring one position unjustly, you'll want to do a bit more research to balance your approach. Your reference librarian should be able to point you to resources you can use to identify and locate diverse points of view, particularly on controversial subjects. Several publications specialize in oppositional views: *Current Controversies*, *Ideas in Conflict*, and the aptly named *Opposing Viewpoints* series.

15c Consider whether you need to revise your purpose

One of the most rewarding—and occasionally frustrating—aspects of research is that you learn a tremendous amount about your topic. It's rewarding because you expand your knowledge, and it can be frustrating because sometimes the things you learn will contradict the beliefs you started out with. This isn't unusual; in fact it's a validation of the purpose for doing research in the first place: to discover the truth as revealed by the evidence. Reflect on what you've learned in researching and reading about your topic and gauge whether your beliefs or opinions have changed since you began. Do you see the topic in a different light now? Have the things you've learned altered your perceptions in any way? Are you beginning to feel that your original purpose for the research project is changing, that maybe a different focus or a different approach or a different research question might work better? If you find yourself answering yes to any of these questions, then you may want to consider revising your purpose.

Imagine that you began a research project on standardized testing, intending to see it as a question of cause and effect (see Section 3d), setting out to assess its effects on classroom instruction. As you conduct your research, however, you find a lot of disputes over just exactly what "standardized testing" is. Some people talk about national tests, some about state tests, and some about tests at individual schools. Some people talk about multiple choice tests, and others talk about essay tests. The more you read, the more you might realize that what's really needed is a clearer definition of "standardized testing." If that's the case, you may find that you want to revise your purpose from a question of cause and effect to a question of definition (see Section 3b).

Don't be afraid to modify your purpose at this point. This is just the right time to do it—when you have all your materials in front of you, before you start to organize and draft your project.

15d Consider whether you need to refine your claim

Sometimes when you conduct research you find that your original topic—the one you felt would be limited and easily manageable—turns out to be larger and more complex than you thought. A research project on the Bay of Pigs incident in 1963, for instance, might seem to be a narrow, well-focused topic for investigation. Once you get into the research, however, you may find yourself immersed in articles about the Cold War,

United States policy toward Cuba, Cuban exiles and refugees, and President John F. Kennedy's relationship with Fidel Castro. Even those articles that center on the day of the invasion itself could point in many directions, with widely varying opinions about what happened and who was responsible. Suddenly your narrow topic has broadened considerably, and you need to refine that topic further.

When you find yourself in this position, don't despair! In the next chapter we show you strategies you can employ to make your topic manageable again. While it's certainly easy to be sidetracked by new discoveries and research topics only slightly related to your subject, you have to know when to stop doing research and move on to the next phase of your project.

⟲ FOCUS ON . . . Toulmin Logic

Toulmin logic, named after Stephen Toulmin, a British logician and philosopher, is a method for structuring arguments. Basically, it divides an argument into three parts: the *claim*, the *grounds*, and the *warrant*.

CLAIM	Your main point or assertion.
GROUNDS	The facts or evidence on which your claim is based.
WARRANT	The link between your claim and the grounds on which it is based. To be effective, a warrant must be something you can expect your reader to know or believe.

In order to prove your *claim*, you must present the *grounds* on which you base your claim, connected by a *warrant* with which your reader will agree. Warrants are often left unstated in arguments, but they are always there nonetheless. If your warrant is arguable, however, then your claim will remain ungrounded—that is, unproven—until you prove your warrant by providing *backing*. You may also need to *qualify* your claim. In the following example, the writer does not assert that Mina *will* do well in college; instead, the claim is qualified by the word *should*.

15.2

Claim	Warrant	Grounds
Mina should do well in college.	Working at a restaurant is good preparation for college.	She has worked at her parents' restaurant for six years.
⬆	**Backing**	
	Restaurant workers must work under pressure and juggle several tasks at once—skills that are necessary for success in college courses.	

WWW Web Sites Worth Knowing

15.3

- "Revising"—University of Arizona Library,
  http://www.library.arizona.edu/rio/write8.html

- Library Resources for Opposing Viewpoints—New England Institute of Technology,
  http://library.neit.edu/argument.htm

- "The Toulmin Method," Colorado State University Writing Center,
  http://writing.colostate.edu/references/reading/toulmin/index.cfm

GETTING INVOLVED

1. Read an opinion piece on the editorial or op-ed page of your local newspaper or on an issue-oriented Web site. How does the type of writing in this piece differ from that in a research project such as yours? How much research does the author appear to have done? Has attention been paid to alternative viewpoints? Are they handled fairly? In what way might opinion pieces such as these be shaped by the medium they appear in?

2. Collect a list of statements or beliefs from your classmates that you think no one could reasonably disagree with—"Pleasure is preferable to pain" and "People should have savings accounts," for instance. Then create a list of arguments or reasons in support of the opposite point of view. How can you make these arguments seem equally reasonable? Where would you go to find supportive evidence? Share these arguments and sources with your class.

MANAGING YOUR PROJECT

1. Review the list of possible purposes for a research project (see Chapter 3) and compose research questions or hypotheses for each purpose that your research findings might be able to address. Which of these purposes seems the most interesting to you now? the most manageable? the most relevant to you or your community? Gauge whether you are still satisfied with your original purpose or if an alternative approach might be preferable.

2. Divide a sheet of paper into two columns. In one column list all the evidence, arguments, and resources in support of your research question or hypothesis; in the other column list all the information and resources that argue against your position or that hold an alternative view. Do the two columns seem unbalanced? If they seem clearly uneven, you might want to do additional research to shore up the weaker side. If they are almost perfectly balanced, you might want to consider revising or qualifying your claim to accommodate the perspectives of the other side.

3. What is the relationship between the "big picture" (overall context) and the "little picture" (specific topic) in your research project? Has your research provided you with enough background information to show readers why your project is important to a larger community? Conversely, do you have enough specific information to answer the particular research question you've posed for yourself? If you feel something is lacking in one or the other of these areas, you should do further research to fill in the gaps.

CHAPTER

16

Refining
Your Claim

In most cases you'll want to narrow the scope of your project early in the writing process and give it a design that reinforces clear, though not necessarily simple, points. Some projects will support specific thesis statements or arguments; others may explore alternatives to the status quo or offer proposals to solve problems; still others might invite readers to join in a conversation. Your role is to create whatever framework will work to make your project an effective response to the original assignment. This shaping must be deliberate and strategic. In a research project, you usually can't rely on chance to bring the parts together.

16a Be sure you have a point to make

It doesn't matter whether your research supports a report, an argument, a Web site, or a series of online conversations; you need to have a point and a purpose. But don't be surprised if you (and your co-authors in collaborative work) have uncertainties about that purpose throughout the research process. All the while you're reading, responding, taking notes, and conducting surveys or interviews, you should be testing your preliminary assumptions and objectives. As we've indicated in previous chapters, you may want to revise your original purpose or rethink your initial focus based on what you learn from your research. Use the checklist on page 187 to test potential theses or project ideas against the material you are reading or gathering.

16b Grab your reader's attention

For many writers, developing a significant point or thesis is the real challenge of a research project. The thesis is the claim you make as the result of your research, the answer to your research question or the confirmation of your original hypothesis (see

CHECKLIST

Evaluating Your Thesis

If the purpose of your research project is primarily argumentative—that is, if its thesis makes a strong claim about where you stand on an issue and supports that position with evidence from your research—then you should ask:

○ Does the project focus on a substantial issue that deserves readers' attention?

○ Does the project focus on a debatable issue?

○ Will the issue affect or interest your audience?

○ Will readers understand how the issue affects them?

○ Does the information you are finding support your hypothesis or research claim?

○ Are you using information from your sources to support your own claim, or are you merely repeating a claim made by others?

○ Do you need to qualify your hypothesis and claim? In other words, would it make more sense to say your position or approach is true under *some* rather than *all* circumstances?

If the purpose of your research project is primarily informational—that is, if it intends to educate your audience and deepen its understanding of an issue by presenting the results of your research—then you should ask:

○ Does the project focus on a substantial issue that deserves readers' attention?

○ Does the project focus on an issue or a topic that your readers are presently unfamiliar with?

○ Will the issue affect or interest your audience?

○ Will readers understand how the issue affects them?

○ Does the project present information your audience is not likely to know?

○ Are you using sources to supplement your own presentation, or are you relying on them too heavily?

○ Do you need to narrow the scope of your project to keep from being too general or too lengthy and detailed?

WWW

16.1

Chapter 15). It is tempting to rely on thesis statements that only break huge research ideas into smaller parts because the material then seems easy to organize:

> Child abuse is a serious problem with three major aspects: causes, detection, and prevention.

> Some scientists favor human exploration of the planet Mars while others think robots can do a better job.

> Common types of white-collar crime are embezzlement, mail fraud, and insurance fraud.

Just as the artist pictured here seeks to shape the clay, you need to find the shape of your project from among the myriad of ideas you have discovered.

Simple classifications like these can work well when you need to divide issues or ideas into their components—as you might when designing a Web site home page or a brochure—but for research projects that make arguments, theses that just break an idea into parts can seem more like shopping lists than engagements with compelling ideas. The breadth of the statements deadens the argument by preventing readers (and writers too) from considering underlying concepts—for example, how child abuse might be prevented if we could understand what causes it, or why white-collar crime poses a threat to the work ethic. When issues are laid out piece by piece, readers can lose a sense of what connects them.

One way to avoid such loose structures is to focus on problems and conflicts connected to your life or community. Look for claims that demand the attention of readers and that place a burden on you to provide convincing supporting evidence.

> TENTATIVE THESIS   Students who read extensively may perform no better on academic achievement tests than those who hardly read at all.

You may quickly learn that the point you're developing can't be supported by reliable studies. If that's so, share this discovery with readers.

> FINAL THESIS   If you think you can do well on achievement tests without cracking a book, you're flat wrong.

Ask basic questions about your topic, particularly *how* and *why*. Get to the heart of a matter in defining a topic. Examine issues that affect people.

> LIFELESS   Child abuse is a serious problem with three major aspects: causes, detection, and prevention.

> CHALLENGING   Prosecutors in some communities have based charges of child abuse on types of hearsay evidence that now receive tougher scrutiny from judges.

> LIFELESS   Common types of white-collar crime are embezzlement, bank fraud, and insurance fraud.

CHALLENGING   White-collar crime is rarely punished severely because many people think that misdeeds aimed at institutions are less serious than
crimes against people.

🔅 FOCUS ON . . . **Refining Your Claim**

Refining your original claim can sometimes be difficult, particularly when you have invested a good deal of time thinking about and researching your topic. You may feel discouraged at the thought of having to start again with a new thesis. Take heart. Revising
your thesis doesn't mean climbing a new mountain; it means you're at the top of a
mountain and deciding on the best route to get to where you already are! Here's a short
list of ways to help you refine your claim:

- What issues or questions keep coming up over and over again in your research? What do other writers seem to be focusing on? You might pick one
  or two of these more specific issues as the central point of a revised thesis.
- Where are most disagreements coming from? Find a critical point of the debate and take your stand on that point alone.
- Look for broad terms in your original thesis (standardized testing, the
  young, cloning) and break them into smaller parts (*cloning*: human cloning,
  animal cloning, body-parts cloning, etc.). Use one of these subcategories as
  the central topic of your revised thesis.

16c Limit your claim

The more you learn about a subject, the more careful you're likely to be in making
claims. The thesis that eventually guides your project will almost certainly be more specific, restrictive, and informative than your initial research question or hypothesis. If
nothing else, the thesis itself or the paragraph surrounding it should address questions
such as *who, what, when, where, under what conditions, with what limits, with what scope?*

Remember that no matter what sort of research project you are putting together,
you will be making a series of linked claims. The biggest of these claims will be the thesis, the claim that provides the foundation and purpose for your entire project. But a
thesis cannot stand alone; it is invariably supported by subclaims you will make—and
support—along the way. These subclaims will often appear as topic sentences of paragraphs (or other guideposts such as the headings of Web pages, pamphlets, or information sheets), and they should relate clearly to the thesis and be equally specific.

The shape you give a project will depend on what your thesis promises. One way
to understand that commitment is to recall the point of your research inquiry (see
Chapter 3). Does it ultimately involve a claim of *fact*, a claim of *definition*, a claim of
value, a claim of *cause*, or a claim of *policy*? You'll want to refine your thesis to make a
distinct and limited claim and then follow through with the appropriate support and
evidence.

16.2

ORIGINAL CLAIM OF *FACT*

AIDS is the greatest killer of the young.

CLAIM SPECIFIED AND LIMITED BY RESEARCH

In the United States, AIDS has recently replaced automobile accidents as the leading cause of death among teenagers.

COMMITMENTS
- Present figures on mortality rates among young people.
- Find figures on deaths from auto accidents.
- Find figures on deaths from AIDS.
- Draw out the implications of the studies for AIDS prevention.

ORIGINAL CLAIM OF *DEFINITION*

Zoos constitute cruelty to animals.

CLAIM SPECIFIED AND LIMITED BY RESEARCH

Confining large marine mammals in sea parks for public amusement is, arguably, a form of cruelty to animals.

COMMITMENTS
- Define specific criteria for "cruelty."
- Examine what experts say about the condition of animals in marine parks or do fieldwork in such a park.
- Find statistics on animal health in and out of marine parks.
- Show that conditions in marine parks meet or do not meet criteria for "cruelty to animals."

ORIGINAL CLAIM OF *VALUE*

Frankenstein is one of the most influential books of all time.

CLAIM SPECIFIED AND LIMITED BY RESEARCH

Because of its strong technological elements and its focus on the moral questions that accompany any new scientific achievement or discovery, Mary Shelley's *Frankenstein* is considered to be the first great work of science fiction, one that had a lasting impact on that literary genre.

COMMITMENTS
- Examine the work of scholars who study and define science fiction.
- Demonstrate that the features which define science fiction as a genre appear in *Frankenstein*.
- Present statements from literary scholars and current science fiction writers attesting to the book's influence.

ORIGINAL CLAIM OF *CAUSE*

Higher speed limits are not the cause of increased traffic deaths.

CLAIM SPECIFIED AND LIMITED BY RESEARCH

The general gradual rise in traffic deaths is not due to recent higher speed limits on interstate and limited-access highways.

COMMITMENTS
- Provide accurate facts on increase in traffic deaths.
- Explain where, when, and by how much speed limits have increased.
- Refute the inference that the rate of traffic deaths has risen uniformly on four-lane, limited-access highways.
- Present other potential causes for any observed increase—including increases in travel, number of vehicles and drivers, road rage.

ORIGINAL CLAIM OF *POLICY*
Standardized testing should be eliminated in schools.

CLAIM SPECIFIED AND LIMITED BY RESEARCH
Standardized tests should not be used as measures of school performance because they discriminate against poor school districts and fail to measure student learning adequately.

COMMITMENTS
- Demonstrate the relationship between test scores and school funding.
- Show the limited range of skills and knowledge measured by standardized tests.
- Offer an alternative proposal to show how such tests could be used fairly.
- Defend the advantages and feasibility of the proposal.

One result of thinking about your project in terms of its thesis, claims, and commitments at this stage is that you will begin to get a sense of the structure you need to develop as you organize your project. Considering how to introduce the topic, what background information to provide, what order your points should be presented in, and which pieces of evidence should be included will be key to the success of your project and the effect it will have on your audience. In the next chapter we examine useful rhetorical strategies for organizing research materials.

WWW Web Sites Worth Knowing

- "Developing a Thesis Statement"—University of Illinois Writers' Workshop, **http://www.english.uiuc.edu/cws/wworkshop/advice/developing_a_thesis.htm**
- "Thesis Construction"—TeachWeb at the University of Pennsylvania, **http://www.english.upenn.edu/Grad/Teachweb/thesis.html**

WWW
16.3

GETTING INVOLVED

1. Study the table of contents of a textbook or a major reference tool (one that is not arranged alphabetically). How is the volume arranged? What are its major divisions and subdivisions? Can you appreciate why the book is arranged as it is? Can you imagine alternative arrangements?

2. Working with a team, gather as many examples as you can of claims that are carefully qualified. You can look everywhere, from editorial columns in newspapers to toothpaste packages. What different purposes do these qualifications serve? Summarize your findings in a brief report for all your classmates.

● MANAGING YOUR PROJECT

1. Can you connect your project in some way to your world or local community? Why should readers care about what you have discovered? How will they benefit, directly or indirectly? Consider how you can give your project significance.

2. What limits on your thesis can help make your project both more true to the facts you are uncovering and more manageable? Write out your thesis fully, stating both your claim and supporting reasons. Then either add the necessary qualifications or note the qualifications already in the statement.

3. How would you characterize your project and thesis: are you making a claim of *fact, definition, value, cause,* or *policy?* Or does your project fall between categories, combine them, or fit in another realm entirely? (Review Chapter 3 on these categories.) If you are unable to categorize the nature of your claim, it may be because your claim is either changing or still unfocused. This might be a time to ask an instructor or your colleagues for suggestions.

4. What commitments does your project make? Writers sometimes underestimate what they have to explain to readers, especially in setting the context for their work and providing background information (or helpful links to related works). Be honest with yourself about enumerating the commitments your work involves. If necessary, plan more research to meet those expectations.

Organizing Your Project

From the humblest two-page research report to the most complex Web site, structure matters. Structure helps readers move purposefully from point to point in a project—whether they are heading in straight lines as they usually do in most papers or blazing paths of their own through the nodes of a Web site.

Organizing a project might seem easy. We even have the classic academic design for papers, the five-paragraph essay, that looks like a model of clarity. Make a statement in an introductory paragraph, prove it with at least three paragraphs of supporting evidence, tack on a conclusion, and you've got a paper.

> Introduction: Thesis
>> Argument 1 + examples/illustrations
>> Argument 2 + examples/illustrations
>> Argument 3 + examples/illustrations
> Conclusion

Unfortunately, a statement isn't proven just because you can line up three ideas in a row to support it. Three or more reasons can be marshaled in favor of most propositions, and using such a pattern of organization can produce sheer nonsense:

THESIS: LARGE DOSES OF RADIATION MUST BE BENEFICIAL TO HUMAN HEALTH.
- Atomic power produces useful energy.
- Energy powers satellites.
- Radiation is used to cure cancer.

You may feel like you're putting together an impossible jigsaw puzzle as you attempt to make the pieces of your project fit together. You may need to reconsider the structure and organization of your project now so you will not be tempted to force information where it does not fit.

These "supporting arguments" aren't related to the main point or to each other, and they certainly don't prove that radiation in large doses is good for people. Yet some writers will believe that they have done their jobs just because they have corralled ideas into a similar five-paragraph structure.

When organizing research materials, you want a plan that reflects the complexity of your ideas while serving your readers' need for clarity; no single formula will work for all your projects.

17a Create a blueprint for your project

The design of your paper, brochure, Web site, or other project may initially be too rough to offer the precise lines and dimensions blueprints typically offer, but you do need to sketch out a shape of some kind. For a paper, that shape may be a scratch outline that does no more than list what you know you must cover.

I. Thesis
II. Background information
III. Claim
IV. Evidence
V. Conclusion

The equivalent of a scratch outline for a Web project or brochure might be a *storyboard,* a drawing that positions the major features or elements of a design. Scratch outlines and storyboards help you set large-scale priorities in arranging and positioning information.

Organizing your research effort means deciding what parts or features a project must have and in what order they'll appear. At least five priorities will typically compete for your attention.

Logical order. You will want material to follow a pattern that seems coherent to readers, with claims and reasons backed by evidence. Or you may want to enforce some other logical pattern of induction or deduction. Readers should have the impression that ideas are being presented thoroughly, fairly, and systematically. Even a simple division of a topic into its component parts represents a logical order—the kind you might use in a Web site or field report.

Chronological order. In some cases the structure of a project will follow a sequence: *first, second, third; beginning, middle, end; step 1, step 2, step 3.* Portions of a project may follow chronological order even when the rest of the work doesn't. For example, a section at the beginning of a technical report might review what other researchers have had to say on the subject, beginning with the oldest sources and working up to the most recent.

Order defined by genre. In some cases the structure of a project will be determined for you by precedent or professional guidelines. This will be the case with laboratory or research reports in many fields. Even items as simple as email messages or business letters have structures dictated by conventions that you violate at your own risk.

Order of importance or significance. In some projects, especially papers that present arguments, you may need to present the most compelling evidence near the end of the presentation where readers will remember it. Questions of significance may similarly arise when you have to decide whether information belongs in the body of a paper, in notes, or in an appendix. With a Web site, order of significance may play a major role in determining what goes on the home page and how "deep" the site goes. Readers should be able to find important information with just a few clicks.

Order of interest. Depending on your purpose, interest may be a consideration in arranging material. You may decide that it is necessary to present important information early just to keep readers involved. In a Web site or a brochure, you may decide to forgo the most logical arrangement in order to present an appealing face.

It's up to you to manage these competing interests as you create a design for your work. **17.1**

17b Consider general patterns of organization

Projects that prove a thesis can be organized in various ways, and your choice of organizational pattern will depend on your topic, your hypothesis, the evidence you've gathered, and the effect you want to have on your audience. Each piece of writing will have its own unique structure, but some research hypotheses will lend themselves to common organizational patterns. You may want to consider adopting or modifying one of them to fit the needs of your own project. The following patterns may be useful when your project builds a connected sequence of arguments, makes an evaluation, establishes a cause-and-effect chain, or proposes a solution to a problem.

Connected sequence of arguments. In a connected sequence of arguments, each claim is based on the one that precedes it: "If *X* is so, then *Y* is true, and if *Y* is true, then so is *Z*." A structure of this kind presents arguments that build on each other. You cannot remove any portion of such a structure without demolishing the whole.

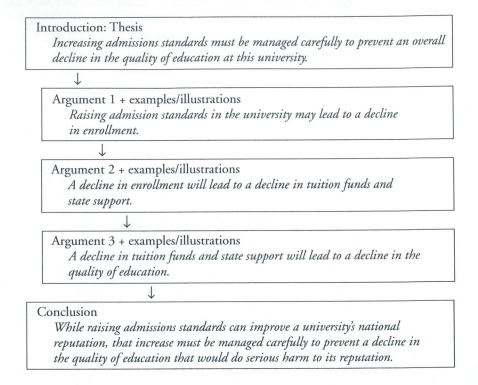

Introduction: Thesis
Increasing admissions standards must be managed carefully to prevent an overall decline in the quality of education at this university.

↓

Argument 1 + examples/illustrations
Raising admission standards in the university may lead to a decline in enrollment.

↓

Argument 2 + examples/illustrations
A decline in enrollment will lead to a decline in tuition funds and state support.

↓

Argument 3 + examples/illustrations
A decline in tuition funds and state support will lead to a decline in the quality of education.

↓

Conclusion
While raising admissions standards can improve a university's national reputation, that increase must be managed carefully to prevent a decline in the quality of education that would do serious harm to its reputation.

This pattern of organization is potentially more complex than the basic five-paragraph essay because each part of the project depends on its connection to a previous part, not to the thesis statement alone. However, the axiom that a chain is only as strong as its weakest link also applies here. A writer has to be sure that readers follow the chain of evidence from link to link, so strong transitions are essential.

Evaluations. Similar organizational patterns may seem simple in outline but will grow in complexity as you fill in the blanks. When your project involves evaluating something, you know the project has to fulfill certain commitments:

- To provide a rationale for the evaluation
- To establish criteria for making evaluative judgments
- To measure the subject against the standards
- To provide evidence that the standards are or are not met

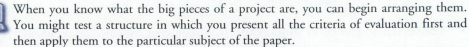

When you know what the big pieces of a project are, you can begin arranging them. You might test a structure in which you present all the criteria of evaluation first and then apply them to the particular subject of the paper.

17.2

Introduction: What's being evaluated
This evaluation judges whether standardized testing produces the positive results its advocates claim.

↓

Criteria for evaluation presented

Criterion 1
Standardized testing should fully measure student abilities.

Criterion 2
Standardized testing should lead to improvements in low-performing schools.

Criterion 3
Standardized testing should lead to improvements in teaching.

↓

Evaluation/judgment of subject

By criterion 1
Standardized tests measure only a limited range of student abilities, but do not measure these abilities very well.

Evidence/counterevidence

By criterion 2
Standardized tests only confirm that poorly funded schools have poor student achievement. These results do not lead to additional funding to improve the schools that need it most.

Evidence/counterevidence

By criterion 3
The pressure put on teachers to improve their students' standardized test scores discourages creativity and drives many of the best teachers out of the profession.

Evidence

↓

Conclusion
High-stakes standardized testing achieves none of the goals its advocates claim and may in fact worsen the situation for many schools and teachers. For these reasons, a strong emphasis on standardized test scores as the basis for rewarding or punishing school systems seems misguided.

Should you decide that readers will be able to follow your evaluation argument more easily if you explain individual criteria of evaluation in the same part of the paper where they are applied, you would craft a different outline.

Introduction: What's being evaluated
This evaluation judges whether standardized testing produces the positive results its advocates claim.

↓

Evaluation of the subject

Criterion 1
Standardized testing should fully measure student abilities, but tests measure only a limited range, and do not even measure these abilities very well.

Evidence/counterevidence

Criterion 2
Standardized testing should lead to improvements in low-performing schools, but it only confirms that poorly funded schools have poor student achievement. These results do not lead to additional funding to improve the schools that need it most.

Evidence/counterevidence

Criterion 3
Standardized testing should lead to improvements in teaching, but the pressure put on teachers to improve their students' standardized test scores discourages creativity and drives many of the best teachers out of the profession.

Evidence/counterevidence

↓

Conclusions
High-stakes standardized testing achieves none of the goals its advocates claim and may in fact worsen the situation for many schools and teachers. For these reasons, a strong emphasis on standardized test scores as the basis for rewarding or punishing school systems seems misguided.

Which pattern will work best? That's a question you alone can answer, knowing the purpose of your work, your audience, your evidence, your medium, and your own preferences.

Cause and effect. A project that examines a cause-and-effect question offers similar structural options. Once again, you'd begin by determining the project's major components. The typical cause-and-effect paper will probably make at least two major commitments:

- To examine a phenomenon or event
- To explore causes and effects of the event

The first part of such a project might introduce the phenomenon or situation the project will explore, explaining it in some detail by answering the questions *who, what, where, when.* The bulk of the project will then be concerned with interpreting the phenomenon, probably answering the question *why.*

Effect(s)
    The current recession in the U.S. economy.

↓

Cause 1
    A tax rebate that wiped out the previous budget surplus and increased the national debt.

Cause 2
    Uncertainty caused by the election of a new president.

Cause 3
    The dotcom bust: many new Internet companies with inflated stock prices failing.

Cause 4
    A drop in consumer confidence as a result of terrorist attacks.

This arrangement is solid and simple, yet it still might require rearranging the causes from the most obvious, specific, or noncontroversial to the more subtle, abstract, and challenging ones.

Effect(s)
    The current recession in the U.S. economy.

↓

Cause 1   Most obvious
    The dotcom bust: many new Internet companies with inflated stock prices failing.

Cause 2
    A tax rebate that wiped out the previous budget surplus and increased the national debt.

Cause 3
    A drop in consumer confidence as a result of terrorist attacks.

Cause 4   Least obvious, "deepest"
    Uncertainty caused by the election of a new president.

Proposals. Sometimes the components of a project don't fall to hand as easily as they do for evaluative or cause-and-effect projects. That's often the case when you are proposing a solution for a problem. The project will likely have several parts, each organized by a different principle. You might have to explain the history of a problem, evaluate the seriousness of the situation, explain the causes of the current situation, enumerate alternatives, and argue for your own solution. Each of these considerations might require its own section of the project. Again, you'd want to set down the essential components of the paper and arrange them in a coherent order based on the principles described in Section 17a.

The problem
A continuing occurrence of typos and layout mistakes in the local newspaper.

History of the problem
For nearly as long as anyone can remember, the Herald *has had typos and other mistakes in every issue. The newspaper's problems have become a standing joke among members of the local community, particularly those who teach journalism at the local college.*

Causes of the problem
Small-town newspaper, underfunded, with a poorly trained staff, deadline pressures, and low standards.

Crisis: need for solution
An embarrassment to the community.

Alternatives to the current situation (rejected)

Alternative 1: advantages/disadvantages
Hire more and better proofreaders: Would solve the problem, but the newspaper's budget won't permit it.

Alternative 2: advantages/disadvantages
Rely more frequently on pretyped wire stories from the Associated Press: They'd still need to be proofread, and they wouldn't cover the local news.

Alternative 3: advantages/disadvantages
Publish less frequently: More time for proofreading, but news would be less current and subscribers might cancel.

The proposed solution
Increase subscription fees by a small percentage.

> **Explanation of solution**
> *The increased revenue would pay for additional and/or better-qualified proofreading staff.*

> **Feasibility of solution**
> *An increase in subscription rates is easy to implement and announce; the increased revenue would easily pay for a staff person; qualified people can be hired from the local college community.*

> **Disadvantages**
> *Some people might cancel their subscriptions because of increased rates.*

> **Advantages**
> *Increased professional appearance of newspaper; increased respect inside and outside the community; more people might subscribe; new job(s) created.*

> **Implementation of solution**
> *Recommendation to newspaper's board of directors, editors, and accounting department.*

In research this complex, the key points in the scratch outline may eventually become headings within the project itself.

Remember that patterns such as these are not simply "writing containers" into which your content can be poured; even when one of them looks like it will work for you, you will probably have to modify the pattern to fit your particular evidence, audience, and rhetorical goals.

17c Accommodate dissenting voices

In many projects you must deal with opposing arguments by presenting them fairly and strategically. If you don't acknowledge them, your project may seem unbalanced, uninformed, or narrow. So the structure of your project must accommodate contrary or alternative opinions, and it must deal with them. This is not just a matter of dividing positions into "those in favor" and "those against." Most debatable issues offer a range of positions, and most problems have a variety of solutions; you will need to recognize these positions and demonstrate why your position is the more reasonable, logical, or preferable one. You do this by using *counterargument*. Counterarguments can be explored anywhere in a project, though generally it is better not to conclude with objections to your thesis because readers often recall best what they have read last. Here are two sample scratch outlines that take counterarguments into account; the first deals with all objections to a thesis at once and the second deals with objections one by one.

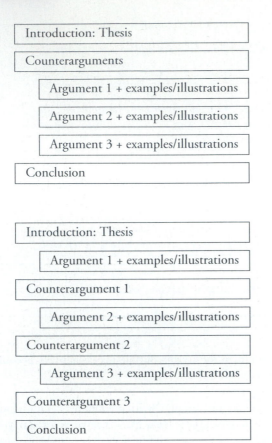

Introduction: Thesis

Counterarguments

> Argument 1 + examples/illustrations

> Argument 2 + examples/illustrations

> Argument 3 + examples/illustrations

Conclusion

Introduction: Thesis

> Argument 1 + examples/illustrations

Counterargument 1

> Argument 2 + examples/illustrations

Counterargument 2

> Argument 3 + examples/illustrations

Counterargument 3

Conclusion

Notice that these models suggest that all components of an essay would receive comparable treatment. This is a distortion: in practice, you would give your best points more attention, using all the examples and illustrations you need to make your case. Minor points would receive less coverage than major ones.

17d Follow professional templates

For some projects you will have to learn and apply the conventions of organization already established within a profession or field. If you're asked to prepare a scientific research report, your project may require some or all of the following parts:

Abstract

Introduction

Review of the literature

Methods

Results

Discussion

Summary

References

Appendixes

These parts make up your organization. As you flesh out each section, you create your report. We present sample research papers following MLA manuscript format (page 261), APA format (page 384), and CMS format (page 415).

Some software will walk you through the task of creating newsletters, brochures, and other kinds of presentations. Many newer word-processing packages include templates for typical MLA and APA style reports, as well as electronic presentations for various purposes and samples of spreadsheets and databases for common uses. Before using the templates, however, make sure they conform to the requirements of your project (see Chapter 1), and learn how you can customize them to best suit your purpose.

If your project is a Web site, you will find yourself constricted by the "interfaces" of online communication—the places where you and your readers meet the computer. Just as print reports restrict readers and writers because of the technology used (that is, paper, word-processing applications—even the cost of printing—restrict the choices that authors can make), what you present will be defined by the tools available to you and the expectations readers have for Web sites and Web designs.

Even a project as seemingly open-ended as preparing a brochure will quickly be defined by certain expectations. For example, if the brochure is a sheet of paper folded into six panels, readers will expect certain information on the "cover" and other information on the back panel. They will likely peruse the sections of the brochure in a certain order, too, so you have to arrange information to meet their expectations. In all cases, readers must easily be able to grasp the logic of your design and find information they need. You will want to check with your instructor about the shape of your project; he or she may provide you with appropriate models or templates to follow. In Part V you will learn more about designing documents following professional guidelines.

With an organizational plan in place, one that reflects the purpose of the project, your audience's needs and expectations, and your personal goals, you should be ready to begin your first full draft. The research and groundwork you have done thus far should have prepared you to take this next step with confidence.

WWW Web Sites Worth Knowing

- Yale C/AIM *Web Style Guide*, **http://info.med.yale.edu/caim/manual/contents.html**
- LSU Library List of Style Manuals in Selected Scientific Disciplines, **http://www.lib.lsu.edu/sci/chem/guides/srs115.html**
- Purdue University's OWL, "Developing an Outline," **http://owl.english.purdue.edu/handouts/general/gl_outlin.html**

17.3

GETTING INVOLVED

1. Study the structure of a half-hour television news program such as the nightly news shows on the networks, the hourly news programs on cable outlets (CNN, Fox, MSNBC), and the weekly Sunday morning political forums on all the major networks. You may need to watch a program several times to grasp its underlying design. Note what comes first in the show, where commercials are typically placed, how credits are presented, how the program typically closes. Once you have uncovered the structure of the program, consider how that design shapes the way news is being presented to viewers. What do viewers see—and not see? How does the program separate what is supposedly important news from what is less significant? What does the regularity of the structure do for (and to) viewers of the news?

2. Find a lengthy report or news article, copy it, and then underscore or highlight every paragraph, sentence, phrase, or word that might be considered transitional (defining the term broadly). Hand the piece to a second and even a third reader to hunt for transitional devices you may have missed. When you are satisfied that all transitions have been discovered, estimate what percentage of the entire piece is working to move readers from one thought to another.

MANAGING YOUR PROJECT

1. Create scratch outlines or storyboards for your overall project. Identify the major divisions of your work—the four or five divisions under which all information might be organized. Don't settle too quickly on a single design; try alternatives. Be sure to examine these tentative outlines (or storyboards) from the point of view of readers coming to your project with no idea of what you may be doing.

2. Once you have settled on the major divisions of your project, prepare a more formal outline or sketch that subdivides each of the major headings into component parts. You may discover places where a traditional paper might repeat itself or where a Web site might run into navigational problems (such as dead ends, where users might not understand how to return to a main page). It's easier to see opportunities and to eliminate problems at this stage than to revise a project that has been fully drafted or constructed.

3. If you have kept your notes on cards, you might now lay out the entire project. Create note cards for all your major heads and subheads, then arrange your other cards under those headings in the order you expect to follow in the project. When you have a satisfying design, "read" through it as you might a paper, imagining the transitional paragraphs, sentences, and words you might employ. Modify the design as you see fit. Many writers find that laying out their projects on cards in this way helps them keep their thoughts organized.

CHAPTER

18

Drafting and Revising Your Project

There comes a moment in every major research project when the work *really* begins. You'll recognize the moment because it often takes so much effort to reach that point and then to push beyond it. You need to have confidence in your ideas, in your hypothesis, in the thoroughness of your research, in your overall design. At this delicate moment it can be tempting to retreat into more research or reading, to promise yourself to "think about it tomorrow," to go to a movie. That's precisely when you have to gather up your confidence, your determination, and your co-authors—and push ahead. It's time to write.

18a Prepare a version of your project early

Think of the first draft as the prototype for your project. Many years before new automobiles are introduced to the public, hand-built versions are run thousands of miles on test tracks to simulate road conditions. In a similar way, a draft tests your project under demanding conditions. Will it stand up to calls for facts, evidence, logical argumentation? Will it survive potential counterarguments? Will it keep readers interested and engaged? Will readers understand references to events or people? In the illustration on page 206, for example, your readers would probably not recognize James Meredith or know what he did or how it relates to your project without a caption and a discussion of his relevance.

Plan on finishing the first version of a project, one on which you can get serious feedback from colleagues, about halfway through the time allotted for the assignment (see Chapter 1). If you have a month for a project, resolve to have a draft in hand in two weeks.

Why draft so early? You need to plan ahead because you'll want plenty of time to revise, fill in gaps, or redesign your presentation. You may have to return to the library or the Web to gather additional material, or you may need to conduct follow-up

In drafting your project, use precise language that answers basic questions readers might have. For example, readers looking at this photograph might expect a caption to identify who is pictured here (James Meredith), what he did (he changed higher education for minorities in the 1960s), and how this happened (a Supreme Court ruling enabled him to attend and graduate from the University of Mississippi).

experiments or surveys. You may need to reorganize what you have written, polish the style, improve the graphics. The more time you give yourself between your prototype and the final version, the better your project is likely to be.

Remember, too, that the final stages of producing a research project involve steps not required in other work: from doing an outline and preparing a Works Cited page to checking Web page links and graphics or tinkering with a color printer. You have to allocate time for all these activities, appreciating that something can always go wrong.

18b Draft your project for an audience

Reflecting on the needs and interests of your audience, as we've said, is important throughout your research project, but it's vital at the drafting stage. Here you will make critical choices about how to present your material, what to include, and what can be safely left out. While there are no simple charts or graphs that will allow you to determine exactly who your readers will be or exactly what they will know about your topic, you should be able to make reasonable guesses about your readership and adjust your presentation accordingly. The checklist that follows offers ways in which you can accomplish this.

CHECKLIST
Keeping Your Readership in Mind

○ **Tailor your examples, illustrations, and allusions to the group you are addressing.** With a professional audience, you can select technical sources and explain them, knowing that many concepts, theoretical assumptions, and terms will be familiar. Among experts the body of shared common knowledge will be quite large. With a less knowledgeable audience, you'll have to surround technical materials with more detailed explanations or choose less daunting evidence and examples.

○ **Write in language suited to your audience.** Language changes from audience to audience, and you'll find differences in tone, style, organization, and vocabulary in the work of writers who want to be "heard" by their various readers. To address an academic setting, you must master something vaguely described as *college writing.* Managing an academic style isn't easy when you are a novice writer beginning work in a major or a professional specialty, yet learning that professional language is one purpose of most college research projects. College writing is semiformal in tone, careful about grammar and mechanics, and scrupulous about evidence and documentation.

○ **Convince readers that your project deserves attention.** You may be certain that your subject is important, but readers presented with a paper, brochure, Web site, or other project need some reason to take notice. If you've decided (against all advice) to examine the death penalty in the United States, you'll have to provide a motive for readers to visit that shopworn subject one more time. Maybe you can offer a new angle on crime statistics, new survey information, or a newsworthy local case that might compel renewed attention. Somehow you need to give the subject *presence.* This isn't a matter of grabbing readers with sensational claims or pulsing graphics; it *is* about supplying a rationale for your work based on your own thoughtful study of an issue or a problem. The type of rationale you supply may depend on the audience you must reach: members of a professional audience will attend to your research if it promises to advance what they already know; a general audience may need more coaxing to develop an interest.

18c Present your material strategically

The organization of your research project (see Chapter 17) will guide many decisions you make about content and the coverage of your subject, but certain general principles and practices apply as you draft any project.

State ideas clearly. Explain your ideas in language as directly as the facts will allow (see also Section 18f), answering as many basic questions as readers are likely to have. Here, for example, is a topic sentence that would leave most readers puzzling over *who* is doing *what* to *whom.* It's from a paper examining the causes of an increasing pregnancy rate among teenagers.

```
The most evident and changeable factor in the pregnancy
increase in the past thirty years directly relates to the
media.
```

In this sentence you won't find an explanation for the rising pregnancy rate, only the suggestion that some evident and changeable factor *relates* to the media. *Relates* is an ambiguous verb; in what sense is this factor connected to the media? Indeed, what is the factor? The topic sentence doesn't tell you. The sentence needs to be revised to make the causal connection clear so that the project (or paragraph) that follows from it will have direction.

```
The clearest blame for the increase in teenage pregnancies in
the past thirty years belongs to the national media—newspapers,
magazines, films, and television filled daily with articles
that make teens believe that early sexual activity is both
normal and healthy.
```

That's quite an indictment. A reader might disagree with the claim, but at least he or she has something to disagree with: an argument stated clearly and directly. Who would react to the original version of the topic sentence in the same way?

Provide evidence for all key claims. You don't prove an assertion by merely restating it or contradicting it, no matter how confident you are of your views. You must analyze and argue. Show readers how you came to your judgments. If possible, give them an opportunity to arrive at similar conclusions. Consider this passage from a paper about battered spouses:

```
A common belief in society today is that spouses who put up
with beatings over a long period of time are probably
masochists who come to regard the assaults as signs of love.
This belief is obviously not true.
```

The second sentence, no doubt based on the writer's research and probably an accurate statement, carries little weight as part of an argument or proof because it is presented as a mere assertion. In fact, the first sentence is not *obviously* false; if it were, the belief would not be common. The writer needs to do more work, to provide evidence and alternative explanations for the willingness of spouses to put up with long-term abuse.

Qualify generalizations. You'll have a much easier time proving claims that are limited rather than sweeping in scope. In writing about conditions in the United States, for instance, be specific; don't assume that readers will understand what you are talking about if you haven't defined your scope:

```
Throughout history, minorities were barred from institutions of
higher learning until the civil rights movement broke those
barriers.
```

Because college audiences are likely to include international students, the claim needs to be appropriately qualified:

In the United States, minorities were barred from most
institutions of higher learning until the civil rights movement
of the 1960s broke those barriers.

Cite authorities whenever you support assertions with figures or other data. Don't expect readers to take your word for any arguable claim, and don't assume that you know what the facts are because you've heard some generalizations. Statements as sweeping as the following would need statistical backing if they were to appear in a research project:

It is a scientific fact that a marijuana cigarette kills more
brain cells than a night of free drinks on Bourbon Street.

There is no evidence that capital punishment serves as a
deterrent to crime.

Athletes perform at the same academic level as students in the
general population.

Use multiple sources to support your thesis. Readers will probably not find your project or thesis convincing if you rely heavily on a small number of sources. Your readers might think you haven't done a very good job of researching your topic; worse, they might think you are purposefully showing bias by excluding relevant information. Your audience will be far more likely to accept your claims when you provide facts and opinions from several sources that bolster your arguments rather than just one or two. Again, it doesn't matter how authoritative you think your source is—be it the *Encyclopedia of American Biography* or the King James version of the Bible—you can't assume that all members of your audience will find that source so powerfully credible or valid that they'll consider other references unnecessary.

18d Write a strong introduction and conclusion

Introductions and conclusions can sometimes be the hardest parts of a research project to write because they serve as a frame into which the contents of your research and critical thinking are poured. Introductions draw readers into a project and persuade them to keep reading; conclusions ease readers out of a project report and convince them that what they read was meaningful and worthwhile. Perhaps the most useful advice we can give you here is that you don't have to write introductions first, and you don't have to write conclusions last! For extended research projects, it often makes sense to write a draft of your conclusion at the start. That way, you'll have a reasonably clear sense of what you want to "get to" as you draft the rest of your project.

By the same reasoning, you may want to write your introduction last. After all, how can you introduce your research project effectively without knowing what appears in your final draft?

For those who are uncertain how to write an introduction or a conclusion without sounding dry and formulaic, we summarize the tried-and-true techniques that authors have been using since the time of Aristotle. You may find that one of them works for you.

SUMMARY

Strategies for Introductions

Begin with a narrative. Many professional authors will begin a piece with an attention-getting narrative or anecdote that catches their readers' attention and sparks interest in the topic. Most readers love stories, and a brief, well-told tale can draw readers in and make the topic more "real" for them.

Begin with a question or a series of questions that relate to your topic. The rhetorician Richard Whately calls this the Introduction Inquisitive, and it's intended to show readers that your subject is curious, provocative, interesting, or just plain puzzling. When you ask a question of your readers, they can't help but think about how to respond, and that draws them into your presentation.

Begin by quoting a key source. Have you come across a statement from an expert, an interview subject, or another source in your research that expresses a key issue more vividly than you could in your own words? If so, don't hesitate to begin your opening paragraph with a quote. Sometimes this quote can be set off by itself before the introductory paragraph—the quote is then called an epigraph; more often it is integrated into the introduction itself.

Begin by showing that your subject has long been neglected, misunderstood, or misrepresented. Whately refers to this as the Introduction Corrective, and it can be especially useful when you're writing about a subject that your audience thinks it knows relatively well. An introduction that begins, "Most people's assumption that standardized testing is a benign, relatively harmless procedure is contradicted by virtually all the available evidence," cannot help but increase a reader's interest.

Begin with your thesis. Sometimes you will do best to open your essay by simply telling your readers exactly what you are going to write about. Such openings work well for many papers you write in college courses, for reports you write on the job, and for many other kinds of factual, informative prose.

SUMMARY

Strategies for Conclusions

Summarize the main points you have made. Often you'll want to bring your paper to a close by reemphasizing your main points. When you do this, however, avoid merely repeating what you have said in the same words or sounding like you can't think of anything else to do. One phrase that instructors hate to see in conclusions is "As I have shown in this paper . . ." because it generally forecasts a dry, unimaginative, formulaic repetition of what has come before. Your summary's goal should be to link the project's main points together into a coherent argument or narrative.

Make a recommendation when one is appropriate. Any recommendation should grow out of the issue you have been discussing. This strategy brings a paper to a positive ending and closes the topic.

Link the end to the beginning. To tie your conclusion back to your beginning is a good way to frame and unify your paper. If you began with a narrative or opening anecdote, it might be effective to show how the information revealed in your research project might have affected the people or the action in the narrative had circumstances been different.

Place your argument in a larger context. When readers reach the end of a piece, they may want to know how what you've told them is relevant to larger issues or conversations: For example, does your analysis of a problem have implications for the community or for others studying your topic? Concluding paragraphs that suggest these sorts of connections are common in academic research projects.

Stop when you're finished. Probably the most important thing to remember about closing a paper or an essay is not to overdo your conclusion. When you have covered all your points and you are reasonably well satisfied with what you've said, quit. Don't bore your reader by tacking on further recapitulation or adding a paragraph of platitudes.

18e Make connections and use transitions

It is not enough to have pattern or structure within a project; you must also help readers follow it. In papers and other written work, we designate the components that hold a piece together as *transitions*.

For the sake of economy, writers often—and understandably—omit connectors when taking notes. They become so conversant with a subject that they understand a lot of information that was not obvious when they first found the subject. Unfortunately, writers often fail to restore some of those connectors when they come to write about a subject themselves, mistakenly assuming that readers are just as familiar with the material as they are. The result can be sentences of information unsupported by connective tissue.

> Physicians will usually perform artificial insemination only for married women. When a single woman wants a baby, she will often be rejected. Single parenthood, it is believed, is not good for a child.

This cluster of sentences frustrates readers more than it informs them. Readers will have to rewrite the paragraph to make sense of it. Worse, readers may infer meanings not intended by the author. The writer needs to make the connections implied in the sentences more explicit, spelling out the relationships.

> Physicians will usually perform artificial insemination only for married women **who are having trouble conceiving naturally.** Believing that single parenthood is not good for a child, **doctors** will often reject a single woman who wants to have a baby **by this method**.

The concluding sentence of a paragraph can also function as a kind of connector. Not every paragraph requires a concluding statement that reinforces the theses of the project. But when you've furnished considerable evidence in a paragraph, don't leave it up to readers to reckon how that evidence supports your thesis. Make the connection yourself in a competent concluding sentence.

You can also make connections in an essay by using helpful transitional words and expressions such as the following.

Transitional Words

although	however	moreover	consequently
first, second (etc.)	not only, but	for example	then
next	similarly	alternatively	finally
because	since	instead	thus

Although transitional words may seem like small items, a timely *nevertheless* or a phrase such as *on the other hand* can help a reader enormously. As you will see in Chapter 21, the strategic placement of headings and subheadings is highly effective and important. Even a well-chosen title—one that previews succinctly the content of a paper or project—can add to the coherence of a project.

WWW
18.1

18f   Write stylishly

"One size fits all" does not apply to the writing style of a research project. You'll write one way when assembling a research report for a psychology course, another way entirely when posting a Web site designed to help elementary school children understand aspects of African American history. Many of your choices of language will seem fairly obvious: you know better than to joke around in a physics lab report or to present the case for capping tuition in language that insults the very people who have the power to change the situation. You've probably been drilled, too, in the virtues of sentence economy—of cutting your prose to a minimum so readers don't waste their time. Here we explore general principles that apply to research reports and arguments. As always, the guidelines should be applied judiciously.

Find language that addresses readers intelligently. Be confident about the research you have done, but don't assume that positions other than your own aren't plausible. Remember that the readers most interested in your research may be suspicious of it. Make sure that the language you use welcomes skeptics and doesn't make them personally defensive. Put your own case in positive terms (when that's possible), and don't alienate readers by assuming a lofty moral tone that suggests that only you have special insight or sensitivity on the issue.

Use specific details. Writing that uses a lot of abstract language is often harder to understand and less pleasurable to read than writing that states ideas more specifically. Abstract terms like *health-care provider system, positive learning environment,* and *two-wheeled vehicle* are usually harder to grasp than concrete terms like *hospital, classroom,* and *Harley.* Of course you have to use abstract words sometimes; it's impossible to discuss big ideas without them. But the more you use specific details, the clearer your sentences will be. For example, specialists might understand the following sentence from a scholarly book, but stating its ideas more concretely gives the statement broader appeal.

ABSTRACT   It is also important to recognize that just as we can learn from knowledge about the efficacy of alternative bargaining structures, we can also benefit from knowledge of alternative approaches to welfare and employment policies.
            —William Julius Wilson, *The Truly Disadvantaged*

REVISED   We should recognize that just as it helps us to learn more about how groups bargain in other countries, it would also help us to learn more about how they handle welfare and unemployment.

State ideas positively. Negative statements can be surprisingly hard to read. When you can, turn negative statements into positive ones. Your writing will seem more confident and may be more economical.

DIFFICULT   Do we have the right **not to be victims** of street crime?
CLEARER   Do we have the right **to be safe** from street crime?

DIFFICULT   It is **not unlikely** that I will attend the conference.
CLEARER   I **will probably** attend the conference.

"Chunk" your writing. Consider breaking lengthy sentences into more manageable pieces or creating a list to present unusually complex information. People can comprehend only so much material at one time. Chunking is the principle behind dividing telephone and social security numbers into smaller parts: the breaks make the long strings of numbers easier to recall. It's also a principle operating on many Web pages, where information is constricted to fit relatively small screens.

Too Long

Citing an instance in which a 16-year-old student was working 48 hours a week at Burger King in order to pay for a new car and simultaneously trying to attend high school full time, New York educators have recently proposed legislation that prohibits high school students from working more than 3 hours on a school night, limits the total time they can work in a week to 20 hours when school is in session, and fines employees who violate these regulations as much as $2000.

In many respects this long sentence is admirable. It uses parallelism to keep a complex array of information in order. Yet most readers would probably like to see its wealth of information broken into more digestible chunks.

Revised

Educators in New York have recently proposed legislation that prohibits high school students from working more than 3 hours on a school night. In support of the proposal, they cite the example of a 16-year-old student working 48 hours a week at Burger King in order to pay for a new car while simultaneously trying to attend high school full time. The proposed law would limit the total time students can work in a week to 20 hours when school is in session and would fine employers who violate these regulations as much as $2000.

Condense sprawling phrases. Some long-winded expressions often just slow a reader's way into a sentence, especially at the beginning.

Why write . . .	When you could write . . .
in the event that	if
in light of the fact that	since
on the grounds that	because
regardless of the fact that	although
on the occasion of	when
at this point in time	now
it is obvious that	obviously
on an everyday basis	routinely
with regard/respect to	for

We are so accustomed to these familiar but wordy expressions that we don't notice how little they convey.

WORDY	**Regardless of the fact that** Marisol graduated from the police academy just last year, she has the confidence of a seasoned officer.
REVISED	**Although** Marisol graduated from the police academy just last year, she has the confidence of a seasoned officer.

WORDY	**At this point in time,** the committee hasn't convened.
REVISED	The committee hasn't convened **yet.**

Cut nominalizations. Nominalizations are nouns made by adding endings to verbs and adjectives. The resulting words tend to be long and abstract. Worse, nominalizations are often grafted onto terms that are themselves recent coinages of dubious merit.

Word	Nominalization
connect	connect**ivity**
customize	customi**zation**
historicize	historici**zation**
knowledge	knowledge**ableness**
merchandise	merchant**ability**
prioritize	prioriti**zation**
victimize	victimi**zation**

Unfortunately, writers in college, business, and government sometimes think that readers will be more impressed by prose laden with these grand abstractions. Here's a parody of a "bureaucratic" style.

> The **utilization** of appropriate **documentation** will achieve a **maximization** of **accountability,** assuring a **prioritization** and ultimate **finalization** of our budgetary requisitions.

Writing larded with nominalizations gives simple thoughts the appearance of complexity and vacuous thinking the cover of darkness. Avoid such sludge.

Condense long verb phrases to focus on the action. To show tense and mood, verb phrases need auxiliaries and helping verbs: I *could have* gone; she *will be* writing. But many verb phrases are strung out by unnecessary clutter. Such expressions sap the energy from sentences.

Why write . . .	When you could write . . .
give consideration to	consider
make acknowledgment of	acknowledge
have doubts about	doubt
is reflective of	reflects
has an understanding of	understands
put the emphasis on	emphasize

Similarly, don't clutter active verbs with expressions such as *start to, manage to,* and *proceed to.*

CLUTTERED VERBS	Malls and markets **always manage to irritate me** when they **start to display** Christmas paraphernalia immediately after Halloween.
REVISED	Malls and markets **irritate me** when they **display** Christmas paraphernalia immediately after Halloween.

Cut down on expletive constructions. Expletives are short expressions such as *it was, there are,* and *this is* that function like starting blocks for pushing into a sentence or clause. For example:

It was a dark and stormy night.

There were five of us huddled in the basement.

There are too many gopher holes on this golf course!

It is a proud day for Bluefield State College.

Some expletives are unavoidable. But using them habitually to open your sentences will make your prose tiresome. In many cases, sentences will be stronger without the expletives.

WITH EXPLETIVE	Even though **it is** the oldest manufacturer of automobiles, Mercedes-Benz remains innovative.
EXPLETIVE CUT	The oldest manufacturer of automobiles, Mercedes-Benz still remains innovative.

Why write . . .	When you could write . . .
There is a desire for	We want
There are reasons for	For several reasons
There was an expectation	They expected
It is clear that	Clearly
It is to be hoped	We hope

Avoid vague evaluative terms. Writers often report information in evaluative terms too vague to make much of an impression. If you find yourself tempted to overuse the following terms, you may want to reconsider.

Vague Terms

bad	effective	good	little	nice
big	fine	great	neat	poor

Also avoid expressions that begin with vague qualifiers such as *pretty, sort of, kind of, such a,* and *so.*

The point of most research is to make ideas more robust, not to bury claims under vacuous adjectives. You can't be content with vague terms. Every time you use a

vague evaluative term in a draft, circle it and ask yourself, What do I mean by
_____? What exactly makes my subject _____? Then incor-
porate those specifications into your prose, as shown in these examples:

Why write . . .	When you could provide details?
good evidence	three refereed articles in *JAMA*
a bad estimate	an estimate 125 percent too high
sort of hot	a surface temperature of 104°F
nice music	lush, romantic orchestration

Qualify sweeping statements. Sweeping statements are those that attempt to
generalize from too small a sample. You may have seen advertisements that claimed or
suggested that a product is the "physician's choice." The inference here is that *all* physicians would choose it, when the more likely fact is that all (or most, or some) of the
physicians *they surveyed* chose it. Can you support all the evaluative statements and
judgments you make? Qualifiers, such as the following, help limit your liability.

Qualifiers

almost	many	occasionally	some
in a few cases	most	possibly	sometimes
in many cases	often	probably	with these exceptions

18g Revise your draft

When you revise an early version of a paper or a project, you are not correcting it.
You're making much bigger changes, the kind that might affect its subject, focus, structure, even its genre. Bring a fresh eye to your work and make major changes wherever
they're needed—painful as such revisions may be. Ask yourself frankly whether you like
the paper or the project and believe it has potential. If you really dislike what you've
produced, consider starting over, perhaps by mining a vein in the original that shows
more promise.

Review your purpose. Someone reading your draft should quickly understand
what you are trying to accomplish. Ask yourself:

- Will readers appreciate the point of the project? Research papers, reports, and
  editorials obviously need direction and focus. But so do slide presentations,
  Web sites, and personal narratives.

- Have I chosen a project that I think is important and interesting to my readers
  or the community?

- Do I really know what I want to achieve with my project?

Check the focus of the project. Is your topic so broad that the work seems su-
perficial or rambling? Ask these questions:

- Does the thesis sentence present a limited claim that you can support with specific evidence?
- Have I made broad generalizations I can't prove in the space available?

Recall your audience. Your first draft is very likely to be "writer-centered," which means that its ideas are stated mostly from your point of view. If so, it's time to become more "reader-centered"—that is, to adapt your writing to the needs and expectations of your audience. Ask these questions:

- Have I decided whom I want to reach with this project? What would their interest in my work be?
- What do I know about this group (or these groups—you may have more than one type of reader in mind)? To what kinds of examples and reasons will they respond?
- How much do my readers already know about the subject? What questions might they have?
- What tone and style of writing is appropriate for these readers? Should my language or presentation be more or less formal?

When revising, your greatest asset is a clear sense of your audience.

Evaluate the organization of your project. Friends and fellow writers can often help you spot organizational problems. Ask them whether they can follow your work easily. If they become lost or confused, have them show you where. Then ask yourself these questions:

- Does the project have a clear pattern that is easy to follow? If I read the first sentence of each paragraph, does it give me a kind of summary? Does the home page of a Web site array its information logically?
- Does the project meet the expectations raised by its opening? Do I deliver on my promises?
- Does the project need more signposts to keep readers on track? more logical divisions? better headings and subheadings? a site map or other graphics?

It's hard to get an overview of organization when you're reading a paper from a computer screen. Work from a printed copy if it helps you.

18.4

Review the content of your project. You may need to add information and more detail to your project to make it important to readers. Don't be satisfied with a minimum number of sources or a series of generalizations without texture or grip. Ask yourself these questions:

- Have I answered the journalist's questions—*who, what, when, why, where,* and *how?*
- Do I need to quote authorities or offer more specific examples to give weight to my essay and add interest?
- Have I supported my claims with acceptable evidence?

Drafting your research project is likely to be a time-consuming process as you can see by examining the sample student draft at the end of Chapter 19, but you will be well rewarded by the satisfaction you feel once you have a completed draft. At this point you should see the whole project—in all its component parts—coming together and you should be prepared to move into the last phase of the task: verifying that all necessary documentation has been completed and preparing the project for presentation.

FOCUS ON . . . Writing Centers

One of the most valuable resources available to you as a college student is the campus writing center, a place where skilled, interested writers and/or instructors will look over what you've written and give you valuable feedback. Writing centers are not just for "poor" writers, and they aren't just places where you can have your paper proofread for grammar mistakes. In fact, writing centers tend to be visited most by "good" writers who want to be even better, and writing center consultants are generally trained to look first at the "higher order" issues of discourse: organization, development, tone, argumentation, use of evidence, and focus on audience.

If you would like to get additional response to what you have written as well as suggestions for how your project's rhetorical goals might be better achieved, you should find out where your campus writing center is located and make an appointment to see one of the consultants. They won't fix all your mistakes or write your paper for you, but they might be able to identify options or possibilities that you overlooked.

WWW Web Sites Worth Knowing

18.5

- Writing a First Draft, **http://daphne.palomar.edu/handbook/firstdraft.htm**
- William Strunk's *Elements of Style*, **http://www.bartleby.com/141/**
- Strategies for Overcoming Writer's Block,
  http://www.english.uiuc.edu/cws/wworkshop/advice/writersblock.htm
- International Writing Center Association Homepage, **http://iwca.syr.edu**

GETTING INVOLVED

1. You know what procrastination is. In a group, talk about the problem as it affects writers and researchers. When do *you* typically procrastinate? What underlies the procrastination: Is it fear of failure? a sense of inadequacy? sheer laziness? How have you suffered in the past from decisions to put off what you might have finished quickly? How have you overcome procrastination?

2. Review several papers you have written for past classes and list the comments and corrections your instructors have made. What sorts of comments, both rhetorical and grammatical, have appeared with regularity? What areas of organization or development have teachers commented on, and why? Keep this list handy as you draft and revise your paper.

3. In a small group, look at the introductory and concluding paragraphs in several short articles from popular magazines, an anthology, or even other student papers. Decide among yourselves what *types* of introductions and conclusions they are and consider how effective they are at fulfilling their rhetorical purpose and interesting readers.

MANAGING YOUR PROJECT

1. Clear out both physical and temporal spaces to work on drafting your project: a place to work and a time to work. Don't underestimate the importance of this preparation. Gather all the materials you need in one location so that you don't have to interrupt your writing. Also claim the time you need from friends, other projects, and other concerns. Make yourself comfortable, too.

2. Review the timetable for completing your project, and adjust it to fit any changes in your project to date (see Chapter 1). Be sure the schedule remains specific and reasonable. You'll be more successful if you break the project into manageable parts and set goals that you can realistically meet.

3. Schedule a visit to your campus writing center and prepare for the visit in advance. What sorts of questions do you have about your draft? What things concern you most, and what would you like help with? Go in with a list of specific issues you would like to discuss.

19

Reviewing Documentation in Your Project

Documentation is the evidence you provide to support the ideas you present in a research project. Effective documentation gives the material you offer readers credibility and authority, and it encourages further dialogue. Anthony Grafton, professor of history at Princeton University, explains this dual mission in "The Death of the Footnote (Report on an Exaggeration)," published in *The Wilson Quarterly* (Winter 1997). Footnotes, he writes, "give us reason to believe that their authors have done their best to find out the truth [. . .] they give us reason to trust what we read." That's the contribution documentation makes to gathering information.

But the dialogic dimension of research—the unending conversation of ideas that makes academic work an adventure—is always present too, as Grafton explains: "[Footnotes] also suggest ways that the author's own formulations can be unraveled. Devised to give texts authority, footnotes in fact undermine. They democratize scholarly writing: they bring many voices, including those of the sources, together on a single page." Footnotes, in-text notes, and electronic hyperlinks encourage the conversation that has become essential to contemporary academic work.

Traditional documentation usually points readers to sources of information: books, articles, statistics, and so on. It may also cite interviews, software, films, television programs, databases, images, audio files, and online conversations. Various systems for managing sources and documentation have been devised. Presented in this handbook are systems of the Modern Language Association (MLA), the American Psychological Association (APA), the *Chicago Manual of Style* (CMS), the Council of Science Editors (CSE), and the *Columbia Guide to Online Style* (COS). Specific guidelines for formal documentation appear in Chapters 23 through 27. This chapter examines general principles for acknowledging and using sources.

19.1

Authors of successful projects pay attention to details. Make sure that it's clear where the information you use in your project came from, using in-text notes where appropriate and paying close attention to every entry in your bibliography or Works Cited page to ensure accuracy and completeness.

19a Provide a source for every direct quotation

A direct quotation is any material repeated word for word from a source. (For integrating quotations in your project, see Chapter 14.) Direct quotations in college projects often require some form of parenthetical documentation—that is, a citation of author and page number (MLA) or author, date, and page number (APA).

> **MLA**   It is possible to define literature as simply "that text which the community insists on having repeated from time to time intact" (Joos 51-52).

> **APA**   Hashimoto (1986) questions the value of attention-getting essay openings that "presuppose passive, uninterested (probably uninteresting) readers" (p. 126).

Some systems signal notes with raised or highlighted numbers in the body of a text keyed either to individual footnotes or endnotes (Chicago style) or to sources on a References page (CSE style).

> **CMS**   Achilles can hardly be faulted for taking offense to this incident, as it "threatened to invalidate . . . the whole meaning of his life."[2]

> **CSE**   Oncologists[1] are aware of trends in cancer mortality.[2]

Many electronically accessed sources—especially Web pages—do not have page numbers. For these types of sources, the parenthetical note or footnote would usually include only the author's last name. (For more on citing electronic sources, see Chapter 23.)

You are similarly expected to identify the sources for any diagrams, statistics, charts, or pictures in your project. In fact, when you request permission to use a copyrighted photograph or illustration, you likely will be asked to provide a credit line as a condition of use. (See Chapter 9 on academic responsibility and intellectual property.)

Graphics and other artwork may not need to be listed in your Works Cited or References page; however, you will still need to provide source information.

Famous sayings, proverbs, and biblical citations do not need formal documentation as they are considered forms of common knowledge; however, if in doubt, it is better to give too much information than too little. You are likely to quote more often in papers and projects within the humanities and the arts than in scientific articles and projects, but all systems of documentation provide forms for direct quotation.

19b Provide a source for all paraphrased material

Even when you present information completely in your own words, if that information came from other sources, you will need to document it. Paraphrases and summaries of another person's ideas or information can be cited by placing a parenthetical note at the end of the paraphrase or summary, indicating the author's last name (see Chapter 13). Include page number(s) when you are summarizing or paraphrasing a specific section of the text. For example,

```
Though so-called single-track trails might put mountain bikers

in conflict with the hikers, such tracks are often empty and

underutilized (van der Plas 106).
```

When you are summarizing or paraphrasing a complete work (book, article, movie), omit the page number. For example:

```
Problems on the Russian space station Mir make it clear why a

human mission to Mars may not be a good idea: people in space

cause problems that robots don't (Roland).
```

When a work is important enough to summarize or paraphrase, you may want to cite the author in the text to lend your use of the information greater credibility. For example:

```
Recent problems on the Russian space station Mir, Alex Roland

argues in a USA Today editorial, make it clear why a human

mission to Mars may not be a good idea: people in space cause

problems that robots don't.
```

APA and other scientific styles also include the date of publication either in the text after the author's name or in the parenthetical note if the author's name is not mentioned in the text (see Part VI).

19c Document all ideas not from common knowledge

Common knowledge includes facts, dates, events, information, and concepts that an educated person can be assumed to know. You may need to check an encyclopedia to find out that the Battle of Waterloo was fought on June 18, 1815, but that fact belongs to common knowledge and for that reason you don't have to document it.

You may also make assumptions about *common knowledge within a field*. When you find that a given piece of information or an idea is shared among several of the sources you are using, you need not document it. (For example, if in writing a paper on anorexia nervosa you discovered that most authorities define it in the same way, you probably don't have to document that definition.) What experts know collectively constitutes the common knowledge within a field; what they claim individually—their opinions, studies, theories, research projects, and hypotheses—is the material you *must* document in a paper.

COMMON KNOWLEDGE

```
The Internet is a vast network of computers that connects
millions of people from many areas of the world.
```

NOT COMMON KNOWLEDGE

```
The Internet is a vast network of computers used by over 300
million people worldwide (USIC).
```

```
OR
```

```
The Internet is a vast network of computers which, according to
the United States Internet Council, is used by over 300 million
people worldwide.
```

When you're not sure whether the information you are using is common knowledge, document it. You should also consider documenting information if your readers are likely to question it or if your argument depends on your readers' accepting the information as credible (see Section 19e).

19d Document information from field research

Some of the information you present may be the result of your own original research. While this information may not be included in your list of Works Cited or References, you will still need to acknowledge the source of your information in the body of your paper or project. The mere assertion that two out of three students in your class spent more than $50 on a pair of sneakers in the past year is not convincing, but you can make it convincing by providing the source of your information:

```
A survey of students in Dr. Smith's English 101 class at State
University conducted during Spring Semester 2002 indicated that
two out of three students spent more than $50 on a pair of
sneakers during the 2000-01 school year.
```

For more formal research projects, you may need to provide information about your methodology. (How did you select students to survey? How many students were surveyed? How was the survey administered?) Sometimes the survey and complete results will be included as appendixes.

Similarly, citing the authority of interviewees can help corroborate the information you include.

> "Timed in-class writings are not usually the best way to assess
> students' writing abilities," cautioned Dr. Jones, Professor of
> English at XYZ University, in an email interview with the
> author.

You may need to include the transcripts of interviews as appendixes as well; check with your instructor for specific requirements for your project.

19e Document all material that might be questioned

When your subject is controversial, you may want to document even those facts or ideas considered common knowledge. When in doubt, document. Suppose that, in writing about witchcraft in colonial America, you make a historical assertion that is well known by historians but likely to surprise nonspecialists. Writing to nonspecialists, you should certainly document the assertion. Writing to historians, you would probably skip the note.

Sometimes people's biases can be reflected in what they think of as common knowledge. General statements such as "Men make better soldiers than women" and "Reagan was one of our country's best presidents" are common knowledge only to people who feel the same way. Don't confuse personal opinion with fact. If your sources provide you with evidence to back up these claims, then you need to cite them.

Understand, too, that the documentation you provide should give readers confidence in your source. A traditional citation for a book usually tells them (at minimum) the name of the author, the title of the book, the place and date of publication, and the identity of the publisher—enough information to support a judgment about the authority of the work.

> Gass, William. <u>Habitations of the World</u>. Ithaca: Cornell UP,
> 1997.

Electronic sources may provide less information. Some Web sites have no traditional authorship, no pagination, no publisher, no supporting institution. What can a reader learn from a Works Cited entry such as the following?

> "The Advances in Cloning." http://daphne.palomar.edu/di/
> spring2000/garrison001/essay4.htm (29 Dec. 2001).

The reader won't learn much. The electronic address places the Web site at an educational site (*edu*), but readers may have no clue who the author is, nor will they know whether the material on cloning has much authority. As a writer, you should avoid sources that offer so little documentary information; they will undermine your credibility unless you can back them up.

19f Furnish source information for all graphics, audio files, and other borrowings

If you include graphics (either downloaded or scanned in), audio, video, or other types of files in your project, you will need to provide source information. Make sure you have permission to use the files or graphics, and follow any instructions the permission specifies for citing your source (see Chapter 9). For online projects you will usually include a link to the original as well. Often these kinds of sources will not appear in your list of Works Cited or References. Instead, you may include the source information as a "credit line" following the title of a figure or table (see Chapter 20). Alternatively, you may be asked to compile a separate Credits page (see page 431), especially if you make extensive use of copyrighted material such as audio or video files.

19g Furnish dates and other useful information

Provide dates for important events, major figures, and works of literature and art. Also identify any people readers might not recognize.

```
After the great fire of London (1666), the city was . . .

Henry Highland Garnet (1815-82), an American abolitionist and
radical, . . .

Pearl (c. 1400), an elegy about . . .
```

In the latter example, *c.* stands for *circa,* which means "about" or "approximately."

When quoting from literary works, help readers to locate the passages you cite. For novels, identify page numbers; for plays, give act, scene, and line numbers; for long poems, provide line numbers and, when appropriate, division numbers (book, canto, or other divisions). Some Internet sources will provide paragraph numbers or links to specific sections of a page, usually indicated in the URL by a pound sign (#) followed by the name of the target (for example, #AT2).

```
NCSA's "A Beginner's Guide to HTML" at http://archive.ncsa
.uiuc.edu/General/Internet/WWW/HTMLPrimerAll.html explains how
to add alternate text for images (#AT2), which is often
recommended to facilitate ADA compliance.
```

The reader may access the specific section cited by adding the information in parentheses to the end of the URL (**http://archive.ncsa.uiuc.edu/General/Internet/ WWW/HTMLPrimerAll.html#AT2**).

19h Use links to document electronic sources

Creating a link in a Web page to the original source (if it is online) can function as a type of documentation: such links take readers directly to supporting material or sources. However, it's important that readers understand where a highlighted passage is leading them; when they select a link, they should know where they are going. One way to ensure that readers will know where a link will take them—or why they should click on a link—is to provide information in ALT tags (see Chapter 22). Most Web browsers now show this information to users when the mouse is positioned over the link.

Hyperlinks should be offered judiciously to provide real information. Don't overwhelm a Web page with links that do not contribute significantly to the project; such a project can seem as fussy as a paper with too many footnotes. Note, too, that you may still be expected to provide a References page or traditional documentation in a scholarly paper that is posted online. The hypertext link may supplement but it won't necessarily supplant more traditional documentation—at least not yet.

❧ FOCUS ON . . . Avoiding Plagiarism

It was discovered recently that the famous historian Stephen Ambrose, author of *Wild Blue* and other books, "lifted" several passages from other sources. An article in *Newsday* by Aileen Jacobson at **http://library.newsday.com** notes that "Quotation marks may soothe his critics, but they may never repair Stephen Ambrose's reputation." While some instances of plagiarism are outright instances of theft of intellectual property, sloppy note-taking can also lead to unintentional plagiarism. In either case the result may be the same: your reputation as both an honest and a reliable communicator may be damaged beyond repair.

Citing direct quotations is not enough; you must also cite information such as statistics, paraphrased or summarized material, and graphics, tables, and figures that you borrow from other sources. For citations to online sources, make certain that the URLs you provide will actually take your readers to the original source; for other types of sources, be certain that your bibliographic entries are accurate and that notes in the text clearly designate the bibliographic entry. Part VI presents both in-text and bibliographic formats for citing sources following the COS, MLA, APA, CMS, and CSE style guidelines.

Pay scrupulous attention to your use of information from other sources. Reviewing the documentation in your project may seem a tedious job, but it can make the difference between a successful project and a damaged reputation.

Now is the time to review your project carefully. Make sure that you have met all the requirements of the assignment (the hard points), that your focus is clear and consistent, your arguments and supporting evidence sound and logical, and your sources correctly documented. Next comes the fun part: designing the presentation, testing it, and submitting the final project professionally. In Chapter 20 you will learn the basics of good design for both print and electronic projects.

WWW Web Sites Worth Knowing

- *The English Pages* Online Citation Guides – COS Humanities Style, http://www.awl.com/englishpages/citation_walker_citing_h.htm
- "Using Quotations Effectively," http://www.virtualsalt.com/quotehlp.htm
- University of Wisconsin–Madison Writing Center's "Using Literary Quotations," http://www.wisc.edu/writing/Handbook/QuoLitIncorporating.html

GETTING INVOLVED

1. Have each member of a small group (four or five people) locate a book or article that uses footnotes or endnotes extensively. Study how the notes function in these works. What do the notes tell you about the research done to prepare the project? Can you tell how thorough the research has been? Can you tell anything about the field from the sources cited? How up-to-date were the sources when the piece was published? When does the author use sources? Are the notes in any way "dialogic," as Anthony Grafton claims they might be, "suggest[ing] ways that the author's own formulations can be unraveled"?

2. Which of the following items would be common knowledge? Which would you probably feel the obligation to document? Discuss the examples in class. You may find that you would prefer to document even some items regarded as common knowledge—on the grounds that readers might still want to look at your sources.

   - In a psychology textbook, an informal definition of *split personality*
   - The most recent unemployment figures from the Department of Labor
   - Newton's third law of motion
   - Mae West's comment "When I'm good I'm very good, but when I'm bad, I'm better"
   - The population of Atlanta, Georgia, in 1960
   - Judge Antonin Scalia's dissenting opinion in a Supreme Court case
   - Average price of a quart of milk at three local grocery stores today
   - An author's proposal for improving the safety of air-traffic control procedures
   - Complete text of the Constitution of the United States of America
   - Percentage of registered voters who participated in the last presidential election

MANAGING YOUR PROJECT

An important decision you will make is to determine what system of documentation best suits your project. Consider these matters:

- Did the assignment sheet ask you to use a specific form of documentation?
- Do you expect to document electronic sources? You may want to use COS style for electronic items (see Chapter 23).
- Are you preparing a project in the arts or humanities? If so, you'll want to choose either MLA (Chapter 24) or CMS style (Chapter 26). Notes in these systems focus on individual authors and on particular passages within works.
- Are you preparing a project in the social sciences? If so, you'll want to use APA style (Chapter 25). Notes in this system focus on complete research studies (rather than on individual passages) and the dates of their publication.
- Are you preparing a project in the natural sciences? If so, you'll want to use CSE style (Chapter 27).
- Do you prefer using in-text notes? If so, your options are MLA (Chapter 24) and APA style (Chapter 25).
- Do you prefer traditional footnotes? If so, use CMS style (Chapter 26).

Sample Introduction and Conclusion for a Research Project

The following passages are first attempts at an introduction and a conclusion for an extended research project on standardized testing. The writer includes notes to himself, uses different ways of expressing ideas, and asks questions. As he makes changes to other parts of the project, he will make corresponding changes in the introduction and conclusion.

My Research Project on Standardized Testing

Possible working titles: "Will Standardized Testing Kill Our Schools?" "Surviving Standardized Testing" "Standardized Tests: In Whose Interests?" "Standardized Tests and Learning: A Failed Experiment?"

First draft of an Introduction

In Seeking Diversity **[SHOULD THIS BE UNDERLINED OR ITALICIZED? CHECK BOOKMARKS!]**, a book ~~about English teaching~~ on teaching middle school language arts, Linda Rief ~~a teacher~~ **[DO I NEED TO SAY WHO SHE IS?]** says, "I expect good reading and writing, in which process and product are woven tightly into literate tapestries of wonder and awe" (10). Rief ~~talks about~~ describes an ideal goal for writing instruction here: a classroom where students learn to write because they want to become better writers and not just because they're concerned with getting good grades. ~~Grades are definitely not everything~~. This kind of environment would teach students to write by turning them into writers. Unfortunately, our education system today isn't even teaching students the basic skills they need to survive. ~~Quotes~~ Statements by teachers that "the greater number of the young people we teach [. . .] do not know how to read, spell, write, use correct grammar, do simple math, remember, use logic" **[DO I NEED TO HAVE A CITATION HERE IF IT'S FROM THE SAME PLACE AS THE NEXT QUOTE?]** are supported by studies that show "that only 55% of the nation's 17-year-olds and 49% of out-of-school adults are able to write an acceptable letter ordering a product by mail" (Neill 18). Yet the way some people, ~~such as legislators and boards of education~~, seem to be dealing with this problem-- through an increase in (increasing?) the amount of competency testing in our public schools--may be turning writing into a

formulaic exercise, destroying any regard students may have for
how language is used, **[COMMA HERE?]** and not actually helping
students write any better at all. **[DO I NEED TO INCLUDE WHAT I
THINK WE SHOULD DO?]**

First draft of a Conclusion

Under ~~circumstances~~ conditions like these, where students have
to spend a lot of their valuable class time writing formulaic
(routine? repetitious? highly structured?) practice essays so
they can do well on the standardized tests they have to take,
students learn to hate writing. ~~How could they do anything else?~~
They see it as a boring chore they have to complete rather than
a process that ~~lets them~~ will allow them to produce something
they can actually ~~be proud of~~ take pride in. As soon as they
learn to write the type of dry, five-paragraph essay that says
nothing of value and does so in the least exciting or interesting way, they stop growing as writers. **[SAY SOMETHING MORE ABOUT
WHY THIS HAPPENS? HAVE I INCLUDED SUFFICIENT EVIDENCE TO SUPPORT
THIS?]** The perfect writing classroom Rief describes is still
possible, even if students have to take standardized tests, but
it requires creative faculty willing to bet their jobs that students can pass these tests without drills. Not many teachers are
going to be willing to make such a tradeoff. **[ADD SOMETHING
ABOUT FAMILIES AND BILLS HERE?]** And, when school superintendents
get calls from angry parents whose children aren't going to
graduate, the right thing to do can take a back seat to what is
easiest. Rather than place the blame where it belongs--on parents who don't take active roles in their children's learning;
on legislatures which fail to provide (withhold? deny?) the
funds for adequate schools, supplies, and teacher salaries; or
on the basic inadequacies of the tests themselves--it's sometimes more convenient to blame the teachers and focus all the
attention on ~~poor~~ the ~~weakest~~ least capable students. The consequences are terrible. In the rush to raise the scores of those
who can't meet the state objectives, creativity is crushed in
those who can. **[SHOULD I HAVE SOME SORT OF PITHY QUOTE HERE TO
END THE ESSAY?]**

V

Completing Your Project

Don't miss . . .

- **The guidelines for selecting a project format in Chapter 20.** Choose the presentation method that works best for your material, your audience, and your goals.
- **The principles of document design in Section 21a.** Good document design will give your project impact and help readers understand how all the parts work together.
- **The advice for submitting your project professionally in Section 21d.** Make sure your project reflects all the hard work you've put into it.
- **The overview of design principles for electronic environments in Section 22b.** Your Web pages will be seen on an assortment of computers, monitors, and browsers. Learn how to accommodate their differences through careful design.

Technology Spotlight

WEB AUTHORING TOOLS

Almost all Internet Service Providers offer their customers a few megabytes of memory to host an individual Web page, and millions of people around the world have taken advantage of the opportunity. Web pages take up little memory, and they are an easy way for businesses to advertise merchandise or for individuals to present themselves to the rest of the world. Even so, the number of home pages available on the Web would be far fewer were it not for the development of sophisticated GUI (Graphical User Interface) Web authoring programs.

Web pages may look simple when they are displayed in browsers, but underneath the visually stimulating, colorful pages is a complex set of text-based commands in a specialized language called HTML (Hypertext Markup Language). If you open up a Web page with a text editor, you can see what these commands look like.

It's easier than ever to create and publish a page on the World Wide Web, but learning to design and author pages that are both appealing and effective is still a challenge.

In the early days of the Web, programmers had to learn HTML commands and type them in by hand. If they wanted to create a link to another site, for example, they would have to write a command that looked like this: <a href="http:// www.some-site.com>LINK</a>, and this was just one of the many command lines they would have to write even for the simplest Web page. Few computer users wanted to expend the effort necessary to design a single Web page, let alone an entire Web site.

Fortunately, it wasn't long before a few creative entrepreneurs designed Web authoring tools to simplify the process. Programs such as Netscape *Composer*, *PageMill*, and Microsoft *FrontPage* now help users construct entire Web sites without their having to know a single word of HTML. To make text appear in bold or italic fonts, all you have to do is highlight it with a mouse and click on a "Bold" button; the program will write the HTML code for you. Inserting graphics, sounds, tables, and discussion lists into a Web site has become as easy as pushing a button, and many writing classes can cover the basics of Web page design and construction in just a few class periods.

C H A P T E R

20

Choosing a Format for Your Project

It is important to remain focused as you bring a long project to completion. Don't be the ballcarrier who celebrates before crossing the goal line—only to fumble. Make sure your project meets all its requirements, looks good, and arrives on time. If you created a successful management plan for your project early on (see Chapter 1), you'll reap your reward now with a schedule that can accommodate even the inevitable last-minute glitches.

Depending on your purpose and audience and on the requirements of your assignment and topic, you will now need to decide on a format in which to present your project. This chapter will help you choose the best format.

20a Consider the formats your project might take

A research project may take a variety of forms, depending on your audience, your topic, and your purpose. If your purpose is to present information from research to an academic audience, you will probably want to write a research paper. In the humanities, you will need to follow the guidelines set forth by the Modern Language Association (MLA); in the social sciences, you may follow American Psychological Association (APA) guidelines; and in the hard sciences, you may need to follow the Council of Science Editors (CSE) style.

Or your purpose may dictate other formats. A letter to the editor of your school or local newspaper would look very different from an academic essay, while a newsletter article or brochure might allow you to include different font types, colors, and graphics. You need to decide on a format that makes sense for your project within the confines of the assignment.

Even presenting a more-or-less traditional research paper as a Web site entails a considerable number of choices. A Web page requires formatting in Hypertext Markup Language (HTML), and then you need to decide how to "chunk" the information—that is, whether to present your project on one Web page or to divide the material and present it on separate pages with links from one page to another. You will need to make decisions about formatting headings, paragraphs, and even your list of Works Cited or References, as well as whether to include graphics, tables, lists, external links, multimedia, and other features allowed by electronic publishing.

All these choices will depend on your analysis of the specific rhetorical situation for your project, including the hard points of the assignment (see Chapter 1). Before you decide, be sure to check with your instructor if she or he has not specified a format.

FOCUS ON . . . The Rhetorical Situation

The choices you make throughout your project—the arguments to present, the types of evidence to include, the level of diction, or language, to adopt, and the format in which to present your project—all depend on your analysis of the rhetorical situation. Every project is distinct, and your considering the elements of the specific rhetorical situation for your project—audience, purpose, occasion, and medium—will guide you in your decisions.

Audience. Who is the primary audience for your project? What are their needs and expectations, including their expectation(s) about language and level of diction, structure, and format? Consider the needs and expectations of secondary audiences as well.

Purpose. For what purpose(s) are you writing? What do you want your reader to know or do with the information you present? How does this purpose affect your choices of language, structure, and medium? How will your choice of format help you to achieve your purpose(s)?

Occasion. What occasions (or causes) you to write about this topic at this time? Obviously, your project is partly occasioned by the fact that you have been assigned to research a topic and present the results of your project to an audience for a purpose. Beyond that, however, consider what is going on in the world that has prompted you to choose a specific topic, audience, and purpose for your project. Consider, too, how your choice of format may be at least partially—if not substantially—affected by the occasion within which you write. (For example, twenty years ago the occasion for a college writing project would not have allowed students the choice to format their project as a Web page!)

Medium. The choice of medium depends on many factors, chief of which is the audience's expectations. For your particular audience(s), what are the usual choices of medium? Why would a particular format be appropriate for certain types of media and not for others? These choices are predicated on an author's determination of audience, purpose, and occasion. How does your choice of medium affect the presentation of your message? What formatting choices are allowed—or prohibited—by your choice of medium?

20b Review the structure of your project

Organizing a sizable project involves seeing that all its parts fit together. Is the information in the body of your report clearly supported by the tables and charts you've placed in its appendixes? Will the separate panels in your brochure or the slides in your presentation work well together in an actual presentation? Does a home page provide a logical map or entrance to all the material you've collected in your Web site? These are the kinds of questions you face.

Sometimes you may be too close to your own project to review the material objectively yourself. It makes sense to encourage others from outside your project group to review an early draft and give you feedback. You might then ask yourself and any reviewers these basic questions:

- Is the point of the project clear?
- Are the links between claims and evidence solid?
- Will readers understand the relationship between separate parts of the project?
- Are connections or transitions between parts of the project adequate?
- Do titles, headings, and other devices contribute to the coherence of the project?
- Does the project need a more explanatory opening, one with more background information?
- Does the closing require more summary?
- Do the verbal and visual elements of the project cohere?

For a print structure—a long academic paper, a brochure, a newsletter article—use the following method to check your structure:

- **Underline the topic idea, or thesis, in your draft.** It should be clearly stated in the first few sentences or paragraphs.

- **Underline just the first sentence in each subsequent paragraph.** If the first sentence is very short or closely tied to the second, underline the first two sentences.

- **Read the underlined sentences straight through as if they formed an essay in themselves.** Ask whether each sentence advances or explains the main point or thesis statement. If the sentences—taken together—read coherently, chances are good that the paper is well organized. Make sure the headings are in the right order, the various sections follow in correct sequence (especially when a brochure is folded), and that all pertinent information is included (your name and course identification for a paper; phone numbers and addresses for a brochure).

- **If the underlined sentences don't make sense, reexamine those paragraphs or sections not clearly related to the topic idea.** If the ideas really aren't related, delete the entire paragraph or section. If the ideas are related, consider how to revise your structure to make the connection clearer. A new lead sentence for a paragraph or a new section heading will often solve the problem of incoherence. Pay attention to transitions, too—those places where you can give readers helpful directions: *first of all, on the other hand, to summarize.*

- **Test your conclusion against your introduction.** Sometimes conclusions contradict their openings because of changes that occurred as the project developed. When you've completed a draft, set it aside for a time and then revisit the entire piece. Does it hang together? If not, revise.

You can test other types of documents in a similar manner. For a Web site, try to imagine how a reader encountering it for the first time might search for information: will users find what they are seeking with a minimum number of clicks? Do all the links work in both directions? Make sure there are no dead ends and that every page on your site provides a way to return to your home page or to go to another helpful location in the site. Make sure you include directions for returning to your site from any external links, if necessary. Also:

- **Print out a copy of your Web project and underline the topic or main idea.** Your reader should be able to ascertain the purpose of your Web page or site on the first screen.

- **Underline or highlight transitions between paragraphs, sections, or pages within your site.** Your reader should be able to understand how linked information relates to your main idea. Ask yourself whether it is clear why a reader should follow a given link.

- **Check that links to external sites are clearly connected to your topic idea or thesis.** If the links really aren't related, consider deleting them. If they are related, consider how to make the connections clearer.

  WWW
  20.1

- **Revise your project for coherence.** Add or delete section headings, links, or other navigational features to achieve greater coherence. Include helpful transitional words or phrases—*first of all, on the other hand, to summarize*—to ensure that your reader can follow the logic of your presentation.

- **Test your conclusions against your introduction.** Make sure that, regardless of the path or paths your reader may follow through your Web site, your purpose is clear and that any conclusions you reach are consistent with what you promised in your introduction. When you've completed a draft of your project—on paper or online—set it aside for a time and then revisit it. Does it still hang together and make sense as a whole? If not, revise again.

20c Determine the format for your project

To determine a format for your final project, consider the following factors:

- Your purpose in preparing the project
- The potential audience(s) for the project
- The time available to complete the project

  WWW
  20.2

- Your access to necessary equipment and programs, such as presentation or desktop publishing software, scanners, and graphics programs
- Your technical skill in using that equipment.

Purpose. Regardless of the framework you choose for your project, you need to make a point. Will your purpose be to persuade? to inform? to entertain? to move to action? The design of your project will have to support such goals. Often your purpose may be obvious: a college project designed generally to present information will likely follow a familiar academic format such as that recommended by the MLA or APA style manual.

Purposes can also be much more narrow and pragmatic. For example, if one purpose of a project is to encourage readers to respond to your work, you'll have to make it easy for them to do so—perhaps by furnishing an email address, a telephone number, or a mailing address. Or if you want readers to pressure their congressional representatives on an issue, your project might include a list of the representatives' names and addresses, as well as a sample letter identifying key points to make. For similar reasons, brochures and mailings might include tear-off response forms. The format you choose is important because it demonstrates your grasp of effective communication skills.

Audience. The intended audience will necessarily influence the design of your work. For instance, academic audiences (instructors, colleagues in a field, students) have expectations that differ substantially from those of business executives or general readers. Analyze the needs and capabilities of any audience you hope to address.

- What information is your typical reader already likely to have?

- What materials will you have to furnish?

- What tools will your intended audience need in order to gain access to the information you provide?

Then you need to provide cues for navigating your project. In traditional papers, such cues may be as basic as transitional words and phrases or headings and subheadings. Or they may be as complex as graphs, tables, and full appendixes.

For electronic documents, the navigation requirements may be quite different. On a Web page you may need to supply hypertext links or page anchors as well as instructions for downloading applications or plug-ins readers will need in order to use your site. You'll also want to offer your information in formats that general audiences can readily access. For Web sites, that may mean avoiding the use of Javascripts or other advanced programming techniques if most readers in your audience can't open them. Keep in mind, too, that readers may want to print copies of Web documents. When that's the case, be sure that all important elements of your electronic document will survive the translation into print. (For instance, be sure that the URLs for your links will be visible in printed copies.)

Consider, too, the best media to reach your intended audience(s): by mail, by telephone, in person, in print, via email or the Web? You may even need to combine or overlap formats to reach your whole audience. For instance, on the World Wide Web, you may want to provide a text-only version of your Web pages (many of which will feature images) to accommodate users without access to graphical browsers such as Netscape *Navigator* or *Internet Explorer* as well as the visually impaired, who may need to access the Web through programs that read texts to them. Similarly, you may decide to offer your materials in simple form by email or in text-only versions on the Web while also providing them in downloadable formats (such as portable document format, or PDF) that retain your document formatting codes. In any case, always be sure that readers can gain access to the programs necessary to read your documents and files.

Time. The time available to complete your project may determine how you will present it. For instance, you'll have to weigh the benefit of trying a new technology against the time it will take you to learn it. If creating pie charts is a mystery to you, you might want to avoid them in writing a paper due in just a few days. If you have never designed a Web page, learning advanced HTML authoring techniques may demand more time than you can afford—even with the help of software designed to speed Web authoring. Creating graphics may be similarly time-consuming; fortunately, many word-processing and desktop publishing applications include ready-to-use clip art packages, and you may also incorporate images available for free online in your Web designs. So you have to make intelligent choices, sometimes sticking with technologies you know, at other times exploring new, if more risky, possibilities.

Consider the constraints on your readers, too, when designing your projects. For instance, large electronic files may be time-consuming to download or access online. On the Web, break this complex information into smaller segments, and offer a table of contents or an index page to give readers direct access to the information they need. When a lengthy report might supply more detail than many readers require, include an abstract to summarize the piece, or consider creating a brochure to highlight the most compelling information.

Medium. Your choice of medium will dictate some design considerations. For example, print documents such as research papers, brochures, and newsletters often adhere to traditional formats: they need to be produced with a quality printer (preferably a laser or ink-jet printer), usually on plain white paper with black ink. The fonts and colors you choose will depend on the capabilities of your printer. Your use of graphics may build, at least in part, on your familiarity with your word processor's capabilities, your proficiency with various text art or drawing programs, and your access to scanners, clip art files, and other equipment. You could include graphics by the old-fashioned cut-and-paste method (literally pasting cutout copies of graphics onto your document pages), but this option is limiting. You'll produce better, more professional documents when you master the intricacies of graphics programs.

For Web projects you will have to know how to create and/or incorporate graphics, fonts, hypertext links, and other important elements of page design, making sure all the pieces work together to deliver information to readers. And you will need to have permission to post your files to an Internet service that allows Web access.

The format of a document tells readers—at a glance—something about its audience and purpose. Figure 20.1 on page 240 lists some common document formats.

Whether your final project will be completed for print or electronic publication, you need to ensure that it is coherent and that it conforms to the requirements of the specific rhetorical situation, including the hard points of your assignment. Once you have determined the appropriate format, you will find many similarities among formats—for instance, both print and electronic documents require transitional devices to help the reader to follow the writer's arguments and logic. However, there are important differences between projects for print and those for electronic publication. In Chapter 21 we guide you through the process of completing a print project such as a research paper, a brochure, or a newsletter article. Chapter 22 presents guidelines for authoring a Web site.

Document Formats

TRADITIONAL PRINT FORMATS

Letters	Résumés	Papers/Reports	Booklets
Memorandums	Articles	Flyers	Spreadsheets
Pamphlets	Brochures	Books	Newsletters

COMMON ELECTRONIC FORMATS

Email	Web pages (.htm, .html)	Message forums
Word-processing files	Graphics files	Spreadsheets
Help files	Sound files	Animation files
Program scripts	Style sheets	Databases
Rich Text Format (.rtf)	Portable Document Format (.pdf)	

OTHER PRESENTATION FORMATS

Speeches	Slide shows	Video clips
Dramatic performances	Colloquiums	Debates

Figure 20.1 Document Formats

WWW Web Sites Worth Knowing

20.3

- The Rhetorical Situation, **http://www.bristol.mass.edu/department_pages/quest_writing_lab/writing/rhetoric.htm**

- Writer's Center at Colorado State University, "Guides about Types of Documents," **http://writing.colostate.edu/references/documents.cfm**

GETTING INVOLVED

1. Instructors will rarely accept computer failure as an excuse for a late project. In a group, share any experiences you may have had with untimely electronic glitches and discuss ways that such problems can be avoided or circumvented.

2. Research papers seem to have lots of extra elements, but that is because they represent preprofessional work. Examine a professional article or scholarly book, listing all the separate parts included before or after the main body of the piece. You might encounter features such as title pages, publication and copyright information, outlines, tables of contents, prefaces, appendixes, indexes, and author biographies. Discuss the function of each item.

3. Examine the structure of a scholarly Web page or site. List the various parts of the site, including pages within the site, internal and external navigational cues (links, headings, etc.). Determine how fonts, colors, tables, and other formatting elements

are used to help signify different types of information or different sections of the site. Discuss the functions of the various elements and whether you think they are effective.

MANAGING YOUR PROJECT

1. Write an analysis of the rhetorical situation for your project. Who is your primary audience? What are their needs and expectations? What is your purpose in presenting your information to this audience? What is the occasion for presenting the information? What medium (paper or electronic) have you chosen and why? Discuss your analysis with your peers, orally or by email, and compare your formatting decisions.

2. If you are writing a paper, check the structure of your project as suggested in Section 20b. If you are preparing another kind of project, carefully examine its structure. For example, have friends test-drive a brochure you've designed. Does its arrangement of panels make sense? Are its headings logical? Will readers know where to go for additional information? For a Web site, ask an outsider to navigate the site. Does the structure direct readers logically to important information? Can readers navigate all levels of the site easily? Can they always return quickly to the home page?

C H A P T E R
21

Completing a Print-Based Research Project

Once you have determined that the best medium to present the results of your research is a print-based one, you will want to consider appropriate formats. For example, you might want to format your paper following MLA, APA, or CMS guidelines for traditional, academic audiences. On the other hand, you might need to format your document for submission to a publisher or, for a general audience, as a brochure or newsletter article. Depending on your choice of topic, audience, and purpose, you may even need to prepare a technical report or an oral or visual presentation. In this chapter you will learn to understand the principles of print document design and to apply these principles to a variety of document types.

21a Understand the principles of document design

Unlike writing style, which focuses on word choice, sentence structure, and the figurative language you use in writing, document design is concerned with the ways in which you present your writing through formatting and media. In Figure 21.1 you can see how a document makes use of colors, fonts, images, lines, and boxes to set off elements of the text, show relationships, and lead the reader's eye to important information.

You need to be familiar with the more common elements of document design whether you are planning to present your document in a print or an electronic medium.

Page size, margins, and line spacing. Most academic projects for print will use standard paper sizes (in the United States, 8 1/2 x 11 inches) with standard margins, usually one inch on all four sides. For projects that will be bound, the left-hand margin may be increased to one-and-a-half inches; if the bound project will have type on both sides of each page, the right-hand margin may be increased to one-and-a-half inches on

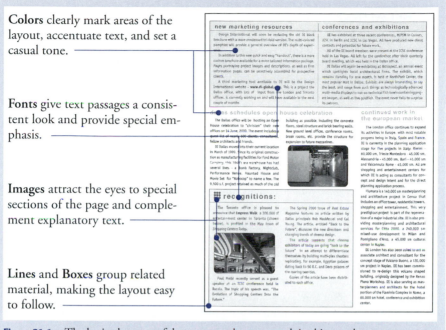

Colors clearly mark areas of the layout, accentuate text, and set a casual tone. ────

Fonts give text passages a consistent look and provide special emphasis. ────

Images attract the eyes to special sections of the page and complement explanatory text. ────

Lines and **Boxes** group related material, making the layout easy to follow. ────

Figure 21.1   The basic elements of document style are at work in this newsletter page.

even-numbered pages. Headers, required for many types of academic papers, are usually positioned one-half inch from the top margin. The document should usually be double-spaced throughout. Specifications for MLA and APA papers are given in Chapters 24 and 25 respectively.

Newsletters and brochures may use considerably smaller margins. Newsletters are often formatted in columns (see Figure 21.1) and may be printed on either standard or legal size (8 1/2 x 14 inches) paper. A brochure may use either size paper, formatted in "panels" to allow it to be folded. Unlike most academic papers, newsletters and brochures may be printed on both sides of a single sheet of paper.

Headings and subheadings. In academic papers, specific guidelines for headings and subheadings often apply. A short research paper (five or six pages) may need only a title. Longer papers may require subheadings that announce the content of major sections. Subheadings should be brief, parallel in phrasing, and consistent in format. MLA style provides fairly loose standards for headings and subheadings, with titles ordinarily centered on the first page and first-level headings flush with the left-hand margin. Subsequent levels of headings, when necessary, may be designated with italics or underlining, or with boldfaced type. APA style (see Chapter 25) defines five levels of headings for professional articles, more than you are likely to need for most academic projects. Figure 21.2 illustrates how you might handle headings for a typical academic project. While the rules vary, most styles agree that you must have at least two headings at each level and that you should be consistent in how you format headings and subheadings in your document.

First-level Heading

First-level headings are flush with the left-hand margin and follow the same rules of capitalization as titles (capitalize the first word and all major words). An extra line space usually precedes the first-level heading in the body of the document. No extra line spacing follows the first-level heading.

Second-level Heading

Second-level headings are usually italicized or underlined and follow the same rules of capitalization as for titles and first-level headings. Notice that no extra line spacing precedes or follows the second-level heading.

Third-level heading. Third-level headings may be italicized, underlined, or boldfaced. Only the first word and proper nouns are capitalized. It is followed by a period and then immediately by the text. No extra line spacing precedes or follows the third-level heading.

Figure 21.2 Formatting Headings for Academic Papers

Newsletters and brochures also use different levels of headers to indicate major and minor divisions. However, in addition to boldface, italics, and underlining, you may be able to choose different font sizes, faces, and colors, or you may use text boxes or background coloring to draw your reader's attention.

Fonts and colors. Mixing too many font styles or colors can be distracting and unattractive. For most academic projects, use a simple *serif* font (see Figure 21.3) such

Font Styles

SERIF FONTS
Serif fonts are the most easily readable. The "feet" lead the reader's eye and help in recognition of letters and words. Use serif fonts for most body text. These are some of the more common serif fonts.

- Courier
- Times or Times New Roman
- Bookman Old Style

SANS SERIF FONTS
Sans serif fonts are generally not as easy to read as serif fonts, but they have a clean look that stands out. Use sans serif fonts for headings. These are examples of common sans serif fonts.

- Arial
- Futura
- Helvetica

Figure 21.3 Choose the font style to suit your project.

as Times Roman 10- or 12-point type. Fonts that are too large can be as difficult to read as those that are too small. Use a quality printer and white paper to increase contrast for easy readability.

With print projects such as brochures or newsletters you have more freedom for artistic expression than with academic essays. For example, you can use colors and fonts for visual emphasis. But the same rules apply—using too many colors can be distracting; it can also be expensive to reproduce projects since commercial printers charge extra for each additional color.

Tables, figures, and graphics. Tables, figures, and other graphics can help readers understand your ideas better than words alone can do. In your own work you might want to use pie charts, graphs, and tables to make statistics easier to interpret or trends easier to spot. Graphics have been shown to aid in reader understanding and retention, especially when complicated or complex statistical information is being given.

Choose the right format to present information:

- Use *tables* to present complicated data in an easy-to-apprehend format and allow comparisons among items.
- Use *bar charts* to allow ready comparison of quantities.
- Use *line charts* to show changes in quantities over time.
- Use *pie charts* to show the distribution of parts of a whole when exact quantities are not essential.
- Use *Gantt charts* to show progress over time toward a goal (see Chapter 1).
- Use *maps* to indicate geographic locations and relations.
- Use *flowcharts* to illustrate steps in a process or procedure.

Be careful, though, not to clutter your work with what design experts call "chartjunk." Develop an eye for clean and attractive presentations on paper or screen.

For academic papers, MLA format requires that you label tables (columns of data) and figures (pictures or illustrations), number them, and briefly identify what they illustrate. Spell out the word *table* and place the head above the table, flush left. Following are a properly prepared table and figure.

Table 1

Economic Dimensions of the Bond Market, 1980-90

Type of Issuer[a]	Year-End Amounts Outstanding (in billions)		
	1980	1985	1990
U.S. Treasury	$159.8	$427.0	$1,023.6
U.S. agencies	17.6	276.1	447.3
States and municipalities	144.4	322.3	734.9
Corporations	181.0	421.7	752.3
Total	$502.8	$1,447.1	$2,958.1

Sources:Federal Reserve Bulletin, U.S. Treasury Bulletin, and Survey of Current Business.

[a]Excludes institutional issues; data are not available.

Figure, which is usually abbreviated in the caption as *Fig.,* appears below the illustration, flush left.

Fig.1. A well-prepared figure of a mountain bike.

When preparing an APA paper, you may want to check the complete coverage of figures and tables in the *Publication Manual of the American Psychological Association,* fifth edition. For APA-style student papers, figures (including graphs, illustrations, and photos) and tables may appear in the body of the text. Longer tables and all figures are placed on separate pages, immediately following their mention in the text.

Chromosomes consist of four different nucleotides or bases--
adenine, guanine, thymine, and cytosine--which, working
together, provide the code for different genes (see Figure 1).

Short tables may appear on the same page as text material.

Figures and tables are numbered consecutively. A figure caption appears below the figure. When the illustration is borrowed from a source, you must get permission to reproduce it. Acknowledge a borrowing in this manner:

Figure 1. The four bases of the genetic code: adenine (A),
guanine (G), thymine (T), and cytosine (C). Note. From Your
Genes, Your Choice, by C. Baker, 1997. Copyright 1997 by the
American Association for the Advancement of Science. Reprinted
with permission.

A table title appears above the table; the source of information appears below the table.

TABLE 1 Unemployment in the United States, 1999

	Unemployed Persons	Unemployment Rate	Unemployment Rate Rank	Total Labor Force	Labor Force as % of Population	% of Population Rank
Alabama	87,600	4.0%	24	2,170,300	49.9%	41
Alaska	19,100	6.0	2	316,700	51.6	34
Arizona	106,900	4.4	19	2,406,100	51.5	35
Arkansas	58,500	4.7	14	1,258,000	49.6	45
California	881,700	5.3	6	16,605,300	50.8	38
Colorado	69,000	3.0	39	2,286,900	57.6	2
Connecticut	44,800	2.6	46	1,706,500	52.1	30
Delaware	13,300	3.3	36	398,200	53.6	18
Florida	286,100	3.8	26	7,468,500	50.1	39
Georgia	148,900	3.7	28	4,059,600	53.1	22
Hawaii	32,000	5.4	5	596,700	50.0	40
Idaho	33,300	5.0	8	659,900	53.7	17
Illinois	293,500	4.6	15	6,388,700	53.0	23
Indiana	73,100	2.4	50	3,081,100	52.2	27
Iowa	42,800	2.7	45	1,597,300	55.8	7
Kansas	48,600	3.4	35	1,449,700	55.1	8
Kentucky	80,200	4.1	22	1,955,000	49.7	43
Louisiana	97,100	4.7	12	2,054,500	47.0	48
Maine	27,800	4.1	21	670,000	53.8	15
Maryland	108,900	3.9	25	2,815,300	54.8	10
Massachusetts	105,500	3.2	37	3,286,700	53.5	20
Michigan	175,300	3.4	31	5,092,000	51.9	31
Minnesota	81,000	3.0	42	2,740,600	58.0	1
Mississippi	60,300	4.7	13	1,281,700	46.6	49
Missouri	103,100	3.5	29	2,911,800	53.5	19
Montana	22,600	4.8	11	475,300	54.0	14
Nebraska	22,400	2.4	49	933,400	56.1	6
Nevada	36,600	3.8	27	955,500	54.7	11
New Hampshire	16,600	2.5	48	671,300	56.6	5
New Jersey	206,000	4.8	9	4,250,900	52.4	26
New Mexico	50,000	6.0	3	832,100	47.9	47
New York	461,800	5.2	7	8,910,200	49.0	46
North Carolina	113,900	3.0	41	3,845,900	51.0	37
North Dakota	9,800	2.9	43	341,100	53.4	21
Ohio	266,400	4.6	16	5,848,600	52.2	28
Oklahoma	57,500	3.5	30	1,661,600	49.6	44
Oregon	97,200	5.5	4	1,763,000	53.7	16
Pennsylvania	255,200	4.3	20	5,979,200	49.8	42
Rhode Island	20,800	4.1	23	509,400	51.5	36
South Carolina	66,600	3.4	34	1,980,200	51.6	33
South Dakota	10,300	2.6	47	400,400	54.2	13
Tennessee	96,000	3.4	33	2,813,700	51.8	32
Texas	464,500	4.5	18	10,308,800	52.2	29
Utah	37,900	3.4	32	1,105,400	52.6	25
Vermont	10,700	3.1	38	340,000	57.5	3
Virginia	96,300	2.7	44	3,593,900	52.9	24
Washington	148,600	4.8	10	3,120,600	54.9	9
West Virginia	49,800	6.1	1	813,900	44.9	50
Wisconsin	88,200	3.0	40	2,964,100	56.7	4
Wyoming	11,800	4.5	17	261,600	54.4	12
DC	16,300	6.0	—	271,500	51.9	—
US	5,947,200	4.3	—	139,254,000	51.5	—

Source: U.S. Bureau of Labor Statistics

> ### 🕸 FOCUS ON . . . **Creating Graphics and Visuals**
>
> It makes sense to learn how to manipulate the graphics software available in word-processing or data management programs. In the former you may be offered a wide range of drawing tools. In the latter you can typically choose how to present data (in tables, bar graphs, pie charts); the program itself produces the actual image, which you can modify to suit your needs. Presentation programs, too, make it easy to create professional-looking slides and overheads. Some presentation programs even allow you to include sound and may allow you to publish your presentation automatically on the World Wide Web. Desktop publishing programs are more complex, but you can learn to use them to design sophisticated projects, including magazines and books.
>
> If you have access to the Web, you can download pictures and other visual items for your projects, but you must both document the borrowings and get permission to use them from the authors or owners of the material. If you scan images from published work, you need to document the borrowing and obtain permission to use it in your published project as well (see Chapter 9).

Photos and other visuals. Photographs provide a realistic view of a person, place, or thing. They can be useful when you want to "humanize" a project, for example, by including photographs of people in a newsletter or brochure. Other types of visuals can depict what photographs cannot. Line drawings may show a rendering of a product that has not yet been developed; exploded views and cutaway drawings can allow readers an inside view of something—a machine or even a person's body (see Figure 21.4). Choose the right visual for the information you need to convey.

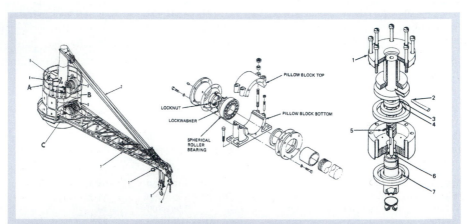

Figure 21.4   Line drawing, exploded view, and cutaway drawing used in technical reports. *(Source: Naval Systems Data Support Activity, U.S. Navy, Technical Manual Management Program, "Hull Mechanical and Electrical Equipment/Systems Technical Manual Production and Style Guide."* **http://nsdsa.phdnswc.navy.mil/tmmp/axgyd010/toc.htm** *)*

Lists and text boxes. Complicated information or instructions that must be followed in a specific order may be best presented online as either an ordered list (if the instructions must be followed in sequence) or an unordered, or bulleted, list (when the order of operations is not essential). Ordered lists usually use numbers or letters to designate the sequence.

1. Take out two slices of fresh bread.
2. Spread one slice of bread with a thin layer of peanut butter.
3. Spread the other slice of bread with a layer of your favorite jam or jelly.
4. Place the two slices of bread together, coated layers facing each other.
5. Enjoy.

Bulleted lists highlight key ideas that do not require a specific order.

- Use bulleted lists to highlight key ideas that do not require a specific order.
- Use ordered lists to present ideas that must occur in a certain sequence.

Text boxes are useful in newsletters and brochures to set off headlines or other information that you wish to stand out. You can fill in the background of boxed text with shades of gray (for a black-and-white project) or colors, but be careful: make sure there is enough contrast between text and background to allow for easy reading.

21b Apply design principles for print documents

Since the invention of movable type in the fifteenth century, people have relied on printed texts for much of their information. Thanks to powerful software and high-speed printers, almost anyone today can produce documents that rival those from a print shop. But many writers have abused this design capability, sometimes forgetting that design should enhance a message, not become the message itself. Fortunately, most professional and academic disciplines offer sensible guidelines for formatting documents. You will want to consult the style guide for your field whenever you begin a major project—whether it's a paper or something less conventional. You don't want to waste time creating projects you ultimately cannot use.

Consider the following guidelines for specific types of print projects.

Designing academic papers and essays for final print copy. Most academic papers are relatively restrained in appearance, using diverse fonts, colors, and graphics only minimally. However, within limits, academic essays do include specific design criteria you must consider. The sample essays at the end of this chapter (MLA) and Chapter 25 (APA) illustrate design concepts you will need to follow. You will want to take advantage of the automatic formatting features of your word processor, such as italics, block indent, hanging indent, page numbering, headers, centering, and so on. Some word-processing packages include templates or style sheets that can help you set up your document following generic "research paper" guidelines; compare those style guidelines with the requirements of your project. Make sure you spell check your document, use a good quality printer and paper, and proofread your work carefully.

Most word processors include built-in help to make learning these features easier. If necessary, consider taking a course on word processing (perhaps one is offered by your school) or purchase one of the many books available to help you get the most from your software.

The following checklist presents important considerations for traditional research projects.

CHECKLIST

Checklist for Research Projects

○ For academic papers, have you placed your name, your instructor's name, the date, and the course name on the first or title page, if appropriate?

○ Is the title centered? Are only the major words and any proper nouns capitalized? (Do not use boldfaced type, underlining, italics, or different font sizes or types for titles.)

○ Did you number the pages? Are they in the right order?

○ Have you double-spaced your text?

○ Are tables and figures labeled correctly and introduced in the text?

○ Have you provided transitions and navigational aids such as subheadings, if appropriate?

○ Have you used quotation marks and parentheses correctly and in pairs? (The closing quotation mark and parenthesis are often forgotten.)

○ Have you indented all direct quotations of four typed lines or more (MLA) or of forty words or more (APA)?

○ Have you remembered that indented quotations are not placed between quotation marks?

○ Did you introduce all direct quotations with some identification of their author, source, or significance?

○ Have you handled titles correctly, italicizing the titles of books and putting the titles of articles between quotation marks?

○ Did you include a Works Cited or References page? Is it alphabetized correctly? Did you handle the formatting correctly?

○ Have you proofread your work carefully for errors? (Use a spelling checker if available but carefully proofread your final documents as well before declaring them finished.

Designing articles for submission in hard copy to publishers. Many publishers follow the same guidelines for preparing manuscripts as outlined in MLA, APA, or another of the major style guides. However, some publishers have their own formatting requirements, which must be followed meticulously. Most prefer that design elements in manuscripts be kept to a minimum and that authors use few if any of the automatic formatting features available in their word processors. Instead, some require the use of special codes, or "tags" (similar to Hypertext Markup Language tags; see Chapter 22), to tell a printer exactly how to treat various elements. The following checklist contains important considerations when submitting copy to a publisher.

CHECKLIST

Submitting Articles to Publishers in Hard Copy

- ⭕ Have you followed the editor's instructions for placement of name and affiliation?
- ⭕ Have you included all the parts required by the submission guidelines (abstract, author biography, etc.)?
- ⭕ Have you followed the editor's or required style guidelines *exactly,* including guidelines for formatting the document, for use of nonsexist language, and for citation of sources?
- ⭕ Did you include the required number of copies?
- ⭕ Did you include envelopes or sufficient attached or unattached postage as required by the editor's or publication's guidelines?
- ⭕ Have you included a cover letter with additional information?
- ⭕ Did you double-check the name and address to submit your manuscript?

Follow the style manual or publisher's guidelines as required for your project, respecting any recommendations about length, margins, spacing, and placement of notes or references. Make sure your printouts are clean and legible and that you include separate camera-ready copies of all artwork, as required.

Designing newsletters and brochures. Desktop publishing software such as Adobe *PageMaker* and Broderbund *Print Shop* enables you to create newsletters and brochures that rival those from print shops, and many word processing packages include templates to help you design effective publications, such as the newsletter shown in Figure 21.5.

Newsletters are often printed on both sides of a single sheet of paper, although some newletters include multiple pages. Brochures are usually printed on both sides of a single sheet of paper, in "panels" (similar to columns), so that they can be easily folded. Pay attention to the order of information in both. Use type sizes that are large enough to read (even though you may be tempted to use smaller fonts to squeeze in more information), and use colors, graphics, or other techniques for emphasis sparingly and only when necessary. Often newsletters and brochures fully justify the margins; that is, text continues to the very edge of the right-hand margin. But be careful—unless you are using a proportional font, full-justification may leave wide gaps between words on a line, requiring you to insert hyphens and word breaks manually; "ragged" right-hand margins (called "left justification" because only the text on the left-hand margin is even) is easier to read with most font styles. High contrast and ease of readability are as important for newslet-

FRONT PAGE OF A NEWSLETTER

The **masthead** identifies a newsletter with a specific organization, often showing logos or catchphrases members recognize immediately. Mastheads also include publication date and issue number.

Lead articles appear on the front pages of newsletters—they reflect the most important recent events appearing in the issue.

Images are wrapped by text so that the space on each page is used efficiently, and related material is closely grouped.

Borders are *sometimes* used to frame text or decorate the margins.

PAGE THREE OF A NEWSLETTER

Running heads often include the same information appearing in the masthead and sometimes page numbering.

Standard articles are introduced with enhanced headlines. This example uses a left-justified block style of paragraphing.

Regular features are columns that appear in each issue; they are often framed or otherwise distinguished from standard articles so they can be easily recognized.

Footers can include page numbering and information appearing in the masthead.

Figure 21.5   Designing an Effective Newsletter

ters and brochures as they are for other types of projects. Of course, when your newsletter or brochure is to be professionally typeset, you may have more choices.

The following checklist presents important considerations for creating newsletters.

CHECKLIST
Newsletters

○ Select the size of paper and the method of binding, and plan the number of pages you will use. Choose a margin width that allows for binding or folding.

○ Determine whether you'll use images and how many colors you want to show. Colorful designs are more costly.

○ Decide whether you'll use multicolumn pages. More columns usually mean more planning, but when formatted carefully multiple columns make more efficient use of space.

○ Map out each page with two goals in mind: (1) showcasing the most important articles and (2) preventing your reader from having to jump from page to page to read a single article.

○ For your masthead, use a distinctive font that reflects the spirit of the organization represented by the newsletter. Adjust headlines according to their importance, but maintain a consistent font size and style throughout the body of the articles.

○ Write short paragraphs to avoid long, unbroken stretches of print, especially when you're using narrow columns.

Brochures usually strive to stimulate interest or provide specific information about an organization, its activities, and its concerns. Figure 21.6 illustrates design principles that you will want to consider.

The following checklist will help ensure that your design suits your purpose effectively.

CHECKLIST
Brochures

○ Decide on the purpose of the brochure. Is it to introduce your organization? to talk about events or activities? How do you want your audience to respond to the brochure? Choose content accordingly.

○ Plan the layout of the brochure carefully, keeping in mind how it will fold and how both sides will look. If the brochure is to be mailed, leave one panel blank for the address.

○ Sketch out, or storyboard, each panel to visualize how you'll lay out information in the brochure.

○ If possible, make each panel of the brochure a self-contained unit, so that it will still make sense when read in its folded state.

○ Limit the amount of information to what readers can absorb in a few minutes, but tell them how they can learn more.

FRONT PANEL OF BROCHURE

Use **graphics** and **colors** to attract the eyes of readers. Keep in mind that most brochures must compete for attention.

The **logo** for the organization should appear on the front panel. This logo begins building a persona that the following panels will develop.

Show **addresses** and **contact** information so that readers get a clear idea of the organization's affiliations and institutional relationships.

INSIDE PANELS OF BROCHURE

Each **panel** includes a main heading with related passages of text. Panels have consistent layouts so readers can easily see the central points.

Headings are set apart from other text using inverted background and foreground colors. Provocative, eye-catching phrases draw readers in.

Contact information and the organizational **logo** reappear on the end panel, reminding readers that further details are available if they are interested.

Images have been carefully selected to portray themes and activities related to the organization. Here the images form a collage extending across **all** panels.

Paragraphs focus on the highlights of the organization, especially those that will seem most intriguing to the target audience.

Figure 21.6 **Designing an Effective Brochure**

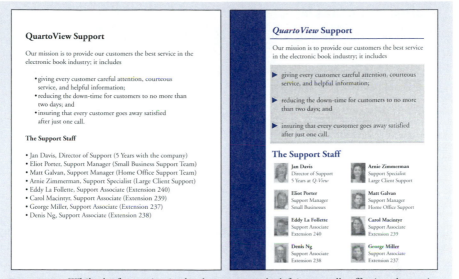

Figure 21.7 While the formatting in the document on the left is generally effective, the version on the right has enhanced the layout with images, multiple type styles, and simple graphics.

Designing technical reports. Many companies have their own in-house style guidelines for technical reports. You will want to follow these guidelines scrupulously. When designing technical reports, you can usually include photographic images, line drawings, graphs, and tables. Some reports, such as corporate annual reports or technical manuals, may incorporate full-color reproductions, photographs, and other complex graphical elements. These reports may be costly and will have to be professionally printed. Thus most technical reports use color sparingly, if at all.

Readers will find your report easy to follow when you use features such as headings or section numbers, lists, and tables to highlight significant information. You might also include a table of contents or an abstract that summarizes important information, especially for lengthy documents. Figure 21.7 compares two versions of the presentation of the same material for a published report.

Review the following checklist to make sure your report includes all the necessary information.

CHECKLIST

Technical Reports

○ Have you followed the appropriate format for your report? If no specific format is required, have you chosen one that suits the information you are providing?

○ Have you included all the necessary parts, such as a title page, an abstract, a table of contents, appendixes, and/or a bibliography?

(Continued)

Technical Reports *(Continued)*

○ Do the page numbers on your table of contents or index page match those in your document?

○ Are headings and subheadings used appropriately? Are headings and subheadings at the same level formatted consistently, and are they parallel in grammatical structure?

○ Have you used figures, tables, and graphics appropriately? Have you stated the source of the information contained in them?

○ Does your conclusion follow logically from the evidence you have provided? Does it agree with your stated purpose?

21.1 **Designing oral and visual presentations.** Oral presentations are not, strictly speaking, print projects; however, an effective oral presentation is usually carefully planned, often written on note cards, and may make extensive use of posters or electronic slide shows to present information. Most oral presentations follow the same sequence as a formal written report: an introduction, a body, and a conclusion.

For most presentations you would do well to heed the sage advice of professionals—begin by telling your audience what you will tell them; tell them; then conclude by telling the audience what you have told them. Repetition, often berated in scholarly papers, is considered a key to effective oral presentations for its aiding memory and reinforcing of important ideas.

For many presentations you will prepare posters, electronic slide shows, or handouts to accompany the information you present orally. Beginners often make the mistake of providing too much or too little information on a slide. You need a title and a few bulleted points on each slide—enough to keep the audience interested and on track. Crowd too much information on a slide, and you will distract viewers and may make the slide hard to read; offer too little information, and the slide will seem irrelevant, maybe even distracting. Remember, it is up to you to provide the details orally.

For your slides you can vary both font sizes and colors. Begin by considering the size of the room in which you will make your presentation and the projection equipment you will need. For electronic presentations you may want to consider using sans serif fonts: use a size large enough to be read easily, and use high contrast (white backgrounds and dark text or dark backgrounds with light text) for easy visibility. Use graphics or multimedia elements and colors with care—make sure they are important to your presentation and do not distract your audience's attention from what you have to say. Always test your slides to be certain they are readable by your audience. Also proofread them carefully—your audience will have plenty of time to spot errors!

Most presentation software, such as Microsoft *PowerPoint* and Corel *Presentations*, includes templates for various types of presentations and slide shows as well as context-sensitive help, as shown in Figure 21.8.

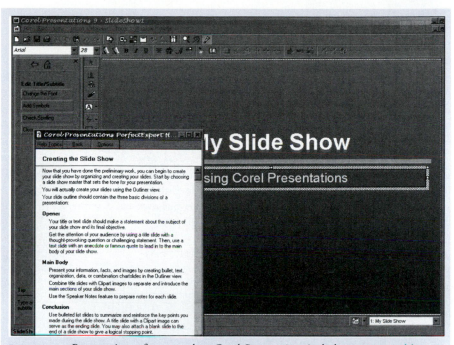

Figure 21.8 Presentation software, such as Corel *Presentations*, includes context-sensitive help to guide you. *(Source: Corel Presentations 9 Copyright © 1999 COREL CORPORATION and COREL CORPORATION LIMITED. All rights reserved.)*

CHECKLIST

Presentations

○ Does your introduction adequately announce the purpose of the presentation and what information it will include? Don't forget to introduce yourself to your audience as well.

○ Have you chosen appropriate figures, graphics, or tables to illustrate difficult or complex information?

○ Do handouts, posters, or slides use bulleted points to set off important items, or have you crowded too much information on them?

○ Are visual aids large enough to be seen by everyone in your audience?

○ Have you prepared a summary for your conclusion to reinforce the points you make in your oral presentation?

○ Have you timed your presentation? If it is too long, you will need to cut information; if it is too short, are you sure you have included sufficient details?

○ Have you practiced your presentation sufficiently? Do you have note cards or an outline to help you keep track of what you want to say?

21c Include all the parts your project requires

Before submitting a research project, reread the specifications of the instructor or the professional society to which you are submitting your paper. Must you, for instance, include an abstract or an outline? What leeway (if any) do you have in arranging the title page, notes, bibliography, and other features? A research paper, for example, typically follows a specific order. The sample research essay at the end of this chapter presents a model paper in MLA style, and the essay on pages 384–402 presents a paper in APA style. For a more complex paper such as a master's thesis or a doctoral dissertation, you might follow the order recommended in *The MLA Style Manual* (MLA) or the *Publication Manual of the American Psychological Association* (APA). Many schools publish their own guidelines for submitting graduate-level theses.

Use the checklist that follows or create one of your own (see Chapter 1) to ensure that you have included all required parts of your project.

C H E C K L I S T

> ### Checklist for a Research Project

- ○ Title page (not recommended in MLA; required in APA).
- ○ Outline (optional; begins on its own page; requires separate title page).
- ○ Abstract (optional, but common in APA; usually on its own page).
- ○ Body of the essay (Arabic pagination begins with the body of the essay in MLA; in APA, Arabic pagination begins with the title page).
- ○ Content or bibliographic notes.
- ○ Works Cited/References (begins on its own page separate from the body of the essay and any content or bibliographic notes).

21d Submit your project professionally

Whether you've written a paper, designed a brochure, or composed a technical report, be sure the work meets appropriate standards as required by the hard points of the assignment (see Section 1b) or the style guide you are required to follow. Examine what you've produced to see that everything looks "detailed": the writing is sharp and correct, the images are crisp and labeled, the pagination is right, the documentation is solid.

Don't overdo it. Bind a research paper modestly with a staple or a paper clip. Nothing more elaborate is needed, unless an instructor asks you to place the essay in a folder along with all materials you used in developing it. For newsletters or brochures, make sure the information flows from one page to the next or from one panel to the next. If you have printed a newsletter on two sides of a single page, make sure that the print goes in the same direction on both sides! For brochures, you want to make sure the reader can follow the text from one panel (or "page") to the next and that space for a mailing address or contact information is in the appropriate place.

When you submit an article for publication, be sure to follow all instructions for submission provided by the editors. Note in particular how many clean copies they require of your work, to whom those copies should be sent, and whether you should furnish a self-addressed, stamped envelope or separate, unattached postage for the return of your work.

When files are to be submitted electronically (you may need to submit your work to a drop box in WebCT or Blackboard, or you may need to email it as an attachment to your teacher or submit it on disk to teachers, fellow students, or publishers), you will want to be certain the file is in a format that is readable by your audience. Luckily, there are formats that are readable across platforms and applications. For example, you can save your work as text-only, usually as ASCII-DOS Text or MS-DOS Text. Unfortunately, text-only files will strip your document of any special formatting features (italics, boldfaced fonts, colors, graphics). A better choice might be to save your word-processed files as PDF (Portable Document Format) or RTF (Rich Text Format).

In Part VI we present specific guidelines for using Columbia Online Style (COS), Modern Language Association Style (MLA), American Pscyhological Association Style (APA), *Chicago Manual of Style* (CMS), and Council of Science Editors Style (CSE) for documenting sources. In addition, you will find sample Works Cited or References pages for COS, CMS, and CSE. A complete sample paper for MLA is included at the end of this chapter. Chapter 25 contains a sample paper in APA style. While these chapters are primarily for reference purposes, you may find the information well worth the time and effort you spend reading them as you near completion of your research project. Pay special attention to the sample research papers—how they are designed, how they incorporate information from research, how they use figures or special elements, and how they handle the citation of sources. For projects that include references to electronic or electronically accessed sources, you may want to consider following the guidelines presented in Chapter 23, Columbia Online Style (COS-humanities for MLA-style projects and COS-scientific for APA-style projects).

Many of the design principles for print projects apply to other types of projects as well. As you have seen, an oral presentation often makes use of graphical aids, some of them electronically produced. In Chapter 22 you will find more about how to apply design guidelines to electronic projects, and basic advice about authoring a Web page.

21e Sample MLA paper

The sample paper by Ben Brenneman, a senior English major at the University of Texas at Austin, is accompanied by checklists designed to help you set up a paper correctly in MLA style. When your work meets the specifications on the checklists, it should be in proper form.

The assignment that generated this paper asked students to prepare a report of roughly 1,500 words on a subject related to language. Brenneman chose to write about a subject from his own experiences as a student teacher in Texas high schools—the effect of standardized testing on students and instructors. The report developed into an argument highly critical of standardized testing.

We have numbered the paragraphs in "Can Quality Survive the Standardized Test?" for easy reference in classroom discussions; do *not* number the paragraphs in a paper unless an instructor or editor instructs you to do so.

Brenneman 1

Ben H. Brenneman

Professor Ruszkiewicz

English 379

2 March 2000

Can Quality Survive the Standardized Test?

¶1   In <u>Seeking Diversity</u>, a book on teaching middle
school language arts, author and teacher Linda Rief says,
"I expect good reading and writing, in which process and
product are woven tightly into literate tapestries of
wonder and awe" (10). Rief thus describes the Holy Grail of
writing instruction: a classroom in which students learn to
write because they care about the final product and want to
do excellent work. Such an environment would give students
the ability to write by turning them into writers.
Unfortunately, the American education system today is
failing to teach many students even the basic skills they
will need to survive. Statements by teachers that "the
greater number of the young people we teach [. . .] do not
know how to read, spell, write, use correct grammar, do
simple math, remember, use logic" are supported by
statistics showing "that only 55% of the nations 17-year-
olds and 49% of out-of-school adults are able to write an
acceptable letter ordering a product by mail" (Neill 18).
Yet the dominant response to this problem--competency
testing in our public schools--may be destroying any regard
students may have for language by turning writing into a
formulaic exercise.

¶2   Many states, in fact, have already responded to
problems in their educational systems by passing laws
mandating the skills that students must learn by a
specified grade. The students' ability to reach the
objectives and the faculty's ability to teach this
"standards-based curriculum" are then measured by statewide

CHECKLIST

Title Page—MLA

MLA does not require a separate cover sheet or title page. If your instructor expects one, center the title of your paper and your name in the upper third of the paper. Center the course title, your instructor's name, and the date of submission on the lower third of the sheet, double-spacing between the elements.

The first page of a paper without a separate title page will look like the facing page. Be sure to check all the items in this list.

○ Place your name, your instructor's name, the course title, and the date in the upper left-hand corner, beginning one inch from the top of the page. These items are double spaced.

○ Identify your instructor by an appropriate title. When uncertain about academic rank, use *Mr.* or *Ms.*

Dr. James Duban   Professor Rosa Eberly
Ms. Evelyn Westbrook   Mr. John Kinkade

○ Center the title a double space under the date. Capitalize the first and last word of the title. Capitalize all other words *except* articles (*a, an, the*), prepositions, the *to* in infinitives, and coordinating conjunctions—unless they are the first or last words.

```
Can Quality Survive the Standardized Test?
```

○ Do not underline or boldface the title of your paper. Do not use all caps, place it between quotation marks, or end it with a period. Titles may, however, end with question marks or include words or phrases that are italicized, underlined, or between quotation marks.

```
Violence in Shakespeare's Macbeth

Dylan's "Like a Rolling Stone" Revisited
```

○ Begin the body of the essay two lines (a double space) below the title. Double-space the entire essay, including quotations.

○ Use one-inch margins at the sides and bottom of this page.

○ Number this first page in the upper right-hand corner, one-half inch from the top, one inch from the right margin. Precede the page number with your last name.

Brenneman 2

standardized tests. Students and schools that fall short of the mark can then be identified for improvement. As Neill explains, "the strongest argument in support of competency requirements is the potential for motivating students, schools, and districts" (8). The results of testing are carefully monitored and publicized to show continuing improvement in the performance of public schools (see Table 1).

Table 1

Percentage of Students Passing All Texas Assessment
  of Academic Skills Exams (TAAS)

	1994	1995	1996	1997	1998	4 Yr. Gain
Grade 3	58	66	70	74	76	18
Grade 4	54	64	67	72	78	24
Grade 5	58	66	73	79	83	25
Grade 6	56	60	69	77	79	23
Grade 7	55	58	67	75	78	23
Grade 8	49	50	59	67	72	23
Grade 10	52	54	60	68	72	20

Source: Texas Business and Education Coalition, School
  Gains. 1999. 27 Feb. 2000. <http://www.tbec.org/
  gains.HTML>.

¶3   In many states this progress has been motivated by attaching increasingly serious consequences to the results of these tests. Students who fail the state aptitude test may be held back a grade, or they may even be denied a high school diploma. Teachers are also under increasing pressure to get test scores up. Jack Kaufhold, a professor of educational psychology, notes that principals have been warned, "If your test scores don't go up, you may lose your job." He adds, "Teachers also know that if their students' achievement test scores fluctuate too much from year to year, they too could be demoted or dismissed" (14).

CHECKLIST

Body of the Essay—MLA

The body of an MLA research paper continues uninterrupted until the separate Notes page (if any) and the Works Cited page. Be sure to type or handwrite the essay on good-quality paper.

○ Use margins of at least one inch all around. Try to keep the right-hand margin reasonably straight. Do not hyphenate words at the end of lines.

○ Place page numbers in the upper right-hand corner, one inch from the right edge of the page and one-half inch from the top. Precede the page number with your last name.

○ Indent the first line of each paragraph one-half inch, or five spaces if you use a typewriter.

○ Indent long quotations one inch, or ten spaces if you use a typewriter. In MLA documentation, long quotations are any that exceed four typed lines in the body of your essay. Double-space these indented quotations.

¶4   State officials justify these types of high-stakes
assessments on the grounds that the skills the tests focus
on are those students will need to function in society.
They argue, moreover, that students who receive a quality
education should have little trouble fulfilling the minimum
requirements. For instance, the standards for writing set
in Texas, called the "Texas Essential Knowledge and Skills"
or TEKS, state that students who graduate high school must
"write in a variety of forms using effective word choice,
structure, and sentences with an emphasis on organizing
logical arguments [. . .]; write in a voice and style
appropriate to audience and purpose; and organize in
writing to ensure coherence" (Texas Education Agency). In
other words, everyone who receives a high school diploma
should be able to communicate effectively in writing.
Students demonstrate their skill during the Texas
Assessment of Academic Skills (TAAS) by composing an essay.
As Mary argues on a WWW forum sponsored by Teachers.Net,
"The TEKS based TAAS are a reflection of the specific
standards the children of our state should meet. That's
precisely what we should be teaching." Many teachers,
however, find that their curriculums are already adequate.
Their response to these requirements is like Sheri Arni's:
"My answer has been to leave unchanged most of what happens
in my classroom" (76). Rief, for example, gives her
students "a two-day crash course [. . .] just before they
take the state-mandated achievement tests [. . .] Two days
is all I allow" (180).

¶5   Unfortunately some schools fall short of the mark.
The administrators in these institutions are then forced to
make changes to the curriculum in order to raise scores
quickly. In Maryland, teachers responded to a writing test
that they felt was too difficult by creating writing labs,
increasing the amount of writing done in regular English,

and cooperating between departments to focus on writing in all disciplines (Corbett and Wilson). This is the type of reform the tests were intended to produce. The instructors at this school improved their curriculum by finding innovative ways to teach their students how to write. Anne Shaughnessy, when preparing her students for the Florida assessment, had them discuss their responses to a sample prompt. She showed them that the qualities they felt made an essay successful were the same criteria that would be used to score their tests. She then had them use the actual rubric to score their essays in class. In this way Shaughnessy gave her students some insight into the logic behind the test, making it more than simply an arbitrary exercise. She writes, "Clearly I was teaching to the test, but I was also introducing activities that extended rather than displaced the writing curriculum" (56).

¶6   These improvements are certainly commendable. They occur when schools are blessed with creative teachers who are willing to take risks. However, many educators, when faced with the possibility of unemployment, turn to the tried-and-true method the army uses to train new recruits: drill, drill, drill. In the Maryland case, for example, Corbett and Wilson note that "teachers would stop what they were doing with students [. . .] and inject an intense period of [. . .] 'drill and review' specifically related to the test" (124). When preparing for a writing exam, students spend this period responding to practice prompts, often from previous tests that have been released by the state. A teacher in Texas reported that she "had to give a writing test AND a reading test every six weeks" (Melissa). In teaching circles this strategy is known as the "drill-and-kill" approach. In other words, students are drilled until all genuine interest in the subject is killed by weeks of prompt writing.

Brenneman 5

¶7   Teachers are alarmed by the drill-and-kill approach to test preparation. They fear that the focus of their instruction has shifted from producing excellent writing for a general audience to producing adequate writing in order to avoid the wrath of the state. This attitude is communicated to the students simply by the time spent in practice. As one Texas teacher laments, "from mid-January through April we are not teachers, we are masters of how to take a test" (Linda/tx). In this environment students begin to believe that mastery of the test is the goal of their education. They often create, or are even taught, ways to improve their scores by manipulating the test. According to Donna Garner, any student who got a high score on the essay portion of the TAAS could miss most of the questions on the grammar-oriented part of the test and still pass. She says that, when students understand this,

> it's rather hard to get them to see the
> seriousness of correct grammar, spelling,
> punctuation, capitalization, and sentence
> structure. Once the students learn to "play the
> TAAS game" by scripting their essays to a set
> pattern, the accuracy of the content is of little
> importance to them.

These students see writing as a task they will have to perform once in order to graduate, not as a skill they will need to communicate effectively in the real world.

¶8   Kaufhold describes this mindset as "convergent thinking." He says that these types of tests emphasize "the need to search for one right answer. Creative ideas or divergent thinking is discouraged as students narrow the scope of their thinking toward what will be on the test" (14). Ironically, such narrowing is actually endorsed by A. D. Rison in his 1990 book designed to help students pass the language arts portion of the TAAS. He supports the use

Brenneman 6

of a "Rison Design," basically the typical hourglass shape
long used to teach the five-paragraph theme. He believes
that students should use this design so that "many
competing functions, thinking, writing, vision, and other
unnecessary movements are lessened" (136). And yet for
years, many teachers of composition have complained that
such a standard form "almost inevitably encourages dull,
formulaic writing" (Irmscher 97) and that, when these forms
were taught, "all of the students seemed to write exactly
alike" (104). By focusing on formulaic essays, teachers
encourage convergent thinking by giving students the
impression that there is only one correct way to write. In
a 1990 article in the English Journal, John Dinan says that
students "believe that barren, formulaic writing is what we
want from them. Standardized tests of English cultivate
this belief [. . .] because they implicitly define the
writing process as mechanistic and impersonal" (54). The
concept of writing as a mechanical process is very
different from that advocated in Rief's ideal classroom.

¶9   As dull as these exercises are for teachers to
grade, they are even duller for students to write. Rief
makes the comment, "I cannot immerse my students in
literature I don't like, anymore than any of us can write
effectively on topics in which we have little interest"
(19). One of the sample prompts Rison gives for fourth
graders consists of a picture of a man sitting in a hole
eating a sandwich. Beside him lie a pick and a lunchbox.
The caption says, "This is a picture of a construction
worker. Look at this picture and describe what you see on
two sheets" (143). Is this topic supposed to produce a
student's best writing? Are there aspects of a construction
worker's life to which fourth graders can relate their own
experiences? Why should they care about the construction
worker at all? Nothing in this exercise has any application

Brenneman 7

beyond preparation for answering similarly bland test prompts in the future. When confronted with one such prompt, Rief cut it out of the test books for her class and replaced it with "Write about anything you care deeply about. Try to convince the reader how much you care" (121).

¶10   The prompts Rison gives for tenth graders are not much better: "Your school wants to add a new course. Your principal has asked for suggestions. Write a letter to your principal telling what courses you would add and give convincing reasons for your choice" (180). The work can seem mindless. Students in Maryland were forced to sit through drill sessions even after they had passed the state-mandated tests for graduation (Corbett). Imagine, day after day of tedious prompt writing for no purpose whatsoever. No wonder Dinan complains,

> To take such a test is to become bored, to become
> a machine--that is, to take on the
> characteristics of a dull, lifeless writer
> [. . .] most students simply don't <u>like</u>
> writing very much, they are apprehensive about
> it, beleaguered by it, inclined to do it only on
> demand. (55)

Drilling students for these tests undermines the writing teacher's attempts to create an environment in which students are interested in and feel comfortable with their writing.

¶11   Under these conditions students learn to hate writing. They see it as a boring chore, a task they must complete in order to please a higher authority rather than a process intended to produce something they themselves can take pride in. As soon as they learn to write the type of dry, five-paragraph essay that puts professors to sleep, their growth as writers ends. The type of idyllic writing classroom Rief describes is still possible under the

pressure of a high-stakes test, but it requires creative
faculty willing to bet their jobs that students can pass
these tests without drills. Unfortunately, when
superintendents are receiving calls from angry parents
whose children aren't going to graduate, what is good can
take a back seat to what is expedient. In the rush to raise
the scores of those who can't meet the state objectives,
creativity is crushed in those who can.

Brenneman 9

Works Cited

Arni, Sherry. "I Can Live With It." English Journal 79
(Nov. 1990): 76.

Corbett, H. Dickson, and Bruce L. Wilson. Testing, Reform,
and Rebellion. Norwood: Ablex, 1991.

Dinan, John. "Standardized Tests: Multiple Choices of the
Wrong Kind." English Journal 79 (Oct. 1990): 54–56.

Garner, Donna. "RE: A Special Note on the TAAS Series." 29
Jan. 2000. Online posting. EducationNews.org Bulletin
Board. 13 Feb. 2000 <http://www.educationnews.org/
cgi/webbbs/article/article_list.pl>.

Irmscher, William F. Teaching Expository Writing. New York:
Holt, 1979.

Kaufhold, Jack. "What's Wrong With Teaching for the Test?"
The School Administrator 55 (Dec. 1998): 14–16.

Linda/tx. "RE: Teaching to the TAAS Criticism Getting to
Me." 4 Feb. 2000. Online posting. Texas Teachers
Chatboard. 13 Feb. 2000
<http://texas.teachers.net/chatboard/>.

Mary. "RE: Teaching to the TAAS Criticism Getting to Me." 4
Feb. 2000. Online posting. Texas Teachers Chatboard.
13 Feb. 2000 <http://texas.teachers.net/chatboard/>.

Melissa. "RE: Does Your School Give a Released TAAS Test?"
14 Jan. 2000. Online posting. Texas Teachers
Chatboard. 13 Feb. 2000
<http://texas.teachers.net/chatboard/>.

Neill, Shirley Boes. The Competency Movement: Problems and
Solutions. Sacramento: Educational News Service, 1978.

Rief, Linda. Seeking Diversity. Portsmouth: Heinemann,
1992.

Rison, A. D. A. D. Rison's Teacher's and Parents' Guide to
Pass the TAAS Test: Language Arts, Reading and
Writing. Austin: Sunbelt, 1990.

CHECKLIST

The Works Cited Page—MLA

The Works Cited list contains full bibliographical information on all the books, articles, and other resources used in composing the paper. For more about the purpose and form of this list, see Chapter 24.

○ Center the title "Works Cited" at the top of the page.

○ Include in the Works Cited list all the sources actually mentioned in the paper. Do not include materials you examined but did not cite in the body of the paper itself.

○ Arrange the items in the Works Cited list alphabetically by the last name of the author. If no author is given for a work, list it according to the first word of its title, ignoring articles (*The, A, An*).

○ Be sure the first line of each entry touches the left-hand margin. Subsequent lines are indented five spaces.

○ Double-space the entire list. Do not quadruple-space between entries unless that is the form your instructor prefers.

○ Punctuate items in the list carefully. Don't forget the period at the end of each entry.

○ Follow this form if you have two or more entries by the same author:

van der Plas, Rob. The Mountain Bike Book: Choosing, Riding
      and Maintaining the Off-Road Bicycle. 3rd ed. San
      Francisco: Bicycle, 1993.

---. Mountain Bike Magic. Mill Valley: Bicycle, 1991.

Brenneman 10

Shaughnessy, Anne. "Teaching to the Test: Sometimes a Good

    Practice." <u>English Journal</u> 83 (Apr. 1994): 54-56.

Texas Education Agency. <u>Texas Education Agency</u>

    <u>Administrative Rules.</u> Chapters 110 and 128, subchapter

    C. 1 Sept. 1998. 6 Mar. 2000 <http://www.tea.state.tx

    .us/rules/tac/ch110_128c.html>.

WWW Web Sites Worth Knowing

- About APA Style, **http://www.apastyle.org/aboutstyle.html**
- Modern Language Association (MLA) Home Page, **http://www.mla.org**
- Tips on Designing Brochures,
  http://www.peachpit.com/features/ndmonth/brochures.html
- Newsletter Design Tips, **http://graphicdesign.about.com/library/weekly/**
  aa121400a.htm?iam=spkask&terms=designing
- IEEE Standards Style Manual for Technical Publications,
  http://standards.ieee.org/resources/glance_at_writing_new.html
- The Art of Communicating Effectively,
  http://presentingsolutions.com/effectivepresentations.asp

WWW

21.2

GETTING INVOLVED

1. Find a print document that you think is either extremely effective or extremely in-effective in communicating its message to readers. Working with a small group of classmates, identfy specific features of document format and document style that make the piece successful or unsuccessful.

2. Explore the templates in your word-processing, desktop publishing, or presentation software. For what kinds of documents are templates available? Compare the formatting features in the templates with the guidelines you need to follow. Can you create your own templates? Some word-processing packages let you use pre-defined "styles" or define your own. Read the "Help" feature of your software package to determine how to use these features. Prepare an oral presentation for your classmates explaining how to use one of these features.

MANAGING YOUR PROJECT

1. To be certain you bring your project to timely completion, decide in advance how you will reward yourself when you finish. Be specific. Give yourself something real to work for—in addition to the satisfaction (not insignificant) of completing a noteworthy research project.

2. Before submitting a conventional research paper, ask yourself the following questions:

   - Have you placed your name, the instructor's name, the date, and the course name on the first or title page?
   - Is the title centered? Are only major words capitalized? (Your title should not be underlined.)

- Did you number the pages? Are they in the right order?
- Have you used quotation marks and parentheses correctly and in pairs? (The closing quotation mark and parenthesis are often forgotten.)
- Have you placed quotation marks around all direct quotations that are shorter than four lines?
- Have you indented all direct quotations of more than four typed lines (MLA) or of forty words or more (APA)?
- Have you remembered that indented quotations are not placed between quotation marks?
- Did you introduce all direct quotations with some identification of their author, source, or significance?
- Did you use the correct form for parenthetical notes?
- Have you handled titles correctly, italicizing book titles and putting the titles of articles between quotation marks?
- Did you include a Works Cited or References list? Is your list of works cited alphabetized? Did you indent the entries correctly?

CHAPTER

22

Completing a Web-Based Research Project

In many ways, writing for the World Wide Web is similar to writing for print. You will still rely on text to convey a good deal of your message, and you are still writing to an audience—for a purpose and in reponse to an occasion. However, writing for electronic media involves additional constraints as well as additional opportunities. Depending on your audience, purpose, and message—as well as on the time and expertise you have for your project—you may need to choose a traditional medium such as a brochure or an academic paper. When the situation warrants, however, creating a Web site for your research project can be incredibly rewarding, especially when your project reaches a wider audience outside the classroom.

Web pages are useful for publishing information quickly to a wide audience—if your intended audience has access and can find your page. You may have to register your URL with appropriate search engines, include specific keywords in special tags, or request that other pages include links to yours. It is also possible for someone to stumble onto your page even when you haven't publicized it, so be careful about what your work says about you.

Only a few years ago, authoring a Web page required learning Hypertext Markup Language (HTML), which designates the features of a page (font sizes or colors, paragraph breaks, etc.) using special tags. Understanding basic HTML can give you greater control over your pages. However, to simplify the process of Web site creation, most people now use one of the many visual Web page editors available. Some of them, such as Macromedia's *Dreamweaver* and Microsoft's *Front Page,* can help you include features that rival any professional Web developer's pages; a simple but very effective Web page editor, *Composer,* comes bundled for free with the Netscape browser. Yet regardless of what you use to create your page, you will need to develop an eye for good design.

In this chapter you will learn to understand the principles of Web design and to apply these design principles to creating your own Web page.

22a Understand the principles of Web design

The most important consideration—for both print and electronic projects—is that your project meet the needs of your reader. In Figure 22.1, the Web site creator provides three means of entry into the site to meet the needs of readers with various levels of access. Since large graphics, frames, and other features can considerably increase the time it takes a page to load, readers are offered a version with smaller-sized graphics and one with no graphics at all.

Many Web page design elements you need to know about are the same ones that you use for print documents. However, for Web projects some of them need to be reconsidered. Following are the basic elements of design which you need to be familiar with for Web-based projects.

Page size, margins, and line spacing. For electronic documents, the "page" size often depends on the software used to view the document, the size of the screen, the browser window, and other factors. While some formats (such as Adobe PDF files) emulate print documents exactly, others, such as World Wide Web pages, allow readers to make choices that affect the amount of text or graphical elements that will fit on the screen.

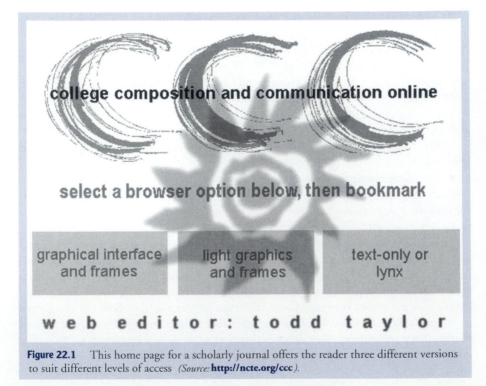

Figure 22.1 This home page for a scholarly journal offers the reader three different versions to suit different levels of access *(Source:* **http://ncte.org/ccc***).*

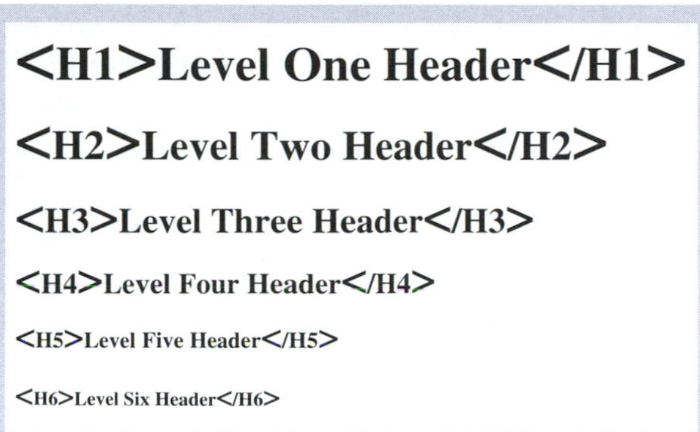

<H1>Level One Header</H1>

<H2>Level Two Header</H2>

<H3>Level Three Header</H3>

<H4>Level Four Header</H4>

<H5>Level Five Header</H5>

<H6>Level Six Header</H6>

Figure 22.2   Six levels of HTML headers.

While a Web page may not have "margins" in the traditional sense, some Web page designers argue that information should be "chunked" to fit on one screen; most agree that formatting that forces readers to scroll to the right or left should be avoided. Trying to force line breaks to emulate double spacing or the hanging indents used in print documents can result in a mess if your reader views your project with a different Web browser, screen size, or font than you intended. You will also need to ensure that your page design includes "white space": areas of the page with no text or graphics, to enhance readability and avoid clutter.

Headings and subheadings.   Hypertext Markup Language (HTML) designates six levels of headers, as shown in Figure 22.2. You can also choose different font styles, sizes, or colors to designate various levels of headings. But be careful with your choices; professionals caution that mixing too many different font styles or colors makes a page difficult to read. Many professionals also suggest using *sans serif* fonts for headings.

Headings and subheadings help the reader to navigate your page and locate information quickly. They also help to break up the text into chunks, allowing additional white space to make your page more attractive and less intimidating. Note the differences in the two pages in Figure 22.3: both pages use subheadings, but the right-hand page includes more white space, making that page more inviting.

Fonts, colors, and multimedia.   For electronic projects, the cost of reproduction is not a consideration as it is with print projects, but mixing too many colors on a page may result in a distracting mishmash. Use different font types (see the chart, Font Styles, on page 244), sizes, and colors to enhance your project, to make elements stand out, or to designate related information, but don't be tempted to fall into the "because I can" trap; use features to enhance your presentation, not simply because the technology allows them. If you want to insert multimedia elements like animated graphics, video, sound effects, or background music, make certain you have a legitimate reason for doing so; too many bells and whistles can distract your audience and obscure the point you're trying to make. As in print documents, high contrast (that is, dark backgrounds with light-colored text, or light-colored backgrounds with dark text) is easier to read; avoid "busy" backgrounds that make information hard to read.

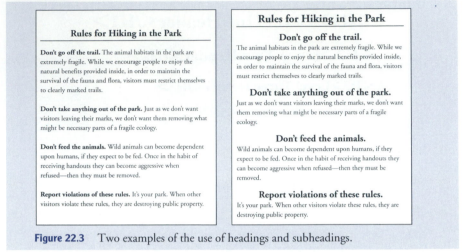

Rules for Hiking in the Park

Don't go off the trail. The animal habitats in the park are extremely fragile. While we encourage people to enjoy the natural benefits provided inside, in order to maintain the survival of the fauna and flora, visitors must restrict themselves to clearly marked trails.

Don't take anything out of the park. Just as we don't want visitors leaving their marks, we don't want them removing what might be necessary parts of a fragile ecology.

Don't feed the animals. Wild animals can become dependent upon humans, if they expect to be fed. Once in the habit of receiving handouts they can become aggressive when refused—then they must be removed.

Report violations of these rules. It's your park. When other visitors violate these rules, they are destroying public property.

Rules for Hiking in the Park

Don't go off the trail.

The animal habitats in the park are extremely fragile. While we encourage people to enjoy the natural benefits provided inside, in order to maintain the survival of the fauna and flora, visitors must restrict themselves to clearly marked trails.

Don't take anything out of the park.

Just as we don't want visitors leaving their marks, we don't want them removing what might be necessary parts of a fragile ecology.

Don't feed the animals.

Wild animals can become dependent upon humans, if they expect to be fed. Once in the habit of receiving handouts they can become aggressive when refused—then they must be removed.

Report violations of these rules.

It's your park. When other visitors violate these rules, they are destroying public property.

Figure 22.3   Two examples of the use of headings and subheadings.

Tables, figures, and graphics.   Use tables in Web documents to present information in rows and columns, as shown in Figure 22.4.

For Web documents, tables are one of the most powerful design features, allowing you to place graphical or visual elements on your page in a variety of ways. By changing the size or position of the table on the page or the height or width of rows, columns, or individual cells, by nesting tables inside tables, by changing the width of the table's borders—or eliminating the borders altogether—you can achieve configurations that create the look you desire.

Page designers for print publications have long used a sort of table known as a grid to lay out elements on a page. Text and picture elements can be placed on the design

Festival 2000: Daily Venue Schedules

	Center Stage	East Stage	West Stage	Welcome Stage
Wed.	Classic Rock	World Beat	Punk	Polka
Th.	Funk and Soul	Swing	Reggae and Ska	Metal Mania
Fri.	Rock and Pop	Blues	Hip-hop and R & B	Local Grab Bag
Sat.	Rock and Pop	Jazz	Country	DJ Showcase
Sun.	International Folk	Classical	Gospel	Amateur Contest

Figure 22.4   The rows and columns of a table organize and present information clearly and effectively.

grid, each element taking up one or more cells on a page as needed. You can use tables without borders in your Web pages in the same way to ensure that your layout is effective and aesthetically pleasing.

Figures and other graphical elements are easy to include in Web projects, so easy that authors may often be tempted to fill all available space on a page with animated graphics, scanned-in photographs, and blinking text. Every element on your page should serve a purpose: graphics and figures present data, clarify details, illustrate concepts, draw attention, or enliven your page, but you must use them with caution. A simple horizontal rule that separates information into recognizable chunks can be much more effective than a dozen blinking arrows.

Lists. As you have done in print documents, you will sometimes need to use numbered or bulleted lists to present information or instructions (see Section 21a). For a Web-based research project, you may want to use the "List" feature to format your Works Cited or References list, as shown in Figure 22.5, since the "Hanging Indent" feature in your word processor, which formats the entries in a Works Cited or References list with the first line flush with the left-hand margin and subsequent lines indented, does not work well online.

Most Web page editors, like most word-processing applications, make formatting lists as easy as clicking a "List" button. Remember, however, that you need to introduce

---

Works Cited

- Arni, Sherry. "I Can Live With It." *English Journal* 79 (Nov. 1990): 76.
- Corbett, H. Dickson, and Bruce L. Wilson. *Testing, Reform, and Rebellion.* Norwood: Ablex, 1991.
- Dinan, John, "Standardized Tests: Multiple Choices of the Wrong Kind." *English Journal* 79 (Oct. 1990): 54-56.
  EducationNews.org Bulletin Board. http://www.educationnews.org/cgi/webbs/article_list.pl (13 Feb. 2002).
- Irmscher, William F. *Teaching Expository Writing.* New York: Holt, 1979.
- Kaufhold, Jack. "What's Wrong with Teaching for the Test?" *The School Administrator* 55 (Dec. 1998): 14-16.
- Linda/tx. "RE: Teaching to the TAAS Criticism Getting to Me." 4 Feb. 2000. *Texas Teacher's Chatboard.* http://texas.teachers.net/chatboard/ (13 Feb. 2000).
- Mary. "RE: Teaching to the TAAS Criticism Getting to Me." 4 Feb. 2000. *Texas Teacher's Chatboard.* http://texas.teachers.net/chatboard/ (13 Feb. 2000).
- Melissa. "RE: Does Your School Give a Released TAAS Test?" 14 Jan. 2000. *Texas Teacher's Chatboard.* http://texas.teachers.net/chatboard/ (13 Feb. 2000).
- Neill, Shirley Boes. *The Competency Movement. Problems and Solutions.* Sacramento: Educational News Service, 1978.

Figure 22.5 A Works Cited list online, formatted using the "Bulleted List" feature. Note that references to online sources are formatted as links and follow COS style.

the information contained in lists within the body of your text, and be careful not to clutter your page with different styles of buttons or unnecessary lists.

A good site to visit for more information on Web page design is the Yale C/AIM "Web Style Guide" at **http://info.med.yale.edu/caim/manual/** . While you could take a course in Web design (not a bad idea if you have the time and interest), you can learn much about good (and bad) Web page design simply by casting a critical eye at the pages you visit online. Think about the sites you like, those that are easy to navigate, attractive, and useful, and then consider how the design of those pages contributes to that ease of use. In the next section you will learn how to apply these principles to your own Web project.

22b Apply design principles for electronic documents

When developing a Web site, you need to rely on HTML or Web page editors and other kinds of design software. Gradually you will gain experience with a surprising range of electronic tools for shaping documents. This section and the one that follows will aid you in designing and creating a Web page.

A well-designed Web page or site is not only attractive and easy to read, it fulfills a purpose and provides the reader with something useful—information, links, entertainment value—something that makes time spent visiting the site time well spent. Consider the following elements when designing your site.

Suitability. Almost anyone with access to the Internet can learn to design, create, and publish Web pages, but not every project belongs on the World Wide Web. You have to decide whether and when the Web is a suitable environment for your project by considering five factors.

- *Purpose.* Material on the Web can reach a large audience, so it might be an appropriate place to publish a project when you want to disseminate information widely or make it easy for people to respond to your work. A Web site might not be the best place to post a piece of technical writing or a private meditation.

- *Audience.* A college instructor may expect you to turn in a traditional paper, even when the information might be more appropriately presented on the Internet. On the other hand, an employer might expect reports or documents to be accessible in some form online, or you may have to combine formats to reach the widest possible readership.

- *Time.* If you have never designed a Web page, perhaps you can't afford the time it will take to learn. In that case, stick with more familiar technologies: presentation software, desktop publishing programs, word processing. Alternatively, a significant advantage of the Web is speed of publication—if you need to get information to readers quickly, the Web may be your best choice, assuming that your intended audience can access it.

- *Medium.* The medium you choose has important design implications. You might decide to stick with print because you are familiar with prescribed formats and with the way your software handles fonts and graphics. Moving to a

Web environment will require new skills; you will need to learn something about creating and formatting graphics, fonts, hypertext links, and other elements of Web design. You may also need familiarity with advanced programming techniques if you plan to incorporate sophisticated features into your project.

- *Access.* To create a Web page, you will need access to a computer and to space on the Internet to publish your work. Depending on your project, you may also need graphics programs, scanning equipment, or other applications. You'll want to be sure, too, that your files load quickly and accurately on a variety of browser types and that your audience knows how to access them.

Structure. Web pages offer a great deal of flexibility in design. But just as a traditional essay must follow a logical structure, a Web site needs coherent organization. The design you choose will depend on your purpose and your audience as well as on the nature of the information you are presenting. Figure 22.6 depicts three types of organizational patterns for Web sites: hierarchical, sequential, and hub. Your project may follow any one of these patterns or a combination of them, depending on your rhetorical needs.

Navigability. The reader must be able to locate information on your page or Web site without getting lost. Like printed texts, Web pages need transitional devices. Some of those transitions—such as titles, headings, and numerical sequences—are familiar because they are part of most texts, whether printed or electronic. But hypertext also offers many special devices. For example, you can use page anchors (links to specific sections of a Web page) to scroll readers through lengthy online documents or establish links between pages. You can create arrows, image maps, or buttons to provide graphical transitions and use pop-up browser windows for digressions or explanations. Use these devices to be sure readers always know where they are in your material and how to get where they need to be.

Visual elements and multimedia. Graphics must be appropriate. They can be used to attract the reader's attention to important information (an email icon may alert the reader to information on contacting the author) and for navigational purposes (image maps, "Back" buttons, and other graphical elements can aid the reader in moving through the document). However, a page full of animated graphics and blinking text will probably give your reader eyestrain and detract from what you have to say.

Keep file sizes for visual or multimedia elements small. If the size of your site might cause problems for people downloading it, consider limiting file sizes by including "thumbnail" (reduced-size) images or text descriptions on your pages with links to large multimedia files. Or you might treat interesting but unnecessary material, explanations, or definitions as separate linked files. If your readers might need to download special software plug-ins to access your work, provide the necessary links. Be aware that items such as graphics, frames, and tables may not be readable across different computer platforms. So consider including text-only versions of documents and verbal descriptions of graphic or audio files that some site users might not be able to access.

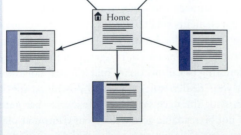

A **hierarchical** pattern organizes pages into increasingly more specific groupings. Readers find material by starting with general categories (topics, areas, units) and working their way down to more specific information. Large organizations (such as colleges) often organize their Web sites this way.

Sequential sites present readers with fewer options. If you are offering a proposal argument, your site might move readers step by step from problem to solution, with each stage of the argument building on material from the preceding screen. Readers are encouraged to click "Next Page" rather than select from a menu of options. Make sure to provide links back to the home page so readers won't reach a dead end.

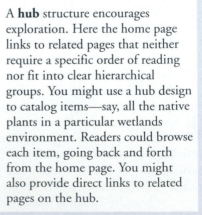

A **hub** structure encourages exploration. Here the home page links to related pages that neither require a specific order of reading nor fit into clear hierarchical groups. You might use a hub design to catalog items—say, all the native plants in a particular wetlands environment. Readers could browse each item, going back and forth from the home page. You might also provide direct links to related pages on the hub.

Figure 22.6 Three organizational patterns for a Web site.

Bibliographical information. Include bibliographical information in your electronic document. Provide your reader with all the information necessary to cite your document and (when necessary) to contact you for permission to use your material. Essential bibliographical information includes the following elements.

1. Your name and email address or email link.

2. Title of your work.

3. Date of publication/creation and/or date of last modification or revision.

4. URL for your document and/or your home page.

Give credit to your sources. Include the source of any graphics or other files you used in your document. Don't just provide a link to an online source; always include full bibliographical information, or at least the URL of the source, in your text. Then people who print out your document from the Web won't lose track of the linked sources—which may print out only as underscored words or phrases.

Use the following checklist to help ensure that your Web page conforms to these guidelines.

CHECKLIST

Good Document Design

○ Make sure all hypertext links are working. For external links, you may want to include a list describing each link in case the intended file moves or is changed.

○ Make sure your graphics print or load accurately and quickly.

○ Check the appearance of your work carefully. For Web documents and files, try a variety of browsers; for documents to be read using electronic means, make sure files will transfer across platforms or applications.

○ Include bibliographical information—your name and a way to contact you (e.g., your email address) if appropriate, the title of your work or site, the date of creation or last modification and the URL for the site if it is on the Web.

○ Give credit in the proper format to any sources you have borrowed from, including the source of any graphics.

22c Create a Web page

Creating a basic Web page is relatively easy and requires not much more skill than it takes to operate word-processing software—if a little more patience. Many Web sites combine diverse design elements such as stylized text, graphics, animation, and even sound: we can't provide you with models and guidelines to suit every possible occasion, but what we can offer here is an outline of the basic processes involved in writing for the Web, which should be enough to get you started.

Plan your Web project carefully. Planning a Web project isn't much different from planning other types of documents (see Figure 22.7). You'll need to determine your audience, assess your resources, choose an effective layout, and make decisions about document style. Web projects, however, do have special demands (see Section 22b).

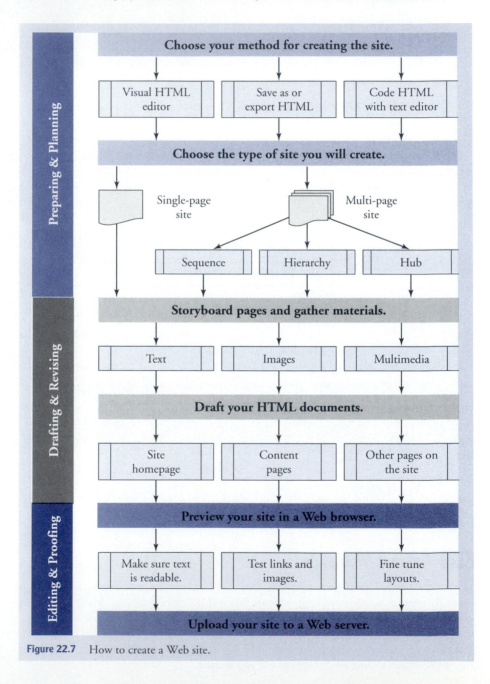

Figure 22.7 How to create a Web site.

Menus and **toolbars** vary with each visual editor, but all are based on standard Web design features.

Header information, such as page title and author, does not appear in the main window of visual editors. Instead you edit this information through the menus of your program.

The **body** looks almost exactly as it would if you were viewing it in a browser. But the editor allows you to modify text, insert pictures and tables, format fonts, and change colors.

Figure 22.8 A personal home page in a visual editor.

First, you'll need to know that Web documents use Hypertext Markup Language tags or codes to tell browsers how to display words and images and how to hyperlink documents to each other. Think about what method you'll use to create your HTML documents, whether you'll use a single-page or a multipage format, and how you'll lay out and link individual pages.

You'll also need to adhere to the publication requirements of the Web. You'll eventually need to "upload" your documents to a Web server to make them accessible to the world. Here we focus on the design of Web pages. Check with your instructor or Internet provider for information on publishing your files.

Choose a method for creating HTML pages. Numerous software programs exist to help you create HTML documents. These tools vary in their user interfaces, their sophistication, and their adherence to Web publishing standards. Later in this chapter we will walk you through the process of creating simple Web pages using each of three basic methods.

- **Visual HTML editors,** or WYSIWYG ("wizzy-wig") editors, which stands for "What You See Is What You Get," are especially useful for new Web writers. The design tools they offer allow you to edit materials as they'd look in Web browsers (in other words, you don't have to edit the HTML codes). But these tools don't always support the latest standards or design features (see Figure 22.8).

- **HTML text editors** are the original tools for creating Web pages. In these programs you must enter HTML codes by hand (so you have to understand the codes). Text editors don't have many user-friendly design tools, but they are extremely flexible, since you can always compose with the latest Web standards and features. Use this method if you like to see what's going on "under the hood" of your Web documents (see Figure 22.9).

- **"Save as" or "Export" HTML** options in word processors and other kinds of software allow you to work on HTML documents as you would any other format. Once you have a finished product, you'll convert your work to HTML using your program's menu options. This method of creating HTML documents is fast and easy, but the pages generated often need fine-tuning to make them appealing.

You can also combine these methods to take advantage of the strengths each has to offer. For example, you might start a page by exporting an existing document to HTML and then add features with a visual editor. Or you might use a visual editor to experiment with page features you're thinking of coding yourself. Even if you begin with a visual editor, you can later tinker with the HTML tags directly.

Choose a single-page or a multipage format. Decide early in your design process how you want to organize your Web page: will you create a single, scrolling page or multiple pages connected by links? When you have a limited amount of information to present—a personal home page or a brief report—consider choosing a single, scrolling page. A single page is simple and clear: readers need only move down the page to find information. If you have more than two or three screens of information or if your material breaks easily into sections, consider a set of pages connected by links.

A site that will consist of multiple pages is harder to create than a single-page site. You have to decide how to arrange your information so readers can navigate the pages easily and intuitively. You'll need to create a home page as the entry into the site, but material deeper in the site may be connected to that home page in different ways—again depending on your purpose and subject—to create a **hierarchy,** a **sequence,** or a **hub** (see Figure 22.6 on page 282).

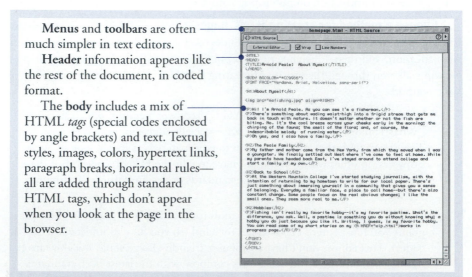

Menus and **toolbars** are often much simpler in text editors.

Header information appears like the rest of the document, in coded format.

The **body** includes a mix of HTML *tags* (special codes enclosed by angle brackets) and text. Textual styles, images, colors, hypertext links, paragraph breaks, horizontal rules—all are added through standard HTML tags, which don't appear when you look at the page in the browser.

Figure 22.9 A personal home page in an HTML text editor.

Storyboard pages. Storyboards are sketches of your page or pages you can draw by hand with pencil and paper. For the sake of simplicity, new Web writers should focus on two types of pages: the *home page,* which clearly conveys the purpose of the site and how to navigate it, and *content pages,* which present, in a consistent and readable manner, the site's most important material.

As you prepare your page layouts, you'll have questions:

- What text do you need to include for the site to achieve its purpose?
- How will you break up text onto separate pages?
- Will you use images or multimedia?
- What materials can you gather from outside sources?
- What materials can you create yourself?
- How will you gather all these materials effectively to create your site?

Gather materials. Whatever materials you add to your site, you'll need to assemble them in electronic formats accessible to those browsing the Web. Although we don't have space here to explain how to digitize photographs, make animations, and record voices—all of which involve an understanding of specific software programs—we can give you guidelines for gathering material already (or easily) converted to Web formats.

- **Create a working folder on your disk.** Place all your materials—HTML files, graphics files, and other media—for the project in this folder. When you're ready to publish your project, all you'll need to do is upload the folder to the Web server.

- **Write the text that will appear on your site.** Web sites may contain less written matter than you'd find in printed sources, but online prose needs to be just as clear and grammatical as any other professional writing. Remember, too, that what you post on a Web page is public. Proofread carefully and edit to eliminate wordiness.

To save an image from the web:

1. Go to an image gallery such as **http://gallery.yahoo.com**

2. Find an image you like.

3. Right-click (Windows) or control-click (Macintosh) to bring up the floating menu.

4. Select "Save Image As . . ." (*Netscape*) or "Save Picture As . . ." (*Internet Explorer*).

5. Choose your Web project folder from the file chooser.

6. Note the online gallery's fair use requirements. If necessary ask for permission by email.

Draft HTML documents. The next few sections take you step by step through the creation of an HTML document, first using a text editor, then a visual editor, and finally the export features of a standard word processor. The instructions will help you compose a simple Web page with a few paragraphs of text, a single image, and a link.

Consider drafting with an HTML text editor. Using a text editor isn't the easiest way for new Web writers to construct HTML documents. We start here, however, because this method shows most clearly the nuts and bolts of all Web pages no matter how they're created. To see what we mean, go to any location in your Web browser and from the "View" menu choose "Source" or "Page Source." You now see a document containing the HTML codes for the page you were just viewing. This document will include the readable text you see in the browser window and a number of HTML tags—those cryptic letters and words that appear between angle brackets.

Depending on the page you're viewing, the HTML tags may seem daunting and difficult to learn. In fact, composing with HTML is relatively easy—if you start with the basics. While these basics won't allow you to make flashy, elaborate sites, they will allow you to publish material on the Web in a clear and organized fashion. Once you feel comfortable with the basics, you can then increase your HTML vocabulary, learning more striking Web design techniques.

- **Choose your editing software.** Both Macintosh and Windows operating systems come with basic text-editing software: *Simple Text* and *Notepad,* respectively. These programs offer all you need to write HTML documents. If, however, you have access to a text editor specialized for HTML documents, such as *BBEdit* on the Macintosh, you will probably want to use it.

- **Create an HTML template.** All HTML documents have a basic structure, a required series of tags that tell browser programs necessary information about the organization of the page. Type the tags shown in Figure 22.10 into a new document using your HTML text editor. Save that document in your working folder as "htmltemplate.html"—you will make a copy of this document every time you start composing a new page, knowing that it will have the required structure.

- **Preview your HTML document in a browser.** This is an action you'll repeat again and again as you draft your Web pages. By using a Web browser to open the pages you save in your working folder, you'll be able to see how they will appear once uploaded. To preview your HTML template, open your Web browser, choose "Open" from the "File" menu, and browse for the file you just saved in your working folder. You should then see something like what is shown in Figure 22.11.

- **Review the basic HTML tags.** Making a simple Web page (as you've just proven) is easy, but the template itself doesn't do much. To achieve the design you want, you'll need to learn more about HTML tags (see Figures 22.12, 22.13, and 22.14). First let's consider the function of the tags we just used to create the template.

```
htmltemplate.html - Notepad
File   Edit   Search   Help

<HTML>

<HEAD>

 <TITLE>HTML Template</TITLE>
 <META NAME="Author" CONTENT="your name">
 <META NAME="Date of Creation" CONTENT="day/month/year">

</HEAD>

<BODY>

  HTML Template

</BODY>

</HTML>
```

Figure 22.10 You can create an HTML template by typing the tags and words into your text editor exactly as shown above. Later, when you start making pages or customized templates, you'll put more personalized information into the areas highlighted above. The area between the <BODY> . . . </BODY> tags will contain the main content for each page. *(Microsoft ® Notepad is a trademark of Microsoft. Title bar screen shot reprinted by permission of Microsoft Corporation.)*

Notice how nearly all tags come in pairs. The first in each pair is the *opening tag;* the second, which always includes a slash before the tag name, is the *closing tag.* All text between the opening and closing tags is formatted in a special manner, depending on the tag. Some tags, such as *<BODY>, <HEAD>,* and

```
HTML Template - Microsoft Internet Explorer - [Working Offline]
File   Edit   View   Favorites   Tools   Help

Back ▾  ➡ ▾  ⊗  ⬙  ⌂   Search   Favorites   History        »   Links »

HTML Template



Done                                      My Computer
```

Figure 22.11 Preview your template and notice how little of what you typed appears on the final product. Browsers hide all HTML tags or convert them to special kinds of content such as images or empty lines. You'll need to review what different tags do in order to know how they can help you achieve the layout you want. *(Title bar screen shot reprinted by permission of Microsoft Corporation.)*

Basic HTML Tags

HTML TAGS	WHAT THEY DO
<HTML> </HTML>	Appears as the first and the last tags in an HTML document. These tags tell browser programs to translate codes on the page to a readable format.
<HEAD> </HEAD>	Follows the opening <HTML> tag in a document. Tags between the <HEAD> tags provide information about the document, but this material does not appear in the browser window.
<TITLE> </TITLE>	Identifies the title that will appear in the title bar on the browser when a page opens. The page title appears between the tags.
<META...>	Provides extra information about the document, data often used by Web search engines to index the document once it has been uploaded to a Web server.
<BODY> </BODY>	Brackets the material in the body of the page, including the text, images, and any formatting that will appear in the browser window.

Figure 22.12 Basic HTML Tags

<HTML>, help the browser software identify parts of the document. Other tags, such as those in the list below, add stylistic features to the text they surround.

Some tags don't come in pairs, among them the *<META>* and *<HR>* tags (see Figures 22.12 and 22.13). These tags add special content to the page. The *<IMG>* tag, for example, tells the browser to insert an image; the *<HR>* tag creates a horizontal rule.

Now that you know how to create a template for your Web page and how to use basic HTML tags, the best way to learn to create a Web page using an HTML text editor is to practice. The following steps guide you through the process of drafting a simple Web page that includes text, an image, a hypertext link, and a footer.

Step 1. Create and draft the body of your new Web page.

- Make a copy of the template you created on pages 288–89 naming it something appropriate like "homepage.html" or "topic1.html." Store this copy in your project folder.

- Open the new document (the copy of your template) in your HTML text editor and change the words between the opening and closing <TITLE> tags to match the content it will contain.

- Enter the text you've prepared for the page between the <BODY> . . . </BODY> tags in the new document. If you don't have the text written yet, make up something with which you can experiment.

- Just below the opening <BODY> tag, create a page heading by typing your title between the <H1> . . . </H1> tags.
- Format paragraphs by surrounding them with <P> . . . </P> tags.

More HTML Tags	
HTML TAGS	**WHAT THEY DO**
<B></B>	Boldfaces text between the tags.
<I></I>	Italicizes text between the tags.
<P></P>	Formats text between the tags as a simple paragraph.
<CENTER></CENTER>	Centers text between the tags.
<H1></H1>	Forms a level-one heading—the largest HTML heading size. See Figure 22.2.
<A...></A>	Hyperlinks the text between the tags.
<FONT...></FONT>	Sets the font for text between the tags.
<UL><LI><LI><LI> ...</UL>	Creates a bulleted list. Place the <LI> tag before each item in the list.
** **	Inserts a line break. All text following the tag appears on the next line.
<HR>	Inserts a horizontal line across the page.
<IMG...>	Inserts an image onto the page.

Figure 22.13 More HTML Tags

Step 2. Change the background color of your page and insert an image.

- Some HTML tags allow you to set *elements,* or special features of document style. All elements appear in the opening tag followed by an equal sign and a value (between quotation marks). The <BODY> tag provides an element—BG-COLOR—that lets you set the background color of the page. Change the background color for your HTML document by modifying your <BODY> tag:

  <BODY BGCOLOR="TAN">

  Different tags allow you to modify different elements of your page. Check your HTML guide to learn more about formatting options.
- The <IMG> tag allows you to add pictures to your Web page. Add the following text to your document just below the header, setting the SRC element to

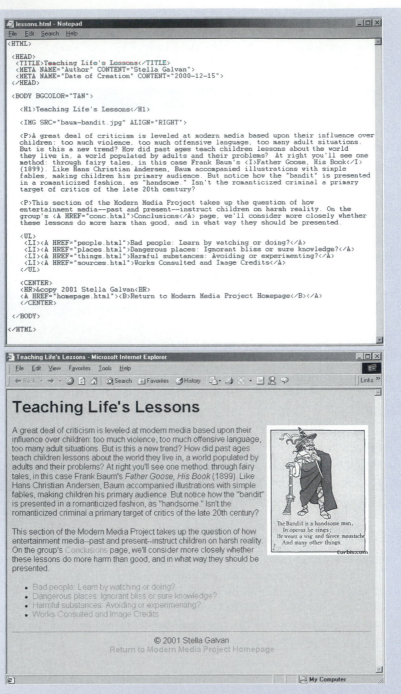

Figure 22.14   The top window shows the HTML codes used to generate the lower window for the page titled "Teaching Life's Lessons." *(Microsoft ® Notepad is a trademark of Microsoft. Title bar screen shot reprinted by permission of Microsoft Corporation.)*

match the name of a graphics file in your working folder and the ALIGN element to RIGHT:

<IMG SRC="yourimage.jpg" ALIGN="RIGHT" >

When you preview your page in a browser you'll see the image aligned to the right of your text.

Step 3. Add a hypertext link and attach a page footer.

- Using the <A> tag (also called the "anchor tag"), link your page to others, either within your Web project or at another location on the Web. To link to the Internet search engine Google, for example, you would enter this text:

<A HREF="http://www.google.com" >Search at Google</A>

The HREF element allows you to specify an Internet address to which the text between the <A> . . . </A> tags will be linked. To link to another page in your project, set the HREF element to match the name of another HTML document in your working project folder.

- Footers on Web pages are useful places to unobtrusively credit yourself and others and to link readers to the site's home page (from content pages). You can create a simple footer using the same codes:

<CENTER>

<HR>&copy 2001 Stella Galvan

<A HREF="homepage.html" > Return to Media Project Homepage </A>

</CENTER>

Review the tags above using the list in Figure 22.13. (You won't find &*copy* on the list—this code creates the copyright symbol.) Check your HTML guide for more extensive lists of codes.

Step 4. Fine-tune your text.

- Use HTML tags to change font face and style where it's appropriate. The <FONT> tag includes three important elements: *COLOR, FACE,* and *SIZE.* In combination with the <I> (italics) and <B> (boldface) tags, you can have nearly as much control over the style of your text as you do with a word processor. For example, the text between the <I> . . . </I> tags below will be Helvetica, a size larger than normal, red, and italicized. (Notice that quotation marks surround element values):

<FONT COLOR="RED" SIZE="+I" FACE="Helvetica" >

<I> . . . </I>

</FONT>

- To adjust the layout of text, use the list tags <UL> and <OL> and the line break tag <BR>. The <BR> tag is especially useful for presenting text that doesn't extend a full line but shouldn't be double-spaced (such as lines in poems). The list tags are useful for presenting all kinds of materials. You can make a hypertextual table of contents for your site by creating a list that links each item to a separate page. Review the list of tags in Figure 22.13 on page 291 as you fine-tune the text on your page. For more advanced options, consult your HTML guide.

Consider drafting with a visual HTML editor. If you aren't concerned about the nuts and bolts of HTML, or if you need to produce an attractive Web document quickly, try a visual Web authoring program. The quality of the page you finally produce will depend on the software you have available—but most programs generate suitable layouts.

- **Choose your editing software.** Visual editors often cost money, but some computers come with them preinstalled. *Netscape*'s suite of Internet applications comes with both a Web browser (*Communicator*) and an editor (*Composer*); Microsoft's *Internet Explorer* often comes with a version of *Frontpage*. Other editors include *Dreamweaver* and *Claris Homepage*. Predictably, the more features offered, the more expensive the program.

- **Create a new HTML document.** In most programs all you'll need to do is select "New" from the "File" menu, just as you would in a word processor. Save the blank page in your project folder. Note that your editing software might provide pre-designed templates. Choose a template for your new document if you find one that's appropriate. Make sure to adjust the template to suit your needs.

- **Set the document title.** Unlike HTML text editors, visual editors allow you to use the program's menus and dialog boxes to make modifications to your document. For this reason you'll need to explore your software for a few minutes, learning the available options. In particular, look for an option that allows you to change the title of your HTML document. This menu item often appears under "Format" and "File" menus. Having found this option, your editor will display a dialog box that allows you to modify various properties of your document, including the name of the author (see Figure 22.15). The options will vary with the software you use.

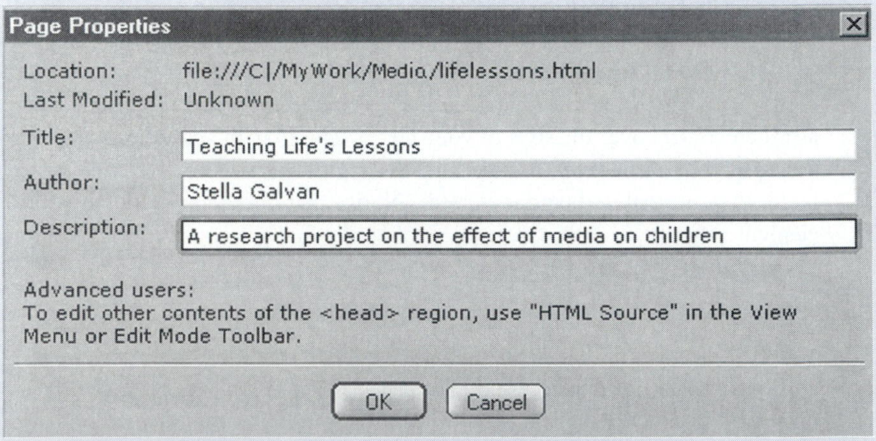

Figure 22.15 The Page Properties dialog box from *Netscape Composer* allows you to specify the title (as it will appear in the browser's title bar), the author, and a brief description, which search engines will use to index your page. After filling in the boxes, press the "OK" button.

- **Insert the text you have written into the new document.** If you already have the text stored in a word-processing document, you can cut and paste the material using your program's "Edit" menus. Otherwise type your words into the visual editor as you would into any other program. Notice, however, that you'll have less flexibility in the way you format your paragraphs, which will normally appear in single-spaced block style (this is the Web standard). You can change font and alignment by using options found in your program's formatting menus and toolbars.

- **Preview your page in a Web browser.** Most visual editors have a preview option among their menus and toolbars. This option will display your page in a Web browser program, allowing you to see how it will appear to readers on the Web. Ideally, your page won't change much from the editor to the browser program—that is, after all, the claim of WYSIWYG software. If the page does look significantly different, try upgrading either your editor or your browser; the versions you have may not have the latest standards. Most software makers provide free updates on the Web.

- **Insert an image into your page.** Most WYSIWYG editors have an "Insert" menu that allows you to add nontextual content to your page, such as pictures, tables, and horizontal rules. After moving your cursor to the location where you want the picture, select the menu option that allows you to place an image on your page. Select an image you have already saved in your Web project folder. After clicking "OK" in the dialog box, you should see the image on your page, as it will appear to browsers on the Web.

- **Link your page to another.** Set the cursor where you want to add a link to another page. Type the text you would like to be linked, such as "Search at Google" or "Next Page." Select the text you just typed and choose the option to insert a link from your editor's menus. In the dialog box that appears, type the Internet address or page name. To link to a page in your working folder, simply enter the filename, as shown in Figure 22.16. Some editors allow you to edit other elements of the link, such as the target window. To link to sites outside your folder, use the full Web page URL including the protocol (e.g., http://).

- **Change the page's background color.** One especially useful feature of visual editors is their ability to assign colors according to how they appear on the screen, rather than through codes or names. To change the background color of your page, choose the appropriate menu option, probably "Change Background" or "Format Page." You will then see a dialog box displaying color options. To select your color, click on the box with the desired hue and then select the "OK" button. When you return to the editor's main window, the background will have changed. A similar dialog box is often used to assist in picking colors for fonts, rules, and tables.

- **Add a footer.** Using the knowledge you have so far, try building a footer for your page. Insert a horizontal rule, a copyright symbol followed by the year and your name, and a link to your project's home page. Finally, use your editor's alignment tools to center the footer material.

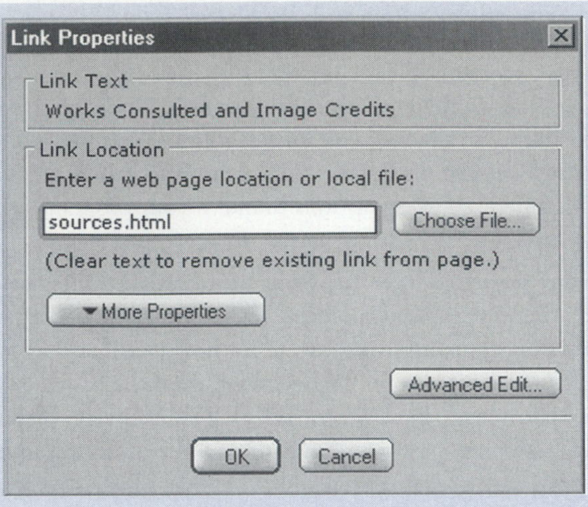

Figure 22.16 Creating hypertext links is easy with a Web page or WYSIWYG editor.

Your editor window should now look something like it would appear if it were viewed in a Web browser. What shows up in the browser may differ from the page you created in the program, but the inconsistencies don't usually outweigh the ease of laying out pages with a visual editor. If you wanted to use the visual editor to create an exact image of what your readers will see, you could probably come close but you might have to do some tweaking with the program's menus and dialog boxes.

We suggest, rather, that you focus on the important parts of your page, namely its ease of reading and navigation. It is often a good idea to leave some control over the layout of a page to your readers, who may have preferred settings for browsing the Web, such as large type, reduced colors, and text-only. If you make your page so that readers with special needs can't use their preferences, they may decide not to read your page at all.

Draft by exporting from your word processor. This is the fastest and easiest method for creating Web documents. The latest word processors and spreadsheets allow you to open any existing document and convert it to HTML within seconds. The resulting pages may not have the layouts you expect, but they will be Web compatible (which may be all you care about).

- **Open the text you've prepared in your word processor.** To make your text more readable onscreen, create block paragraphs. Feel free to use bullets and numbers for lists, and if your word processor allows, set background and font colors. Be aware that some word processors accommodate standard Web layouts, allowing you to identify different levels of headings to help organize your material.

- **Select the export option.** Some word processors allow you to "Save as" HTML, others permit you to "Export" the document to HTML. After selecting the appropriate option, you'll be prompted to name the file and storage location. Create a name that is compatible with Web standards and store the document in your project folder. Note that your word processor may generate files besides the HTML document you explicitly name; this often occurs when you have images in your document. When you publish your document on the Web, you'll need to upload to the server all files and folders created by your word processor.

- **View the generated page in a browser.** To see the results created by your word processor, open the new HTML document in a Web browser. If the results aren't satisfactory, return to your word processor, experiment with simpler layouts, and try again. Alternatively, edit the HTML document directly using one of the other two methods discussed in this chapter.

Edit and proof your Web page. Although Web pages have many special features, the writing that appears on them requires the same care and attention that you would give to a print document. Besides editing for style and clarity, keep in mind some basic document design concerns. Will readers be able to move through the material in the manner you expect? Are the colors you have chosen readable onscreen? Have you cited your images correctly?

22d Submit your project professionally

When you publish your files on the World Wide Web, you will want to double-check them, preferably using different browsers and even different computers, to make sure they appear the way you want them to. Be certain that you uploaded any graphics files along with your HTML files (unlike print, graphics on the Web remain separate files), that you have set the necessary permissions to make your files readable online, and that your links and file names all work. File names on the Web are case sensitive; you may want to use only lowercase letters for your file names to avoid problems. Avoid file names with spaces or special characters in them.

HTML files are readable regardless of the platform (DOS, Windows, MacIntosh). However, embedded applications such as Javascript or audio or video files may require certain browsers or plug-in applications. When this is the case, you can either include links to these applications or include a notice that your reader needs to acquire them before they can access your site. For example, if your online research paper is posted in PDF format, your reader must download the free Adobe Acrobat reader (a program so popular that it is now included with most browsers). Just in case, you may want to include a link to the Adobe site where your reader can download the application. You may even want to include links to text-only versions of your pages; this will help to make sure your files are accessible to the visually handicapped, who may use text-readers to access the Web. Remember, too, that not everyone has access to the latest hardware and software applications. Design your files with these limitations in mind.

Designing Web pages can be both frustrating and fun. It can take hours to find just the right graphic, to painstakingly proofread your work, and to eliminate all the bugs, but most students feel that the result is well worth the time and effort. Of course, Web pages aren't the only projects that require "de-bugging"; you'll pay the same careful attention to your print projects as you do to those published online. And you will want to take special care to give credit to all your sources in the proper format. Part VI contains chapters for five major styles of documentation, with more than 160 examples: Columbia Online Style (COS)—both humanities and scientific formats, MLA, APA, CMS, and CSE. In addition, you will find a complete paper that follows APA format. See Chapter 21 for a complete paper that follows MLA format.

22e Annotated sample Web page

1. Background image suits the topic and doesn't interfere with text or visuals.
2. Title is presented in a table with white background to stand out.
3. Page includes information about the paper.
4. Author's name is formatted as a link to student's email address.
5. Table of contents links to different sections of the page and to other pages.
6. Text and images are laid out on the page using tables without borders.
7. Paragraphs are smaller than traditional research papers.
8. Double spacing between paragraphs with no indention adds white space.
9. Table with borders is used to present statistical information.
10. Link to online source.
11. Small graphic consistent with the topic adds interest.
12. Subheadings in tables are color consistent with background.

13. "Teaser" entices reader to go to the next page for more information.
14. Arrow graphic is a link to the next page.
15. Credit line links to source of graphics as requested by copyright owner.
16. Bibliographic information helps others evaluate and cite this page.

WWW Web Sites Worth Knowing

- Yale C/AIM Web Style Guide, **http://info.med.yale.edu/caim/manual/contents.html**
- Tutorials from the Web Developer's Virtual Library, **http://www.wdvl.com/Authoring/Tutorials/**
- NCSA's "A Beginner's Guide to HTML," **http://archive.ncsa.uiuc.edu/General/Internet/WWW/HTMLPrimer.html**
- Grids for Desktop Publishing, **http://desktoppub.about.com/msub16grids.htm**

22.2

GETTING INVOLVED

1. Choose one of the "Daily Sucker" Web pages at "Web Pages That Suck" at **http://www.webpagesthatsuck.com/**. Prepare a presentation to the class analyzing the design features of the page. Include your recommendations for improving the design.

2. If you have access to a visual Web page editor such as Netscape *Composer* or Microsoft *Front Page*, explore the features—especially the "Help" feature—included with it. Discuss what you have learned with your group.

MANAGING YOUR PROJECT

1. Using pencil and paper, sketch a layout for your Web site. If your site will include more than one page, include arrows designating links between pages. Review the design structures on page 282. Does your design fit any of these basic structures? Prepare a one-page written explanation of your design choices and share it and your sketches with your peers. Ask for feedback and suggestions.

2. Create a basic template for your Web page, using either a visual or HTML editor. Experiment with different layouts using the table feature to place elements on your page. Save the different layouts to your disk and share them with your classmates. Ask classmates to review your designs and offer suggestions for improvement.

VI

Documentation

Don't miss . . .

- **The overview of COS documentation in Section 23a.** When you expect to use many electronic sources in a project, Columbia Online Style (COS) may be your best choice of documentation system.
- **The explanation of MLA documentation in Section 24a.** If you are preparing a paper in language, literature, or the humanities, you may want to use MLA documentation.
- **The explanation of APA documentation in Section 25a.** If you are preparing a paper in the social sciences, you may want to use APA documentation.
- **The explanation of CMS documentation in Section 26a.** If you are preparing a paper in language, literature, or the humanities, you may want to use CMS documentation—especially if you prefer footnotes or endnotes to in-text parenthetical notes.
- **The explanation of CSE documentation in Section 27a.** If you are preparing a paper in the natural sciences, you may want to use CSE documentation.

Technology Spotlight

NEWSGROUPS AND CHAT ROOMS

Like bibliographies and in-text citations, the Internet is all about making connections—not just through hyperlinks to other sites but also through conversations with other users. Messages, personal and professional, can be written quickly and sent instantaneously, making it possible for a student in Los Angeles, California, to correspond with a friend in Paris, France, dozens of times in a single day for less than the cost of a postage stamp. And while email is certainly one of the best known methods for engaging in these electronic conversations, it is by no means the only one. Usenet newsgroups are popular places for like-minded people to gather electronically, trading ideas, arguments, and files with conviviality and abandon. MUDs (Multiple User Domains/Dungeons), MOOs (MUDs, Object Oriented), IRC (Internet Relay Chat), and chat rooms also provide "virtual spaces" where many people can meet electronically, conversing with one another as if they were all meeting together in the same room. Remember, though, that each newsgroup and chatroom has its own rules for behavior; you have to conform to these rules if you want to participate, just as you will need to conform to certain bibliographical rules in preparing your project.

Instant messaging and chat rooms make it possible to connect with people from all over the world. Some chat rooms offer features such as audio and video conferencing and file sharing.

Many class Web sites now include discussion areas where students can share their thoughts on course materials and ask questions; a great many writing classes make use of programs such as *Daedalus Interchange,* which facilitates online discussions among class members. So, while the Internet's value as a storehouse of information and a resource for active researchers is undeniable, its greatest contribution to our society and the world at large may be the manner in which it links us all together without respect to national boundaries or cultural differences.

CHAPTER

23

COS Documentation

In preparing a college research project, you may use a wide variety of electronic sources and services. When the time comes to document these items, however, conventional citation systems may prove inadequate. Either they don't mention the types of sources you are using, or the guidelines for documenting them are unwieldy. That's not surprising; most citation systems were originally designed for printed documents, so they wobble as they try to accommodate sources without authors, titles, or page numbers.

An exception is the system of documentation presented in *The Columbia Guide to Online Style* (1998) by Janice R. Walker and Todd Taylor (**http://www.columbia.edu/ cu/cup/cgos/idx_basic.html**). Columbia Online Style (COS), designed expressly for electronically accessed material, acknowledges that online and computer sources differ from printed sources and yet have a logic of their own that makes reliable citation possible. We recommend that unless specifically instructed otherwise, students should use the appropriate COS style to document electronic sources: COS-humanities style for projects following MLA and CMS guidelines and COS-scientific style for projects following APA and CSE guidelines. For other styles, COS guidelines can easily be adapted to conform to the specific format required.

23a How do you use COS documentation?

COS doesn't replace MLA, APA, CMS, or CSE styles. Instead it is designed to work with all of them so that writers can document electronic sources consistently and appropriately *within* the style they are expected to use in school or at work. To use COS style, simply follow it consistently for all electronic sources in a project, choosing the COS form best suited to the documentation style you are using for printed sources. To make this adaptation simple, COS offers forms for both major types of documentation—the author–page number form favored in humanities systems (MLA, CMS) and the author-date style preferred in the sciences (APA, CSE). In this chapter we provide separate COS form directories for humanities-style citations (Section 23b) and science-style citations (Section 23d).

Like the MLA and APA systems (see Chapters 24 and 25), Columbia Online Style documentation involves two basic steps: (1) inserting a note at each point where a paper or project needs documentation and (2) recording all sources used in these notes in a Works Cited or References list.

(Step 1) In the body of your paper, place a note in the appropriate form for every item you must document. The purpose of a parenthetical note is to guide your reader to the full citation in the list of Works Cited or References. If the entry in your Works Cited or References list begins with the author's last name, the parenthetical note will, too. If it begins with the name of a corporate author or government agency, so will your parenthetical note. And if it begins with a title, you will use that title, or a shortened version of it if the title is very long, formatted appropriately (italics for book titles, quotation marks for article titles), in your parenthetical note.

In addition, the parenthetical note designates the exact location of information or quotations within the original source, as appropriate. When your source provides page numbers (as do most PDF or full-image sources accessed through online databases), include the page number after the author's name or the title, following the same format as you do for print sources. For a **humanities** paper in MLA style, the in-text note will appear as follows.

```
(Weinberg 38)
```

Most electronic sources, however, do not have page numbers—which are, after all, a convention of printed texts. Since specific references in electronic sources can be easily located using "Search" or "Find" features built into most software packages, designating the specific location of a reference within an electronic text is usually unnecessary. For electronic sources without page numbers or other consistent divisions (such as paragraph numbers), place the author's last name in parentheses after a passage that requires documentation.

```
Jim Lehrer may be America's most trusted newsperson, its new
Walter Cronkite (Shafer).
```

If an electronic source has no conventional author or other person responsible for the information (a common occurrence), identify the source by its title or by a brief description of the file when no title is given (such as for a graphics file). When the title is very long, use a shortened version. The title of the following source is "Tobacco Wields Its Clout."

```
USA Today was among those to editorialize against the tobacco
industry's continuing influence on Congress ("Tobacco").
```

Many Web pages are sponsored by business, government, or nonprofit organizations. Often these pages do not list an individual author or person responsible for maintaining the page; instead, the sponsoring organization itself is considered the author. For example:

```
The Educational Testing Service, or ETS, is a nonprofit
organization that develops and administers educational
assessment tests for schools throughout the world (ETS).
```

When you cite a source without page numbers multiple times, you will need to repeat the author's name (or short title if there is no author) for each citation. But try to keep intrusions to a minimum—for example, by using a single note at the end of a paragraph when one source is cited throughout it. You can also eliminate a parenthetical note by naming the author or title of a source in the body of the paper.

```
Shafer claims in a Slate column that PBS's Jim Lehrer is the
new Walter Cronkite, America's most trusted newsperson.

In "Tobacco Wields Its Clout," USA Today editorializes against
the tobacco industry's continuing influence on Congress.
```

When citing a message from email, listservs, or other electronic forums such as MOO or chat room discussions, you may have to cite an author's alias or nickname.

```
In a recent posting to the newsgroup alt.sport.paintball,
jireem argued . . . .
```

Note that electronic addresses are *not* enclosed in parentheses or angle brackets in COS style.

Some styles, such as Chicago, require that you use **footnotes or endnotes** instead of most parenthetical references. For a **humanities** paper using *Chicago Manual of Style* (CMS) footnotes or endnotes, a note consists of a raised number in the text keyed to a full note either at the bottom of the page or in a separate "Notes" list at the end.

```
20. Paul Skowronek, "Left and Right for Rights," Trincoll
Journal, 13 March 1997. http://www.trincoll.edu/~tj/tj03.13.97/
articles/comm2.html (23 July 1997).
```

The COS form for CMS notes can be adapted from the COS Humanities Form Directory in Section 23b. You will need to study both the COS forms in that section and the CMS footnote forms in Sections 26a and 26c.

For **scientific** papers following APA or CSE styles for print sources, the in-text note will include an author's last name followed by a date of publication in parentheses.

For most types of publications, give only the year even when the source furnishes day and date.

```
Jim Lehrer may be America's most trusted newsperson, its new

Walter Cronkite (Shafer, 1996).
```

You can also name the author in the body of your text, following the name with year of publication in parentheses.

```
Shafer (1996) claims in a Slate column that PBS's Jim Lehrer

is the new Walter Cronkite, America's most trusted newsperson.
```

Some electronic sources such as pages on the World Wide Web may not have dates of publication or any dates at all. In such cases for science-style references, record the date you accessed the source, giving day, month, and year.

```
Slipstream (21 May 1997) argues that the research design is

flawed, but ksmith (22 May 1997) rejects that claim.
```

As a general rule, make all parenthetical notes as brief and inconspicuous as possible. Remember that the point of a note is to identify a source of information, not to distract readers.

(Step 2) On a separate page at the end of your paper, list every source you cited in a parenthetical note. This alphabetical list of sources is usually titled "Works Cited" in humanities projects and "References" in scientific projects. You must have a Works Cited/References list for MLA and APA projects; in Chicago style such a page is optional because the notes themselves include all essential bibliographical information. (We show a general Chicago model on page 309 but do not include specific CMS models in the COS form directories.)

Like other systems, COS items are assembled from a few basic components.

- **Author.** In humanities styles, list the full name of the author, last name first, followed by any additional authors, their names given in the usual order.

```
Walker, Janice R., and Todd Taylor.
```

In scientific styles, list the author's last name and initials, followed by any additional authors.

```
Walker, J. R., & Taylor, T.
```

Many electronic sources do not have authors in the conventional sense. A Web site, for example, may be a collaborative effort or may represent an entire institution or a corporation; even for many singly authored electronic sources, the author's name may be missing or may be an alias or a nickname. List an author when you can clearly identify someone as responsible for a source, text, or message. List an alias if you don't know the actual name of the person. For example, the author of an email message from cerulean @mail.utexas.edu would be cerulean. Do not include the author's email address.

`cerulean.` "Re: Bono Rocks." Personal email (25 Jul. 1997).

Note that COS style does not hyphenate the word *email.* When no author can be identified, list the source on a Works Cited/References page by its title or subject line.

- **Title.** Depending on whether you are adapting COS to MLA or APA documentation styles, titles of electronic works might be italicized, placed between quotation marks, or left with no special marking, following the format specified for print-based sources. There is one important difference, however: COS does *not* use underlining to designate book or journal titles since, in computer environments, underlining indicates a hypertext link. Be careful not to mix formatting; if you are following MLA format for print-based sources and COS-humanities format for electronically accessed sources, you will need to format *all* book, journal, and similar titles using italics.

- **Editor, translator, or compiler.** Include the name of an editor, translator, or compiler, if not listed earlier. In humanities styles, give the appropriate abbreviation (*Ed., Trans.,* or *Comp.*) immediately followed by the full name. In scientific styles, the abbreviation is enclosed in parentheses and follows the name.

- **Print or previous publication information.** Many works online are based on printed sources with conventional publication histories. This information should be listed just before the electronic publication information. For other online sources, the electronic address or pathway is the essential publication information. Specifying a "publication medium" (*CD-ROM, Internet, online, WWW*) for an electronic source is usually unnecessary since the information is evident in the electronic address and since the same information may be available in more than one medium. Follow print publication information, if applicable, with the online publication information (see below).

- **Date of publication and/or access.** While print publications are routinely dated and archived, these conventions don't always suit electronic sources, which allow for more frequent revisions and may be moved or even deleted without notice (see Section 10f on the timeliness of research materials). When an online or electronic source is based on a printed source or appears in a dated format (such as the online version of a newspaper or magazine), give the original publication date of the material. For Web sites, check the home page or the source code for dates of posting or updates.

   For most electronic sources, provide a date of access—the day, month, and year you examined the material—enclosed in parentheses and following the electronic address. This date is important for establishing the version of the material you looked at in an environment that might be changing rapidly. When the date of publication of a source is the same as the date of your access (as it might be when you're reading an online news source), you need to give only the date of access.

- **Electronic address.** In citations of online items, the information most important to a researcher may be the pathway or electronic address, the means by which a given source can be located. For many sources in undergraduate research projects, that electronic address is likely to be a World Wide Web uniform resource locator (URL), that is, the familiar Web address beginning http://. URLs must be copied accurately so that researchers can locate the material you are documenting. To ensure accuracy, you can usually cut and paste an address directly from a Web browser into your project document.

  Unfortunately, some URLs are quite long and will produce odd line breaks. Never introduce a space or hard return into a URL just to fill an awkward gap in your citation. That empty space will ruin the citation for researchers who might copy and paste it directly from your document to their Web browsers. Let the word wrap capability of your word processor break the URL (but turn off the auto hyphenation feature).

```
Holmes, Steven. "Black English Debate: No Standard
     Assumptions." The New York Times 30 Dec. 1996.
     http://search.nytimes.com/search/daily/bin/fastweb?
     getdoc+site+site+8836+4+wAAA+%28suspension%29%26OR%26%28
     bridges%29%26OR%26%28%29 (28 July 1997).
```

Sometimes you can avoid long and unwieldy URLs by pointing to the main URL for a given site and then listing the links or search terms followed to access the particular site or document. For example, the *New York Times* article shown above can be located through the paper's searchable index by going directly to the search URL at **http://search.nytimes.com/search/daily/** and typing in the search terms ("Black English Debate").

```
Holmes, Steven. "Black English Debate: No Standard
     Assumptions." The New York Times 30 Dec. 1996.
     http://search.nytimes.com/search/daily/ "Black English
     Debate" (22 Feb. 1998).
```

Note that a single blank space separates the URL from the search terms.

Some newer versions of word processors have incorporated features that automatically reformat URLs and email addresses in a text document. For documents being read on a computer with Internet access, the address in the document becomes a link that automatically opens a browser or email client and connects to the designated URL. For documents in print, the font size and/or color may be changed, and the address is usually underlined automatically to designate a hypertext link.

http://www.ala.org/acrl/ilcomstan.html

When you include this address within a citation, the word processor will automatically reformat it for you.

```
Association of College and Research Libraries. "Information
     Literacy Competency Standards for Higher Education." 28
     Jan. 2002. American Library Association.
```
http://www.ala.org/acrl/ilcomstan.html (4 Feb. 2002).

Unless you are using a color printer, the colored text will appear in a slightly lighter shade than the surrounding text. Columbia Online Style recognizes that hypertext is becoming a feature of both print *and* online sources; thus, if your word processor reformats the text for you for an electronic address and automatically treats it as a hypertext link, you should not attempt to change it. However, do not attempt to emulate it on your own, either—merely underlining an electronic address will not create a hypertext link in your file.

COS also suggests that, for works to be published on the Web, citation entries be listed using the hypertext "unordered list" feature rather than trying to force hanging indents. For traditional print projects, however, COS follows the "hanging indent" feature of other styles, with the first line of each bibliographic entry flush with the left-hand margin and subsequent lines indented one-half inch or five spaces. In the sample COS entries in the form directories (Sections 23b and 23d), we follow this convention.

COS does not surround electronic addresses with angle brackets (< >). This additional and potentially confusing punctuation is not necessary to separate an electronic address from other elements in an entry. Moreover, these characters could cause problems if you were to copy and paste them into a word-processed document or a hypertext composition.

Use the following checklists to understand the basic elements of citation for electronic sources.

CHECKLIST

Basic Format—COS-Humanities (MLA)

A typical **Columbia Online Style Works Cited entry for an MLA-style paper in the humanities** includes the following basic information.

○ Author, last name first, followed by a period and one space.

○ Title of the work, followed by a period and one space. Book titles are italicized; article titles appear between quotation marks.

○ Publication information (if any), followed by a period and one space. This will ordinarily include a date of publication if different from the date of access. List previous publication information (including print publication information), if known, followed by information on the electronic publication.

○ The electronic address and any path or directory information, followed by a space. No period follows the electronic address.

○ The date you accessed the information, in parentheses, followed by a period.

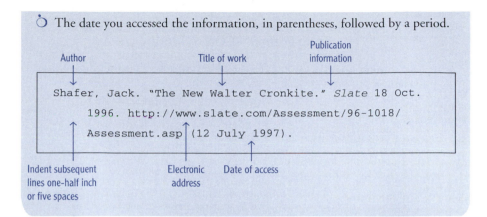

Author   Title of work   Publication information

```
Shafer, Jack. "The New Walter Cronkite." Slate 18 Oct.
     1996. http://www.slate.com/Assessment/96-1018/
     Assessment.asp (12 July 1997).
```

Indent subsequent lines one-half inch or five spaces   Electronic address   Date of access

---

CHECKLIST

Basic Format—COS-Humanities (CMS)

A typical **Columbia Online Style Works Cited entry for a CMS-style paper in the humanities** includes the following basic information.

○ Author(s), last name first, followed by a period and one space.

○ Title of the work, followed by a period (or other final punctuation mark) and enclosed between quotation marks.

○ Publication information, followed by a period. This will ordinarily include a date of publication if different from the date of access. List previous publication information (including print publication information), if known, followed by information on the electronic publication.

○ The electronic address and any path or directory information, followed by a space. No period follows the electronic address.

○ The date you accessed the information, in parentheses, followed by a period.

Authors   Title of work   Publication information

```
Benbow, Camilla Persson, and Julian C. Stanley.
     "Inequity in Equity: How 'Equity' Can Lead to
     Inequity for High-Potential Students." Abstract.
     Psychology, Public Policy, and Law. 2 June 1996.
     http://www.apa.org/journals/law/696ab.html#4
     (30 July 1997).
```

Indent subsequent lines one-half inch   Date of access   Electronic address

CHECKLIST

Basic Format—COS-Scientific (APA)

A typical **Columbia Online Style "References" entry for an APA-style paper in the sciences** includes the following basic information.

○ Author(s), last name first, followed by a period and one space.

○ Date of publication in parentheses, followed by a period and one space. Give the year first, followed by the month (do not abbreviate it), followed by the day (if applicable) for periodical publications; give only the year of publication for other works.

○ Title of the work, capitalizing only the first word and any proper nouns, followed by a period and one space.

○ Publication information (if any), followed by a period and one space. List previous publication information (including print publication information), if known, followed by information on the electronic publication.

○ The electronic address and any path or directory information, followed by a space. No period follows the electronic address.

○ The date you accessed the information, in parentheses, followed by a period.

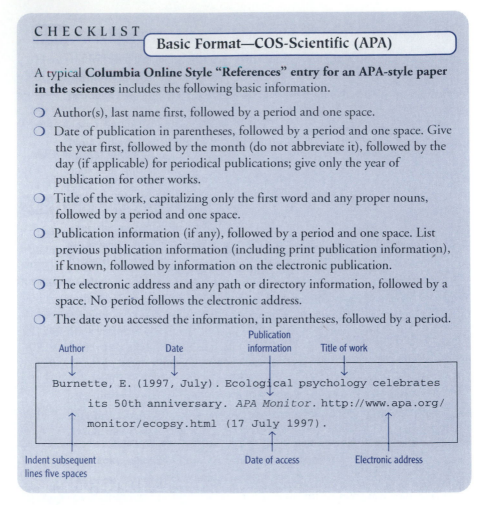

Because there are so many variations in these general entries, you will want to check the COS form directories that follow in Sections 23b (humanities) and 23d (sciences) for the correct format of a particular entry.

23b COS Form Directory—Humanities (MLA)

Here you will find the COS humanities-style forms for a variety of electronic sources. Use these forms when you are writing a paper in which you use an author–page number citation system (such as MLA) for nonelectronic sources.

Note that the items in this section adhere to MLA style for the names of authors and the titles of works and for print publication information but follow COS guidelines for the electronic portions of the citation.

To find the form you need, look in the Format Index for the type of source you need to document and then locate that item by number in the COS Form Directory itself. To handle more complex electronic sources and to learn more about developing standards for online style, consult *The Columbia Guide to On-line Style* by Janice R. Walker and Todd Taylor (New York: Columbia University Press, 1998) or its regularly updated online version at **http://www.columbia.edu/cu/cup/cgos/index.html**

COS Format Index— Humanities (MLA)

WORLD WIDE WEB CITATIONS

1. Web page—COS/MLA
2. Web site—COS/MLA
3. Web site, revised or modified—COS/MLA
4. Web site with a group or institutional author—COS/MLA
5. Web site, no author or institution—COS/MLA
6. Web site maintained by an individual—COS/MLA
7. Web site—government—COS/MLA
8. Web site—corporate—COS/MLA
9. Web site—book, printed, available online—COS/MLA
10. Web site—book, published electronically—COS/MLA
11. Web site—online article—COS/MLA
12. Web site—article from a news service or online newspaper—COS/MLA
13. Web site—article from an archive—COS/MLA
14. Web site—with frames—COS/MLA
15. Web site—graphic, audio, or video file—COS/MLA

ONLINE REFERENCES AND DATABASES

16. Online encyclopedia article—COS/MLA
17. Online dictionary or thesaurus entry—COS/MLA
18. Material from a CD-ROM—COS/MLA
19. Material from an online database—COS/MLA

EMAIL, LISTSERVS, NEWSGROUPS

20. Personal email—COS/MLA
21. Listserv—COS/MLA
22. Newsgroup—COS/MLA
23. Message from an archive—COS/MLA

GOPHER, FTP, AND TELNET SITES

24. Material from a Gopher or FTP site—COS/MLA
25. Material from a telnet site—COS/MLA
26. Synchronous communications (MOOs, MUDs, chat)—COS/MLA

SOFTWARE

27. Software—COS/MLA

1. **Web Page—COS/Humanities (MLA)** The title of a Web page appears in quotation marks.

Works Cited

"Essential Elvis (UK)." http://ourworld.compuserve.com/
    homepages/elvisfanclub/ (16 Jan. 2002).

2. **Web Site—COS/Humanities (MLA)** The title of an entire Web site is italicized. Titles of individual pages within the site are enclosed in quotation marks.

Works Cited

Humara, Miguel. "The Relationship between Anxiety and
    Performance: A Cognitive-Behavioral Perspective."
    Athletic Insight: The Online Journal of Sport Psychology
    1.2 (1999). http://www.athleticinsight.com/VollIss2/
    Cognitive_Behavioral_Anxiety.htm (10 Dec. 2001).

3. **Web Site, Revised or Modified—COS/Humanities (MLA)** You may specify a date that a page or a site was revised or updated when such a date is given. Your date of access follows the electronic address.

Works Cited

Currents in Electronic Literacy. Updated Nov. 2001.
    http://currents.cwrl.utexas.edu/ (30 Dec. 2001).

4. **Web Site with a Group or Institutional Author—COS/Humanities (MLA)** Groups, organizations, and government agencies will often co-author a document under the name of the group, organization, or agency instead of listing the names of individuals as authors.

Works Cited

Committee on the Right to Read. National Council of Teachers of
    English. "The Students' Right to Read." Mod. 12 Jan. 2000.
    http://www.ncte.org/censorship/right2read.shtml (16 Jan.
    2002).

5. **Web Site, No Author or Institution—COS/Humanities (MLA)** When no author or institution can be assigned to a site, begin the entry with the title of the page or the site. A title is italicized when it identifies an entire Web site.

Works Cited

The Official Web Site of the British Monarchy. http://
    www.royal.gov.uk/ (15 Jan. 2002).

6. Web Site Maintained by an Individual—COS/Humanities (MLA) A maintained site is one that usually contains links, routinely updated, to materials not created by the author(s) of the site. The site can be listed either by the person(s) maintaining it or by its name, depending on which emphasis suits your project.

Works Cited

Ley, Michael, maint. "DPLP Computer Science Bibliography."
    2002. Universität Trier. http://dblp.uni-trier.de/ (16
    Jan. 2002).
"DPLP Computer Science Bibliography." Maint. Michael Ley.
    Universität Trier. http://dblp.uni-trier.de/ (16 Jan.
    2002).

7. Web Site—Government—COS/Humanities (MLA) No date is given for this frequently updated Web site because it would be the same as the date of access. Government agencies are treated like corporate authors.

Works Cited

United States Congress. *Thomas: Legislative Information on the
    Internet.* http://thomas.loc.gov/home/ (28 Nov. 2001).

8. Web Site—Corporate—COS/Humanities (MLA) The corporation or institution should be listed as author.

Works Cited

Cedar Fair, L. P. "Spinning in Circles: Carousels." 2001.
    http://www.cedarpoint.com/public/news/carousel/index.cfm
    (4 Jan. 2002).

9. Web Site—Book, Printed, Available Online—COS/Humanities (MLA)
Give the name of the author, the title of the work, and the publication information for the printed version if known. Then provide the title of the electronic version, if different from the original title, and the electronic publication information.

Works Cited

Austen, Jane. *Pride and Prejudice*. 1813. *Pride and Prejudice*

Hypertext. Ed. H. Churchyard. 1994. http://www.pemberley

.com/janeinfo/pridprej.html (29 May 2001).

10. Web Site—Book, Published Electronically—COS/Humanities (MLA) Provide author, title, and date of publication. In this example the publication of the book is sponsored by an organization listed after the title.

Works Cited

Baker, Catherine. *Your Genes, Your Choice: Exploring the Issues*

Raised by Genetic Research. American Association for the

Advancement of Science. 1999. http://www.nextwave.org/

ehr/books/index.html (16 July 2001).

11. Web Site—Online Article—COS/Humanities (MLA) The title of the article in quotation marks is followed by the italicized title of the journal in which it appears. The volume number of the periodical is given, followed by a period and an issue number (if available) and date of publication.

Works Cited

DeFrancesco, Laura. "Beta Stem Cells: Searching for the

Diabetic's Holy Grail." *The Scientist* 15.21 (29 Oct.

2001). http://www.the-scientist.com/yr2001/oct/

research1_011029.html (16 Jan. 2002).

12. Web Site—Article from a News Service or Online Newspaper—COS/Humanities (MLA) When no author's name is given, list the name of the news source (such as Reuters or Associated Press), followed by the title of the article, the name of the news service or online newspaper, the date of the article if different from the date accessed, the electronic address, and the date accessed.

Works Cited

Associated Press. "Alaska Ruling Starts Debate on Gun Permits

for Mentally Ill." *New York Times on the Web* 11 Jan. 2002.

http://www.nytimes.com/2002/01/11/national/11ALAS.html (16

Jan. 2002).

13. Web Site—Article from an Archive—COS/Humanities (MLA) Provide author, title, journal or collection, and date as you would for a printed article, followed by the name of the archive site if applicable, the electronic address, and the date of access. For articles in archives with very long URLs or without direct access, give the address of the main page and include the publication information (if available), link names, or search terms used.

Works Cited

Shaw, Anna Howard. *The Story of a Pioneer*. New York: Harper and
    Brothers, 1915. U.S. Library of Congress. *American Memory*
    Collection. http://memory.loc.gov/cgi-bin/query/r?ammem/
    lhbum:@field(DOCID+@lit(M184331)) (12 Jan. 2002).

Shaw, Anna Howard. *The Story of a Pioneer*. New York: Harper and
    Brothers, 1915. U.S. Library of Congress. *American Memory*
    Collection. http://memory.loc.gov Search/woman
    suffrage/The story of a pioneer (12 Jan. 2002).

14. **Web Site—with Frames—COS/Humanities (MLA)** A Web site that uses frames may present material from other sites as well as material from within its own site. To determine the URL for the material, you may be able to right click inside the frame and choose "Open Frame in New Window" (*Netscape*) or "Open Link in New Window" (*Internet Explorer*). When you cannot determine the original URL of such material, list the documents by author, title, and other publication information; then give the name of the site where the source appears in a frame. Provide the electronic address of the site with frames, followed by a single blank space and the path or links necessary to access the specific article or site (separating individual links by a forward slash). Conclude the entry with the date of access.

Works Cited

Burney, Fanny. *Dr. Johnson and Fanny Burney*. London, 1842. "The
    Unsex'd Females and Women Writers Hypertext." *Women of the*
    Romantic Period. 1997. http://www.cwrl.utexas.edu/~worp/
    worp.html Frances Burney/Dr. Johnson and Fanny Burney (13
    Jan. 2002).

15. **Web Site—Graphic, Audio, or Video File—COS/Humanities (MLA)** Cite a multimedia file in one of two ways: either by its own URL (which you can usually find in the Netscape browser by selecting "View Page Info") or by the Web page on which the file appears. For a graphic alone, identify the author, photographer, or artist (if known); then identify the title or file name, followed by the date of

publication (if known). Then furnish the electronic address and date of access. For audio and video files, you may include the name of the artist, composer, or director if known.

Works Cited

```
Van Gogh, Vincent. Fourteen Sunflowers in a Vase. 1888.
     http://192.41.13.240/artchive/v/van_gogh/thumbs/sunflowers
     .jpg (16 Jan. 2002).
```

To cite the file as it appears on a particular page, identify the artist, the title of the file, and the date of creation, if known. Then name the site on which it appears, followed by any publication information and the electronic address for the page.

Works Cited

```
Van Gogh, Vincent. Fourteen Sunflowers in a Vase. 1888. Web
     Gallery of Art. http://www.artchive.com/artchive/V/
     van_gogh/sunflowers.jpg.html (17 Jan. 2002).
```

Audio and video files are similar to graphic files: you may cite the direct address or cite the file as a link from a Web site. Note that the file extension indicates the type of application necessary to access the file (.mp3, .ra, .mov, etc.).

Works Cited

```
"Cherokee Traditional: Stomp Dance." http://realdl.ket.org/
     ramgen/realmedia/humanities/music/cherokee.ra/
     dnet.ra?usehostname (17 Jan. 2002).
"Cherokee Traditional: Stomp Dance." The Kentucky Network
     Distance Learning Site. 2002. http://www.dl.ket.org/
     Humanities through the Arts/Music/Other Music (17 Jan.
     2002).
```

16. **Online Encyclopedia Article—COS/Humanities (MLA)** Give the author of the article (if available), the title of the article or term, enclosed in quotation marks, and the name of the encyclopedia in italics. If the encyclopedia is based on a printed work, give place of publication, publisher, and date. For electronic publications, include online publication information, if known, the electronic address, including any directories and pathways, and the date accessed.

Works Cited

```
Brown, James Robert. "Thought Experiments." 28 Dec. 1996. Mod.
     4 Jan. 1997. Stanford Encyclopedia of Philosophy. Ed.
```

Edward N. Zalta. Stanford, CA: Stanford U, 2001.
http://plato.stanford.edu/entries/thought-experiment/ (30
Dec. 2001).

Often online encyclopedias and reference works are available only through subscription. You may have free access through your library's portal or through an Internet or Information Service Provider such as *America Online*. When this is the case, you need to give enough information to allow your reader to find the source regardless of the portal they use for access. Give the URL if it allows direct access.

Works Cited

"Cathode Ray." *Encyclopaedia Britannica Online*. http://
search.eb.com/bol/topic?eu=22155&sctn=1 (30 Dec. 2001).

Stern, Robert M. "Eurodollar." *World Book Online Americas
Edition*. http://www..aolsvc.worldbook.aol.com/wbol/
wbPage/na/ar/co/186620 (30 Dec. 2001).

When you are unable to determine a URL for the article, give what information you have, including, where applicable, the name of the portal or service and any keywords or search terms that differ from the title.

Works Cited

"Cathode Ray." *Encyclopaedia Britannica Online. Galileo.
Henderson Library, Georgia Southern University,
Statesboro, GA* (30 Dec. 2001).

Stern, Robert M. "Eurodollar." *World Book Online Americas
Edition. America Online.* Keyword: World Book (30 Dec.
2001).

17. **Online Dictionary or Thesaurus Entry—COS/Humanities (MLA)** List the entry by the word looked up, enclosed in quotation marks, followed by the name of the dictionary. If the dictionary is based on a printed work, give place of publication, publisher, and date. Give any publication information about the electronic version, including the service offering it (for example, *America Online*), the electronic address, links or keywords used to access the source, and the date accessed.

Works Cited

"Assessment." *Merriam-Webster's Collegiate Dictionary. 2002.
Merriam-Webster Online.* http://www.m-w.com (17 Jan. 2002).

"Assessment." *Thesaurus by Merriam Webster. America Online.*
    Research and Learn/thesaurus (17 Jan. 2002).

18. Material from a CD-ROM—COS/Humanities (MLA) Provide an author (if available), the title of the entry or article (if applicable), and the name of the CD-ROM program or publication. Furnish any edition or version numbers, a series title if applicable, and available publication information. No date of access is necessary for CD-ROM publications. (See also model 27.)

Works Cited

Bruckheim, Allan H. "Basic First Aid." *The Family Doctor.*
    Vers. 3. Portland: Creative Multimedia, 1993.

19. Material from an Online Database—COS/Humanities (MLA) Identify the author and the title of the entry or article, and give publication information for items that have appeared in print. Identify the database or information service in italics, the name of the database publisher (if known), and furnish any retrieval data (if applicable) including the date of access. Remember that your goal is to provide as much information as possible to help your reader locate the source; however, unless the URL allows direct access to the source, do not include it. Include file or other identifying numbers if available before the date of access.

Works Cited

Jonas, Peter M., Don Weimer, and Kim Herzer. "Comparison of
    Traditional and Nontraditional (Adult Education)
    Undergraduate Business Programs." *Journal of Instructional
    Psychology* 28.3 (2001): 161-70. *Academic Search Premier.*
    Ebsco Host. AN #5338536 (7 Jan. 2002).

Perucci, Dori R. "When Pension and Unemployment Checks Don't
    Mix." *New York Times* 13 Jan. 2002, late ed.: sec. 3: 8.
    Lexis-Nexis Academic Universe (17 Jan. 2002).

Often online databases are available only through subscription. You may have free access through your library's portal or through an Internet or Information Service Provider such as *America Online.* When this is the case, you may want to include information on the portal or service you used to access the database.

Works Cited

Heinze, Denise. "Toni Morrison." *Dictionary of Literary
    Biography.* Vol. 143: American Novelists Since World War
    II, 3rd series. Gale Group, 2001: 171-87. *Gale Literary*

Databases. Henderson Library, Georgia Southern University, Statesboro, GA (21 Jan. 2002).

Taylor, John M. "The General and the Historians." *Columbiad* Winter 2000. *XanEdu Research Engine.* ProQuest. *America Online.* Research and Learn/History and Biography/U.S. Civil War/Changing Views of Lee Through History (21 Jan. 2002).

20. **Personal Email—COS/Humanities (MLA)** Identify the author of the email and give the title of the message in quotation marks. Then identify the communication as "Personal email." Include the date only if it differs from the date you accessed (or read) the message; otherwise, you need only give the access date in parentheses.

Works Cited

Sherman, Lee. "Coffee Shops." Personal email (5 Mar. 1997).

21. **Listserv—COS/Humanities (MLA)** Identify the author of the message to a list-serv. If no author's name is given, use the author's alias or email name. Then give the subject line of the message (enclosed in quotation marks) as the title, followed by the date of the message (if different from the date of access); the name of the list in italics, if known; the address of the listserv; and the date of access.

Works Cited

Cook, Janice. "Re: What New Day Is Dawning?" 19 June 1997. *Alliance for Computers and Writing Listserv.* acw-l@ttacs6 .ttu.edu (21 June 1997).

22. **Newsgroup—COS/Humanities (MLA)** Give the author's name (or alias), the subject line of the message as the title (enclosed in quotation marks), the date of the message (if different from the date of access), the name and address of the newsgroup or the name and address of the online archive (if applicable), followed by the date of access.

Works Cited

Rigney, Daniel A. III. "Re: Postmodern Theory and African American Lit." 2 Nov. 1994. *alt.postmodern.* http://groups.google.com/groups?hl=en&selm=Cyo9Aw .ELA%40acsu.buffalo.edu (14 July 1997).

23. **Message from an Archive—COS/Humanities (MLA)** Give the author, the title of the message, the date of posting, and the name of the list. Follow with the electronic address if available, or give the name of the archive if available; the electronic

address, followed by a single blank space; any other access information, separating individual links or commands by a forward slash (/). Finally, give the date of access enclosed in parentheses.

Works Cited

```
de Villiers, Michael. "New Generalisations." 14 Jan. 2002.
     geometry.college. http://mathforum.org/epigone/
     geometry-college/gayskiljal (17 Jan. 2002).
de Villiers, Michael. "New Generalisations." 14 Jan. 2002.
     geometry.college. The Math Forum Home Page.
     http://mathforum.org Math Resources by Subject/College
     Geometry/Public Forums/geometry-college (21 Jan. 2002).
```

24. **Material from a Gopher or FTP Site—COS/Humanities (MLA)** Give the name of the author; the title of the work; publication information if the work appears elsewhere; the date of the document; the protocol *(gopher, FTP)* and address, including any directory or path information; and the date of access. If the information is accessed via the World Wide Web, include the electronic address from the browser.

Works Cited

```
Carter, Locke Mitchell. "Arguments in Hypertext: Order and
     Structure in Non-Sequential Essays." Diss. The University
     of Texas at Austin, 1997. ftp://ftp.daedalus.com/
     Dissertations/Carter-Locke.pdf (17 Jan. 2002).
Cole, John Y. "Jefferson's Legacy: A Brief History of the
     Library of Congress." Last update 6 Nov. 1995. gopher://
     marvel.loc.gov/00/loc/history%09%09%2B (30 July 2001).
```

Or the electronic address can be written to indicate the links that lead to a particular document, separating the links from the URL with a single blank space.

```
gopher://marvel.loc.gov Facilities, Publications, and
     Services/History of the Library of Congress (30 July
     2001).
```

25. **Material from a Telnet Site—COS/Humanities (MLA)** Give the author of the material you are citing (if available); the title of the material; the date of publication or creation (if available); the protocol (*telnet*) and address, followed by a single blank space and any steps or commands necessary to access the site; and the date of access.

Works Cited

"Manners." *Connections.* telnet://connections.moo.mud

    .org:3333 help manners (16 Jan. 2002).

26. Synchronous Communications (MOOs, MUDs, chat)—COS/Humanities (MLA) Identify the speaker, the type of communication ("personal interview"), and the date of the interview or discussion. You may also need to include specific information about the location of the interview if requested. If so, give the title of the session or site (if applicable), the electronic address, and any pathways, directories, or commands necessary. Note that, since personal interviews and chats take place in real time, the discussion itself is not available (unless it is archived on a Web site, for example), so you do not need to give a date of access.

Works Cited

Inept Guest. Personal interview. 21 May 2000. *DaMOO.*

    telnet://damoo.csun.edu:7777/ connect guest.

shoe_polish. Personal interview. 21 Jan. 2002. *Yahoo! Chat.*

    Schools & Education/The University Years/Violence in

    Schools.

Jeremy. Personal interview. 22 Jan. 2002. http://

    www.blackboard.com/bin/login.pl?course_id=ENC1101

    &new_loc=/courses/ENC1101 Communication/Virtual Chat.

27. Software—COS/Humanities (MLA) List software by its individual or corporate author. When no author is given or the corporate author is the same as the publisher, list the software by its title. Then identify the version of the software unless the version number is part of its name (*Windows XP, Word 2000*). Give place of publication (if known), publisher, and date of release.

Works Cited

The Norton Utilities. Vers. 3.2. Cupertino, CA: Symantec, 1995.

23c Sample COS pages—Humanities (MLA)

Excerpts from a research paper that uses MLA format for printed sources and COS-humanities style for electronically accessed sources appear on pages 322–23. Note that titles of complete works are italicized rather than underlined. If you compare the examples here with the sample MLA-style paper in Chapter 24, you will notice that the COS entries resemble MLA entries in arrangement, capitalization, and punctuation; the only difference is in how COS references electronic sources.

Although water covers most of the earth's surface, most of
this water is not usable for industrial or human
consumption (Carson 44). The U.S. Environmental Protection
Agency (EPA) estimates as much as 30 to 50 percent of our
water in this country is wasted. "Water is so inexpensive,"
they argue, "that there is little incentive to repair the
leaks that needlessly waste our water" (U.S. Environmental
Protection Agency). Along with water conservation measures
and stricter regulations to preserve water quality,
increasing the amount of available freshwater supplies is
an urgent concern.

One method often suggested to address this problem is
desalination, the process of removing salts from ocean or
brackish water to produce fresh, potable water. There are
several desalination methods, including reverse osmosis,
electrodialysis, flash evaporation, and freezing (Lewin).
Reverse osmosis entails pumping salt water at high pressure
through special membranes that, while allowing fresh water
to pass through, repel the salts (Uehling 83). Tom
Pankrantz notes that "Desalination technology has been
available since the turn of the century. However, economic
considerations have limited its widespread use."

Works Cited

Carson, Rachel. *Silent Spring*. Boston: Houghton, 1962.

Heller, Jean. "Water Woes May Find Salty Solution." *St.
      Petersburg Times* 2 Apr. 1995, state ed., Tampa Bay and
      State: 1B.

Kensmark, John. "Re: Desalination." 15 Sep. 1998.
      news:rec.arts.sf.science (16 Jan 2002).

Lewin, Seymour Z. "Water." *Microsoft Encarta*. Santa Rosa, CA:

    Microsoft, 1993.

Pankrantz, Tom. "Dissecting Desalination." *Water and*

    Environment International 9.64 (2000): 8–9. *Academic*

    Search Premier. Ebsco Host. AN #3058652 (2 Jan. 2002).

Uehling, Mark D., and J. Brenning. "Salt Water on Tap."

    Popular Science 238.4 (Apr. 1991): 82–85.

U.S. Environmental Protection Agency. "Water Conservation."

    http://www.epa.gov/Region7/kids/lawater1.htm (17 Jan.

    2002).

CHECKLIST

Body of the Essay—COS-Humanities Style

Like MLA style, COS-humanities style uses parenthetical or in-text citations to designate material from other sources. The parenthetical reference generally includes the author's last name and a page number, if applicable.

○ A book is cited following MLA format, giving the author's last name and the exact page number of the reference.

○ A Web site is listed by the author's last name (here the author is a government agency). Since page numbers are not designated in the Web site, this information is omitted from the reference. Even when the source is named in the text, a parenthetical note is included for direct quotations.

○ An article from an electronic encyclopedia on CD-ROM does not include pagination and is listed by the author's last name only.

○ Journal and magazine articles, accessed using an online database, are also listed by the author's last name. Page numbers are omitted unless specifically included in the electronic text.

○ A posting to an online newsgroup is cited by the author's last name.

○ A newspaper article of only one page, following MLA format, may omit the page number from the parenthetical reference.

CHECKLIST

Works Cited Page—COS-Humanities Style

The Works Cited list (see pages 322–23) contains full bibliographic information on all sources used in composing the paper. Electronic sources are cited using COS-humanities format; other sources are cited using MLA style. Titles are italicized rather than underlined for both types of sources. Begin the list of works cited on a separate page immediately following the body of the essay; number the pages sequentially throughout the paper (including the Works Cited page).

○ Center the title "Works Cited" at the top of the page.

○ Include full bibliographic information for all sources mentioned in the paper.

○ Arrange the items in the list alphabetically by the last name of the author, or, when no author is given, by the first major word of the title.

○ Use the "hanging indent" feature of your word processor to format entries, with the first line of each entry flush with the left-hand margin and subsequent lines indented five spaces or one-half inch.

○ Double-space the entire list. Do not add extra spacing between entries.

○ Use MLA style to cite nonelectronic sources; for electronic sources, follow COS-humanities style.

23d COS Form Directory—Sciences (APA)

Here you will find the COS science-style forms for a variety of electronic sources. Use these forms when you are writing a paper in which you use an author-date citation system (such as APA) for nonelectronic sources. Note that the items in this section adhere to APA style for the names of authors and the titles of works but follow COS guidelines for the electronic portion of the citation.

To find the form you need, look in the Format Index for the type of source you need to document and then locate that item by number in the COS Form Directory that follows. To handle more complex electronic sources and to learn more about developing standards for online style, consult *The Columbia Guide to Online Style* by Janice R. Walker and Todd Taylor (New York: Columbia University Press, 1998) or its online version at **http://www.columbia.edu/cu/cup/cgos/idx_basic.html**.

COS Format Index—Sciences (APA)

WORLD WIDE WEB CITATIONS

28. Web page—COS/APA
29. Web site—COS/APA
30. Web site, revised or modified—COS/APA
31. Web site with a group or institutional author—COS/APA
32. Web site, no author or institution—COS/APA
33. Web site maintained by an individual—COS/APA
34. Web site—government—COS/APA
35. Web site—corporate—COS/APA
36. Web site—book, printed, available online—COS/APA
37. Web site—book, published electronically—COS/APA
38. Web site—online article—COS/APA
39. Web site—article from a news service or online newspaper—COS/APA
40. Web site—article from an archive—COS/APA
41. Web site—with frames—COS/APA

42. Web site—graphic, audio, or video file—COS/APA

REFERENCES AND DATABASES

43. Online encyclopedia article—COS/APA
44. Online dictionary or thesaurus entry—COS/APA
45. Material from a CD-ROM—COS/APA
46. Material from an online database—COS/APA

EMAIL, LISTSERVS, NEWSGROUPS

47. Personal email—COS/APA
48. Listserv—COS/APA
49. Newsgroup—COS/APA
50. Message from an archive—COS/APA

GOPHER, FTP, AND TELNET SITES

51. Material from a Gopher or FTP site—COS/APA
52. Material from a telnet site—COS/APA
53. Synchronous communications (MOOs, MUDs, chat)—COS/APA

SOFTWARE

54. Software—COS/APA

---

28. **Web Page—COS/Sciences (APA)** Capitalize the first word and any proper noun in the title of a Web page. Do not enclose it in quotation marks or italicize it. Because this site is undated, no date follows the name of the author or title. In a parenthetical citation, however, give the date of access: (Essential Elvis, 16 Jan. 2002).

References

```
Essential Elvis (UK). http://ourworld.compuserve.com/homepages/
    elvisfanclub/ (16 Jan. 2002).
```

29. **Web Site—COS/Sciences (APA)** The title of an entire Web site is italicized with only the first word and any proper noun capitalized. The date of publication, if

known, immediately follows the author's name or the title when no author is given.

References

Harris, R. (2001). Human-factor phenomena in problem solving.
    Virtual salt. http://www.virtualsalt.com/crebok3a.htm (17
    Jan. 2002).

30. **Web Site, Revised or Modified—COS/Sciences (APA)** You may specify a date that a page or site was revised or updated if such a date is given. Your date of access follows the electronic address.

References

Warren, W. H., Jr. (1982). *Bright star catalogue* (4th ed.,
    rev.). New Haven, CT: Yale University Observatory.
    http://astroserver.to.astro.it/dira2/dira2_doc/BSC4.HTML
    (17 Jan. 2002).

31. **Web Site with a Group or Institutional Author—COS/Sciences (APA)** Instead of listing the names of individual authors, sometimes a group or institution will co-author or take responsibility for authorship. List the name of the group or institution in place of an author's name.

References

Committee on the Right to Read. National Council of Teachers of
    English. (12 Jan. 2000). The students' right to read.
    http://www.ncte.org/censorship/right2read.shtml (16 Jan.
    2002).

32. **Web Site, No Author or Institution—COS/Sciences (APA)** When no author or institution can be assigned to a site, begin the entry with the title of the page or the site. The title is italicized when it identifies an entire Web site.

References

The official Web site of the British monarchy. http://
    www.royal.gov.uk/ (5 Dec. 2001).

33. **Web Site Maintained by an Individual—COS/Sciences (APA)** A maintained site is one that contains links, routinely updated, to materials not created by the

author(s) of the site. The site can be listed either by the person(s) maintaining it or by its name, depending on which emphasis suits your project.

References

Ley, M. (Maint.). (2002). DBLP computer science bibliography.
        Universität Trier. http://dblp.uni-trier.de/ (16 Jan.
        2002).

DBLP computer science bibliography. M. Ley (Maint.).
        Universität Trier. http://dblp.uni-trier.de/ (16 Jan.
        2002).

34. **Web Site—Government—COS/Sciences (APA)** In this example no date is given for this frequently updated Web site because it would be the same as the date of access. Government agencies are treated like group or institutional authors.

References

U.S. Congress. *Thomas: Legislative information on the Internet.*
        http://thomas.loc.gov/home (28 Dec. 2001).

35. **Web Site—Corporate—COS/Sciences (APA)** The corporation or institution should be listed as the author.

References

Cedar Fair, L.P. (2001). Spinning in circles: carousels.
        http://www.cedarpoint.com/public/news/carousel/index.cfm
        (4 Jan. 2002).

36. **Web Site—Book, Printed, Available Online—COS/Sciences (APA)** Give the name of the author, the year of publication, the title of the work, and the publication information for the printed version if known. Then provide the title of the electronic version, if different from the original title, and the electronic publication information.

References

Austen, J. (1813). *Pride and prejudice. Pride and prejudice
        hypertext.* H. Churchyard (Ed.). 1994. http://
        www.pemberley.com/janeinfo/prideprej.html (29 May 2001).

37. **Web Site—Book, Published Electronically—COS/Sciences (APA)** Provide an author, date of publication, and title. In this example the publication of the book is sponsored by an organization listed after the title.

References

Baker, C. (1999). *Your genes, your choice: Exploring the issues raised by genetic research.* American Association for the Advancement of Science. http://www.nextwave.org/ehr/books/index.html (16 July 2001).

38. Web Site—Online Article—COS/Sciences (APA) In this entry the complete date of publication is included in the parenthetical note after the author's name. Notice also that in APA style the volume number of the periodical is italicized and all major words in magazine, journal, and newspaper titles are capitalized. Provide an issue number (if available) in parentheses after the volume number. The issue number is not italicized.

References

DeFrancesco, L. (2001, October 29). Beta stem cells: Searching for the diabetic's holy grail. *The Scientist, 15*(21). http://www.the-scientist.com/yr2001/oct/research1_011029.html (16 Jan. 2002).

39. Web Site—Article from a News Service or Online Newspaper—COS/Sciences (APA) When no author's name is given, list the name of the news source (such as Reuters or Associated Press), followed by the date of the article if different from the date accessed, the title of the article, the name of the online news service or newspaper, the electronic address, and the date accessed.

References

Associated Press. (2002, January 11). Alaska ruling starts debate on gun permits for mentally ill. *New York Times on the Web.* http://www.nytimes.com/2002/01/11/national/11ALAS.html (16 Jan. 2002).

40. Web Site—Article from an Archive—COS/Sciences (APA) Provide author, date of publication, title, and publication information (if applicable). Include the name of the archive site (if available), the electronic address, and date of access. For articles in archives with very long URLs or without direct access, give the address of the main page and include the publication information (if available) or search terms used.

References

Shaw, A. H. (1915). *The story of a pioneer.* New York: Harper and Brothers. U.S. Library of Congress. *American memory collection.* http://memory.loc.gov/cgi-bin/quiery/r?ammem/lhbum:@field(DOCID+@lit(M184331)) (12 Jan. 2002).

Shaw, A. H. (1915). *The story of a pioneer*. New York: Harper

and Brothers. U.S. Library of Congress. *American memory*

collection. http://memory.loc.gov Search/woman suffrage/

The story of a pioneer (12 Jan. 2002).

41. Web Site—with Frames—COS/Sciences (APA) A Web site that uses frames may present material from other sites as well as material from within its own site. To determine the URL for the material, you may be able to right click inside the frame and choose "Open Frame in New Window" (Netscape) or "Open Link in New Window" (*Internet Explorer*). When you cannot determine the original URL of such material, list the documents by author, date, and title or other publication information; then give the name of the site where the source appears in a frame. Provide the electronic address of the site with frames, followed by a single blank space, and the path or links necessary to access the specific article or site. Conclude the entry with the date of access.

References

Burney, F. (1842). *Fanny Burney and Dr. Johnson*. London. The

unsex'd females and women writers hypertext (1997). *Women*

of the Romantic Period. http://www.cwrl.utexas.edu/~worp/

worp.html Frances Burney/Dr. Johnson and Fanny Burney (13

Jan. 2002).

42. Web Site—Graphic, Audio, or Video File—COS/Sciences (APA) Cite a multimedia file in one of two ways: either by its own URL (which you can usually find in the Netscape browser by selecting "View Page Info") or by the Web page on which the file appears. For a graphic alone, identify the author, photographer, or artist (if known); then give the date of creation or publication (if known); and the title of the work followed by a description of the source in square brackets. For files with no title information available, you may use the file name (sunflowers.jpg) instead.

References

Van Gogh, V. (1888). *Fourteen sunflowers in a vase* [painting].

http://92.4.3.240/artchive/v/van_gogh/thumbs/sunflowers

.jpg (16 Jan. 2002).

To cite the file as it appears on a particular page, identify the artist, date of creation, and title of the file, then name the site on which it appears, followed by any publication information and the electronic address for the page.

References

Van Gogh, V. (1888). *Fourteen sunflowers in a vase* [painting].

    Web gallery of art. http://www.artchive.com/artchive/V/

    van_gogh/sunflowers.jpg.html (17 Jan. 2002).

Audio and video files are similar to graphic files; you may cite the direct address or cite the file as a link from a Web site. Note that the file extension indicates the application necessary to access the file (.mp3, .ra, .mov, etc.). In the second example the year of publication refers to the Web site, not the audio file being cited.

References

Cherokee traditional: Stomp dance [audio file]. http://realdl

    .ket.org/ramgen/realmedia/humanities/music/cherokee.ra/

    dnet.ra?usehostname (17 Jan. 2002).

Cherokee traditional: Stomp dance [audio file]. *The Kentucky*

    network distance learning site. (2002). http://

    www.dl.ket.org/Humanities through the Arts/Music/

    Other Music (17 Jan. 2002).

43. Online Encyclopedia Article—COS/Sciences (APA) Give the author of the article (if available), the date of the article, its title, and the name of the encyclopedia. If the encyclopedia is based on a printed work, identify the place of publication and the publisher. Give any publication information about the electronic version, including the electronic address and any directories and pathways, as well as the date accessed.

References

Brown, J. R. (1996, December 28). Thought experiments. (Mod. 4

    Jan. 1997). In E. N. Zalta (Ed.), *Stanford encyclopedia of*

    philosophy. (2001). Stanford, CA: Stanford University.

    http://plato.stanford.edu/entries/thought-experiment (30

    Dec. 2001).

Often online encyclopedias and reference works are available only through subscription. You may have free access through your library's portal or through an Internet or Information Service Provider such as *America Online*. When this is the case, you need to give enough information to allow your reader to find the source regardless of the portal they use for access. Give the URL if it allows direct access.

References

Cathode ray. (2001, December 30). In *Encyclopaedia Britannica*

    online. http://search.eb.com/bol/topic?eu=22155&sctn=1 (30

    Dec. 2001).

```
Stern, R. M. Eurodollar. In World Book online Americas edition.
    http://www.aolsvc.worldbook.aol.com/wbol/wbPage/na/ar/co/
    186620 (30 Dec. 2001).
```

When you are unable to determine a URL for the article, give what information you have, including, where applicable, the name of the portal or service and any keywords or search terms that differ from the title.

References

```
Cathode ray. (2001, December 30). In Encyclopaedia Britannica
    online. Galileo. Henderson Library, Georgia Southern
    University, Statesboro, GA (30 Dec. 2001).
Stern, R. M. Eurodollar. In World book online Americas edition.
    America Online. Keyword: World Book (30 Dec. 2001).
```

44. Online Dictionary or Thesaurus Entry—COS/Sciences (APA) List the entry by the word looked up, followed by the date of publication and the name of the dictionary or thesaurus. If the dictionary is based on a printed work, give the place of publication and the publisher. Give any publication information about the electronic version, including the service offering it (for example, *America Online*), the electronic address, links or keywords necessary to access the source, and the date accessed.

References

```
Assessment. (2002). Merriam-Webster's collegiate dictionary.
    Merriam-Webster online. http://www.m-w.com (17 Jan. 2002).
Assessment. (2002). Thesaurus by Merriam-Webster. America
    Online. Research and Learn/thesaurus (17 Jan. 2002).
```

45. Material from a CD-ROM—COS/Sciences (APA) Provide an author (if available), the date of publication, the title of the entry or article, and the name of the CD-ROM program or publication. Furnish any edition or version numbers, a series title, and available publication information. No date of access is necessary for CD-ROM publications. (See also model 54.)

References

```
Bruckheim, A. H. (1993). Basic first aid. The family doctor
    (Version 3). Portland, OR: Creative Multimedia.
```

46. Material from an Online Database—COS/Sciences (APA) Identify the author, the date of publication, and the title of the entry or article, and give publication information for items that have appeared in print. Identify the database or information service in italics, the name of the database publisher (if known), and furnish retrieval data and a date of access. Remember that your goal is to provide as much information as possible to help your reader locate the source; however, unless the URL allows direct access to the source, do not include it. Include the file or other identifying number if available before the date of access.

References

Jonas, P. M., Weimer, D., & Herzer, K. (2001). Comparison of
    traditional and nontraditional (adult education)
    undergraduate business programs. *Journal of Instructional*
    Psychology, 28(3), 161–170. *Academic Search Premier*. Ebsco
    Host. [AN #5338536]. (7 Jan. 2002).

Perucci, D. R. (2002, January 13). When pension and
    unemployment checks don't mix. *New York Times*. Late ed.,
    sec. 3, p. 8. *Lexis-Nexis Academic Universe* (17 Jan.
    2002).

Often online databases are available only through subscription. You may have free access through your library's portal or through an Internet or Information Service Provider such as *America Online*. When this is the case, you may want to include information on the portal or service you used to access the database.

References

Heinze, D. (2001). Toni Morrison. In *Dictionary of Literary*
    Biography. Vol. 143: American novelists since World War II
    (3rd series). Gale Group: p. 171–187. *Gale Literary*
    Databases. Henderson Library, Georgia Southern University,
    Statesboro, GA (21 Jan. 2002).

Taylor, J. M. (2000, Winter). The general and the historians.
    Columbiad. XanEdu Research Engine. ProQuest. *America*
    Online. Research and Learn/History and Biography/U.S.
    Civil War/Changing Views of Lee Through History (21 Jan.
    2002).

47. Personal Email—COS/Sciences (APA) In APA style, you do not include personal email messages in the References list.

48. Listserv—COS/Sciences (APA) Identify the author of the message to a listserv. If no author's name is given, use the author's alias or email name. Then give the date followed by the subject line of the message as the title; the name of the list, if known, in italics; the address of the listserv; and the date of access.

References

Cook, J. (1997, June 19). Re: What new day is dawning? *Alliance for Computers and Writing Listserv.* acw-l@ttacs6.ttu.edu (21 June 1997).

49. Newsgroup—COS/Sciences (APA) Give the author's name (or alias), the date of the posting, the subject line of the message as the title, the name and address of the newsgroup, and the date of access.

References

Rigney, D. A. III. (1994, November 2). Re: Postmodern theory and African American lit. *alt.postmodern.* http:// groups.google.com/groups?hl=en&selm=Cyo9Aw.ELA%40acsu .buffalo.edu (14 July 1997).

50. Message from an Archive—COS/Sciences (APA) Give the name of the author, the date of the message, the title of the message, and the name of the list (if applicable). Follow with the electronic address if available, or give the name of the archive, the electronic address followed by a single blank space, and any other access information, separating individual links or commands by a forward slash (/). Finally, give the date of access enclosed in parentheses.

References

de Villiers, M. (2002, January 14). New generalisations. *geometry.college.* http://mathforum.org/epigone/ geometry-college/gayskiljal (17 Jan. 2002).

de Villiers, M. (2002, January 14). New generalisations. *geometry.college. The math forum home page.* http://mathforum.org Resources by Subject/College Geometry/Public Forums/geometry-college (21 Jan. 2002).

51. Material from a Gopher or FTP Site—COS/Sciences (APA) Give the name of the author; the date; the title of the work; publication information if the work appears elsewhere; the protocol (*gopher, FTP*) and address, including any directory or path information, and the date of access. If the information is accessed via the World Wide Web, you may include the electronic address from the browser.

References

Cole, J. Y. (1995, November 6). Jefferson's legacy: A brief history of the Library of Congress. gopher://marvel.loc .gov/00/loc/history%09%09%2B (30 July 2001).

```
Carter, L. M. (1997). Arguments in hypertext: Order and
    structure in non-sequential essays. Unpublished doctoral
    dissertation, The University of Texas at Austin.
    ftp://ftp.daedalus.com/Dissertations/Carter-Locke.pdf (17
    Jan. 2002).
```

Or the electronic address can be written to indicate the links that lead to a particular document, separating the electronic address from the directory or path information by a single blank space.

```
gopher://marvel.loc.gov/ Facilities, Publications, and
    Services/History of the Library of Congress (30 July
    2001).
```

52. Material from a Telnet Site—COS/Sciences (APA) Give the author of the material you are citing (if available); the date of creation or publication (if available); the title of the material; the site name; the protocol (*telnet*) and address, including any steps or commands necessary to access the site; and the date of access.

References

```
Manners. Connections. telnet://connections.moo.mud
    .org:3333 help manners (16 Jan. 2002).
```

53. Synchronous Communications (MOOs, MUDs, chat)—COS/Sciences (APA) Identify the speaker, the date and type of communication and/or the title of the session, and the title of the site (if available). Then give the electronic address and date of access. In giving an address, furnish any pathways, directories, or commands necessary. Note that personal communications are not usually included in the References list in APA style. However, they must be noted within the body of the paper (see Section 23b).

References

```
Inept Guest. (2000, May 21). Personal interview. DaMOO.
    telnet://damoo.csun.edu:7777.
shoe_polish. (2002, January 21). Personal interview. Yahoo!
    Chat. Schools & Education/The University Years/Violence in
    Schools.
Jeremy (2002, January 22). Personal interview. http://www
    .blackboard.com/bin/login.pl?course_id=ENC1101&new_loc=/
    courses/ENC1101/Communication/Virtual Chat.
```

54. **Software—COS/Sciences (APA)** List software by its individual or corporate author. When no author is given or the corporate author is the same as the publisher, list the software by its title. APA style does not italicize the title of software in a References list. Note also the placement of the version number in parentheses and the description of the source in brackets, both following the title.

```
                        References
The Norton utilities (Version 3.2) [Computer software]. (1995).
     Cupertino, CA: Symantec.
```

23e Sample COS pages—Sciences (APA)

Excerpts from a research paper that uses APA format for printed sources and COS-sciences style for electronically accessed sources appear on pages 336–37. You will notice that the COS entries resemble APA entries in arrangement, capitalization, and punctuation. However, COS electronic entries are more compact than comparable APA entries.

CHECKLIST

Body of the Essay—COS-Sciences Style

Like APA style, COS-sciences style uses parenthetical or in-text citations to designate material from other sources. The parenthetical reference generally includes the author's last name and the year of publication. APA requires that page numbers be included for citing a specific part of a text and for direct quotations. In COS-sciences style, however, page numbers may be omitted for electronically accessed sources that do not specifically designate pagination.

○ An article in a print journal is cited in the paper by the author's last name and the year of publication, separated by a comma. Since this reference is to the work as a whole, no page number is given.

○ A Web page with no author specified is cited by a shortened version of the title, followed by a comma and the year of publication.

○ A Web site authored by an organization (in this case, a government agency) is listed by the name of the organization, followed by the year of publication.

○ For both print and electronic sources, when the author's name is given in the essay, the parenthetical reference directly follows it and includes only the year of publication.

Sanders 2

The human genome project began a decade ago in 1988 when the Congress of the United States allocated approximately $3 billion to support a 15-year multi-university endeavor to complete the mapping of the human genome (Caskey, 1994). The human genome is the set of 23 chromosomes and 60,000 to 80,000 genes that provide the blueprint for our bodies ("Human genome," 1997). . . . .

Throughout the project, scientists also hope to identify some of the key ethical issues in gene research, to address the societal implications of the research, to bring genetic issues to public attention, and to formulate policy options designed to benefit both individuals and society (U.S. Department of Energy, 1995). Swinbanks (1992) observes, however, that since many scientists believe that

---

Sanders 10

References

Caskey, T. C. (1994). Human genes: The map takes shape. *Patient Care, 28,* 28–32.

Human genome project frequently asked questions. [FAQ]. http://www.ornl.gov/hgmis/faq/faqs1.html#q1 (5 July 1997).

Swinbanks, D. (1992). When silence isn't golden. *Nature, 368,* 368–370.

U.S. Department of Energy. (1995). Understanding our genetic inheritance: The U.S. Human Genome Project. *Human Genome Project research.* http://www.ornl.gov/TechResources/ Human_Genome/project/5yrplan/science2.html (1 July 1997).

CHECKLIST

References Page—COS-Sciences Style

○ List sources used in the paper alphabetically by the author's last name or, when no author is given, by the first major word of the title. Use italics rather than underlining for titles throughout.

○ Begin the list of references on a separate page immediately following the body of the essay; number the pages sequentially throughout (including the References page).

○ Center the title "References" at the top of the page.

○ Include full bibliographical information for all sources mentioned in the paper.

○ Use the "Hanging Indent" feature of your word processor to format entries, with the first line of each entry flush with the left-hand margin and subsequent lines indented five spaces or one-half inch.

○ Double-space the entire list. Do not add extra spacing between entries.

○ Use APA style to cite nonelectronic sources; for electronic sources, follow COS-sciences style.

24

MLA Documentation

In many professional fields in the humanities (including both English and rhetoric and composition) writers are expected to follow the conventions of documentation and format recommended by the Modern Language Association (MLA). The basic procedures for MLA documentation are spelled out in this chapter. If you encounter documentation problems not discussed here, you may want to refer to the *MLA Handbook for Writers of Research Papers,* fifth edition (1999), by Joseph Gibaldi. Style updates are available at the MLA Web site at **http://www.mla.org/**.

Citing Electronic Sources in the Humanities

Current MLA guidelines do not include forms for many electronic sources and environments, and there is considerable debate over the forms they do present. When citing electronic sources, you can use MLA format or you may instead use the documentation style recommended by the *Columbia Guide to Online Style;* it was developed explicitly for electronic environments. Columbia Online Style (COS) for humanities papers is described in Chapter 23. MLA items that have a Columbia equivalent are marked in the MLA Form Directory in this chapter with a distinctive icon: COS p. 000 . COS-humanities style is designed to work with MLA format for citing print sources and to replace MLA recommendations for citing electronic sources. Consult your instructor about using Columbia Online Style in your research project.

   Note an important difference between MLA and Columbia Online Style (COS) styles: COS requires italics, not underlining, to designate the titles of books and other major works to avoid confusion between underscored text and hypertext links. MLA suggests that, because italics are not always recognizable in certain fonts, students may wish to underline titles instead. Do not mix the two formats, however; if you use COS-humanities style—with italics—to cite electronic sources, then *all* titles of major works in your project, and in your list of Works Cited, should be italicized.

MLA's use of angle brackets (< >) to surround electronic addresses can cause problems in some applications. You may need to change the default settings in your word processor to deal with them or use special characters in HTML files. COS style, of course, avoids these problems. But consistency in citation formats is important if the elements are to be easily understood by readers. If you decide to follow MLA format for electronic sources, do so for all of them; if you decide to follow COS-humanities style for electronic sources, see Chapter 23.

24a How do you use MLA documentation?

MLA documentation involves two basic steps: (1) inserting an in-text note at each point where you have used information, ideas, or quotations from sources and (2) recording all these sources in a Works Cited list.

(Step 1) In the body of your paper, place a note in parentheses to identify the source of each passage or idea you must document. Such a note ordinarily consists of an author's last name and a page number—or a paragraph number for the few sources that have them. Here is a sentence that includes a direct quotation from *Ralph Bunche: An American Life,* by Brian Urquhart.

```
Ralph Bunche never wavered in his belief that the races
in America had to learn to live together: "In all of his
experience of racial discrimination Bunche never allowed
himself to become bitter or to feel racial hatred"
(Urquhart 435).
```

The author's name and the page number of the source are separated by a single typed space.

Page numbers are not preceded by *p.* or *pp.* or by a comma.

Also note that you do not need to repeat the first digit of the page number when it is over one hundred.

```
(Bly 253-54)
```

You can shorten a note by naming the author of the source in the body of the essay; then the note consists only of a page number. This is a common and readable form, one you should use regularly, since it also accomplishes the important goal of helping your reader to discern the authority behind your use of the information.

Brian Urquhart , a biographer of Ralph Bunche, asserts that "in
all of his experience of racial discrimination Bunche never
allowed himself to become bitter or to feel racial hatred"
(435) .

Note that the period is placed outside the parenthetical note; a single blank space separates the closing quotation marks from the opening parenthesis.

As a general rule, make all parenthetical notes as brief and inconspicuous as possible. The point of a note is to identify a source of information, not to distract or impress readers. A parenthetical note should begin with the same name as the entry in your list of Works Cited as shown in Figure 24.1; indicate the exact location of information in the source by providing a page number, if available.

The parenthetical note is usually placed after a passage needing documentation, typically at the end of a sentence, before the final punctuation mark. When a quotation is long enough (more than four typed lines) to require indention, the parenthetical note falls after the final punctuation mark. Compare the following examples.

SHORT QUOTATION (**NOT INDENTED**)

Ralph Bunche never wavered in his belief that the races
in America had to learn to live together: "In all of his
experience of racial discrimination Bunche never allowed
himself to become bitter or to feel racial hatred"
(Urquhart 435) . He continued to work . . .

The note is placed inside the final punctuation mark.

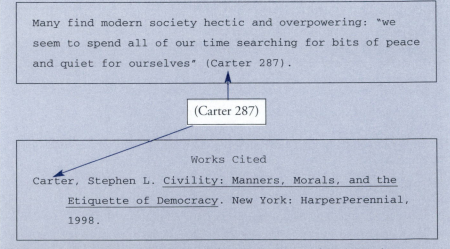

Many find modern society hectic and overpowering: "we
seem to spend all of our time searching for bits of peace
and quiet for ourselves" (Carter 287).

(Carter 287)

                    Works Cited
Carter, Stephen L. Civility: Manners, Morals, and the
        Etiquette of Democracy. New York: HarperPerennial,
        1998.

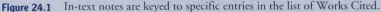

Figure 24.1   In-text notes are keyed to specific entries in the list of Works Cited.

Long quotation (indented ten spaces)

```
Winner of the Nobel Peace Prize in 1950, Ralph Bunche, who died
in 1971, left an enduring legacy:

        His memory lives on, especially in the long struggle

        for human dignity and against racial discrimination

        and bigotry, and in the growing effectiveness of the

        United Nations in resolving conflicts and keeping the

        peace. (Urquhart 458)
```

The note is placed outside the final punctuation mark.

Generally you will want to rely on primary sources in your research projects (see Chapter 5). When you need to cite a quotation included in another source and you are using only the quoted material, note that you obtained it secondhand by including "qtd. in" in the parenthetical note.

```
One handbook includes a quote from Roger Parker's Looking Good

in Print that makes even more sense as we begin considering

rhetorical concepts for hypertextual writing: "Graphic design

should provide a road map that steers your readers from point

to point" (qtd. in Hairston et al. 268).
```

The Hairston book would be listed on your Works Cited page, not Roger Parker's book. In this way you protect yourself—if there are errors in the quotation, they are Hairston's, not yours—and you show that you are honest—you cited the source where you actually found the information. If at all possible, and to eliminate any chance of error or academic dishonesty, you should check the original for yourself.

Another situation you may encounter is a quote within a quote. In this case, alternate your use of double and single quotation marks: the entire quotation will be surrounded by double quotation marks, the interior quotation enclosed within single quotation marks.

```
Walker notes that "Mikhail Bakhtin segregates language into

three aspects--thematic content, style, and compositional

structure, in which all three are 'inseparably linked to the

whole of utterance'(945)."
```

Make sure you close both sets of quotation marks.

Use the following guidelines when preparing in-text notes.

1. **When two or more sources are cited within a single sentence,** the parenthetical notes appear right after the statements they support.

```
While the budget cuts might go deeper than originally
reported (Kinsley 42), there is no reason to believe that
"throwing more taxpayers' dollars into a bottomless pit"
(Doggett 62) will do much to reform "one of the least
productive job training programs ever devised by the
federal government" (Will 28).
```

Notice that a parenthetical note is always placed outside quotation marks but before any punctuation, including the period that ends the sentence.

2. **When you cite more than one work by a single author in a paper,** a parenthetical note listing only the author's last name could refer to more than one book or article on the Works Cited page. To avoid confusion, place a comma after the author's name and use a shortened title to identify the particular work being cited. For example, a Works Cited page might list four works by Richard D. Altick:

```
                    Works Cited
Altick, Richard D. The Art of Literary Research. New York:
        Norton, 1963.
---. The Shows of London. Cambridge: Belknap-Harvard, 1978.
---. Victorian People and Ideas. New York: Norton, 1973.
---. Victorian Studies in Scarlet. New York: Norton, 1977.
```

The first time—and every subsequent time—you refer to a work by Richard Altick, you need to identify it by a shortened title in the parenthetical note.

```
(Altick, Shows 345)
(Altick, Victorian People 190-202)
(Altick, Victorian Studies 59)
```

3. **When you need to document a work without an author**—an unsigned article in a magazine or newspaper, for example—give the title, shortened if necessary, and the page number. Remember that the goal is to help your reader locate the citation in your list of Works Cited.

```
("In the Thicket" 18)
("Students Rally" A6)
```

```
                    Works Cited
"In the Thicket of Things." Texas Monthly Apr. 1994: 18.
"Students Rally for Academic Freedom." The Chronicle of
        Higher Education 28 Sept. 1994: A6.
```

4. **When you need to cite more than a single work in one note,** separate the citations with a semicolon.

```
(Polukord 13-16; Ryan and Weber 126)
```

5. **When a parenthetical note would be awkward,** refer to the source in the body of the essay itself.

```
In "Hamlet's Encounter with the Pirates," Wentersdorf

argues . . .

Under "Northwest Passage" in Collier's Encyclopedia . . .

The Arkansas State Highway Map indicates . . .

Software such as Microsoft's FoxPro . . .
```

Occasions when parenthetical notes might be awkward include the following:

- When you wish to refer to an entire article, not just to a passage or several pages
- When the author is a group or institution—for example, the editors of *Time* or the Smithsonian Institution
- When the citation is to a personal interview or an unpublished speech or letter
- When the item doesn't have page numbers: a map, a cartoon, a work of art, a videotape, a play in performance
- When the item is a reference work arranged alphabetically
- When the item is a government document with a name too long for a convenient in-text note
- When the item is computer software or an electronic source without conventional page numbers (see Section 23a on using parenthetical notes with electronic sources)

Individual entries in the MLA Form Directory (Section 24b) indicate when to avoid an in-text parenthetical note.

(Step 2) On a separate page at the end of your project, list every source included in the parenthetical notes. The alphabetical list of sources is titled "Works Cited" and begins on the page immediately following the body of your essay. (See the sample essay beginning on page 261.) A Works Cited entry for Brian Urquhart's biography of Ralph Bunche would look like this:

```
Urquhart, Brian. Ralph Bunche: An American Life. New York:
       Norton, 1993.
```

The first entries on a full Works Cited page might look like this.

Subsequent lines indented
one-half inch or five spaces   "Works Cited" centered   All items double spaced

Works Cited

"Bataan Death March." Encyclopaedia Britannica:
Micropaedia. 1985 ed.

Berger, Joseph. "Once Rarely Explored, the Holocaust Gains
Momentum as a School Subject." New York Times
3 October 1988, sec. A: 16.

Hoyt, Edwin P. Japan's War. New York: McGraw, 1986.

McGill, Peter. "A Cover-up for a Death Camp." Maclean's
20 May 1985: 32.

The Works Cited page itself follows the body of the essay (and endnotes, if there are any). It lists bibliographical information on all the materials you used in composing an essay. (You do not include sources you examined but did not cite in your paper). For a sample Works Cited list, see page 272.

When an author has more than one work on the Works Cited list, those works are listed alphabetically under the author's name. (See page 342.)

Works published since 1900 include the publisher's name. Publishers' names should be shortened whenever possible. Drop the words *Company, Inc., Ltd., Bros.,* and *Books.* Abbreviate *University* as *U* and *University Press* as *UP.* When possible, shorten a publisher's name to one word. Here are suggested abbreviations.

Barnes and Noble Books	Barnes
Doubleday and Co., Inc.	Doubleday
Harvard University Press	Harvard UP
University of Chicago Press	U of Chicago P
The Viking Press	Viking

CHECKLIST

Basic Format—Books

A typical MLA Works Cited entry for a book includes the following basic information.

○ Author, last name first, followed by a period and one space.

○ Title of the work, underlined or italicized, followed by a period and one space.

○ City of publication (including two-letter state designation for cities that are not well known), followed by a colon.
○ Name of publisher (see list of abbreviations), followed by a comma and one space.
○ Date of publication, followed by a period.

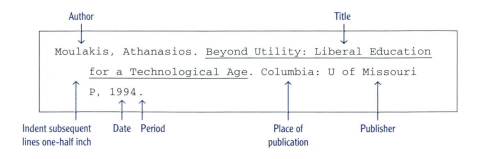

Author — Title

Moulakis, Athanasios. Beyond Utility: Liberal Education for a Technological Age. Columbia: U of Missouri P, 1994.

Indent subsequent lines one-half inch   Date   Period   Place of publication   Publisher

CHECKLIST

Basic Format—Scholarly Journals

A typical MLA Works Cited entry for an article in a scholarly journal (where the pagination is continuous throughout a year) includes the following basic information.

○ Author, last name first, followed by a period and one space.
○ Title of the article, followed by a period (or other final punctuation mark) and enclosed between quotation marks.
○ Name of the periodical, italicized or underlined, followed by one space.
○ Volume number, followed by one space.
○ Date of publication in parentheses, followed by a colon.
○ Page or location, followed by a period. Page numbers should be inclusive, from the first page of the article to the last, including notes and bibliography.

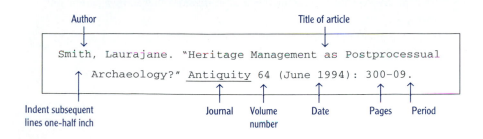

Author   Title of article

Smith, Laurajane. "Heritage Management as Postprocessual Archaeology?" Antiquity 64 (June 1994): 300–09.

Indent subsequent lines one-half inch   Journal   Volume number   Date   Pages   Period

CHECKLIST
Basic Format—Magazines and Newspapers

A typical MLA Works Cited entry for an article in a popular magazine or newspaper includes the following basic information.

○ Author, last name first, followed by a period and one space.
○ Title of the article, followed by a period and enclosed between quotation marks.
○ Name of the periodical or newspaper, underlined or italicized, followed by one space.
○ Date of publication, followed by a colon and one space. Abbreviate all months except May, June, and July.
○ Page and/or location (section number for newspapers), followed by a period. Pages should be inclusive.

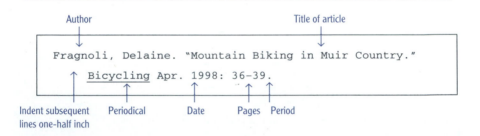

Author · Title of article

Fragnoli, Delaine. "Mountain Biking in Muir Country."
    Bicycling Apr. 1998: 36–39.

Indent subsequent   Periodical   Date   Pages Period
lines one-half inch

CHECKLIST
Basic Format—Electronic Sources

A typical MLA Works Cited entry for an electronic source may include the following information, though few will require all the elements. (See also COS-humanities style in Chapter 23.)

○ Author, last name first, followed by a period and one space.
○ Title of the work, followed by a period and one space. Book titles are underlined or italicized; article titles appear between quotation marks.
○ Print publication information (if any), followed by a period and one space.
○ Title of the electronic site, underlined or italicized followed by a period and one space.
○ Editor (if any) of the electronic site, database, or text, with role indicated (for example, *Ed.*), followed by a period and a space.
○ Version or volume number (if any) of the source, usually followed by a period.
○ Date of electronic publication or most recent update, followed by a period.

○ Identity of institution or group (if any) sponsoring the electronic site, followed by a period and a space.
○ The date you accessed the information, followed by a space.
○ The electronic address between angle brackets (< >), followed by a period.

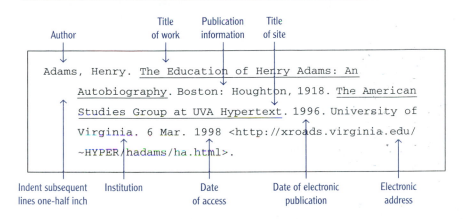

Because there are so many variations to these general entries, you will want to check the MLA Form Directory that follows for the correct format of any unusual entry.

24b MLA Form Directory

Here you will find the MLA Works Cited and parenthetical note forms for more than sixty kinds of sources. First find the type of source you need to cite in the Format Index, then locate that item by number in the list that follows. The "COS" icon next to an entry indicates that a Columbia Online Style (COS) form is available for that source (see Chapter 23 on COS).

MLA Format Index

BOOKS AND DISSERTATIONS

55. Book, one author
56. Book, two or three authors or editors
57. Book, four or more authors or editors
58. Book, revised by a second author
59. Book, edited—focus on the editor
60. Book, edited—focus on the editor, more than one editor
61. Book, edited—focus on the original author
62. Book, written by a group
63. Book with no author
64. Book, focus on a foreword, introduction, preface, or afterword
65. Work of more than one volume
66. Book, translation—focus on the original author
67. Book, translation—focus on the translator

68. Book in a foreign language
69. Book, republished
70. Book, part of a series
71. Book, a reader or anthology
72. Book, a second, third, or later edition
73. Chapter in a book
74. Book published before 1900
75. Book issued by a division of a publisher—a special imprint
76. Dissertation or thesis—published (including publication by UMI)
77. Dissertation or thesis—unpublished
78. Book review—titled or untitled

ARTICLES AND MAGAZINE PIECES

79. Article in a scholarly journal
80. Article in a popular magazine
81. Article in a weekly or biweekly magazine
82. Article in a monthly magazine
83. Article or selection from a reader or anthology

NEWSPAPERS

84. Article in a newspaper
85. Editorial in a newspaper—author not named
86. Letter to the editor
87. Cartoon

REFERENCE WORKS

COS 88. Reference work or encyclopedia (familiar or online)
89. Reference work (specialized or less familiar)
90. Bulletin or pamphlet
91. Government document

ELECTRONIC SOURCES

COS 92. Computer software
COS 93. Web page—generic
COS 94. Web—online book
COS 95. Web—online scholarly journal
COS 96. Web—online popular magazine
COS 97. Web—online newspaper editorial
COS 98. Web—personal home page
COS 99. Listserv/Newsgroup/Usenet newsgroup
COS 100. Synchronous communication (MOOs, MUDs)
COS 101. Email
COS 102. CD-ROM/diskette database or publication

MISCELLANEOUS ENTRIES

103. Microfilm or microfiche
104. Biblical citation
105. Videotape
106. Movie
107. Television program
108. Radio program
109. Personal interview
110. Musical composition
111. Recording
112. Speech—no printed text
113. Speech—printed text
114. Lecture
115. Letter—published
116. Letter—unpublished
117. Artwork
118. Drama or play

55. Book, One Author—MLA Give the author, last name first, followed by the title of the book in italics or underlined, city of publication, name of publisher, and year of publication.

Works Cited

Weinberg, Steven. <u>Dreams of a Final Theory</u>. New York:

    Pantheon, 1992.

Parenthetical note: (Weinberg 38)

56. Book, Two or Three Authors or Editors—MLA The names of second and third authors are given in normal order, first names first.

Works Cited

Collier, Peter, and David Horowitz. <u>Destructive Generation:</u>

    <u>Second Thoughts About the '60s</u>. New York: Summit, 1989.

Parenthetical note: (Collier and Horowitz 24)

57. Book, Four or More Authors or Editors—MLA You have two options. You may name all the authors in both the Works Cited entry and any parenthetical note.

Works Cited

Guth, Hans P., Gabriele L. Rico, John Ruszkiewicz, and Bill

    Bridges. <u>The Rhetoric of Laughter: The Best and Worst of</u>

    <u>Humor Night</u>. Fort Worth: Harcourt, 1996.

Parenthetical note: (Guth, Rico, Ruszkiewicz, and Bridges 95)

Alternatively, you may name only the first author listed on the title page, followed by the Latin abbreviation *et al.*, which means "and others."

Works Cited

Guth, Hans P., et al. <u>The Rhetoric of Laughter: The Best and</u>

    <u>Worst of Humor Night</u>. Fort Worth: Harcourt, 1996.

Parenthetical note: (Guth et al. 95)

58. Book, Revised by a Second Author—MLA Sometimes you may need to cite a book by its original author, even when it has been revised. In such a case, place the editor's name after the title of the book.

Works Cited

Guerber, Hélène Adeline. <u>The Myths of Greece and Rome</u>. Ed.

    Dorothy Margaret Stuart. 3rd ed. London: Harrap, 1965.

Parenthetical note: (Guerber 20)

59. Book, Edited—Focus on the Editor—MLA When you cite an edited work by the editor's name, identify the original author after the title of the work.

```
                       Works Cited
Noyes, George R., ed. The Poetical Works of John Dryden. By
        John Dryden. Boston: Houghton, 1950.
```
Parenthetical note: (Noyes v-vi)

60. **Book, Edited—Focus on the Editor, More Than One Editor—MLA** Treat multiple editors just as you would multiple authors, but place the abbreviation for editors (*eds.*) after their names.

```
                       Works Cited
Detweiler, Robert, John N. Sutherland, and Michael S.
        Werthman, eds. Environmental Decay in Its Historical
        Context. Glenview: Scott, 1973.
```
Parenthetical note: (Detweiler et al. 3)

61. **Book, Edited—Focus on the Original Author—MLA** Because the sample Works Cited entry shown here is an edition of Shakespeare, the parenthetical note furnishes the act, scene, and line numbers for a particular play—not the author and page numbers one might expect with another kind of book.

```
                       Works Cited
Shakespeare, William. The Tragedy of Coriolanus. Ed. Reuben
        Brower. New York: Signet, 1966.
```
Parenthetical note: (Cor. 3.3.119-35)

62. **Book, Written by a Group—MLA** In the Works Cited entry, treat the group as the author. But to avoid a confusing parenthetical note, identify the group author in the body of your paper and place only relevant page numbers in parentheses. For example, you might use a sentence such as "The Reader's Digest *Fix-It-Yourself Manual* explains the importance of a UL label (123)."

```
                       Works Cited
Reader's Digest. Fix-It-Yourself Manual. Pleasantville:
        Reader's Digest, 1977.
```

63. **Book with No Author—MLA** List the book by its title, alphabetized by the first major word (excluding *The, A,* or *An*).

```
                       Works Cited
Illustrated Atlas of the World. Chicago: Rand, 1985.
```
Parenthetical note: (Illustrated Atlas 88)

64. Book, Focus on a Foreword, Introduction, Preface, or Afterword—MLA
The note below refers to information in Tony Tanner's introduction, not to the
text of Jane Austen's novel.

Works Cited

Tanner, Tony. Introduction. <u>Mansfield Park</u>. By Jane Austen.

Harmondsworth, Eng.: Penguin, 1966. 7–36.

Parenthetical note: (Tanner 9–10)

65. Work of More Than One Volume—MLA When you use only one volume of
a multivolume set, identify both the volume you used and the total number of
volumes in the set.

Works Cited

Spindler, Karlheinz. <u>Abstract Algebra with Applications</u>.

Vol. 1. New York: Dekker, 1994. 2 vols.

Parenthetical note: (Spindler 17–18)

If you use more than one volume of a set, list only the total number of volumes in
that set. Then, in your parenthetical notes, identify the specific volumes as you
cite them.

Works Cited

Spindler, Karlheinz. <u>Abstract Algebra with Applications</u>.

2 vols. New York: Dekker, 1994.

Parenthetical note: (Spindler 1: 17–18); (Spindler 2: 369)

66. Book, Translation—Focus on the Original Author—MLA Include the name
of the translator preceded by the abbreviation *Trans.* after the title of the book.

Works Cited

Freire, Paulo. <u>Learning to Question: A Pedagogy of Liberation</u>.

Trans. Tony Coates. New York: Continuum, 1989.

Parenthetical note: (Freire 137–38)

67. Book, Translation—Focus on the Translator—MLA In this example the
author is unknown. If known, the author's name would follow the title of the
book, preceded by the word *By.*

Works Cited

Swanton, Michael, trans. <u>Beowulf</u>. New York: Barnes, 1978.

Parenthetical note: (Swanton 17–18)

68. Book in a Foreign Language—MLA Copy the title of the foreign language work exactly as it appears on the title page, paying special attention both to accent marks and to capitalization.

Works Cited

Bablet, Denis, and Jean Jacquot. <u>Les Voies de la création</u>
     <u>théâtrale</u>. Paris: Editions du Centre National de la
     Recherche Scientifique, 1977.

Parenthetical note: (Bablet and Jacquot 59)

69. Book, Republished—MLA Give the original year of publication after the title of a work of fiction that has been through many editions and reprints.

Works Cited

Herbert, Frank. <u>Dune</u>. 1965. New York: Berkeley, 1977.

Parenthetical note: (Herbert 146)

70. Book, Part of a Series—MLA Give the series name just before the publishing information. Do not underline or italicize a series name or enclose it in quotation marks.

Works Cited

Kirk, Grayson, and Nils H. Wessell, eds. <u>The Soviet Threat:</u>
     <u>Myths and Realities</u>. Proceedings of the Academy of
     Political Science 33. New York: Academy of Political
     Science, 1978.

Parenthetical note: (Kirk and Wessell 62)

71. Book, a Reader or Anthology—MLA When you quote from the front matter of the collection, the page numbers for a parenthetical note may sometimes be Roman numerals. (To cite a selection within an anthology, see model 83.)

Works Cited

Lunsford, Andrea, and John Ruszkiewicz, eds. <u>The Presence of</u>
     <u>Others: Voices That Call for Response</u>. 2nd ed. New York:
     St. Martin's, 1997.

Parenthetical note: (Lunsford and Ruszkiewicz xvii-xix)

72. Book, a Second, Third, or Later Edition—MLA The edition number follows the title of the book.

Works Cited

Rombauer, Marjorie Dick. <u>Legal Problem Solving: Analysis,</u>

    <u>Research, and Writing</u>. 5th ed. St. Paul: West, 1991.

Parenthetical note: (Rombauer 480-81)

73. **Chapter in a Book—MLA** Give the name of the author(s) of the chapter, followed by the title of the chapter enclosed in quotation marks, and the title of the book in italics or underlined. Include the name(s) of the book's author(s) or editor(s), if different from the chapter's author(s), after the book title (see model 83).

Works Cited

Owens, Delia, and Mark Owens. "Home to the Dunes." <u>The Eye of</u>

    <u>the Elephant: An Epic Adventure in the African</u>

    <u>Wilderness</u>. Boston: Houghton, 1992: 11-27.

Parenthetical note: (Owens and Owens 24-27)

74. **Book Published Before 1900—MLA** Omit the name of the publisher in citations of works published prior to 1900.

Works Cited

Bowdler, Thomas, ed. <u>The Family Shakespeare</u>. 10 vols. London,

    1818.

Parenthetical note: (Bowdler 2: 47)

75. **Book Issued by a Division of a Publisher—a Special Imprint—MLA** Attach the special imprint (Vintage in this case) to the publisher's name with a hyphen.

Works Cited

Hofstadter, Douglas. <u>Gödel, Escher, Bach: An Eternal Golden</u>

    <u>Braid</u>. New York: Vintage-Random, 1980.

Parenthetical note: (Hofstadter 192-93)

76. **Dissertation or Thesis—Published (Including Publication by UMI)—MLA** If the dissertation you are citing is published by University Microfilms International (UMI), provide the order number as the last item in the Works Cited entry.

Works Cited

Rifkin, Myra Lee. <u>Burial, Funeral and Mourning Customs in</u>

    <u>England, 1558-1662</u>. Diss. Bryn Mawr, 1977. Ann Arbor:

    UMI, 1977. DDJ78-01385.

Parenthetical note: (Rifkin 234)

77. **Dissertation or Thesis—Unpublished—MLA** The title of an unpublished dissertation appears between quotation marks. *Diss.* indicates that the source is a dissertation.

Works Cited

Altman, Jack, Jr. "The Politics of Health Planning and

    Regulation." Diss. Massachusetts Institute of Technology,

    1983.

Parenthetical note: (Altman 150)

78. **Book Review—Titled or Untitled—MLA** Not all book reviews have titles, so the Works Cited form for a book review can vary slightly. Notice that a book title (*Uncle Tom's Cabin*) within a book title (Uncle Tom's Cabin *and American Culture*) is not underscored or italicized.

Works Cited

Baym, Nina. Rev. of Uncle Tom's Cabin and American Culture, by

    Thomas F. Gossett. Journal of American History 72 (1985):

    691-92.

Keen, Maurice. "The Knight of Knights." Rev. of William

    Marshall: The Flower of Chivalry, by Georges Duby.

    New York Review of Books 16 Jan. 1986: 39-40.

Parenthetical note: (Baym 691-92); (Keen 39)

79. **Article in a Scholarly Journal—MLA** Issues of scholarly journals are usually identified by volume number or season (rather than day, week, or month of publication). Such journals are usually paginated year by year, with a year's work treated as one volume.

Works Cited

Pratt, Mary Louise. "Humanities for the Future: Reflections on

    the Western Cultural Debate at Stanford." South Atlantic

    Quarterly 89 (1990): 7-25.

Parenthetical note: (Pratt 24)

When a scholarly journal is paginated issue by issue, place a period and the issue number after the volume number.

Savolainen, Matti. "Fatal Drops of Blood in Yoknapatawpha: On

    Translations and Reception of Faulkner in Finland." South

    Atlantic Review 65.4 (2000): 51-61.

80. **Article in a Popular Magazine—MLA** Magazines are paginated issue by issue and identified by the monthly or weekly date of publication (instead of by volume number). If an article does not appear on consecutive pages in the magazine, give the first page on which it appears, followed by a plus sign: *64+*.

Works Cited

Sabbag, Robert. "Fear and Reloading in Gun Valley." Men's

    Journal Oct. 1994: 64+.

Parenthetical note: (Sabbag 64)

81. **Article in a Weekly or Biweekly Magazine—MLA** Give the entire date of publication in day-month-year format as stated on the issue.

Works Cited

Smolowe, Jill. "When Violence Hits Home." Time 18 July 1994:

    18-25.

Parenthetical note: (Smolowe 20)

82. **Article in a Monthly Magazine—MLA** Give the month and year, abbreviating any month longer than four letters.

Works Cited

Hudson, Elizabeth. "Hanging Out with the Bats." Texas Highways

    Aug. 1994: 14-19.

Parenthetical note: (Hudson 15)

83. **Article or Selection from a Reader or Anthology—MLA** List the item on the Works Cited page by the author of the piece you are citing, not the editor(s) of the collection. Then provide the title of the particular selection, the title of the overall collection, the editor(s) of the collection, and publication information. Conclude with the page numbers of the selection.

Works Cited

Rohrer, Matthew. "Found in the Museum of Old Science." The

    Presence of Others: Voices That Call for Response. Ed.

    Andrea Lunsford and John Ruszkiewicz. 2nd ed. New York:

    St. Martin's, 1997. 290-91.

Parenthetical note: (Rohrer 290)

When you cite two or more selections from a reader or an anthology, list that collection fully on the Works Cited page.

```
Lunsford, Andrea, and John Ruszkiewicz, eds. The Presence of
     Others: Voices That Call for Response. 2nd ed. New York:
     St. Martin's, 1997.
```

Then, elsewhere in the Works Cited list, identify the authors and titles of all articles you cite from that reader or anthology, followed by the name(s) of the editors(s) and the page numbers of those selections.

```
Himmelfarb, Gertrude. "The Victorians Get a Bad Rap." Lunsford
     and Ruszkiewicz 528-32.
Rohrer, Matthew. "Found in the Museum of Old Science."
     Lunsford and Ruszkiewicz 290-91.
```

When necessary, provide the original publication information first and then give the facts about the collection.

```
Hartman, Geoffrey. "Milton's Counterplot." ELH 25 (1958):
     1-12. Rpt. in Milton: A Collection of Critical Essays.
     Ed. Louis L. Martz. Twentieth Century Views. Englewood
     Cliffs: Spectrum-Prentice, 1966: 100-08.
```
Parenthetical note: (Hartman 101)

84. **Article in a Newspaper—MLA** For page numbers, use the form in the newspaper you are citing; many newspapers are paginated according to sections.

Works Cited

```
Rorty, Richard. "The Unpatriotic Academy." New York Times 13
     Feb. 1994: E15.
```
Parenthetical note: (Rorty E15)

A plus sign following the page number (for example, 7+) indicates that an article continues beyond the designated page but not necessarily on consecutive pages.

Works Cited

```
Peterson, Karen S. "Turns Out We Are 'Sexually Conventional.'"
     USA Today 7 Oct. 1994: 1A+.
```
Parenthetical note: (Peterson 2A)

85. **Editorial in a Newspaper—Author Not Named—MLA** Begin with the title of the editorial, followed by the description *Editorial.*

Works Cited

"Negro College Fund: Mission Is Still Important on 50th

      Anniversary." Editorial. <u>Dallas Morning News</u> 8 Oct. 1994,

      sec. A: 28.

Parenthetical note: ("Negro College" 28)

86. **Letter to the Editor—MLA** Give the author's name, followed by the
description *Letter*. In this example the particular edition of the newspaper is
noted after the date of publication.

Works Cited

Cantu, Tony. Letter. <u>San Antonio Light</u> 14 Jan. 1986, southwest

      ed., sec. C: 4.

Parenthetical note: (Cantu 4)

87. **Cartoon—MLA** To avoid a confusing parenthetical note, describe a cartoon in
the text of your essay. For example, you might use a reference such as "In 'Squib'
by Miles Mathis . . ."

Works Cited

Mathis, Miles. "Squib." Cartoon. <u>Daily Texan</u> 15 Jan. 1986: 19.

88. **Reference Work or Encyclopedia (Familiar or Online)—MLA** With familiar
reference works, especially those revised regularly, identify the edition you are
using by its date. You may omit the names of editors and most publishing
information. No page number is given in the parenthetical note when a work is
arranged alphabetically.

Works Cited

Benedict, Roger William. "Northwest Passage." <u>Encyclopaedia</u>

      <u>Britannica: Macropaedia</u>. 1974 ed.

Parenthetical note: (Benedict)

COS
p. 316

A citation for an online encyclopedia article would include a date of access and an
electronic address. However, the online version might not list an author.

Works Cited

"Northwest Passage." <u>Britannica Online</u>. Vers. 98.1. 1 Nov.

      1997. <u>Encyclopaedia Britannica</u>. 30 Nov. 1997

      <http://www.eb.com:180/cgibin/g?DocF=micro/430/12.html>.

89. **Reference Work (Specialized or Less Familiar)—MLA** With less familiar reference tools, a full entry is required. (See model 88 for the treatment of familiar reference works.)

Works Cited

```
Kovesi, Julius. "Hungarian Philosophy." The Encyclopedia of

     Philosophy. Ed. Paul Edwards. 8 vols. New York:

     Macmillan, 1967.
```
Parenthetical note: (Kovesi)

90. **Bulletin or Pamphlet—MLA** Treat pamphlets as if they were books.

Works Cited

```
Morgan, Martha, ed. Campus Guide to Computer Services. Austin:

     U of Texas, 1997.
```
Parenthetical note: (Morgan 8-9)

91. **Government Document—MLA** Give the name of the government (national, state, or local) and the agency issuing the report, the title of the document, and publishing information. If it is a congressional document other than the *Congressional Record,* identify the Congress and, when important, the session (for example, *99th Cong., 1st sess.*) after the title of the document. Avoid a lengthy parenthetical note by naming the document in the body of your essay and placing only the relevant page numbers between parentheses: "This information is from the *1985–86 Official Congressional Directory* (182–84)."

Works Cited

```
United States. Cong. Joint Committee on Printing. 1985-86

     Official Congressional Directory. 99th Cong., 1st sess.

     Washington: GPO, 1985.
```

To cite the *Congressional Record,* give only the date and page number.

```
Cong. Rec. 8 Feb. 1974: 3942-43.
```

COS
p. 321 92. **Computer Software—MLA** Give the author if known, the version number if any (for example, *Microsoft Word.* Vers. 7.0), the manufacturer, the date, and (optionally) the system needed to run it. Name the software in your text rather than use a parenthetical note: "With software such as Microsoft's FoxPro. . . ."

Works Cited

```
FoxPro. Vers. 2.5. Redmond: Microsoft, 1993.
```

93. Web Page—Generic—MLA The variety of Web pages is staggering, so you will have to adapt your documentation to particular sources. In general, provide author; title of the work; print publication information (if any); title of the electronic site, italicized or underlined; editor, with role appropriately indicated (*Ed.*); version or volume number (if any) of the source; date of electronic publication or most recent update; identity of the institution or group (if any) sponsoring the electronic site; date you accessed the information; and electronic address between angle brackets (< >). Since most Web sites do not have page numbers, avoid parenthetical citations by identifying the site in the text of your project. A citation for a particular page within a site might look like the following.

Works Cited

"Hubble Catches Up to a Blue Straggler Star." Space Telescope

    Science Institute. 29 Oct. 1997. NASA. 28 Nov. 1997

    <http://oposite.stsci.edu/pubinfo/PR/97/35/>.

A citation of the entire site might be somewhat different.

Works Cited

Astronomy Resources at Space Telescope Science Institute Home

    Page. 4 Apr. 2001. NASA. 16 Jan. 2002 <http://

    www.stsci.edu/>.

94. Web—Online Book—MLA Since most online books do not have page numbers, avoid parenthetical citations by identifying the site in the text of your project. Give both an original date of publication of the electronic source and the date you accessed the information.

Works Cited

Dickens, Charles. A Christmas Carol. London, 1843. The

    Electronic Text Center. Ed. David Seaman. Dec. 1997. U of

    Virginia Library. 4 Feb. 1998 <http://etext.lib.virginia

    .edu/cgibin/browse-mixed?id=DicChri&tag=public&images=

    images/modeng&data=/lv1/Archive/eng-parsed>.

95. Web—Online Scholarly Journal—MLA Since most online articles do not have page numbers, avoid parenthetical citations by identifying the site in the text of your paper.

Works Cited

Katz, Seth, Janice Walker, and Janet Cross. "Tenure and

    Technology: New Values, New Guidelines." Kairos 2.1

```
(1997). 20 July 1997 <http://english.ttu.edu/

kairos/2.1/index-f.html>.
```

COS
p. 314

96. Web—Online Popular Magazine—MLA Since most online articles do not have page numbers, avoid parenthetical citations by identifying the site in the text of your project.

Works Cited

```
Shafer, Jack. "The New Walter Cronkite." Slate 19 Oct. 1996.

17 Jan. 2002 <http://slate.msn.com/?id=1814>.
```

COS
p. 314

97. Web—Online Newspaper Editorial—MLA Here the date of the editorial and the date of access to it are the same.

Works Cited

```
"The Proved and the Unproved." Editorial. New York Times on

the Web 13 July 1997. 13 July 1997 <http://www.nytimes

.com/yr/mo/day/editorial/13sun1.html>.
```

Pay special attention to daily publications online; materials may be archived each day, so the URL for today's headline will change tomorrow. Note, too, that for some online publications, the URL you provide may require a subscription or fee to access.

COS
p. 312

98. Web—Personal Home Page—MLA For personal home pages, you may want to supply the description *Home page* after the author's name.

Works Cited

```
Brown, Kiwi. Home page. 31 Dec. 2001. 16 Jan. 2002

    <http://www.geocities.com/shoe_polish/homepage.html>.
```

COS
p. 319

99. Listserv/Newsgroup/Usenet Newsgroup—MLA When citing material from a listserv, identify the author of the document or posting; put the subject line of the posting between quotation marks, followed by the date on which the item was originally posted and the words *Online posting*; give the name of the listserv, followed by the date you accessed the item, and the electronic address of the list in angle brackets. Because there will be no page number to cite, avoid a parenthetical citation by naming the author in the text of your project: "Cook argues in favor of . . . ."

Works Cited

```
Cook, Janice. "Re: What New Day Is Dawning?" 19 June 1997.

    Online posting. Alliance for Computers and Writing

    Listserv. 4 Feb. 1998 <acw-l@ttacs6.ttu.edu>.
```

Heady, Christy. "Buy or Lease? Depends on How Long You'll Keep
the Car." 7 July 1997. Online posting. ClariNet. 14 July
1997 <news:clari.biz.industry.automotive>.

COS
p. 321

100. Synchronous Communication (MOOs, MUDs)—MLA Provide the speaker
and/or site, the title of the session or event, the date of the session, the forum for
the communication (if specified), the date of access, and the electronic address.

Works Cited

Inept Guest. Discussion of disciplinary politics in rhet/comp.
12 Mar. 1998. LinguaMOO. 12 Mar. 1998
<telnet://lingua.utdallas.edu:8888>.

COS
p. 319

101. Email—MLA Identifying the communication in the essay itself is preferable to
using a parenthetical citation. Note the hyphen in *e-mail.*

Works Cited

Pacheco, Miguel. "Re: R-ball?" E-mail to the author. 14 Apr.
1997.

COS
p. 318

102. CD-ROM/Diskette Database or Publication—MLA To cite a CD-ROM or
a similar electronic database, provide basic information about the source itself:
author, title, and publication information. Identify the database, publication
medium (*CD-ROM; Diskette; Magnetic tape*) and the name of the vendor if
available. (The vendor is the company publishing or distributing the database.)
Conclude with the date of electronic publication.

Works Cited

Bevington, David. "Castles in the Air: The Morality Plays."
The Theatre of Medieval Europe: New Research in Early
Drama. Ed. Simon Eckehard. Cambridge: Cambridge UP, 1993.
MLA Bibliography. CD-ROM. SilverPlatter. Feb. 1995.

Parenthetical note: (Bevington 98)

For a CD-ROM database that is often updated (ProQuest, for example), you
must provide publication dates for the item you are examining and for the data
disk itself.

Works Cited

Alva, Sylvia Alatore. "Differential Patterns of Achievement
Among Asian-American Adolescents." Journal of Youth and
Adolescence 22 (1993): 407-23. Proquest General
Periodicals. CD-ROM. UMI-Proquest. June 1994.

Parenthetical note: (Alva 407-10)

Cite a book, encyclopedia, play, or other item published on CD-ROM or diskette just as if it were a printed source, adding the medium of publication (*Diskette, CD-ROM*). When page numbers aren't available, name the author in the text of your project to avoid using a parenthetical citation: "Bolter argues. . . ."

```
                       Works Cited
Bolter, Jay David. Writing Space: A Hypertext. Diskette.
      Hillsdale: Erlbaum, 1990.
```

103. Microfilm or Microfiche—MLA Treat material on microfilm as if you had seen its original hard-copy version.

```
                       Works Cited
"How Long Will the Chemise Last?" Consumer Reports. Aug. 1958:
      434-37.
```

Parenthetical note: ("How Long?" 434)

104. Biblical Citation—MLA Note that titles of sacred works, including all versions of the Bible, are not underlined.

```
                       Works Cited
The Jerusalem Bible. Ed. Alexander Jones. Garden City:
      Doubleday, 1966.
```

Parenthetical note: (John 18:37–38)

105. Videotape—MLA Cite a video entry by title in most cases. Include relevant information about the producer, designer, performers, and so on. Identify the distributor, and provide a date. Avoid parenthetical citations to items on videocassette by naming the work in the body of your essay: "In Oliveri's video Dream Cars of the 50s & 60s . . . ."

```
                       Works Cited
Dream Cars of the 50s & 60s. Compiled by Sandy Oliveri.
      Videocassette. Goodtimes Home Video, 1986.
```

106. Movie—MLA In most cases list a movie by its title unless your emphasis is on the director, producer, or screenwriter. Provide information about actors, producers, cinematographers, set designers, and so on, to suit your purpose. Identify the distributor, and give a date of production. Avoid parenthetical citations to films by naming the works in the body of your paper: as "In Lucas's film American Graffiti . . . ."

Works Cited

American Graffiti. Dir. George Lucas. Perf. Richard Dreyfuss
     and Ronny Howard. Universal, 1973.

107. Television Program—MLA List the TV program by episode or name of series or program. Enclose episode names in quotation marks; italicize or underline program or series' names. Avoid parenthetical citations to television shows by naming the programs in the body of your paper.

Works Cited

"No Surrender, No Retreat." Dir. Mike Vejar. Writ. Michael
     Straczynski. Perf. Bruce Boxleitner, Claudia Christian,
     and Mira Furlan. Babylon 5. KEYE-42, Austin. 28 July
     1997.

108. Radio Program—MLA Avoid parenthetical citations to radio shows by naming the programs in the body of your paper.

Works Cited

Death Valley Days. Created by Ruth Cornwall Woodman. NBC
     Radio. WNBC, New York. 30 Sept. 1930.

109. Personal Interview—MLA Refer to the interview in the body of your essay rather than in a parenthetical note: "In an interview, Peter Gomes explained . . . ."

Works Cited

Gomes, Rev. Peter. Personal interview. 23 Apr. 1997.

110. Musical Composition—MLA List the work on the Works Cited page by the name of the composer. When you have sheet music or a score, you can furnish complete publication information.

Works Cited

Joplin, Scott. "The Strenuous Life: A Ragtime Two Step." St.
     Louis: Stark Sheet Music, 1902.

When you don't have a score or sheet music to refer to, provide a simpler entry. In either case, naming the music in the essay text is preferable to using a parenthetical citation.

Porter, Cole. "Too Darn Hot." 1949.

111. Recording—MLA Song titles are enclosed in quotation marks; album and CD titles are italicized.

```
                          Works Cited
Pavarotti, Luciano. Pavarotti's Greatest Hits. London, 1980.
```

112. Speech—No Printed Text—MLA Include the location and date of the speech.

```
                          Works Cited
Reagan, Ronald. "The Geneva Summit Meeting: A Measure of
        Progress." U.S. Congress. Washington. 21 Nov. 1985.
```

113. Speech—Printed Text—MLA Give the location and date of the speech, followed by the publication information including page numbers.

```
                          Works Cited
O'Rourke, P. J. "Brickbats and Broomsticks." Capital Hilton.
        Washington. 2 Dec. 1992. Rpt. American Spectator Feb.
        1993: 20-21.
```
Parenthetical note: (O'Rourke 20)

114. Lecture—MLA Naming the lecture in the text of your project is preferable to using a parenthetical citation.

```
                          Works Cited
Cook, William W. "Writing in the Spaces Left." Chair's
        Address. Conf. on Coll. Composition and Communication.
        Cincinnati. 19 Mar. 1992.
```

115. Letter—Published—MLA A published letter is cited in the same manner as an article in a collection.

```
                          Works Cited
Eliot, George. "To Thomas Clifford Allbutt." 1 Nov. 1873. In
        Selections from George Eliot's Letters. Ed. Gordon S.
        Haight. New Haven: Yale UP, 1985: 427.
```
Parenthetical note: (Eliot 427)

116. Letter—Unpublished—MLA Identifying the letter communication in the text of your project is preferable to using a parenthetical citation.

Works Cited

Newton, Albert. Letter to Agnes Weinstein. 23 May 1917. Albert

    Newton Papers. Woodhill Lib., Cleveland.

117. Artwork—MLA Titles of works of art are generally underlined or italicized. Include information on the location of the collection, if applicable. Naming the artwork in the text of your essay is preferable to using a parenthetical citation.

Works Cited

Fuseli, Henry. Ariel. Folger Shakespeare Lib., Washington, DC.

118. Drama or Play—MLA Citing the printed text of a play, whether individual or collected, differs from citing a performance. For printed texts, provide the usual Works Cited information, taking special care when citing a collection in which various editors handle different plays. In parenthetical notes give the act, scene, and line numbers when the work is so divided; give page numbers if it is not.

Works Cited

Stoppard, Tom. Rosencrantz and Guildenstern Are Dead. New

    York: Grove, 1967.

Shakespeare, William. The Tragedy of Hamlet, Prince of

    Denmark. Ed. Frank Kermode. The Riverside Shakespeare.

    2nd ed. Ed. G. Blakemore Evans and J. J. M. Tobin.

    Boston: Houghton, 1997. 1183-1245.

Parenthetical note: (Stoppard 11-15); (Ham. 5.2.219-24)

For performances of plays, give the title of the work, the author, and then any specific information that seems relevant—director, performers, producers, set designer, theater company, and so on. Conclude the entry with a theater, its location, and a date. Refer to the production directly in the body of your essay to avoid using a parenthetical citation.

Timon of Athens. By William Shakespeare. Dir. Michael

    Benthall. Perf. Ralph Richardson, Paul Curran, and

    Margaret Whiting. Old Vic, London. 5 Sept. 1956.

C H A P T E R

25

APA
Documentation

In many social science and related courses (anthropology, education, home economics, linguistics, political science, psychology, sociology) writers are expected to follow the conventions of documentation recommended by the American Psychological Association (APA). The basic procedures for APA documentation are spelled out in this chapter. A full explanation of APA procedures is provided by the *Publication Manual of the American Psychological Association,* fifth edition (2001), available in most college libraries. Style updates are also available at the APA Web site at **http://apastyle.org/**

Citing Electronic Sources in the Social Sciences

APA documentation includes forms for some electronic sources, which we present on pages 379–82. For electronic items not covered by specific APA forms, you may want to use the documentation style recommended by the *Columbia Guide to Online Style.* The citation examples in COS-sciences style were developed explicitly for electronic forms and cover more types of sources than any other style. But consistency in citation formats is essential if the elements of the citation are to be readily understood. COS-sciences style is designed to *work with* APA forms for citing conventional print sources and *replace* APA style for the citation of electronic sources. However, when it is necessary to use APA format for citing electronically accessed and published sources, this chapter presents examples following the guidelines in the APA *Publication Manual.* Columbia Online Style (COS) is described on pages 302–37. APA forms that have a Columbia equivalent are marked in the APA Form Directory in this chapter with a distinctive icon: | COS p. 000 | .

25a How do you use APA documentation?

APA documentation involves two basic steps: (1) inserting an in-text note at each point where a paper or project needs documentation and (2) recording all sources cited in these notes in a References list.

(Step 1) In the body of your paper, place a note to identify the source of each passage or idea you must document. In its most common form, the APA note consists of the last name of the source's author, followed in parentheses by the year the material was published. Here is a sentence derived from information in an article by E. Tebeaux, "Ramus, Visual Rhetoric, and the Emergence of Page Design in Medical Writing of the English Renaissance," published in 1991:

> According to Tebeaux (1991), technical writing developed in important ways in the English Renaissance.

Another basic form of the APA note places both the author's last name and a date between parentheses. This form is used when the author's name is not mentioned in the sentence. Notice that a comma follows the author's name.

> Technical writing developed in important ways during the English Renaissance (Tebeaux, 1991).

A page number may be given for indirect citations and *must* be given for direct quotations. A comma follows the date when page numbers are given, and page numbers are preceded by *p.* or *pp.*

> During the English Renaissance, writers began to employ "various page design strategies to enhance visual access" (Tebeaux, 1991, p. 413).

When appropriate, the documentation may be distributed throughout a passage.

> Tebeaux (1991) observes that for writers in the late sixteenth century, the philosophical ideas of Peter Ramus "provided a significant impetus to major changes in page design" (p. 413).

APA parenthetical notes should be as brief and inconspicuous as possible. Because the purpose of a note is to identify a source of information, it should begin with the same name as the entry in your References list, as shown in Figure 25.1.

The page number in a note indicates the exact location within the source for the information you are using. For electronic sources, page numbers are omitted (most electronic sources do not have pagination) since the "Search" or "Find" feature of most applications will allow readers to locate specific words or phrases within the file.

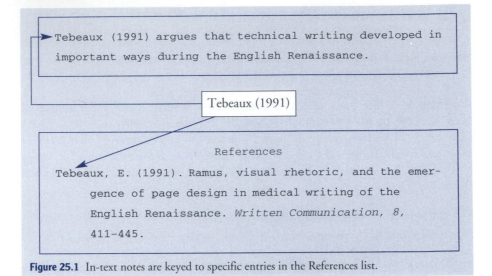

Figure 25.1 In-text notes are keyed to specific entries in the References list.

Use the following guidelines when preparing in-text notes.

1. **When two or more sources are used in a single sentence,** the notes are inserted as needed after the statements they support.

   While Porter (1981) suggests that the ecology of the
   aquifer might be hardier than suspected, "given the size of
   the drainage area and the nature of the subsurface rock"
   (p. 62), there is no reason to believe that the county
   needs another shopping mall in an area described as "one of
   the last outposts of undisturbed nature in the state"
   (Martinez, 1982, p. 28).

   Notice that a parenthetical note is placed outside quotation marks but before the period ending the sentence.

2. **When a single source provides a series of references, you need not repeat the name of the author until other sources interrupt the series.** After the first reference, page numbers are sufficient until another citation intervenes. Even then you need repeat only the author's last name, not a date, when the additional reference occurs within the same paragraph.

   The council vetoed zoning approval for a mall in an area
   described by Martinez (1982) as the last outpost of
   undisturbed nature in the state. The area provides a

"unique environment for several endangered species of birds
and plant life" (p. 31). The birds, especially the
endangered vireo, require breeding spaces free from
encroaching development (Harrison & Cafiero, 1979). Rare
plant life is similarly endangered (Martinez).

3. **When you cite more than one work written by an author in a single year,** assign a small letter after the date to distinguish between the author's works.

(Rosner, 1991a)

(Rosner, 1991b)

The charge is raised by Rosner (1991a), quickly answered by
Anderson (1991), and then raised again by Rosner (1991b).

4. **When you need to cite more than a single work in one note,** separate the citations with a semicolon and list them in alphabetical order.

(Searle, 1993; Yamibe, 1995)

5. **When you are referring to a Web site** (though not to a particular Web document), you can give the electronic address in the text of your paper. The site need not be added to the References list according to APA style. (See Chapter 23 for COS-sciences style on citing electronically accessed sources.)

More information about psychology as a profession is
available on the American Psychological Association's World
Wide Web site at http://www.apa.org/.

In-text notes to specific electronic sources in the body of an APA paper should include the author's last name, a comma, the year of publication followed by a comma, and the page number or, if given in the source, the paragraph number (designated by the symbol ¶).

Ensuring Web site accessibility includes "not only making
the language clear and simple, but also providing
understandable mechanisms for navigating within and between
pages" (W3C, 1999, ¶ 2.2).

For most electronic sources, however, you will not have page or paragraph designations. When this is the case, give the heading or subheading (if applicable) and the number of the paragraph following it. Make certain you count the paragraphs accurately!

```
The first scientific journal was published in 1665 by the
Royal Society of London (Walker, 1998, The Evolution of
Scientific Publishing section, para. 1).
```

(Step 2) On a separate page at the end of your paper, list every source cited in an in-text note. This alphabetical list of sources is titled "References." Tebeaux's article would appear in the References list of a *college paper* in APA "final copy" style in this form:

```
Tebeaux, E. (1991). Ramus, visual rhetoric, and the emergence
        of page design in medical writing of the English
        Renaissance. Written Communication, 8, 411-445.
```

We use hanging indents for APA References entries and italics to designate titles of major works (books, journals, newspapers, magazines, etc.). For projects to be submitted to publishers, see the recommendations in the fifth edition of the APA *Publication Manual*.

Subsequent lines indented one-half inch or five spaces   "References" centered   All items double spaced

```
                              References
    Baocheng, H. (1991, June 17). "Pizhen"--A new acupuncture
         therapy. Beijing Review, 34, 44-45
    Belkin, L. (1992, January 28). Practicing acupuncture made
         easy. The New York Times, p. B1.
    Benson, H. (1979). The mind/body effect. New York: Simon.
    Chang, S.T. (1976). The complete book of acupuncture.
         Millbrae, CA: Celestial Arts.
    Duke, M. (1972). Acupuncture. New York: Jove.
```

CHECKLIST

Basic Format—Books

A typical APA References entry for a book includes the following basic information.

○ Author(s), last name first, followed by a period and one space. Initials are used instead of first and middle names unless two authors mentioned in the paper have identical last names and initials.

○ Date in parentheses, followed by a period and one space.

○ Title of the work, italicized, followed by a period (unless some other information separates the name of the title from the period), and one space. Only the first word of the title, the first word of a subtitle, and proper nouns are capitalized.

○ Place of publication, followed by a colon and one space.

○ Publisher, followed by a period.

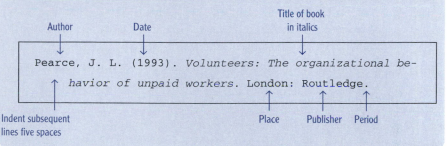

Author | Date | Title of book in italics

Pearce, J. L. (1993). *Volunteers: The organizational be-
    havior of unpaid workers.* London: Routledge.

Indent subsequent lines five spaces | Place | Publisher | Period

CHECKLIST

Basic Format—Scholarly Journals and Scholarly Magazines

A typical APA References entry for an article in a scholarly journal or magazine includes the following basic information.

○ Author(s), last name first, followed by a period and one space.

○ Date in parentheses, followed by a period and one space.

○ Title of the article, followed by a period and one space. Only the first word of the title, the first word of a subtitle, and proper nouns are capitalized. The title does not appear between quotation marks.

○ Name of the periodical, italicized, followed by a comma and one space. Notice that all major words are capitalized in periodical names.

○ Volume number, italicized, followed by a comma and one space.

○ Page numbers, followed by a period.

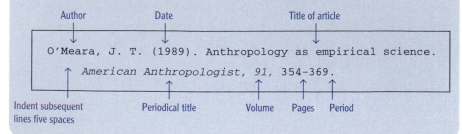

Author | Date | Title of article

O'Meara, J. T. (1989). Anthropology as empirical science.
    American Anthropologist, 91, 354-369.

Indent subsequent lines five spaces | Periodical title | Volume | Pages | Period

CHECKLIST

Basic Format—Magazines and Newspapers

A typical APA References entry for an article in a popular magazine or newspaper includes the following basic information.

○ Author(s), last name first, followed by a period.

○ Date in parentheses, followed by a period and one space. Give the year first, followed by the month (do not abbreviate it) and the day, if necessary.

○ Title of the work, followed by a period and one space. Only the first word and proper nouns are capitalized. The title does not appear between quotation marks.

○ Name of the periodical, italicized, followed by a comma. All major words are capitalized.

○ Page or location, followed by a period.

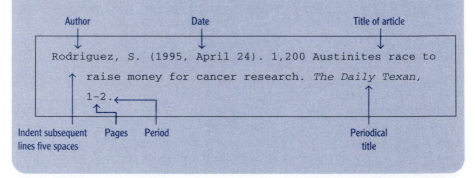

Author   Date   Title of article

Rodriguez, S. (1995, April 24). 1,200 Austinites race to
    raise money for cancer research. *The Daily Texan*,
    1-2.

Indent subsequent   Pages   Period   Periodical
lines five spaces   title

CHECKLIST

Basic Format—Electronic Sources

A typical APA References entry for an online or Web document includes the following basic information. APA offers only a few models for citing electronic sources, and those models may be unwieldy. For papers and projects that follow APA models for citing print sources, consider following COS-science models instead (see pages 324–37).

○ Author(s), last name first, followed by a period and one space.

○ Date of publication in parentheses, followed by a period and one space. Give the year first, followed by the month (do not abbreviate it), followed by the day, if necessary.

○ Title of the work, followed by a period and one space unless other information intervenes.

○ Title of the journal in italics, followed by a comma, a single blank space, and if applicable, the volume number, also in italics, then another comma, a single space, and the page numbers, followed by a period.

○ For Internet articles that are based on a print source, include the description "Electronic version," enclosed in square brackets, after the title of the journal and preceding the period.

○ For Internet-only articles or for articles that you believe are different from the printed version, include the word "Retrieved" followed by the date you accessed the information, a comma, the word "from," and the Internet address. Do not use a period or other punctuation at the end of the URL.

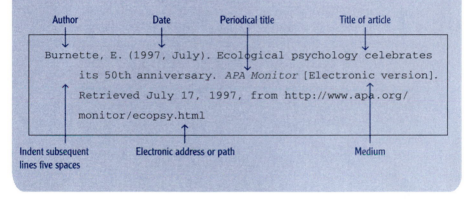

There are many variations to these generic entries, so you should consult the *Publication Manual of the American Psychological Association* (2001) when you do a major APA-style project. For advice on writing a student paper, consult pages 321–326 of the *APA Publication Manual*. For the latest updates on electronic documentation, check the APA Web site at **http://www.apa.org/students**. You may also want to review COS-sciences style in Chapter 23.

The References list appears on its own page following the body of the essay (and any endnote page). It lists bibliographical information for all the materials you used in composing your paper. See page 401 for a checklist on setting up a References list.

25b APA Form Directory

Here you will find the APA References and parenthetical note forms for a variety of sources. First find the type of source you need to cite in the Format Index, and then locate the item by number in the list that follows. The "COS" icon next to an entry indicates that a Columbia Online Style (COS) form is available for that source (see Chapter 23 on COS).

APA Format Index
119. Book, one author
120. Book, two authors
121. Book, three or more authors
122. Book, revised
123. Book, edited
124. Book with no author
125. Book, a collection or anthology
126. Work within a collection, anthology, or reader
127. Chapter in a book
128. Book review
129. Article in a scholarly journal
130. Article in a monthly periodical
131. Article in a weekly or biweekly periodical
132. Article in a newsletter

133. Article in a periodical, no author named
134. Newspaper article, author named
135. Newspaper article, no author named
COS 136. Computer software
COS 137. Online Forums, Usenet Newsgroup, or Email Discussion Groups
COS 138. Web page—generic
COS 139. Web page—online scholarly article
COS 140. Web page—online newspaper article
COS 141. Web page—online abstract
COS 142. Email
143. Movie/videotape
144. Musical recording

119. **Book, One Author—APA** Give the author's last name and initials, followed by a period; the year of publication in parentheses, followed by a period; and the title of the book in italics, capitalizing only the first word, proper nouns, and the first word in subtitles (designated by a colon—see model 120). Then give the city of publication (include the two-letter state designation only when the city is not well known), followed by a colon, and the name of the publisher.

```
                        References
Pearson, G. (1949). Emotional disorders of children.
      Annapolis, MD: Naval Institute Press.
```

Parenthetical notes:

```
Pearson (1949) found . . .

(Pearson, 1949)

(Pearson, 1949, p. 49)
```

120. **Book, Two Authors—APA** An ampersand (&) appears between the authors' names in the References list and in parenthetical notes. *And* is used when the authors are identified in the text.

References

Lasswell, H. D., & Kaplan, A. (1950). *Power and society: A framework for political inquiry.* New York: Yale University Press.

Parenthetical notes:

Lasswell and Kaplan (1950) found . . .

(Lasswell & Kaplan, 1950)

(Lasswell & Kaplan, 1950, pp. 210-213)

121. **Book, Three or More Authors—APA** For books with three to six authors, list all authors' names in both the References list and in the first parenthetical note; subsequent notes will give only the first author's name and the abbreviation "et al."

References

Rosenberg, B., Gerver, I., & Howton, F. W. (1971). *Mass society in crisis: Social problems and social pathology* (2nd ed.). New York: Macmillan.

Parenthetical notes:

First note. Rosenberg, Gerver, and Howton (1971) found . . .

Subsequent notes. Rosenberg et al. (1971) found . . .

First note. (Rosenberg, Gerver, & Howton, 1971)

Subsequent notes. (Rosenberg et al., 1971)

When a work has seven or more authors, give the first six authors' names, followed by "et al." in the References list; for all parenthetical references, including the first, give only the first author's name, followed by "et al." (including the period).

122. **Book, Revised—APA** Provide revision information, enclosed in parentheses, following the book title.

References

Edelmann, A. T. (1969). *Latin American government and politics* (Rev. ed.). Homewood, IL: Dorsey.

Parenthetical notes:

Edelmann (1969) found . . .

```
(Edelmann, 1969)

(Edelmann, 1969, p. 62)
```

123. **Book, Edited—APA** APA uses an ampersand (&) to join the names of two editors or authors.

References

```
Journet, D., & Kling, J. (Eds.). (1984). Readings for
     technical writers. Glenview, IL: Scott, Foresman.
```

Parenthetical notes:

```
Journet and Kling (1984) observe . . .

(Journet & Kling, 1984)
```

124. **Book with No Author—APA** The entry begins with the title of the book, followed by the year of publication, in parentheses, and a period. Notice that the book title is also italicized in the parenthetical note.

References

```
Illustrated atlas of the world. (1985). Chicago: Rand McNally.
```

Parenthetical notes:

```
In Illustrated Atlas (1985) . . .

(Illustrated Atlas, 1985, pp. 88-89)
```

When the author of a work is actually given as "Anonymous," cite the work that way in the References list and a parenthetical note.

```
(Anonymous, 1995)
```

125. **Book, a Collection or Anthology—APA** Begin the entry with the editor(s') name(s), the description "Ed." or "Eds." enclosed in parentheses, and a period.

References

```
Feinstein, C. H. (Ed.). (1967). Socialism, capitalism, and
     economic growth. Cambridge, England: Cambridge University
     Press.
```

Parenthetical notes:

```
Feinstein (1967) found . . .

(Feinstein, 1967)
```

126. **Work Within a Collection, Anthology, or Reader—APA** List the item on the References page by the author of the piece you are citing, not the editor(s) of the collection. Then provide the date of the particular selection, its title, the editor(s) of the collection, the title of the collection, pages on which the selection appears, and publication information.

References

```
Patel, S. (1967). World economy in transition (1850-2060). In
     C. H. Feinstein (Ed.), Socialism, capitalism, and
     economic growth (pp. 255-270). Cambridge, England:
     Cambridge University Press.
```

Parenthetical notes:

```
Patel (1967) found . . .
(Patel, 1967)
```

127. **Chapter in a Book—APA** Give the author's name, followed by the year of publication and the title of the chapter being cited.

References

```
Clark, K. (1969). Heroic materialism. In Civilisation (pp.
     321-347). New York: HarperCollins.
```

Parenthetical notes:

```
Clark (1969) observes . . .
(Clark, 1969)
```

128. **Book Review—APA** Brackets surround the description of an article that has no title. When an article has a title, the title precedes the bracketed description, which would still appear.

References

```
Farquhar, J. (1987). [Review of the book Medical power and
     social knowledge]. American Journal of Psychology, 94,
     256.
```

Parenthetical notes:

```
Farquhar (1987) observes . . .
(Farquhar, 1987)
```

129. **Article in a Scholarly Journal—APA** Scholarly journals are usually identified by volume number or season (rather than day, week, or month of publication) and are paginated year by year, with a full year's work gathered and treated as one volume. Cite articles from these scholarly journals by providing author, date, title of article, journal, volume, and page numbers.

```
                         References
```
Tebeaux, E. (1991). Ramus, visual rhetoric, and the emergence

　　　　of page design in medical writing of the English

　　　　Renaissance. *Written Communication, 8,* 411-445.

Parenthetical notes:

Tebeaux (1991) observes . . .

(Tebeaux, 1991, p. 411)

130. **Article in a Monthly Periodical—APA** To cite a magazine published monthly, give the author's name, the date as given on the publication, title of the article, name of the magazine and volume number if available (in italics), and page numbers.

```
                         References
```
Bass, R. (1995, May/June). The perfect day. *Sierra, 80,* 68-78.

Parenthetical notes:

Bass (1995) notes . . .

(Bass, 1995)

131. **Article in a Weekly or Biweekly Periodical—APA** To cite a weekly or biweekly periodical or magazine, give the author's name, the date (including month and day), title of the article, name of the magazine and volume number if available (in italics), and page numbers.

```
                         References
```
Moody, J. (1993, December 20). A vision of judgment. *Time,*

　　　　142, 58-61.

Parenthetical notes:

Moody (1993) observes . . .

(Moody, 1993)

(Moody, 1993, p. 60)

132. **Article in a Newsletter—APA** To cite a newsletter, give the author's name, date, title of the article, name of the magazine and volume number if available (in italics), and page numbers. If no volume number is given, give as full a date as possible.

```
                         References
```
Piedmont-Marton, E. (1997, July 20). Schoolmarms or language

　　　　paramedics? *The Writer's Block, 4,* 6.

Parenthetical notes:

```
Piedmont-Marton (1997) argues . . .

(Piedmont-Marton, 1997)
```

133. Article in a Periodical, No Author Named—APA Quotation marks are used around titles in the parenthetical notes as well as in the text. Use the full title if it is brief; otherwise, shorten it. Notice that titles in the text and in parenthetical notations capitalize all major words.

References

```
Aladdin releases desktop tools. (1993, October). Macworld, 10,
     35.
```

Parenthetical notes:

```
In "Aladdin Releases" (1993) . . .

("Aladdin Releases," 1993)
```

134. Newspaper Article, Author Named—APA If the article does not appear on consecutive pages in the newspaper, give all the page numbers, separated by a comma. Note that abbreviations for *page* (*p.*) and *pages* (*pp.*) are used with newspaper entries.

References

```
Bragg, R. (1994, October 15). Weather gurus going high-tech.
     San Antonio Express-News, pp. 1A, 7A.
```

Parenthetical notes:

```
Bragg (1994) reports . . .

(Bragg, 1994, p. 7A)
```

135. Newspaper Article, No Author Named—APA The entry begins with the title of the article, followed by the date of publication.

References

```
Scientists find new dinosaur species in Africa. (1994, October
     14). The Daily Texan, p. 3.
```

Parenthetical notes:

```
In the article "Scientists Find" (1994) . . .

("Scientists Find," 1994)
```

COS
p. 335

136. Computer Software—APA Do not underline the titles of software. List authors only when they own a proprietary right to the product. APA does not

require most common software packages (such as Microsoft *Word*) to be
included in the References list.

References

```
Adobe Pagemill 1.0 [Computer software]. (1995). Mountain View,
     CA: Adobe Systems.
```

Parenthetical note:

```
In Adobe Pagemill (1995) . . .
```

COS
p. 332–33

137. Online Forums, Usenet Newsgroup, or Email Discussion Groups—APA
Generally, APA does not require that online discussions of any kind be included in
the list of References; since these postings are not usually peer-reviewed or
permanently archived, APA considers them to be of limited use. Instead, these
types of messages should be cited as personal communication (see model 142). If
you are required to include this information in your References list, give as much
information as possible, including message numbers or other information that will
help the reader locate the source. No period follows Internet or electronic
addresses.

References

```
White, C. E. (2002, January 20). Re: High mileage RAMs--How
     are they holding up? Message posted to news:rec.auto.tech
```

Parenthetical notes:

```
White (2002) reports . . .

(White, 2002)
```

COS
p. 325

138. Web Page—Generic—APA Give the author's name, the date of publication
or last modification, and the title of the page, followed by the word
"Retrieved," the date of retrieval, and the Internet address. No period follows
the URL. When the author is not known, begin with the title of the page,
followed by the date of publication or "n.d." in parentheses if the page is not
dated.

References

```
Johnson, C. W., Jr. (1997, February 13). How our laws are
     made. Retrieved May 27, 1997, from http://thomas.loc
     .gov/home/lawsmade.toc.html
```

Parenthetical notes:

```
Johnson (1997) explains . . .

(Johnson, 1997)
```

COS
p. 328

139. Web Page—Online Scholarly Article—APA Because it is immediately obvious that the source is an article from a scholarly journal, no bracketed explanation of the medium is necessary. If the article is based on a print source with no apparent differences, then omit the retrieval information and the URL.

References

```
Fine, M. A., & Kurdek, L. A. (1993). Reflections on determining

     authorship credit and authorship order on faculty-student

     collaborations. American Psychologist, 48, 1141-1147.

     Retrieved July 17, 1997, from http://www.apa.org/journals/

     amp/kurdek.html
```

Parenthetical notes:

```
Fine and Kurdek (1993) report . . .

(Fine & Kurdek, 1993)
```

COS
p. 328

140. Web Page—Online Newspaper Article—APA Include the date of publication as well as the date of retrieval and the Internet address. Note that the URL should directly link to the article if possible; however, many online newspapers archive messages and may charge a subscription fee to access older items. APA allows you to "break" a URL after a slash or before a period if necessary. COS recommends that you allow your word processor to automatically wrap the lines (see Chapter 23).

References

```
Cohen, E. (1997, January 17). Shrinks aplenty online but are

     they credible? The New York Times. Retrieved May 5, 1997,

     from http://search.nytimes.com/search/daily/bin/

     fastweb?getdoc+site+site+4842+4+wAAA+%28psychology%29%26OR%

     26%28%29%26OR%26%28%29
```

Parenthetical notes:

```
Cohen (1997) asks . . .

(Cohen, 1997)
```

COS
p. 331–32

141. Web Page—Online Abstract—APA Include the word "Abstract" in the retrieval information. For abstracts accessed through online databases, include the name of the database (for example, "PsycINFO database") in place of the URL.

References

Shilkret, R., & Nigrosh, E. (1997). Assessing students' plans

for college. *Journal of Counseling Psychology, 44,*

222–231. Abstract retrieved July 1, 1997, from

http://www.apa.org/journals/cou/497ab.html#10

Parenthetical notes:

Shilkret and Nigrosh (1997) report . . .

(Shilkret & Nigrosh, 1997)

COS p. 332 **142. Email—APA** Electronic communications not stored or archived have limited use for researchers. APA style treats such information (and email) as personal communication. Because personal communications are not available to other researchers, no mention is made of them in the References list. Personal communications should, however, be acknowledged in the body of the paper in parenthetical notes. References to personal communications should include the initials as well as the last name of the speaker.

Parenthetical note:

According to J. G. Rice (personal communication, October 14,

1994) . . .

(J. G. Rice, personal communication, October 14, 1994).

143. Movie/Videotape—APA This is also the basic form for films, audiotapes, slides, charts, and other nonprint sources. The specific medium is described between brackets, as shown here for a motion picture. In most cases APA movie references are listed by the screenwriter, though that varies, as the example shows. Include the country of origin as well as the name of the studio.

References

Zeffirelli, F. (Director). (1968). *Romeo and Juliet* [Motion

Picture]. United States: Paramount Pictures.

Parenthetical notes:

Zeffirelli (1968) features . . .

(Zeffirelli, 1968)

144. Musical Recording—APA Music is ordinarily listed by the composer, followed by the date of copyright and the title of the song. You may include the name of the recording artist if different from the composer, the name of the album or

CD on which the song is recorded, identifying the medium, followed by the location and label. Include the recording date in parentheses if different from the coypright date.

References

Dylan, B. (1989). What was it you wanted? [Recorded by Willie
    Nelson]. On *Across the borderline* [CD]. New York:
    Columbia.

Parenthetical note:

In the song "What Was It You Wanted?" (Dylan, 1989,
    track 10) . . .

25c Sample APA Paper

In the social sciences, articles published in professional journals often follow a form designed to connect new findings to previous research. Your instructor will usually indicate whether you should follow this structure for your paper or report.

The following APA-style research report by Chad Briggs and faculty adviser Fred Ribich originally appeared in volume one of *Psych-E,* an online journal of psychology for undergraduates. We have modified the essay to show how it would look as a paper a student might turn in for a college course. Because of space limitations, we've also shortened the article slightly. But we have not altered its basic style, which reflects the conventions of the social sciences, particularly a heavier use of passive voice than might appear in an MLA or Chicago-style article.

For easy reference, we've numbered the paragraphs (these numbers would *not* appear in an actual APA paper). You can view the original, uncut version online by searching the *Psych-E* archives at **http://www.siu.edu/departments/cola/psycho/journal**. The same site provides additional examples of undergraduate research essays in APA style.

CHECKLIST

The Components of a Social Science Report

○ **An abstract**—a concise summary of the research article.

○ **A review of literature**—a survey of published research that has a bearing on the hypothesis advanced in the research report. The review establishes the context for the research essay.

○ **A hypothesis**—an introduction to the paper that identifies the assumption to be tested and provides a rationale for studying it.

○ **An explanation of method**—a detailed description of the procedures used in the research. Since the validity of the research depends on how the data were gathered, this is a critical section for readers assessing the report.

○ **Results**—a section reporting the data, often given through figures, charts, graphs, and so on. The reliability of the data is explained here, but little comment is made on its implications.

○ **Discussion/conclusions**—a section in which the research results are interpreted and analyzed.

○ **References**—an alphabetical list of research materials and articles cited in the report.

○ **Appendixes**—a section of materials germane to the report but too lengthy to include in the body of the paper.

The Relationship Between Test Anxiety, Sleep Habits,

and Self-perceived Academic Competency

Chad S. Briggs [briggs@siu.edu] and Fred Ribich

Wartburg College

CHECKLIST

Title Page for a Paper—APA

APA style requires a separate title page; use the facing page as a model and review the following checklist.

○ Type your report on white bond paper. Preferred typefaces (when you have a choice) include Times Roman, American Typewriter, and Courier.

○ Arrange and center the title of your paper, your name, and your school.

○ Use the correct form of the title, capitalizing all important words and all words of four letters or more. Articles, conjunctions, and prepositions are not capitalized unless they are four letters or more. Do not underline the title or use all capitals.

○ Give your first name, middle initial, and last name.

○ Number the title page and all subsequent pages in the upper right-hand corner. Place a short title for the paper on the same line as the page number as shown; the short title consists of the first two or three key words of the title.

Test Anxiety 2

Abstract

One hundred and fifty-eight college students completed
questionnaires and tests that measure test anxiety, sleep
habits, and self-perceived academic competency. It was
hypothesized that test anxiety and irregular sleep patterns
will lower college students' self-perceived academic
competency. The results showed that high test anxiety and
poor sleep habits negatively affected students' self-
perceived academic competency. It was also found that high
self-perceived academic competency was positively correlated
with GPA (a measure of performance). This study shows the
need for further research that deals with the relationship
between self-perceived academic competency and academic
performance. This will enable professionals to look at
another variable that affects academic performance in more
detail.

CHECKLIST

Abstract for a Paper—APA

Abstracts are common in papers using APA style.

○ Place the abstract on a separate page, after the title page.
○ Center the word *Abstract* at the top of the page.
○ Place the short title of the essay and the page number (2) in the upper right-hand corner.
○ Double-space the abstract.
○ Do not indent the first line of the abstract. Type it in block form.
○ Strict APA form limits abstracts to 960 characters or fewer.

The Relationship Between Test Anxiety, Sleep Habits, and
Self-perceived Academic Competency

Introduction

¶1   Self-perceived academic competency has been shown to
be a significant contributor to the academic success of
college students. Bandura (1986) defines self-perceived
competency as "people's judgments of their capabilities to
organize and execute courses of action required to attain
designated types of performances" (p. 10). It has been
found by Lee and Babko (1994) that when in a difficult
situation such as a college-type test, a person with a
strong sense of self-perceived academic competency will
devote more attention and effort to the task at hand,
therefore trying harder and persisting longer, than will
those who have lower levels of self-perceived competency.

¶2   Self-perceived academic competency can be affected by
a plethora of variables. In this study, the variables of
test anxiety and sleep habits will be examined in
relationship to college students' self-perceived academic
competency.

¶3   Lewis (1970) defines anxiety as "an unpleasant
emotion experienced as dread, scare, alarm, fright,
trepidation, horror or panic" (p. 63). Test anxiety, then,
is the debilitating experience of anxiety, as described by
Lewis, during the preparation for a test or during the test
itself. Although anxiety is often detrimental, it may be
beneficial if it is not extreme. Simpson, Parker, and
Harrison (1995) convey this through two well-known
principles of anxiety: "A minimal amount of anxiety" (an
optimal amount is more accurate) "can mobilize human beings
to respond rapidly and efficiently," while "excessive
amounts of anxiety may foster poor response and sometimes
inhibit response" (p. 700). Knox, Schacht, and Turner

CHECKLIST

The Body of a Research Paper—APA

The body of the APA paper runs uninterrupted until the separate References page. Be sure to type the essay on good-quality bond paper. The first page of an APA paper will look like the facing page, except for the paragraph numbers, included here for reference only.

○ Repeat the title of your paper, exactly as it appears on the title page, on the first page of the research essay.

○ Be sure the title is centered and properly capitalized.

○ Begin the body of the essay two lines (a double space) below the title.

○ Double-space the body of the essay.

○ Use at least one-inch margins at the sides, top, and bottom of this and all subsequent pages.

○ Indent the first line of each paragraph five to seven spaces.

○ Indent long quotations (more than forty words) in a block five to seven spaces from the left margin. In student papers, APA permits long quotations to be single spaced.

○ Include the short title of the essay and the page number (3) in the upper right-hand corner. Number all subsequent pages the same way.

○ Do not hyphenate words at the right-hand margin. Do not justify the right-hand margin.

○ Label figures and tables correctly. Be sure to mention them in the body of your text: (see Figure 1).

○ Provide copyright/permission data for figures or tables borrowed from other sources.

(1993) state that test anxiety can include performance anxiety and content (e.g., math) anxiety. Both of these make it hard for students to concentrate and perform adequately on tests. Knox et al. (1993) also recognize the consequences of poorly managed test anxiety. "Failure to manage test anxiety can result in failing courses, dropping out of school, a negative self-concept and a low earning potential" (p. 295).

¶4   Research on test anxiety has identified three models that explain the origin of test anxiety: (1) The problem lies not in taking the test, but in preparing for the test. Kleijn, Van der Ploeg, and Topman (1994) have identified this as the learning-deficit model. According to this model, the student with high test anxiety tends to have or use inadequate learning or study skills while in the preparation stage of exam taking. (2) The second model is termed the interference model (Kleijn et al., 1994). The problem for people in this model is that during tests, individuals with test anxiety focus on task-irrelevant stimuli which negatively affect their performance (Sarason, 1975). The attention diverted from the task at hand can be categorized into two types, according to Sarason. The first type of distraction can be classified as physical and includes an increase in awareness of heightened autonomic activity (e.g., sweaty palms, muscle tension). The second type of distraction includes inappropriate cognitions, such as saying to oneself, "others are finishing before me, I must not know the material," or "I'm stupid, I won't pass." The presence of either of these two task-irrelevant cognitions will affect the quality of a student's performance. (3) The third model of test anxiety includes people who think they have prepared adequately for a test, but in reality, did not. These people question their abilities after the test, which creates anxiousness during the next test.

¶5   Sleep patterns are believed to be more irregular among college students, and irregular sleep patterns are believed to affect both self-perceived academic competency and academic performance. Sleep, therefore, seems to be an important factor in a college student's success and self-perceived ability. An optimal sleep pattern, as defined here, is one in which an individual goes to bed and wakes up at about the same time every day while allowing an adequate amount of time in each of the five stages of the sleep cycle. The function of the body that keeps our sleep patterns in this constant waking and sleeping cycle is called the circadian rhythm. During the night a person enters into and out of five different stages of sleep, the most important being REM (rapid eye movement) sleep. When the circadian rhythm of a person's sleep is thrown off, less time is spent in REM sleep (Lahey, 1995). People deprived of REM sleep are likely to experience irritability, inefficiency, and fatigue (Hobson, 1989; Webb & Bonnet, 1979). Furthermore, they are more likely to experience irritability and fatigue when switched from the day shift to the night shift rather than from the night shift to the day shift (Wilkinson, Allison, Feeney, & Kaminska, 1989). This phenomenon known as "jet lag" is consistent with our natural tendency to lengthen our circadian rhythms. For example, one experiment demonstrated that participants' circadian rhythms continued even when they were isolated in constantly lighted chambers. However, their rhythms quickly changed to a twenty-five-hour cycle (Aschoff, 1981; Horne, 1988). This phenomenon suggests that college students are particularly prone to sleep deprivation because college students are notorious for

"cramming" information into their memories the night before
a test. To do this, they stay up longer and wake up earlier
than they usually would. The impact of sleep deprivation on
academic performance is negative; consequently, it is
hypothesized that students with poor sleep habits will have
a lower level of self-perceived academic competency since
each test is taken in a state marked by inefficient,
irritable, or fatigued thinking.

¶6   While there have been numerous studies on self-
perceived competency and academic performance, on test
anxiety and performance, and on sleep and performance,
little direct information exists on the relationship among
these variables taken together. It is believed that in our
findings it will be shown that test anxiety and irregular
sleep patterns will lower college students' self-perceived
academic competency.

Methods

Participants

¶7   One hundred and fifty-eight college students
participated in the study. There were 89 first and second
year students, and 64 third and fourth year students. Among
the participants, there were 67 males and 89 females.
Demographic data obtained from the participants included
gender, age, year in school, major, and their estimated
current grade point average (GPA).

Instruments

¶8   The Test Attitude Inventory (TAI), created by
Spielberger (1980), was used to measure test anxiety. The
TAI subscales measure self-reported worry and emotionality.
The TAI contains twenty items that are situation-specific
to academically related test situations and environments. A
five-point Likert Scale (five represented "usually" and one
represented "never") was used to obtain the participants'
responses.

Test Anxiety 7

¶9   To measure sleep habits, the Sleep Questionnaire
constructed by Domino (1984) was used. The questionnaire
contains fifty-four questions pertaining to various sleep
and related behaviors. The same five-point Likert Scale
that was used for the TAI was used by this instrument as
well. In addition, three closed-ended questions help reveal
the approximate time of sleep-onset, the approximate time
of awakening, and whether or not the participants take naps
during the day.

¶10   The College Academic Self-efficacy Scale (CASES),
created by Owen and Froman (1988), was administered to
determine the degree of confidence participants believe
they have in various academic settings (e.g., note-taking
during class or using the library). A five-point Likert
Scale was also used here, where five represented "a lot of
confidence," and one represented "little confidence." This
scale consists of thirty-three questions covering a wide
variety of academic settings and situations that are
pertinent to the students' overall academic self-competency
rating. Owen and Froman (1988) found the alpha internal
consistency of the CASES, in two different trials, to be .9
and .92.

Procedure

¶11   Packets were prepared which contained a demographic
data sheet, consent form, test anxiety inventory, CASES, and
the sleep habits questionnaire, in that order. Next,
professors in the selected classes were given information on
the purpose of the study, shown the survey instruments, and
told approximately how long it would take for students to
complete the entire packet (20-30 minutes). We were invited
to six different class meetings. The students were informed
verbally that the purpose of the study was to examine the
relationships between test anxiety, sleep habits, and self-
perceived academic competency. The students were also

Test Anxiety 8

informed that participation in the experiment was completely voluntary, and that their responses would be kept anonymous. The students who agreed to participate in the study signed a consent form. These students then filled out the demographic data and then the four surveys. The participants were then thanked for their willingness to participate in the study.

Results

¶12   The mean score for test anxiety was 52.67 (out of a possible 100), with a high score of 95 and a low score of 24. In order to see if differences existed between people with high test anxiety and low test anxiety, the participants' test anxiety scores were divided into three levels (low, moderate, and high) and compared to the CASES using an ANOVA. Those people in the low test anxiety group scored 124.50 (a higher score indicates greater self-perceived academic competency) on the CASES. Those people in the moderate test anxiety group scored 113.75 on the CASES. Those people in the high test anxiety group scored 106.21 on the CASES. The p-value was found to be .001. This finding is represented in Figure 1.

¶13   It was also found that there were significant differences between test anxiety groups and GPA (a measure of performance). The low test anxiety group reported having

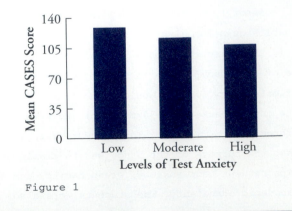

Figure 1

Test Anxiety 9

a 3.29 GPA. The group that reported moderate anxiety had a 3.13 GPA. And, the group with high test anxiety reported having a 3.02 GPA. The p-value was found to be .05.

¶14   Similarly, the sleep scores were also divided into three groups (bad sleep, moderate sleep, and good sleep) for the purpose of comparing mean differences. The mean sleep score was 130.28 (out of 200), with a high score of 163 and a low score of 90. The lower sleep scores represent better sleep habits. The people in the bad sleep group scored 110.42 on the CASES. The moderate sleepers scored 114.98 on the CASES. And the people in the good sleep group scored 119.33. This is represented in Figure 2.

¶15   Furthermore, grade point averages were significantly different depending on which sleep group the student was associated with. Students in the bad sleep group reported having a 3.02 GPA, while students in the moderate sleep group reported having a 3.11 GPA. Also, those students who fell into the good sleep group reported having a 3.31 GPA. The p-value was found to be .03.

¶16   Correlations were also figured for the following variables (shown in Table 1): quality of sleep habits, test anxiety, self-perceived academic competency, and GPA. It was found that the quality of sleep habits and test anxiety

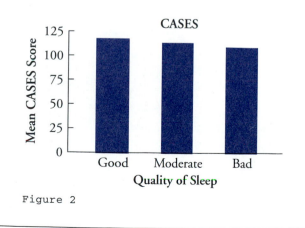

Figure 2

Test Anxiety 10

were negatively correlated at the -.26 level (p-value of
.001). The quality of sleep habits was also found to be
positively correlated with self-perceived academic
competency at the .19 level (p-value of .016).
Additionally, it was found that the quality of sleep habits
was positively correlated with GPA at the .18 level (p-
value of .024). Test anxiety and self-perceived academic
competency were negatively correlated at the -.41 level (p-
value of .001). GPA and test anxiety were negatively
correlated at the -.21 level (p-value of .01). Lastly,
self-perceived academic competency and GPA were positively
correlated at the .47 level (p-value of .001). This can be
seen in Table 1.

Table 1

*Correlations Calculated to Find the Relationships Between
Main Variables in the Study*

	GPA	TA	CASES	Sleep
GPA	1.0			
TA	-.21**	1.0		
CASES	.47***	-.41***	1.0	
Sleep	.18*	-.26***	.19*	1.0

Note. The main variables include test anxiety (TA), sleep
habits (Sleep), self-perceived academic competency (CASES),
and the students' GPA.
*p < 0.05
**p < 0.01
***p < 0.001

Discussion

¶17   The findings presented indicate that bad sleep
habits and high test anxiety negatively affect self-
perceived academic competency, as was hypothesized.
Additionally, it was found that low self-perceived academic
competency negatively affected students' GPA.

¶18   Quality of sleep habits was found to be a factor in self-perceived academic competence. If college students do experience REM sleep deprivation more than the average population, then the findings of this study need to be passed on to college students. The findings in this study suggest that college students with poor sleep habits may perceive themselves as having lower academic competency. The study also showed that self-perceived academic competency was positively correlated to academic performance. Thus, according to Hobson (1989), Webb & Bonnet (1979), and this study, those college students who do have poor sleep habits will negatively affect their academic performance.

¶19   It was also found that test anxiety and grade point average are negatively correlated, and that quality of sleep and grade point average are positively correlated. This, and the fact that quality of sleep and test anxiety are negatively related, suggest interrelationships among the variables test anxiety, sleep habits, self-perceived academic competency and academic performance. This highlights the fact that professors need to instruct their students on how to manage test anxiety. Students also need to be aware of the effects that poor sleep and low self-perceived academic competency have on academic performance. Thus, the phrase, "I think I can, I think I can . . ." may be beneficial only if students reduce their test anxiety and develop better sleep habits. More research needs to be done to find other variables that affect self-perceived academic competence.

Test Anxiety 12

References

Aschoff, J. (1981). *Handbook of behavioral neurobiology* (Vol. 4). Biological rhythms. New York: Plenum.

Bandura, A. (1986). *Social foundations of thought and action: A social cognitive theory.* Englewood Cliffs, NJ: Prentice Hall.

Domino, G., Blair, G., & Bridges, A. (1984). Subjective assessment of sleep by sleep questionnaire. *Perceptual and Motor Skills, 59,* 163–170.

Hobson, J. A. (1989). *Sleep.* New York: Scientific American Library.

Horne, J. (1988). *Why we sleep: The functions of sleep in humans and other mammals.* New York: Oxford University Press.

Kleijn, W. C., Van der Ploeg, H. M., & Topman, R. M. (1994). Cognition, study habits, test anxiety, and academic performance. *Psychological Reports, 75,* 1219–1226.

Knox, D., Schacht, C., & Turner, J. (1993). Virtual reality: A proposal for treating test anxiety in college students. *College Student Journal, 27,* 294–296.

Lahey, B. B. (1995). In M. Lange, S. Connors, A. Fuerste, K. M. Huinker-Timp, & L. Fuller (Eds.), *Psychology: An Introduction.* Dubuque, IA: Brown & Benchmark.

Lee, C., & Babko, P. (1994). Self-efficacy beliefs: Comparison of five measures. *Journal of Applied Psychology, 79,* 364–369.

Lewis, A. (1970). The ambiguous word "anxiety." *International Journal of Psychiatry, 9,* 62–79.

CHECKLIST

References Pages—APA

Sources contributing directly to the paper are listed alphabetically on a separate page immediately after the body of the essay.

○ Center the title (*References*) at the top of the page.

○ All sources mentioned in the text of the paper must appear in the References list, except personal communications; similarly, every source listed in the References list must be mentioned in the paper.

○ Arrange the items in the References list alphabetically by the last name of the author. Give only initials for first names. If no author is given for a work, list and alphabetize it by the first word in the title, excluding articles (*A, An, The*).

○ The first line of each entry is flush with the left-hand margin. Subsequent lines in an entry are indented five spaces.

○ The list is ordinarily double spaced. In student papers, APA style does permit single spacing of individual entries; double spacing is preserved between the single-spaced items.

○ Punctuate items in the list carefully. Do not forget the period at the end of each entry, except those entries that terminate with an electronic address.

○ In the References list, capitalize only the first word and any proper names in the title of a book or article. Within a title, capitalize the first word after a colon.

○ When you have two or more entries by the same author, list them by year of publication, from earliest to latest. If an author publishes two works in the same year, list them alphabetically by title and place a lowercase letter immediately after the year: (1998a).

Test Anxiety 13

Owen, S. V., & Froman, R. D. (1988). *Development of an academic self-efficacy scale.* Paper presented at the annual meeting of the National Council on Measurement in Education, New Orleans, LA.

Sarason, I. G. (1975). Test anxiety and the self-disclosing coping model. *Journal of Consulting and Clinical Psychology, 43,* 148-152.

Simpson, M. L., Parker, P. W., & Harrison, A. W. (1995). Differential performance on Taylor's Manifest Anxiety Scale in black private college freshmen, a partial report. *Perceptual and Motor Skills, 80,* 699-702.

Spielberger, C. D. (1980). *Preliminary Professional Manual for the Test Attitude Inventory.* Palo Alto, CA: Consulting Psychologists Press.

Webb, W. B., & Bonnet, M. H. (1979). Sleep and dreams. In M. E. Meyer (Ed.). *Foundations of contemporary psychology.* New York: Oxford University Press.

Wilkinson, R., Allison, S., Feeney, M., & Kaminska, Z. (1989). Alertness of night nurses: Two shift systems compared. *Ergonomics, 32,* 281-292.

CMS Documentation

Writers who prefer full footnotes or endnotes rather than in-text notes often use the "humanities style" of documentation recommended in *The Chicago Manual of Style,* fourteenth edition (1993). Basic procedures for this CMS documentary-note system are spelled out in the following sections. If you encounter documentation problems not discussed below or prefer the author-date style of CMS documentation, refer to the full manual or to *A Manual for Writers of Term Papers, Theses, and Dissertations,* sixth edition (1996) or check *The Chicago Manual of Style* FAQ at **http://www.press.uchicago.edu/Misc/Chicago/cmosfaq.html**.

A Note on Citing Electronic Sources

Current CMS documentation does not offer specific forms for many electronic sources, although several are presented on pages 413–14. The editors of the *Chicago Manual of Style* have announced a forthcoming edition that promises to include more examples for citing electronic sources. In the meantime, when citing such items, you may use the documentation style recommended by the *Columbia Guide to Online Style,* described in Chapter 23. It was developed explicitly for research in electronic documents and is designed to work *with* CMS-style formats for citing print-based sources. CMS items that have a Columbia equivalent are marked in the CMS Form Directory in this chapter with a distinctive icon: COS p. 000 . Consult your instructor about using Columbia style for electronic sources.

Because notes in CMS humanities style include full publishing information, bibliographies are optional in CMS-style papers. However, both note and bibliography forms are described in the following section.

26a CMS notes

(Step 1) In the text of your paper, place a raised number after a sentence or clause you need to document. These note numbers follow any punctuation mark except a dash, and they run consecutively throughout a paper. A direct quotation from Brian Urquhart's *Ralph Bunche: An American Life* is followed here by a raised note number.

```
Ralph Bunche never wavered in his belief that the races in
America had to learn to live together: "In all of his
experience of racial discrimination Bunche never allowed
himself to become bitter or to feel racial hatred."¹
```

The number is keyed to the first note (see below). To create this raised, or superscript, number, select "Superscript" from your word-processing font options or select the "Endnote" or "Footnote" feature in your word processor.

(Step 2) Link every note number to a footnote or endnote. The basic CMS note consists of a note number, the author's name (in normal order), the title of the work, full publication information within parentheses, and the appropriate page numbers. The first line of the note is indented like a paragraph.

```
     1. Brian Urquhart, Ralph Bunche: An American Life (New
York: Norton, 1993), 435.
```

To document particular types of sources, including books, articles, magazines, and electronic sources, see the CMS Form Directory on page 409.

CMS style allows you to choose whether to place your notes at the bottom of each page (footnotes) or in a single list titled "Notes" at the end of your paper (endnotes). Endnotes are more common now than footnotes and easier to manage—though some word processors can arrange footnotes at the bottom of pages automatically. Individual footnotes are single spaced, with double spaces between them.

Use the following guidelines when preparing notes.

1. **When two or more sources are cited within a single sentence,** the note numbers appear right after the statements they support.

```
While some in the humanities fear that electronic
technologies may make the "notion of wisdom" obsolete,²
others suggest that technology must be the subject of
serious study even in elementary and secondary school.³
```

The notes for this sentence would appear in this form:

```
     2. Sven Birkerts, The Gutenberg Elegies: The Fate of
Reading in an Electronic Age (Boston: Faber and Faber,
1994), 139.
     3. Neil Postman, "The Word Weavers/The World Makers,"
in The End of Education: Redefining the Value of School
(New York: Alfred A. Knopf, 1995), 172–93.
```

Observe that note 2 documents a particular quotation while note 3 refers to a full chapter in a book.

2. **When you cite a work several times in a paper,** the first note gives full information about author(s), title, and publication.

> 1. Helen Wilkinson, "It's Just a Matter of Time," *Utne Reader* (May/June 1995): 66–67.

Then, in shorter papers, subsequent citations require only the last name of the author(s) and page number(s).

> 3. Wilkinson, 66.

In longer papers the entry may also include a shortened title to make references from page to page clearer.

> 3. Wilkinson, "Matter of Time," 66.

When you cite the same work again immediately after a full note, you may use the Latin abbreviation *Ibid.* (meaning "in the same place"), followed by the page number(s) of the citation.

> 4. Newt Gingrich, "America and the Third Wave Information Age," in *To Renew America* (New York, HarperCollins, 1995), 51.
> 5. Ibid., 55.

To avoid using *Ibid.* when documenting the same source in succession, give a page reference—for example: (55)—within the text itself. When successive citations are to the same page, *Ibid.* alone can be used.

> 4. Newt Gingrich, "America and the Third Wave Information Age," in *To Renew America* (New York, HarperCollins, 1995), 51.
> 5. Ibid.

Here's how a sequence of notes using several sources and subsequent short references might look.

Notes

> 1. Helen Wilkinson, "It's Just a Matter of Time," *Utne Reader* (May/June 1995): 66–67.
>
> 2. Paul Osterman, "Getting Started," *Wilson Quarterly* (autumn 1994): 46–55.
>
> 3. Newt Gingrich, "America and the Third Wave Information Age," in *To Renew America* (New York: HarperCollins, 1995), 51–61.

```
4. Ibid., 54.

5. Wilkinson, 66.

6. Ibid.

7. Ibid., 67.

8. Osterman, 48-49.

9. Gingrich, 60.
```

Notice that note 4 refers to the Gingrich chapter and notes 6 and 7 refer to Wilkinson's article.

26b CMS bibliographies

At the end of your project, list alphabetically every source you cited or used. This list is usually titled "Works Cited" when it includes only works actually mentioned in your paper; it is titled "Bibliography" when it also includes works consulted in preparing the project but not cited. Because CMS notes are quite comprehensive, a Works Cited or Bibliography list may be optional, depending on the assignment: check with your instructor or editor about including such a list. Individual entries in a Works Cited or Bibliography list are single spaced, with a double space between each entry (see the sample CMS paper on pages 415–22).

When an author has more than one work in the bibliography, those works are listed alphabetically under the author's name in this form:

```
Altick, Richard D. The Shows of London. Cambridge: Belknap-
     Harvard University Press, 1978.

---. Victorian People and Ideas. New York: Norton, 1973.

---. Victorian Studies in Scarlet. New York: Norton, 1977.
```

The checklists that follow provide general information about citing sources of information following CMS style.

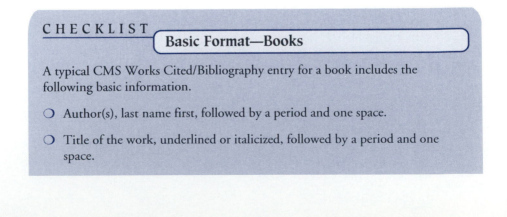

CHECKLIST

Basic Format—Books

A typical CMS Works Cited/Bibliography entry for a book includes the following basic information.

○ Author(s), last name first, followed by a period and one space.

○ Title of the work, underlined or italicized, followed by a period and one space.

○ Place of publication, followed by a colon and one space.

○ Publisher, followed by a comma and one space.

○ Date of publication, followed by a period.

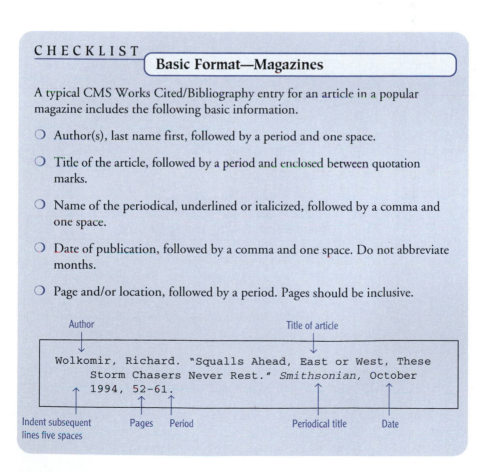

Author · Place of publication · Title

Moulakis, Athanasios. *Beyond Utility: Liberal Education for a Technological Age.* Columbia: University of Missouri Press, 1994.

Indent subsequent lines five spaces · Publisher · Date · Period

CHECKLIST

Basic Format—Magazines

A typical CMS Works Cited/Bibliography entry for an article in a popular magazine includes the following basic information.

○ Author(s), last name first, followed by a period and one space.

○ Title of the article, followed by a period and enclosed between quotation marks.

○ Name of the periodical, underlined or italicized, followed by a comma and one space.

○ Date of publication, followed by a comma and one space. Do not abbreviate months.

○ Page and/or location, followed by a period. Pages should be inclusive.

Author · Title of article

Wolkomir, Richard. "Squalls Ahead, East or West, These Storm Chasers Never Rest." *Smithsonian*, October 1994, 52-61.

Indent subsequent lines five spaces · Pages · Period · Periodical title · Date

Basic Format—Scholarly Journals

A typical CMS Works Cited/Bibliography entry for an article in a scholarly journal (where the pagination is continuous throughout a year) includes the following basic information.

○ Author(s), last name first, followed by a period and one space.

○ Title of the article, followed by a period (or other final punctuation mark) and enclosed between quotation marks.

○ Name of the periodical, underlined or italicized, followed by one space.

○ Volume number, followed by one space.

○ Date of publication in parentheses, followed by a colon and one space.

○ Page or location, followed by a period. Page numbers should be inclusive, from the first page of the article to the last, including notes and bibliography.

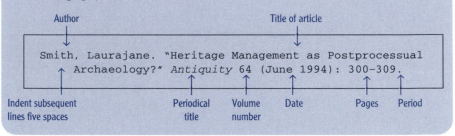

Author   Title of article

Smith, Laurajane. "Heritage Management as Postprocessual Archaeology?" *Antiquity* 64 (June 1994): 300–309.

Indent subsequent lines five spaces   Periodical title   Volume number   Date   Pages   Period

Basic Format—Electronic Sources

A typical CMS Works Cited/Bibliography entry for an electronic source is arranged and punctuated just like a printed source, with some additions.

○ Author and title, arranged and punctuated as for a printed source.

○ Publication information (if available), including city, publisher, and date for books or volume number/date for periodicals, followed by a period and one space.

○ A description of the electronic format or computer source (*database online, CD-ROM, journal online, abstract online*), enclosed in square brackets, followed by a period and one space.

○ An electronic address or pathway following the words *Available from.* For World Wide Web sites, give the URL (that is, the address that begins *http*) and follow it with a semicolon and the word *INTERNET* (in uppercase letters).

○ CMS does not require a date of access; however, if you choose to include one, it can appear either before or after the electronic address. If after, it is separated from that address or pathway by a semicolon and followed by a period.

Author(s)   Title   Publication information/date

```
Benbow, Camilla Persson, and Julian C. Stanley.
    "Inequity in Equity: How 'Equity' Can Lead to
    Inequity for High-Potential Students." Psychology,
    Public Policy, and Law 2 (June 1996). [Abstract
    online]. Available from http://www.apa.org/journals/
    law/696ab.html#4; INTERNET; accessed 30 July 1997.
```

Indent subsequent   Electronic   Description   Date
lines five spaces   address   of source   of access

Because there are so many variations to these general entries, you will want to check the CMS Form Directory below for the correct format of any unusual entry.

26c CMS Form Directory

Here you will find the CMS note and bibliography forms for more than twenty types of sources. The numbered items in the list are the sample note forms, compete with page references; they are followed by their corresponding bibliography entries. The "COS" icon next to an entry indicates that a Columbia Online Style (COS) form is available for that source (see Chapter 23 on COS).

CMS Format Index

145. **Book, One Author—CMS** Give the author's name, the title of the book in italics, and the publication information. Notice that footnotes and endnotes do not invert the author's name and that they use commas to separate information and parentheses to enclose the publication information. The bibliography format uses periods to separate elements and does not enclose the publication information in parentheses, and the author's name is inverted and alphabetized by last name.

> 1. Steven Weinberg, *Dreams of a Final Theory* (New York: Pantheon Books, 1992), 38.

> Weinberg, Steven. *Dreams of a Final Theory.* New York: Pantheon Books, 1992.

146. **Book, Two or Three Authors or Editors—CMS** For footnotes and endnotes, list the names of the authors in normal order; for bibliography citations, invert only the first author's name.

> 2. Peter Collier and David Horowitz, *Destructive Generation: Second Thoughts About the '60s* (New York: Summit, 1989), 24.

> Collier, Peter, and David Horowitz. *Destructive Generation: Second Thoughts About the '60s.* New York: Summit, 1989.

147. **Book, Four or More Authors or Editors—CMS** Use *et al.* or *and others* after the first author's name in a note, but list all authors in the bibliography when that is convenient.

> 3. Philip Curtin and others, eds., *African History* (Boston: Little, Brown, 1978), 77.

> Curtin, Philip, Steve Feierman, Leonard Thompson, and Jan Vansina, eds. *African History.* Boston: Little, Brown, 1978.

148. **Book, Edited—Focus on the Editor—CMS** When you cite an edited work by the editor's name, identify the original author after the title of the work.

> 4. Scott Elledge, ed., *Paradise Lost,* by John Milton (New York: Norton, 1975).

> Elledge, Scott, ed. *Paradise Lost,* by John Milton. New York: Norton, 1975.

149. **Book, Edited—Focus on the Original Author—CMS** In footnotes or endnotes, use the abbreviation *ed.* for *edited by.* In the bibliography entry, either use the abbreviation or spell it out.

> 5. William Shakespeare, *The Complete Works of Shakespeare,* 4th ed., ed. David Bevington (New York: Longman, 1997).

```
Shakespeare, William. The Complete Works of Shakespeare. 4th
     ed. Edited by David Bevington. New York: Longman, 1997.
```

150. Book Written by a Group—CMS List the organization or group name as the author, even if it is repeated in the title or publication information.

```
     6. Council of Biology Editors, Scientific Style and
Format: The CBE Manual for Authors, Editors, and Publishers,
6th ed. (Cambridge: Cambridge University Press, 1994).

Council of Biology Editors. Scientific Style and Format: The
     CBE Manual for Authors, Editors, and Publishers. 6th ed.
     Cambridge: Cambridge University Press, 1994.
```

151. Book with No Author—CMS List the book by its title, alphabetized by the first major word (excluding *The, A,* or *An*).

```
     7. Webster's Collegiate Thesaurus (Springfield: Merriam,
1976).

Webster's Collegiate Thesaurus. Springfield: Merriam, 1976.
```

152. Work of More Than One Volume—CMS Indicate the total number of volumes after the title of the work when you are citing the work as a whole.

```
     8. Karlheinz Spindler, Abstract Algebra with
Applications, 2 vols. (New York: Dekker, 1994).

Spindler, Karlheinz. Abstract Algebra with Applications. 2
     vols. New York: Dekker, 1994.
```

When citing only a particular volume, include the specific volume number only. However, if you reference specific pages within the volume, omit "vol." in the footnote or endnote.

```
     8. Karlheinz Spindler, Abstract Algebra with Applications
(New York: Dekker, 1994), 1:17-18.

Spindler, Karlheinz. Abstract Algebra with Applications. Vol.
     1. New York: Dekker, 1994.
```

153. Work in a Series—CMS Do not underline or italicize a series name. You may omit the series title if the work can be located without it.

```
     9. Grayson Kirk and Nils H. Wessell, eds., The Soviet
Threat: Myths and Realities, Proceedings of the Academy of
Political Science, no. 33 (New York: Academy of Political
Science, 1978), 62.

Kirk, Grayson, and Nils H. Wessell, eds. The Soviet Threat:
     Myths and Realities. Proceedings of the Academy of
     Political Science, no. 33. New York: Academy of Political
     Science, 1978.
```

154. Chapter in a Book—CMS Include the title of the chapter, enclosed by quotation marks, followed by "in" (capitalized for bibliography entries) and the title of the book in italics. If the author of the book is different from the author of the chapter or if the book is edited, you will need to include that information as well (see model 157).

> 10. Delia Owens and Mark Owens, "Home to the Dunes," in *The Eye of the Elephant: An Epic Adventure in the African Wilderness* (Boston: Houghton Mifflin, 1992), 11-27.
>
> Owens, Delia, and Mark Owens. "Home to the Dunes." In *The Eye of the Elephant: An Epic Adventure in the African Wilderness*. Boston: Houghton Mifflin, 1992.

155. Article in a Scholarly Journal—CMS Scholarly journals are usually identified by volume number or season (rather than day, week, or month of publication). Such journals are usually paginated year by year, with a year's work treated as one volume.

> 11. Karl P. Wentersdorf, "Hamlet's Encounter with the Pirates," *Shakespeare Quarterly* 34 (1983): 434-40.
>
> Wentersdorf, Karl P. "Hamlet's Encounter with the Pirates." *Shakespeare Quarterly* 34 (1983): 434-40.

156. Article in a Popular Magazine—CMS Magazines are paginated issue by issue and identified by monthly or weekly dates of publication (instead of by volume number). When an article does not appear on consecutive pages (as in the example below), omit page numbers in the bibliography entry.

> 12. Eleanor Cooney, "Death in Slow Motion: A Descent into Alzheimer's," *Harper's,* October 2001, 43.
>
> Cooney, Eleanor. "Death in Slow Motion: A Descent into Alzheimer's." *Harper's,* October 2001, 43-58.

157. Article or Selection from a Reader or Anthology—CMS Give the author and title of the article being cited, followed by "in" (capitalized for bibliography entries), the book title, the name(s) of editor(s), and publication information. Include the page numbers for the article or selection.

> 13. Matthew Rohrer, "Found in the Museum of Old Science," in *The Presence of Others*, 2d ed., ed. Andrea Lunsford and John Ruszkiewicz (New York: St. Martin's, 1997), 290-91.
>
> Rohrer, Matthew. "Found in the Museum of Old Science." In *The Presence of Others*. 2d ed. Edited by Andrea Lunsford and John Ruszkiewicz. New York: St. Martin's, 1997.

158. Article in a Newspaper—CMS Identify the edition of the newspaper (*final edition, home edition, Western edition*) except when citing editorials or features that appear in all editions. Since an individual story may move in location from edition to edition, page numbers are not ordinarily provided. Section numbers are given for papers so divided. Individual news stories are usually not listed in a bibliography.

> 14. Celestine Bohlen, "A Stunned Venice Surveys the Ruins of a Beloved Hall," *New York Times*, 31 January 1995, national edition, sec. B.

159. Encyclopedia—CMS When a reference work is a familiar one (encyclopedias, dictionaries, thesauruses), omit the names of authors and editors and most publishing information. No page number is given when a work is arranged alphabetically; instead the item referenced is named, following the abbreviation *s.v.* (*sub verbo,* meaning "under the word"). Familiar reference works are not listed in the bibliography.

> 15. *The Oxford Companion to English Literature*, 4th ed., s.v. "Locke, John."

160. Biblical Citation—CMS Biblical citations appear in notes but not in the bibliography. If it is important, you may name the version of the Bible cited.

> 16. John 18.37–38 Jerusalem Bible.

COS
p. 321

161. Computer Software—CMS CMS recommends that references to computer software be included in the text rather than in endnotes or footnotes, with full citation information, if necessary, included in the bibliography. CMS does not italicize the titles of software packages. The version number should be included, but no date of publication is necessary.

> FoxPro Ver. 2.5. Microsoft, Seattle, Wash.

COS
p. 318

162. Electronic Sources—CMS The standards for electronic documentation are in flux. CMS follows the style recommended by the International Standards Organization (ISO), but many issues remain unresolved as new sources and formats evolve. In *The Chicago Manual of Style,* fourteenth edition, the examples of notes for electronic sources generally include three features: a description of the computer source in brackets, such as *[electronic bulletin board]* or *[Web site];* the date the material was accessed, updated, or cited *[cited 28 May 1996];* and an electronic address, following the words *available from.* Models 162 through 165 follow these recommendations as modified in Kate L. Turabian's *Manual of Style for Writers of Term Papers, Theses, and Dissertations,* sixth edition. The resulting citations are quite complex. Some simplification may be in order, or you may wish to consult the chapter on COS style for online sources.

18. Sylvia Atore Alva, "Differential Patterns of Achievement Among Asian-American Adolescents," *Journal of Youth and Adolescence* 22 (1993): 407–23, *ProQuest General Periodicals* [CD-ROM], UMI-ProQuest, June 1994.

Alva, Sylvia Atore. "Differential Patterns of Achievement Among Asian-American Adolescents." *Journal of Youth and Adolescence* 22 (1993): 407–23. *ProQuest General Periodicals.* CD-ROM. UMI-ProQuest, June 1994.

COS
p. 314

163. Web—Book Online—CMS Include previous print publication information if available.

19. Amelia E. Barr, *Remember the Alamo* [book online] (New York: Dodd, Mead, 1888); available from http://etext .lib.virginia.edu/cgibin/browse-mixed?id=BarReme&tag=public &images=images/modeng&data=/lv1/Archive/eng-parsed; INTERNET; cited 12 May 1997.

Barr, Amelia E. *Remember the Alamo.* Book online. New York: Dodd, Mead, 1888. Available from http://etext.lib .virginia.edu/cgibin/browse-mixed?id=BarReme&tag= public&images=images/modeng&data=/lv1/Archive/eng-parsed; INTERNET; cited 12 May 1997.

COS
p. 314

164. Web—Article Online—CMS Include the date of publication or volume numbers, as available, for online articles. No page numbers are included for online publications.

20. Paul Skowronek, "Left and Right for Rights," *Trincoll Journal,* 13 March 1997 [journal online]; available from http://www.trincoll.edu/~tj/tj03.13.97/articles/comm2.html; INTERNET; accessed 23 July 1997.

Skowronek, Paul. "Left and Right for Rights." *Trincoll Journal,* 13 March 1997. Journal online. Available from http://www.trincoll.edu/~tj/tj03.13.97/articles/ comm2.html; INTERNET; accessed 23 July 1997.

COS
p. 319

165. Email—CMS For personal email, include the description, "Email to author"; otherwise include the name of the electronic discussion list and information on accessing the posting ("Available from listserv@ilstu.edu")

21. Robert D. Royer, "Re: Are We in a State of NOMAIL?" Email to author, 22 July 1997.

Royer, Robert D. "Re: Are We in a State of NOMAIL?" Email to author, 22 July 1997.

26d Sample CMS paper

The sample CMS paper was written in spring 1996 by Jeremy A. Corley, a student in Joi Chevalier's course "The Rhetoric of Epic Narratives." The paper provides an example of the sort of literary analysis that might be done for a classics or an English course. The paper has been lightly edited for style and revised to incorporate CMS-style endnotes and a Works Cited page.

The sample paper demonstrates how to use both endnotes and a Works Cited page. However, the Works Cited page is optional in CMS style because the endnotes themselves include full bibliographical information. Following the sample paper, we provide a single page reformatted to demonstrate the use of CMS-style footnotes. If you choose to use footnotes, do not also include endnotes. You may, however, present a Works Cited or Bibliography page. (A Works Cited page lists only those works mentioned in the paper itself; a Bibliography page includes all works cited in the paper as well as sources you consulted but did not mention in the paper.)

The sample paper shows titles italicized. You may either italicize or underline titles in CMS style, but be consistent: do not mix italicized and underlined titles within the same paper. In numbering the pages of CMS papers, count the title page as page one, but do not number it. Note that footnotes are single spaced. Indented quotations are also single spaced. For more on typing student papers in CMS style, see Kate L. Turabian, *A Manual for Writers of Term Papers, Theses, and Dissertations,* sixth edition.

[New Page]

THE UNIVERSITY OF TEXAS AT AUSTIN

DIOMEDES AS HERO OF *THE ILIAD*

E 309K--TOPICS IN WRITING

DIVISION OF RHETORIC AND COMPOSITION

BY

JEREMY A. CORLEY

28 FEBRUARY 1996

[New Page]

Diomedes as Hero of *The Iliad*

Achilles is the central character of *The Iliad,* but is his prominence alone enough to make him the story's hero? There are many examples that would say otherwise. One of the most interesting aspects of the epic is its use of a lesser character, rather than the technical protagonist, as the tale's benchmark for heroism. This lesser character is Diomedes, and his leadership skills and maturity prove to be far superior to those of Achilles. Book V of *The Iliad* is devoted almost entirely to Diomedes' feats, and there are many scenes in which he is presented as a leader and hero throughout the rest of the text. While Diomedes is singled out for his gallantry, Achilles is, by contrast, noted for his immaturity and selfishness. Homer depicts Diomedes in a much more positive light than Achilles, despite the latter's obvious natural superiority as a soldier. It seems evident that Homer is emphasizing the total use of one's abilities, rather than just the presence of those abilities, as the basis of heroism. Diomedes, therefore, is the actual hero of *The Iliad*.

Achilles is immediately placed at the focal point of the story, and his pride and immaturity surface almost instantaneously. In Book I, Agamemnon embarrasses Achilles publicly with an outward display of his power as the Achaians' commander: "Since Apollo robs me of Chryseis . . . I will take your beautiful Briseis . . . to show you how much stronger I am than you are."[1] Achilles can hardly be faulted for taking offense at this incident, as it "threatened to invalidate . . . the whole meaning of his life."[2] Achilles' refusal to fight afterward must be looked at from more than one perspective. This is the first example of Achilles acting according to his pride, as proven by his regard for himself as "the best man of all."[3] While it is understandable for a soldier such as Achilles, who "towers above all the other characters of *The Iliad*," to be hesitant to fight for and under the man who embarrassed him, Agamemnon, it is also folly for a soldier to stop fighting because of anything as relatively unimportant as an insult, even a public one.[4] A soldier's duty is to defend his homeland and fight in its wars, and Achilles misses this greater duty for his own selfishness. This refusal to fight is compounded by his request to his mother, Thetis, to "see if he [Zeus] will help the Trojans and drive the Achaians back to their ships with slaughter!"[5] This is wholly selfish. Achilles is willing to put the fate of the entire Greek army in peril to feed his own wounded ego. Achilles is acting nothing like the leader that his divine gifts give him the power to be. Homer clearly leaves his central character open for some significant character development.

In contrast to Achilles' infantile behavior, which is consistent throughout most of the story, Diomedes is cast in a different light. Athena gives Diomedes "courage and boldness, to make him come to the front and cover himself with glory."[6] While not Achilles' equal as a soldier, "Diomedes was extremely fierce" and proved to be a terrific leader for the Achaians.[7] Diomedes kills off many Trojan warriors in Book V, acting as many hoped Achilles would, and even fighting through an injury suffered from the bow of Pandaros.[8] Rather than back down, Diomedes prayed to Athena for aid and joined the battle even more fiercely than before, slaying even more Trojan soldiers.[9] It is clear at this point that Diomedes is "obviously a paradigm of heroic behavior in Achilles' absence."[10] Diomedes represents a well-behaved, properly subservient soldier in the Achaian army who uses his courage and his honor to accomplish feats that are beyond his natural abilities. Diomedes exhibits self-control above all else, which is the element most wanting in Achilles' character.[11] His courage is further proven when he speaks against Agamemnon at the beginning of Book IX when the Achaian commander is advocating a Greek retreat: "Two of us will go on fighting, Sthenelos and I, until we make our goal!"[12] This is the moment when Diomedes is confirmed as one of the Greeks' greatest leaders, as even in a time when the army was "possessed by Panic,"[13] we see that "all cheered bold Diomedes in admiration."[14] The scene underscores Diomedes' rise to greatness in the Achaian army.

Achilles and Diomedes finally come into direct conflict with one another in Book IX, after Agamemnon has decided to make a peace offering to Achilles in hopes of the latter's return to battle. Agamemnon makes an offer to

Achilles that is outrageously generous in exchange for Achilles' return to battle. Achilles' response is far from heroic and borders on cowardly: "If I go home to my native land, there will be no great fame for me, but I shall live long and not die an early death."[15] These words show utter selfishness on the part of the man who is supposedly the greatest warrior in Greek history, and Achilles is certainly not, at this point, living up to his reputation or his potential. Observing that Achilles "shall appear in battle once more whenever he feels inclined or when God makes him go," Diomedes speaks against Achilles for the first time, effectively casting himself as something of an adversary to Achilles in the hopes of bringing him back into the battle, an action that serves the overall good of the Achaians.[16] Once more, Diomedes is doing what is best for his people and his army while Achilles thinks only of himself. Peter Toohey observes that "Homer likes to juxtapose," and here he uses that device to highlight the stark contrast between the protagonist of the story and the true hero of the story.[17]

Homer centers *The Iliad* around Achilles, whose actions are notably selfish and immature. Homer then uses Diomedes, at first a lesser character, as a dramatic foil. Diomedes comes across as an example of the ideal young Greek soldier. Achilles' capacities as a warrior are far superior to those of any man alive, yet Diomedes betters him in both words and actions throughout most of the story. Achilles is finally brought to realize his supreme military prowess, but it is the death of his friend Patroclos that spurs his fighting spirit, still another example of Achilles' penchant for acting on emotion rather than judgment. Achilles is finally reconciled to Diomedes' example when he meets Priam at the end of the story and responds honorably: "I mean myself to set your Hector free," agreeing to return the corpse of Priam's son for a proper burial.[18] Achilles at last achieves a measure of respect that his abilities could have earned him long before. It is in that time, however, when Achilles was still selfish and immature, that Diomedes shone as the example of leadership and valor. Diomedes is, at least in a measure of consistency, the true hero of *The Iliad*.

NOTES

1. Homer, *The Iliad,* trans. Robert Fitzgerald (New York: Anchor Press, 1974), 14.

2. R. M. Frazer, *A Reading of "The Iliad"* (Lanham, MD: University Press of America, 1993), 12.

3. Homer, 15.

4. Frazer, 11.

5. Homer, 18.

6. Ibid., 58.

7. Scott Richardson, *The Homeric Narrator* (Nashville: Vanderbilt University Press, 1990), 159.

8. Homer, 59.

9. Ibid., 60–61.

10. W. Thomas MacCary, *Childlike Achilles: Ontogeny and Philogeny in "The Iliad"* (New York: Columbia University Press, 1982), 95.

11. G. S. Kirk, *"The Iliad": A Commentary,* vol. 2 (New York: Cambridge University Press, 1990), 34.

12. Homer, 103.

13. Ibid., 102.

14. Ibid., 103.

15. Ibid., 110.

16. Ibid., 115.

17. Peter Toohey, "Epic and Rhetoric: Speech-making and Persuasion in Homer and Apollonius," *Arachnion: A Journal of Ancient Literature and History on the Web* 1 (1995) [journal online]; available from http://www.cisi .unito.it/arachne/num1/toohey.html; INTERNET; accessed 21 February 1996.

18. Homer, 293.

WORKS CITED

Frazer, R. M. *A Reading of "The Iliad."* Lanham, MD.:
    University Press of America, 1993.

Homer. *The Iliad.* Translated by Robert Fitzgerald. New
    York: Anchor Press, 1974.

Kirk, G. S. *"The Iliad": A Commentary.* Vol. 2. New York:
    Cambridge University Press, 1990.

MacCary, W. Thomas. *Childlike Achilles: Ontogeny and
    Philogeny in "The Iliad."* New York: Columbia
    University Press, 1982.

Richardson, Scott. *The Homeric Narrator.* Nashville:
    Vanderbilt University Press, 1990.

Toohey, Peter. "Epic and Rhetoric: Speech-making and
    Persuasion in Homer and Apollonius." *Arachnion: A
    Journal of Ancient Literature and History on the Web* 1
    (1995). Journal online. Available from http://www
    .cisi.unito.it/arachne/num1/toohey.html; INTERNET;
    accessed 21 February 1996.

Sample CMS page with footnotes. In CMS style you have the option of placing all your notes on pages following the body of a paper, as shown on page 421, or you
may locate them at the bottom of each page as they occur in the text.

2

　　In Book I, Agamemnon embarrasses Achilles publicly with
an outward display of his power as the Achaians' commander:
"since Apollo robs me of Chryseis . . . . I will take your
beautiful Briseis . . . to show you how much stronger I am
than you are."[1] Achilles can hardly be faulted for taking
offense at this incident, as it "threatened to invalidate
. . . the whole meaning of his life."[2] Achilles' refusal to
fight afterward must be looked at from more than one
perspective. This is the first example of Achilles acting
according to his pride, as proven by his regard for himself
as "the best man of all."[3] While it is understandable for a
soldier such as Achilles, who "towers above all the other
characters of *The Iliad*," to be hesitant to fight for and
under the man who embarrassed him, Agamemnon, it is also
folly for a soldier to stop fighting because of anything as
relatively unimportant as an insult, even a public one.[4] A
soldier's duty is to defend his homeland and fight in its
wars, and Achilles misses this greater duty for his own
selfishness. This refusal to fight is compounded by his
request to his mother, Thetis, to "see if he [Zeus] will
help the Trojans and drive the Achaians back to their ships
with slaughter!"[5] This is wholly selfish. Achilles is
willing to put the fate of the entire Greek army in peril
to feed his own wounded ego. Achilles is acting nothing
like the leader that his divine gifts give him the

　　1. Homer, *The Iliad,* trans. Robert Fitzgerald (New
York: Anchor Press, 1974), 14.

　　2. R. M. Frazer, *A Reading of "The Iliad"* (Lanham, MD:
University Press of America, 1993), 12.

　　3. Homer, 15.

　　4. Frazer, 11.

　　5. Homer, 18.

CSE Documentation

Disciplines that study the physical world—physics, chemistry, biology—are called the natural sciences; disciplines that examine (and produce) technologies are described as the applied sciences. Writing in these fields is specialized, and no survey of all forms of documentation can be provided here. For more information about writing in the following fields, we suggest that you consult one of these style manuals. Check with your library for availability.

- **Chemistry:** *The ACS Style Guide: A Manual for Authors and Editors,* second edition (1997)—American Chemical Society
- **Geology:** *Suggestions to Authors of Reports of the United States Geological Survey,* eighth edition (1997)—U.S. Geological Survey
- **Mathematics:** *A Manual for Authors of Mathematical Papers,* revised edition (1990)—American Mathematical Society
- **Medicine:** *American Medical Association Manual of Style: A Guide for Authors and Editors,* ninth edition (1997)
- **Physics:** *AIP Style Manual,* fourth edition (1998)—American Institute of Physics

A highly influential manual for scientific writing is *Scientific Style and Format: The CBE Manual for Authors, Editors, and Publishers,* sixth edition (1994). In this most recent edition of the *CBE Manual,* the Council of Biology Editors (now known as the Council of Science Editors, or CSE) advocates a common style for international science but also recognizes important differences between disciplines and even countries. CSE is currently at work on a new edition; in the meantime, updates, corrections, and additional suggestions for citing electronic sources are available on the CSE Web site at http://www.cbe.org.

CSE style offers the choice of two principal methods of documenting sources used in research: a name-year system that resembles APA style and a citation-sequence system that lists sources in the order of their use in a paper. In this chapter we briefly describe the second system.

Citing Electronic Sources in the Natural and Applied Sciences

CSE documentation covers many electronic sources (see page 429 for an explanation), but it does not deal specifically with Web sites and other online environments. When citing such items, you may want to use the documentation style recommended by the *Columbia Guide to Online Style;* it was developed explicitly for newer research situations. Columbia Online Style (COS) for scientific papers, described on pages 324–37, is especially adaptable to CSE-style name-year citations. Consult your instructor about using Columbia style for electronic and computerized sources.

27a Provide in-text citations

Where a citation is needed in the text of a paper, insert either a raised number (the preferred form) or a number in parentheses. Citations should appear immediately after the word or phrase to which they are related, and they are numbered in the order you use them.

```
Oncologists[1] are aware of trends in cancer mortality[2] .
```

```
Oncologists (1) are aware of trends in cancer mortality (2) .
```

Source 1 thus becomes the first item to be listed on the References page, source 2 the second item, and so on.

```
1. Devesa SS, Silverman DT. Cancer incidence and mortality
   trends in the United States: 1935-74. J Natl Cancer Inst
   1978;60:545-571.
2. Goodfield J. The siege of cancer. New York: Dell; 1978.
   240 p.
```

You can refer to more than one source in a single note, with the numbers separated by a dash if they are in sequence and by commas if out of sequence.

IN SEQUENCE

```
Cancer treatment[2-3] has changed over the decades. But Rettig[4]
shows that the politics of cancer research remains constant.
```

OUT OF SEQUENCE

```
Cancer treatment[2,5] has changed over the decades. But Rettig[4]
shows that the politics of cancer research remains constant.
```

If you cite a source again later in the paper, refer to it by its original number.

Great strides have occurred in epidemiological methods[5] despite
the political problems in maintaining research support and
funding described by Rettig.[4]

27b List sources used

On a separate page at the end of your project, list the sources you used in the order they occurred. These sources are numbered: source 1 in the project will be the first source listed on the References page, source 2 the second item, and so on. Notice, then, that this References list is *not* alphabetical. The first few entries on a CSE list might look like this.

Subsequent lines begin under first words of first line   "References" centered   All items double spaced

References

1. Devesa SS, Silverman DT. Cancer incidence and mortality trends in the United States: 1935-74. J Natl Cancer Inst 1978;60:545-571.

2. Goodfield J. The siege of cancer. New York: Dell; 1978. 240 p.

3. Loeb LA, Ernster VL, Warner KE, Abbotts J, Laszo J. Smoking and lung cancer: an overview. Cancer Res 1984; 44:5940-5958.

4. Rettig RA. Cancer crusade: the story of the National Cancer Act of 1971. Princeton: Princeton Univ Pr; 1977. 382 p.

5. Craddock VM. Nitrosamines and human cancer: proof of an association? Nature 1983 Dec 15:638.

CHECKLIST

Basic Format—Books

A typical CSE citation-sequence style References entry for a book includes the following basic information.

○ Number assigned to the source.

○ Name of author(s), last name first, followed by a period. Initials are used in place of full first and middle names. Commas ordinarily separate the names of multiple authors.

○ Title of work, followed by a period. Only the first word and any proper nouns in a title are capitalized. The title is not underlined.

○ Place of publication, followed by a colon.

○ Publisher, followed by a semicolon. Titles of presses can be abbreviated.

○ Date, followed by a period.

○ Number of pages, followed by *p* and a period.

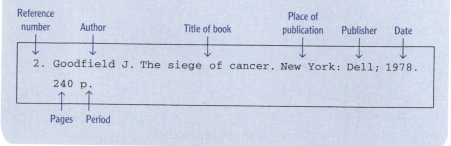

CHECKLIST

Basic Format—Scholarly Journals

A typical CSE citation-sequence–style References entry for an article in a scholarly journal (where the pagination is continuous through a year) includes the following basic information.

○ Number assigned to the source.

○ Name of author(s), last name first, followed by a period. Initials are used in place of full first and middle names. Commas ordinarily separate the names of multiple authors.

○ Title of article, followed by a period. Only the first word and any proper nouns in a title are capitalized. The title does not appear between quotation marks.

○ Name of the journal. All major words are capitalized, and the journal title is not underlined. A space (but no punctuation) separates the journal title from the date. Journal titles of more than one word can be abbreviated following the recommendations in *American National Standard Z39.5-1985: Abbreviations of Titles of Publications.*

○ Year (and month for journals not continuously paginated; date for weekly journals), followed immediately by a semicolon.

(Continued)

Basic Format—Scholarly Journals *(Continued)*

○ Volume number, followed by a colon, and the page numbers of the article. No spaces separate these items. A period follows the page numbers.

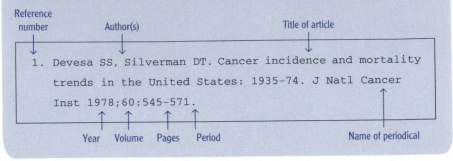

Reference number · Author(s) · Title of article

```
1. Devesa SS, Silverman DT. Cancer incidence and mortality
   trends in the United States: 1935-74. J Natl Cancer
   Inst 1978;60:545-571.
```

Year · Volume · Pages · Period · Name of periodical

CHECKLIST

Basic Format—Magazines

A typical CSE citation-sequence style References entry for an article in a popular magazine includes the following basic information.

○ Number assigned to the source.

○ Name of author(s), last name first, followed by a period. Initials are substituted for first names unless two authors mentioned in the paper have identical last names and first initials.

○ Title of article, followed by a period. Only the first word and any proper nouns in a title are capitalized. The title does not appear between quotation marks. (Where quotation marks are needed, CSE recommends British style. See the *CBE Manual,* pages 180–81.)

○ Name of magazine, abbreviated. All major words are capitalized, but the journal title is not underlined. A space (but no punctuation) separates the magazine title from the year and month.

○ Year, month (abbreviated), and day (for a weekly magazine). The year is separated from the month by a space. A colon follows immediately after the date, followed by page number(s). The entry ends with a period.

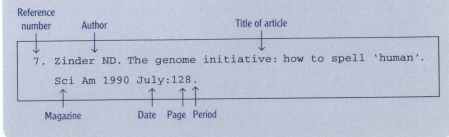

Reference number · Author · Title of article

```
7. Zinder ND. The genome initiative: how to spell 'human'.
   Sci Am 1990 July:128.
```

Magazine · Date · Page · Period

CHECKLIST
Basic Format—Electronic Sources

A typical CSE citation-sequence style References entry for an electronic item includes the basic information provided for a print document (author, title, publication information, page numbers) with the following additions.

○ Electronic medium, identified between brackets. For books and monographs, this information comes after the title *[Internet]*; for periodicals, it follows the name of the journal *[serial on the Internet]*.

○ Date cited, following the year of publication but before the volume and issue numbers.

○ Availability statement, following the publication information or page numbers. No punctuation follows the Internet address

Electronic medium

```
9. Dewitt R. Vagueness, semantics, and the language of
   thought. PSYCHE [serial on the Internet] 1993 [cited
   1995 Apr 26]; 1(1). Available from: ftp.lib.ncsu.edu
```

Date cited   Availability statement

There are so many variations to these basic entries that you will want to consult the *CBE Manual* when you do a major CSE-style paper.

Use the following considerations as a guide when formatting a paper in CSE style.

CHECKLIST
CSE Style

○ CSE style normally requires a separate title page. The title of the essay can be centered about a third of the way down the page, followed by *by* on a separate line and the writer's name, also on a separate line. Other information such as instructor's name, course title, and date can be included on the bottom third of the page.

○ CSE style normally requires an abstract of about 250 words on a separate page immediately following the title page. The title "Abstract" is centered on the page.

○ Double-space the body of a CSE paper. Avoid hyphenating words at the end of lines.

(Continued)

CSE Style *(Continued)*

○ Number pages consecutively in the upper right-hand corner, counting the title page as page one, using the "automatic page numbering" feature of your word processor, if available.

○ Take special care with figures and tables. They should be numbered in separate sequences. The *CBE Manual* includes an entire chapter on handling illustrative material.

○ The References page follows the text of the CSE essay on a new page. Remember that the items on this page are *not* listed alphabetically. References pages can also be titled "Literature Cited" or "References Cited."

○ All works listed on the References page should be cited at least once in the body of your paper.

○ Entries on the References page are single spaced, with a space between entries.

Credits

AIP Journal Center screen shot. Reprinted with permission. Copyright 2002, American Institute of Physics (AIP).

AltaVista screen shots. Reproduced with the permission of AltaVista Company. All rights reserved.

Brenneman, Ben H. "Can Quality Survive the Standardized Test?" (March 2, 2000). Reprinted by permission of The University of Texas at Austin.

Briggs, Chad S., and Fred Ribich. "The Relationship Between Test Anxiety, Sleep Habits, and Self-perceived Academic Competency," *Psych-E,* Vol. 1 (Dec. 1, 1998). Reprinted by permission of Chad S. Briggs.

Citation 8 screen shot. Reprinted by permission of Oberon Development.

Cody, Anthony. "Tests Undermine Teachers," *Oakland Tribune* (May 5, 2001). Reprinted by permission of Anthony Cody.

College Composition and Communication. Home page for CCC (College Composition and Communication). Web design by Todd Taylor. Copyright by the National Council of Teachers of English. Reprinted with permission.

Corel Presentations screen shot. Copyright © 1999 Corel Corporation and Corel Corporation Limited. Reprinted by permission.

Corley, Jeremy A. "Diomedes as Hero of *The Iliad*" (Feb. 28, 1996). Reprinted by permission of The University of Texas at Austin.

Google screen shots. Reproduced with the permission of Google Inc.

HotBot screen shots. HotBot ® is a registered trademark and/or service mark of Wired Ventures, Inc., a Lycos Company. All rights reserved. Reproduced with the permission of Lycos, Inc.

Microsoft screen shots. Reprinted by permission from Microsoft Corporation.

Netscape Composer. Netscape website © 2002 Netscape Communications Corporation. Screen shot used with permission.

***The New York Times* on the Web.** Copyright © 2002 by the New York Times Co. Reprinted by permission.

ProCite 5 screen shot. Reprinted by permission from ISI ResearchSoft.

***Professional Communications Center* brochure.** Reprinted by permission of the Professional Communications Center at the University of South Carolina College of Engineering & Information Technology.

Roland, Alex. "Leave the People Home," *USA Today Online* (July 7, 1997). Reprinted by permission of Alex Roland.

Seward, Dan. Personal home page in visual editor and personal home page in HTML text editor created by Dan Seward. Reproduced by permission of Dan Seward.

Sigma Tau Delta Newsletter. From the Spring 2000 issue of the *Sigma Tau Delta Newsletter.* Copyright © 2000 by Sigma Tau Delta International English Honor Society. Reprinted by permission.

UTNE Reader screen shot. Reproduced with permission from UTNE Reader Online (**www.utne.com**).

UTnetCat online library catalog at the University of Texas at Austin. Provided courtesy of The General Libraries, The University of Texas at Austin.

van der Plas, Robert. *The Mountain Bike Book.* San Francisco: Bicycle Books, 1993. Reprinted by permission of Robert van der Plas.

***The Weekly Standard* screen shot.** Home page is reproduced by permission of *The Weekly Standard.*

WorldCat online database. Screen shot courtesy of OCLC Online Computer Library Center, Inc.

Yahoo! screen shots. Reproduced with permission of Yahoo! Inc. © 2000 by Yahoo! Inc. YAHOO! and the YAHOO! logo are trademarks of Yahoo! Inc.

PHOTO CREDITS

Page 1: Steve Perez/Apex Productions. Page 3: AP/Wide World Photos. Page 16: Thomas del Brase/Stone/Getty Images. Page 27: Courtesy of NASA. Page 36: Jay Freis/The Inage Bank/Getty Images. Page 51: Bruce Laurance/Getty Images. Page 53: Stone/Getty Images. Page 77: David Young-Wolff/PhotoEdit. Page 91: Jason Laure. Page 101: Hulton Archive/Getty Images. Page113: Courtesy of W3.org. Page 115: Kobal Collection.

Page 126: Rhoda Sidney/PhotoEdit. Page 136: Bettmann Archive/CORBIS. Page 143: AP/Wide World Photos. Page 152: Everett Collection. Page 163: Howard Berman/The Image Bank/Getty Images. Page 179: SuperStock. Page 181: Jake Rajas/Stone/Getty Images. Page 188: Mel Curtis/PhotoDisk/Getty Images. Page 194: Mel Curtis/PhotoDisk/Getty Images. Page 206: UPI-Bettmann Archive/CORBIS. Page 222: Super-Stock. Page 233: Courtesy MicroSoft. Page 301: Courtesy of AOL-Time Warner.

Index

Glossary

address   The route or path followed to access a specific file or person. An email address usually consists of a log-in name and a domain name. A web address usually includes a domain name, a directory or directories, and a file name.

asynchronous   In Internet communication, electronic mail and other communication wherein messages are not dependent on timing.

BBS   Bulletin Board Service. An online service, generally hosted by an individual user, that allows others to post messages and share files.

bookmarks   Called "Favorites" in some browsers, bookmarks are a way of marking a specific file, online address, or location within a file for later retrieval.

Boolean operators   Search terms based on logic that allow you to limit and define search criteria. The most commonly used Boolean operators are AND, OR, and NOT.

browser   Software that allows users to access files on the World Wide Web and move through hypertext links. Some browsers such as *Lynx* offer text-only access, while browsers such as Netscape *Navigator* and Microsoft *Internet Explorer* use graphical interfaces and point-and-click technology.

chat room   A virtual room; an address where multiple users may communicate with each other in real time, usually by inputting text on a keyboard.

cookie   A small piece of computer code stored on PC's by some Web sites. Cookies allow sites to recognize return visitors and often include information such as a user's name and the last time the site was visited.

directory   A structure for organizing files on a computer or host, similar to a file folder containing individual files.

domain name   The unique name assigned to an individual host address, such as **www .whitehouse.gov.**

download   The act of moving a file from a host or server directory to a local storage medium such as your diskette or hard drive.

FAQ   Frequently Asked Questions. A file providing information about a newsgroup, listserv, or other online service, including details of membership, discussion topics, and rules or netiquette guidelines.

FTP   File Transfer Protocol. A means of transferring files between machines.

Gopher   A menu-driven system for organizing and accessing remote files on the Internet.

GUI   Graphical User Interface. An interface that uses icons, pictures, and pointers (such as the Windows and MacIntosh desktops) to control programs.

HTTP   HyperText Transfer Protocol. The process by which hypertext files are transferred between remote computers on the Internet using browser software.

hypertext   Text, graphics, or files that are linked together, as designated by the hypertext author, using a special system of tags called HyperText Markup Language (HTML).

Internet   An international network of computers originally designed by the U.S. Department of Defense to ensure communication abilities in the event of a catastrophe. The Internet today connects millions of individual users, universities, governments, businesses, and other organizations using telephone lines, fiber-optic cabling, and other technologies to link machines to each other.